PEEL, PRIESTS AND POLITICS

———

Sir Robert Peel's Administration
and the Roman Catholic Church
in Ireland, 1841-1846

DONAL A. KERR

D1421661

CLARENDON PRESS · OXFORD

Oxford University Press, Walton Street, Oxford OX2 6DP
London Glasgow New York Toronto
Delhi Bombay Calcutta Madras Karachi
Kuala Lumpur Singapore Hong Kong Tokyo
Nairobi Dar es Salaam Cape Town
Melbourne Auckland
and associates in
Beirut Berlin Ibadan Mexico City Nicosia

Published in the United States by
Oxford University Press, New York

First printed 1982
Reprinted (New as Paperback) 1984

British Library Cataloguing in Publication Data

Kerr, Donal A.
    Peel, priests and politics. —(Oxford historical
    monographs)
        1. Catholic Church in Ireland.   2. Church and
    state in Ireland   3. Ireland—Politics and
    government—1837-1901   4. Ireland—Politics
    and government—1837-1901   5. Ireland—
    History—1837-1901
    I. Title
    941.5081   BX1505

    ISBN 0-19-821891-5   822932-1 (pbk)

Library of Congress Cataloging in Publication Data

Kerr, Donal A., 1927-
    Peel, priests, and politics.

        1. Irish question.   2. Catholic Church—Ireland—
    History—19th century.   3. Peel, Robert, Sir, 1788-
    1850.   I. Title.
    DA950.5.K47   1982   941.5081   82-7896
    ISBN 0-19-821891-5   AACR2
            822932-1 (pbk)

Printed in Great Britain
at the University Press, Oxford

TO

Angus Macintyre

PREFACE

In acknowledging my debt to those who helped me to write this work I wish to thank in the first instance Dr R. Dudley Edwards who first suggested the subject and maintained a lively interest in its progress, and Professor F. X. Martin OSA for his helpful advice on all occasions.

Much unpublished material has been generously placed at my disposal. I acknowledge the gracious permission of Her Majesty the Queen to make use of material in the Royal Archives. I acknowledge my indebtedness to Archbishop Dermot Ryan for permission to use the Dublin Diocesan Archives and to Dr Kevin Kennedy for invaluable assistance in my work there; to Cardinal Tomás Ó Fiaich and Monsignor Michael Olden for access to the Archives of Saint Patrick's College, Maynooth; to the late Cardinal Conway for access to the Armagh Diocesan Archives; to the late Most Reverend Dr O'Doherty for access to the Archives of the Dromore diocese; to the Most Reverend Dr Patrick Mulligan for access to the Clogher Diocesan Archives; to Cardinal Casaroli for access to the Vatican Archives; to Monsignor Charles Burns for facilitating access to some documents from the Archives of the Cardinal Secretary for State; to Cardinal Rossi for access to the Congregation of Propaganda Fide Archives; to Monsignor Éamonn Marron and Dr John Silke for access to the Cullen and Kirby Papers in the Irish College, Rome; to Lord Blake for access to the Derby Papers and to Lord Derby for permission to cite from them; to Lord Eliot for access to the St. Germans Archives; to Sir Charles Graham Bt. for permission to use the Graham Papers; to the Earl of Clarendon for permission to use the Clarendon Papers; to Mr Joseph Martin for access to the archives of the Commissioners of Charitable Donations and Bequests for Ireland; and to Mr and Miss White for access to the Blake Papers. Dr Maurice R. O'Connell generously placed at my disposal the transcripts of his definitive edition of the correspondence of Daniel O'Connell. Dr Ambrose Macaulay furnished me with notes and transcripts concerning the national education controversy.

To the staff of various libraries I express my appreciation: the Bodleian, the British Library, the Public Record Office, the National Library of Ireland, the library of the Jesuit Fathers, Milltown, Dublin, the library of University College, Dublin, and the library of Maynooth College.

My deepest debt of gratitude is due to Dr Angus Macintyre who painstakingly directed my research and whose valuable advice, encouragement, and assistance have been readily forthcoming at all times.

St. Benet's Hall, Oxford, &
St. Patrick's College, Maynooth   DONAL KERR
St. Patrick's Day, 1982

CONTENTS

TABLES AND MAP

Tables

Map

ABBREVIATIONS

AA.EE.SS.	Archivio della Congregazione degli Affari Ecclesiastici Straordinari, Archivio Segreto Vaticano
Acta	Acta congregationum generalium Sacrae Congregationis de Propaganda Fide, Propaganda Fide Archives
Add. MSS	Additional Manuscripts, British Library
AHR	*American Historical Review*
Archiv. Hib.	*Archivium Hibernicum: or Irish historical records*
Cath. Hist. Rev.	*Catholic Historical Review*
Cork Hist. Soc. Jn.	*Journal of the Cork Historical and Archaeological Society*
DDA	Dublin Diocesan Archives
EHR	*English Historical Review*
FO	Foreign Office
Hansard	Hansard's Parliamentary Debates
Hist. Studies	*Historical Studies: papers read before the Irish Conference of Historians*
IER	*Irish Ecclesiastical Record*
IHS	*Irish Historical Studies*
Kerry Arch. Soc. Jn.	*Journal of the Kerry Archaeological Society*
NLI	National Library of Ireland
PRO	Public Record Office
RA	Royal Archives, Windsor Castle
SC Irlanda	Scritture riferite nei congressi, Irlanda, Propaganda Fide Archives
SOCG	Scritture riferite nelle congregazioni generali, Propaganda Fide Archives

THE ROMAN CATHOLIC CHURCH
IN IRELAND BY 1844

If it is true that the main lines of Anglo-Irish relations in the nineteenth century have now been firmly established, our knowledge of some aspects of the period is still limited. It is evident, for example, that in the long period between the final passage of the Catholic Relief Act of 1829 and the furious controversy over 'Papal Aggression' in 1850, the affairs of the churches, Protestant and Catholic, were at the centre of British politics and profoundly influenced Anglo-Irish relations. Much of the detail, however, of this period remains to be investigated, and such examination may, in the end, affect our judgement upon the whole course of affairs. This study deals with that phase of the Catholic question which many statesmen hoped had been settled in 1829 but which remained a persistent focus of political conflict. The policy of concessions pursued by Sir Robert Peel and his government towards Irish Catholics and its effect on the Irish Catholic church, Roman authorities, and Irish public opinion will constitute the central theme. In order to appreciate the corporate response of that church to Peel's policies it will first be necessary to survey the church's organization and life, the relationship between clergy and people, and the careers and characters of those men among the hierarchy who carried most formal responsibility for the evolution of the church's pastoral and political attitudes in the face of present and prospective challenges. Indeed, the situation of the church as it appeared to English politicians in the 1840s helped to shape Peel's policies of reform.

There is as yet no comprehensive published study of the Catholic church in Ireland in the decade before the Great Famine, but official papers, ecclesiastical sources, the press, and the accounts of visitors to Ireland furnish a good deal of information concerning it. In 1835, when the Commissioners of Public Instruction began to publish their reports, contemporaries had for the first time a guide to the religious affiliations of the people. The sheer size of the Catholic population was impressive in itself. When the total population of England and Wales was 13,896,797, Catholics in Ireland alone numbered 6,436,060. They constituted almost 81 per cent of the Irish population. Anglicans numbered 853,160 and Dissenters 664,940.[1] Four-fifths of the Catholics lived on the land. In the west particularly, and to a varying degree in other regions, most of them lived at subsistence level and were growing still poorer. There were also many comfortable and some prosperous farmers, particularly in the eastern half of the country. In the towns there was a well-established middle class of merchants, businessmen, and representatives of the professions. Many members of the professional class had acquired land and constituted the most politically articulate section of the Catholic laity, playing a large part in Daniel O'Connell's parliamentary and popular movements.[2] While they had been the main immediate beneficiaries of the Relief Act of 1829, Emancipation, as it was commonly called, although marred by the inclusion of penal clauses, had given a powerful psychological boost to every section of the church.

Ecclesiastically, the country was divided into the four provinces of Armagh, Dublin, Cashel, and Tuam.[3] Cashel and Tuam, which each consisted of seven dioceses, corresponded broadly to the civil provinces of Munster and Connaught. The Dublin province consisted of only four dioceses and encompassed little more than the southern half of Leinster. The province of Armagh consisted of nine dioceses, including the dioceses of Meath and Ardagh which took in the northern part of Leinster and a small section of Connaught. Cashel and Tuam were almost completely Catholic (96 per cent), with

---

[1] *First Report of the Commissioners of Public Instruction, PP 1835,* xxxiii. 904; T. W. Freeman, *Ireland: a general and regional geography* (1972), p. 119, regards the population figures as too high.

[2] A. Macintyre, *The Liberator: Daniel O'Connell and the Irish Party, 1830-1847* (1965), pp. 73-7.

[3] See map p. xii.

2,229,533 and 1,187,507 Catholics respectively. Armagh had 1,955,319 Catholics (63 per cent) and Dublin 1,063,681 (85 per cent). The most populous dioceses were Tuam, Cloyne and Ross, Dublin, Meath, and Killaloe—each with over 300,000 Catholics. At the other end of the scale, Dromore had only 57,000. In Rome, the affairs of the Irish church were entrusted to the *Sacra Congregatio de Propaganda Fide,* a Congregation which looked after the churches in non-Catholic countries. (This Congregation will be referred to in future as the Congregation of Propaganda or, simply, Propaganda.) The twenty-seven Irish bishops, however, although obliged to furnish regular individual reports on their dioceses to the Congregation, were independent in the daily running of their dioceses; Propaganda interfered only in major policy matters or to settle disputes, correct abuses, and grant authorizations or 'faculties'. Rome disapproved of the meetings of national hierarchies, fearing that they might become a focus for Gallican ideas. Yet the Irish bishops, encouraged by Dr Daniel Murray, archbishop of Dublin, held annual meetings and although the decisions taken were not binding on the bishops, a co-ordinated policy emerged which increased their authority with their clergy and faithful and strengthened their bargaining power with the government.[4] These meetings were an outward sign of the reorganization taking place within the church as the bishops strove to instil greater unity of practice and to bring the Irish church into line with the international church.[5]

Most of the bishops and half of the clergy had been educated at the college founded at Maynooth in 1795 for the education of persons professing the Roman Catholic religion. Many of the older men, however, had trained for the priesthood in France,

[4] These meetings—the first of their kind in the modern history of the Catholic church—probably went back to the necessity of coming together to formulate policies on Maynooth College. Strictly speaking, they were not synods and followed a looser and more democratic form which gave each bishop an opportunity to propose motions on relevant matters. A single, bound handwritten volume in the Dublin Diocesan Archives, entitled 'Meetings of the Irish Bishops 1826-49', preserves the records of the proceedings and decisions of the bishops.

[5] Meetings of the Irish Bishops 1826-49, 11 Feb. 1829, DDA, gives the report of a committee appointed to examine the discipline of the church.

Spain, Italy, or Portugal.[6] Theological activity was slight, and the Irish clergy shared in the defensive and apologetic doctrinal approach of the Counter-Reformation. They shared, too, in the general revival of the Catholic church after the French Revolution. In contrast, however, to their continental counterparts, the political outlook of the Irish clergy was surprisingly liberal. The able and universally respected Dr James Doyle, bishop of Kildare and Leighlin, had warned politicians in 1824 that the clergy 'had imbibed the doctrines of Locke and Paley more deeply than those of Bellarmine or even Bossuet on the divine right of Kings; they know much more of the principles of the Constitution than they do of passive obedience.'[7] In a spirited defence of his own involvement in the anti-tithe campaign, he told a Committee of the House of Lords in 1832:

if we are prevented from pursuing the recovery of a right because in pursuing that right evils may arise, we must abandon ourselves to utter despotism; and your Lordships will not succeed with me, and I believe with the public in general, in so captivating their understanding to the letter of the law, as to preclude them from pursuing what they think is right.[8]

The clergy, if anything, was more radical than Doyle's remarks indicated. Gustave de Beaumont, whose penetrating study of Ireland was published in 1839, was astonished to discover that the Catholic clergy so often elsewhere 'l'appui des princes ou l'allié des corporations privilégiées, est en Irlande, un des plus puissants éléments de liberté et de démocratie.'[9] Alexis de Tocqueville, who travelled Ireland with Beaumont, noted more than once in his diary that the clergy were tending clearly to democracy, seeking the sovereignty of the people and anxious to safeguard the freedom of the press.[10] In Carlow he dined with Dr. Slattery, archbishop of Cashel, four other

---

[6] In 1852-3, 23 of the 29 bishops and 1,222 of the 2,291 parish clergy had been educated at Maynooth. See table 5 pp. 330-1 for the bishops' places of training. The proportional difference between the number of Maynooth-trained bishops (80 per cent) and Maynooth-trained priests (53 per cent) is noteworthy; *Report of HM's Commissioners appointed to inquire into the management of the College of Maynooth, PP 1854-5,* xxii. 33-5; 204-31.

[7] W. J. Fitzpatrick, *The life, times and correspondence of ... Dr Doyle* (1890), i. 437.

[8] *Select Committee on Tithes, Ireland (Lords); PP 1831-2,* xxii. 282.

[9] G. de Beaumont, *L'Irlande sociale, politique et religieuse,* 7th ed. (1863), ii. 47.

[10] A. de Tocqueville, *Journeys to England and Ireland,* ed. J. P. Mayer (1958), pp. 167-8, 172, 191.

bishops and many priests and found that 'the feelings expressed [on politics] were extremely democratic'.[11] In Kilkenny, Bishop Kinsella took Tocqueville's own French clergy to task and gave an amusing and revealing account of his own visit to France shortly before the July revolution of 1830:

Arriving at Rouen, I saw two sentries at the gate of the Archbishop's palace. 'Whats that?' I asked a French ecclesiastic ... 'It is a guard of honour for the Archbishop'. 'I don't like that sort of guard of honour', said I. 'They make people think of your Archbishop as the representative of the King much more than that of Jesus Christ'. After that I saw the Fête-Dieu procession. It went between two lines of soldiers. 'Whats that?' said I again. 'What are those soldiers for? Who wants a military show as part of a religious fête?'.[12]

Kinsella, by his own account, told the French priests with whom he dined that they were using the wrong means to promote religion and even though they laughed at him and called him a revolutionary, he went on to lecture them on the necessity for the clergy to identify with their people.[13] Kinsella was no exception. Archbishop MacHale and other bishops were denounced to Rome for drinking public toasts 'To the people, the source of all legitimate power', and 'Civil and religious liberty for every man'.[14] Even Dr Crolly, the archbishop of Armagh and a bulwark of moderation, told the Roman authorities that the clergy must join the laity in their struggle for liberty.[15] Such democratic sentiments are all the more striking when compared with the two encyclicals which Pope Gregory XVI had issued, *Mirari Vos* in 1832 and *Singulari Nos* in 1834, in which he roundly condemned liberalism, indifferentism, liberty of conscience, and the immoderate freedom of the press. Peel, too, became aware of the unique nature of the problem in Ireland. Briefing the new chief secretary, Lord Lincoln, in 1846 he warned him that 'the spirit of Popery, and its alliance with democratic feelings and Institutions will constitute a very formidable combination against the Peace of Ireland, and the maintenance of cordial union with this country.'[16] The origin

---

[11] Ibid., p. 130.   [12] Ibid., pp. 145-6.   [13] Ibid., pp. 145-7.

[14] J. Broderick, *The Holy See and the Irish Movement for the Repeal of the Union with England, 1829-47* (1951), p. 105.

[15] Ibid., pp. 106-7.

[16] Peel to Lincoln, Mar. 1846, Newcastle MSS. Henry Pelham Pelham-Clinton, styled earl of Lincoln, duke of Newcastle, 1851; chief secretary in Ireland, 1846.

of this democratic outlook among the Irish clergy is not clear. Some placed the blame on the state for subsidizing the education of the clergy: Lord Donoughmore told Thomas Creevey, the diarist, that 'when Pitt established the college at Maynooth, he gave Ireland a republican priesthood'.[17] The ideas of the French Revolution and of Liberal Catholicism contributed to this process of democratization. O'Connell's success in politicizing the clergy may well have been the single most important feature.[18] It is clear that in the 1820s O'Connell, Doyle, and MacHale had given the clergy a new vision of its potential influence in public affairs, and the successful campaign for Emancipation, uniting priest and faithful as an almost irresistible force, had shown what could be achieved. Tocqueville carefully noted a revealing comment by a priest in the west of Ireland with whom he spent some time: 'Any religion which broke away from the people, Sir, would move away from its source and lose its main support. It is necessary to go with the people, Sir. There lies strength and in order to remain united with the people there is no sacrifice which one should regret imposing on oneself.'[19] That was the heart of the matter.

In the absence of published biographies, it is difficult to form an over-all picture of the four archbishops and twenty-three bishops who constituted the Irish hierarchy.[20] Their average age, in 1844, was sixty-one, but most of them were aged between fifty and sixty. On the whole, except for an important division of opinion on the national education system which arose in 1838, they worked well together. A collective portrait of the bishops will emerge from an examination of individuals.[21] All

---

[17] Creevey to Elizabeth Ord, 7 Oct. 1828, *The Creevey Papers*, ed. H. Maxwell (1904), ii. 179-80.

[18] O. MacDonagh, 'The politicization of the Irish Catholic bishops, 1800-50', *Hist. Jn.*, xviii (1975), 37-53.

[19] Tocqueville, *Journeys*, p. 172.

[20] This total of twenty-seven excludes Dr Francis O'Finan, bishop of Killala, living in retirement in Rome.

[21] Except for a few individuals the amount of material concerning the bishops readily available is meagre and of poor quality, being mainly hagiographical in tone. For this reason, the above account deals mainly with the public and political attitudes assumed by the bishops. The following works have been found useful in compiling these pages: P. Mac Suibhne, *Paul Cullen and his contemporaries*, 5 vols. (1961-77); J. Broderick, *The Holy See and the Irish Movement for the Repeal of the Act of Union with England: 1829-47* (1951); M. R. O'Connell, ed. *The correspondence of Daniel O'Connell*, 8 vols. (1971-81); C. S. Dessain, ed. *The letters and diaries of J. H. Newman*, 15 vols.

Table 1

The Irish bishops in 1844

	Date of Accession		Date of Accession
ARMAGH		DUBLIN	
William Crolly (trs from	1835	Daniel Murray (1768-1852)	1823
Down & Connor) (1780-1849)		*FERNS*	
ARDAGH		James Keating (1783-1849)	1819
William Higgins (1793-1853)	1829	*KILDARE and LEIGHLIN*	
CLOGHER		Francis Haly (1783 (?)-1855)	1838
Charles McNally (1787-1864)	1844	*OSSORY*	
DERRY		William Kinsella (1796-1845)	1829
John McLaughlin (1794-1864)	1840		
DOWN and CONNOR		TUAM	
Cornelius Denvir (1791-1866)	1835	John MacHale (trs from Killala)	
DROMORE		(1791-1881)	1834
Michael Blake (1775-1860)	1833	*ACHONRY*	
KILMORE		Patrick McNicholas	1818
James Browne (1786-1865)	1829	(1781?-1852)	
MEATH		*CLONFERT*	
John Cantwell (1792-1866)	1830	Thomas Coen (1764-1847)	1831
RAPHOE		*ELPHIN*	
Patrick McGettigan (1785-1861)	1820	George Joseph Plunket Browne	
		(trs from Galway) (1790-1858)	1844
CASHEL		*GALWAY*	
Michael Slattery (1783-1857)	1834	Laurence O'Donnell (1790-1855)	1844
ARDFERT (KERRY)		*KILLALA*	
Cornelius Egan (1780-1856)	1824	Francis O'Finan (1771-1847)	1835
CORK		Thomas Feeny (1790-1873)	1848
John Murphy (1772-1847)	1815	(appointed administrator in 1839).	
CLOYNE and ROSS		*KILMACDUAGH and KILFENORA*	
Bartholomew Crotty (1769-1846)	1833	Edward French (1774-1852)	1825
KILLALOE			
Patrick Kennedy (1786-1850)	1836		
LIMERICK			
John Ryan (1781-1864)	1828		
WATERFORD and LISMORE			
Nicholas Foran (1784-1855)	1837		

but seven had studied for the priesthood at Maynooth College. In the province of Armagh, William Higgins had been appointed bishop of the straggling diocese of Ardagh and Clonmacnoise in 1829 at the youthful age of thirty-six. Trained for the priesthood in France and in Rome, he had been professor of dogmatic theology in Maynooth and was reputed to be an authority on canon law. A man of the people, proud of his humble origins, he was energetic and forceful but often unnecessarily vehement in language. In close association with Archbishop MacHale he involved himself in clerical and national politics, often identifying the two, and he was one of O'Connell's strongest supporters in his campaign for the Repeal of the Union, declaring on one occasion that 'if they [the government] attempt to ... prevent us from assembling in open fields, we will retire to the chapels and suspend all other instruction in order to devote our time to teaching the people to be Repealers'.[22] His pastoral work may have suffered, for in 1851 Dr Paul Cullen, archbishop of Armagh, in an important letter to Rome in which he discussed the pastoral effectiveness of the bishops of the provinces of Armagh and Tuam, complained that Higgins 'shuts himself up in his house for months on end and receives nobody, neither priests nor laymen. I believe that he is letting himself be conquered by wine and his diocese is much neglected.'[23] The neighbouring see of Clogher, an extensive and heavily populated diocese of south Ulster, two-thirds of which was Catholic, had fallen vacant in 1844 and Dr Charles Mc-

---

(1961-74); J. J. McNamee, *History of the diocese of Ardagh* (1954); J. Monahan, *Records relating to the diocese of Ardagh and Clonmacnoise* (1886); A. Cogan, *The ecclesiastical history of the diocese of Meath* ... 3 vols. (1867-74); W. Carrigan, *The history and antiquities of the diocese of Ossory*, 4 vols. (1905); E. A. D'Alton, *History of the archdiocese of Tuam*, 2 vols. (1928); W. J. Battersby, *The complete Catholic directory* ... (1836-57); W. H. Grattan Flood, *History of the diocese of Ferns* (1916); J. Healy, *Maynooth College, its centenary history*, 1795-1895 (1895); C. Maguire, *A history of the diocese of Raphoe*, 2 vols. (1920); O. J. Burke, *The history of the Catholic Archbishops of Tuam* ... (1882); P. O'Connell, *the Diocese of Kilmore: its history and antiquities* (1937); W. Holland, *History of West Cork and the diocese of Ross* (1949); J. Fahey, *The history and antiquities of the diocese of Kilmacduagh* (1893); P. Power, *Parochial history of Waterford and Lismore during the 18th and 19th century* (1912).

[22] *The Nation*, 20 May 1843.

[23] Cullen to Propaganda, 28 Sept. 1851, SC Irlanda, vol. 30, ff. 712-14, Propaganda Fide Archives, cited in V. A. McClelland, *English Roman Catholics and Higher Education, 1830-1903* (1973), pp. 89-90. Cullen's observations, although written some years after our period, are the informed comments of a zealous, reforming bishop. For Cullen, see pp. 62-3.

Nally, the choice of the majority of the priests, had been appointed bishop, despite the opposition of the metropolitan, Archbishop Crolly.[24] McNally was essentially a product of Maynooth College where he had entered as a student in 1808 and remained on as a member of the staff until his appointment, in 1843, as coadjutor bishop. An independent-minded and able administrator and organizer, and a devoted pastor, he effectively reformed his diocese, bringing it into line with the norms of Roman liturgy and law, and promoting, too, popular devotions, particularly the cult of the Virgin Mary.[25] In the 1850s Cullen, who deplored the steady support McNally gave Archbishop MacHale, nevertheless praised him highly on a number of occasions as a diligent pastor, clever and worthy of every commendation.[26] Strongly O'Connellite in politics, one of his first acts as bishop was to prescribe that the special prayer in the Roman missal 'Pro Constituto in carcere vel in captivitate' be said at all masses for Daniel O'Connell, then in Richmond Jail, and he travelled in person to Dublin to present an address of congratulation to the Liberator on his release.[27] The bishop of Derry, a diocese of whose population 54 per cent was Catholic, was the fifty-year-old John McLaughlin who had succeeded his uncle in 1840. Like McNally he supported Repeal, but by 1844 he was already showing signs of severe mental illness and in 1845 he suffered a complete breakdown. As he never fully recovered, it was necessary in 1846 to appoint a coadjutor, Dr Edward Maginn, an ardent Repealer and Young Irelander, to administer the diocese. In neighbouring Donegal, the bishop of Raphoe was Patrick McGettigan, a cautious prelate, popular with the large and wealthy Protestant section of the county. Cullen was critical of his conduct and complained, in 1851, that he 'speaks without much judgment in many cases'.[28] His

[24] Murray to Crolly, 17 Feb. 1843; Fransoni to Murray, 4 Feb. 1843; Murray to Fransoni, 27 Feb. 1843, Murray Papers, DDA; Clogher clergy to Fransoni, 4 Feb. 1843, McNally Papers, Clogher Diocesan Archives.

[25] McNally to Cullen 13 July 1844; 29 Mar. 1845; 15 Oct. 1848, Cullen Papers.

[26] Cullen to Fransoni, 22 Aug. 1852, Acta, vol. 214, f. 490, Propaganda Fide Archives, cited in Emmet Larkin, *The making of the Roman Catholic Church in Ireland, 1850-1860* (1980), p. 161.

[27] *Address of the Roman Catholic Bishop, Priests and Laity of ... Clogher to ... O'Connell* (1845), McNally Papers, Clogher Diocesan Archives.

[28] Cullen to Propaganda, 28 Sept. 1851, SC Irlanda, vol. 30, f. 712, Propaganda Fide Archives, McClelland, *English Roman Catholics*, p. 90.

main achievement was to provide churches and some schools, notably a convent of Loreto nuns, for his diocese.

In the north-east of the country were the two dioceses in which the Catholics formed a minority—Dromore and the united dioceses of Down and Connor. The bishop of the small diocese of Dromore was the energetic and forceful Michael Blake, now in his seventieth year. While vicar-general in the archdiocese of Dublin he had built the first Catholic church facing on a public street—Saints Michael and John—and defiantly rang the peal of bells for mass, an act of provocation which, but for Daniel O'Connell's intervention, would have involved him in a prosecution. The bishops sent him to Rome in 1815 as one of three delegates to protest against the veto, and he had returned there in 1824 to refound, despite strong Roman opposition, the Irish College for the training of students for the priesthood. Catherine McAuley, who was encountering painful misunderstanding in her attempt to found the Irish Sisters of Mercy in Dublin, owed much to the sturdy support and encouragement of this courageous pastor. When appointed bishop in 1833 he built schools and churches, defended the rack-rented peasants and personally served free meals to poor children. His strong views and vigorous, even difficult, temperament involved him in a long drawn-out dispute with some of his clergy which the intervention of the archbishops of Armagh and Dublin failed to resolve. He was a warm supporter of O'Connell.

Of a far milder disposition was his younger colleague, Cornelius Denvir, bishop of Down and Connor, whose diocese was the most challenging in the country. Catholics there constituted a minority (28 per cent) among a hostile, mainly Presbyterian majority, and the diocese embraced Belfast, the most industrialized and fastest-growing city in Ireland. With a population of about 75,000, possibly a third Catholic, Belfast had just experienced its first major sectarian riot in Sandy Row in 1843 which, following the hostile reception accorded to O'Connell in 1841, marked the end of an era of mutual toleration. Denvir, a kindly but timid man of an academic turn of mind, became increasingly unable to cope with this explosive situation; and by 1863, the primate, Dr Joseph Dixon, archbishop of Armagh, was to report reluctantly that 'the "spiritus timoris'' as regards the Orangemen among whom he [Denvir] lives so predominates in him that he is utterly unfit to be left in the administration of the Church in Belfast.'[29] The populous and centrally-situated diocese of Meath, which was over- whelmingly Catholic (93 per cent), had been ruled since 1830 by the active and socially-concerned John Cantwell. Appalled by the hunger and distress he found among his flock, he became convinced that the only way to remove 'the misery which is so continually before our eyes' was by political action; accordingly, the Repeal of the Union became for him 'a holy cause', indeed 'the only means of making Ireland prosperous and happy and the throne secure'.[30] Following his lead clergy and people flocked into the Repeal movement and many of the more famous monster meetings were held in Meath, culminating in the great meeting on the hill of Tara. Even after the collapse of the Repeal agitation, Cantwell remained committed to the cause of the peasants and gave active support to the Tenant Right movement. By contrast, James Browne, the bishop of the neighbouring diocese of Kilmore, a strongly Catholic area of south Ulster, avoided political activity in the belief that Repeal was impractical, although he allowed free rein to his clergy in the matter. Formerly professor of sacred scripture in Maynooth College he had been appointed coadjutor bishop in 1827 when County Cavan, the major portion of the diocese, had become the centre of the most zealous efforts of the New Reformation.[31] He proved an energetic, reforming bishop, successful in the administration of his diocese. Despite his vigorous pastoral policy, he was moderate in outlook and on occasion mediated between Orangeman and Nationalist. In differences within the hierarchy, too, he took a conciliatory attitude.

There were six suffragan bishops in the southern province of Cashel. The bishop of Cork was the seventy-two year-old John Murphy, a member of the brewing family of that name. He had studied for the priesthood at Lisbon and Paris and had been chosen in 1815 to represent the Irish bishops at Rome during the veto controversy. A shrewd administrator, he was

---

[29] Dixon to Kirby, 31 Oct. 1863, Kirby Papers, cited in F.Heatley, *The Story of St Patrick's, Belfast, 1815-1977* (1977), p. 32.

[30] *Pilot*, 17 August. 1840; 8 Jan. 1841.

[31] For the New Reformation, see pp. 56-7.

conservative in his approach to pastoral problems, showing little enthusiasm either for the expansive schemes of Catherine McAuley's Sisters of Mercy or for Father Theobald Mathew's Temperance movement. He was reputed to own the finest private collection of books in Ireland. 'Old Bishop Murphy is a glorious Johnsonian bookworm', wrote the Young Ireland leader Thomas Davis: 'He'd hardly let me out of his house. But he's a courtier and with all his 100,000 volumes, his book-lined mansion, ... I am not quite sure of him.'[32] Bartholomew Crotty, a weaver's son, was bishop of the united dioceses of Cloyne and Ross. The Cloyne diocese was one of the richest and most populous in Ireland, but the bishop was a native of the smaller, more picturesque west Cork diocese of Ross. Trained in the Irish College in Lisbon, he later became its rector during the difficult years of the Napoleonic wars. He had been appointed president of Maynooth College in 1813 and for almost twenty years had guided that institution through some critical episodes. From those years he had gained the reputation of a stern disciplinarian, but he had proved a good pastor and open-minded in his approach. Owing to his poor health he was unable to attend all the meetings of the bishops, but his prudent counsel was always forthcoming. The bishop of Kerry, Cornelius Egan, had been principal of the diocesan seminary in Killarney, then parish priest of the thriving town of Tralee before being appointed bishop of Kerry in 1824. At O'Connell's request he had written to his clergy to support Morgan John O'Connell in the 1835 election, and his priests were active in the campaign against the payment of tithes to the Established church. Later, however, he became more diffident about playing a leading role in nationalist politics. The bishop of Killaloe, Patrick Kennedy, was less reticent in taking a stand in politics, dis-playing interest in both Federalism and in Repeal. An eloquent speaker, able and fundamentally moderate, he was occasionally over-impulsive. John Ryan, bishop of Limerick since 1828, impressed Newman when he visited the city in 1854 as an open-minded man who welcomed discussion. He was also a reforming bishop who provided his diocese with schools and convents. The most recently appointed bishop in the province was Nicholas

---

[32] C. G. Duffy, *Thomas Davis; the Memoirs of an Irish Patriot, 1840-1846* (1890), p. 162.

Foran who, after a distinguished career at Maynooth, was selected by the clergy of Waterford as *dignissimus* for their diocese as early as 1829. The Duke of Wellington had blocked his appointment on the grounds that it would not be beneficial to the peace of the country. In 1831 he was provided to the see of Galway but fell ill and did not accept it. When the see of Waterford again fell vacant in 1837 he was appointed. He had been president of the diocesan college at Waterford and later parish priest in Lismore and Dungarvan. Doyle described him as 'a man of sincere piety and great good sense'.[33] One of O'Connell's staunchest supporters, Foran did not hesitate to intervene in elections to promote O'Connellite candidates.

There were only three suffragan bishops in the province of Dublin. Francis Haly, bishop of Kildare and Leighlin, was a man of moderate views but was accused by a Dublin priest of being absent when awkward issues arose.[34] One of the most influential of the prelates was the youngest on the bench, William Kinsella, bishop of Ossory, who had been picked and trained by Bishop Doyle. Highly esteemed by his confrères who regarded him as an intellectual, he had more than once successfully represented their views to the government. Tocqueville too, was impressed by him: 'Mgr. Kinsley [*sic*] is a likeable man, very witty and perspicacious, and has enough sense to be impartial (as far as an Irishman can be) and finds pleasure in showing it. In everything he says there is a note of triumph, which shows that he is the leader of a party which has attained power after long oppression.'[35] As Tocqueville surmised, Kinsella was much involved in the politics of the day although in general he took the same moderate line as his patron, Dr Doyle. Through Doyle's influence he had been appointed bishop at the very early age of thirty-two and had co-operated closely with the two reforming bishops, Murray and Doyle. He also kept close contact with some of the Munster bishops. James Keating, bishop of Ferns since 1819, did not figure prominently in public life, but his strong stand against tithes occasioned a short but sharp exchange of letters with Dr Elrington, the

[33] Fitzpatrick, *Doyle*, ii. 150.
[34] See p. 174.
[35] Tocqueville, *Journeys*, p. 140.

Anglican bishop of Ferns. Up to twenty new churches were built in his diocese during his reign. Clarendon described him in 1847 as 'a foolish old man surrounded by furious repealing priests'.[36]

What is remarkable about the Connaught bishops is that, without exception, they took an attitude that was opposed to government policy on the major problems of the day. Their stand can be partly accounted for by the vigorous leadership provided by their metropolitan, Dr John MacHale, but it may also reflect clerical resentment that Connaught, the poorest of the provinces, appeared to be neglected by government, whether in London or Dublin, and at the same time had become a prime target for well-financed proselytism. Whatever the reasons, all the bishops attacked the national system of education introduced by the Whig government and all of them gave enthusiastic backing to the Repeal agitation. The pastoral activity of some Connaught bishops did not measure up to the high standard expected by Cullen. One of those whom he criticized was Edmund French, bishop of Kilmacduagh and Kilfenora, who being old ill and afflicted by scruples concerning his baptism, had not visited his diocese, the smallest and poorest in Ireland, for several years.[37] French, whose parents were Protestant, was ecumenically-minded and had trained for the priesthood in Portugal. He had been Warden of Galway where he had established a convent of Presentation nuns. A Dominican friar, he was the only member of the regular clergy on the bishops' bench since the forced retirement of his fellow-Dominican, Francis O'Finan, from the diocese of Killala. In that latter diocese, Thomas Feeny, an irascible and stern disciplinarian, had been the effective ordinary since 1839. George Browne, who had been recently translated from Galway, was bishop of Elphin. He had been a staunch supporter of O'Connellite policies for many years, and as early as 1834 an alarmed government had begged Propaganda not to consider him for the vacant see of Tuam. His successor in the diocese of Galway and the most recent addition to the bench of bishops was Laurence

---

[36] Clarendon to Russell, 28 Dec. 1847, Clarendon Papers, Letterbook 2.

[37] Cullen to Propaganda, 28 Sept. 1851, SC Irlanda, vol. 30, f. 712, Propaganda Fide Archives, McClelland, *English Roman Catholics*, p. 90.

O'Donnell who also proved a fervent Repealer, attending Repeal banquets with MacHale and Browne. According to Cullen he was, in 1851, old and inactive. The distinction of being the first Maynooth-trained priest to become a bishop belonged to Thomas Coen, appointed coadjutor to the bishop of Clonfert in 1815 and succeeding to that see in 1831. Coen was one of the first students to enrol at Maynooth where later he proved a stern dean of discipline. Another former member of the Maynooth staff, a classical scholar, was Patrick McNicholas, whose see was the small, barren diocese of Achonry. Cullen complained that, due to illness, McNicholas neglected his pastoral duties.[38]

In the formulation, from within the Irish church, of its policy towards the state, the four archbishops were of prime importance. At the head of the church stood Dr William Crolly (1780-1849), regarded by Catholics as archbishop of Armagh and primate of all Ireland, although the law did not permit the assumption of territorial titles.[39] Born in County Down and educated at a school run jointly by a Catholic and a Presbyterian, he had been trained at Maynooth before being appointed parish priest of Belfast, and in 1825, bishop of Down and Connor. He became well liked by the Presbyterians, especially the Unitarians, who offered him places for Catholic students in the recently established Belfast Academical Institution. Later, during the Academic Colleges controversy, Cullen denounced him for his approval of the Academy. Crolly held, however, that as an Ulsterman he was better able to judge what was best for his province. In 1835, he was appointed archbishop of Armagh, and in his farewell discourse on leaving Belfast he promised that 'any influence or authority that I possess shall be constantly exercised to establish concord among christians of every communion which is so necessary for the peace, prosperity and happiness of Ireland.'[40] He was not lacking in courage, as he showed in the controversies concerning education. Unfortunately, his tendency to change course weakened his authority within the church. Kinsella complained of the recurrent 'wavering of our Brother of Armagh', and Yore, a Dublin vicar-general, called him the 'unsteady Pilot' at the head of the

---

[38] Ibid.

[39] See G. Crolly, *Life of the Most Rev. Dr Crolly* (1851), for a brief account of his life.

[40] *London and Dublin Weekly Orthodox Journal*, 26 Sept. 1835.

church.[41] The archbishop of Cashel, Dr Michael Slattery (1783-1857), came of well-to-do farming stock in Tipperary.[42] After taking a law degree at Trinity College, Dublin, he retained a strong fear of the danger which that institution allegedly constituted for Catholic students. He trained for the priesthood at Carlow College. After some years as professor of philosophy and of pastoral work, he was appointed president of Maynooth in 1834 and, later the same year, archbishop of Cashel. He was introspective, describing himself as a retiring man, who shunned the public eye. Cullen, who owed much to his support and yet was impatient at his lack of vigour in implementing synodal decrees, told Kirby in January 1853: 'The poor Archbishop is very timid, and he believes that he is always on the verge of death, even though he is in good health'.[43] John Henry Newman was more understanding, describing him in 1854 as 'a most pleasing, taking man—mild, gentle, tender and broken'.[44] Slattery's pastoral activity in his diocese and the leading role he played in such important national issues as the national education system, the Queen's Colleges, and the Famine, indicate a bishop of considerable organizational powers. Owing to his poor health he rarely attended the bishops' meetings, but by his close contact with his fellow bishops, maintained by a regular correspondence, he kept himself well informed of events. In this way, as well as through his businesslike habits and his not inconsiderable intellectual ability, he exercised a real influence on the church's affairs.

The most outstanding bishop, after the death of Doyle in 1834, was Daniel Murray (1768-1852), archbishop of Dublin.[45] His position in the capital, together with his long experience, considerable achievements, and personal goodness contributed to this pre-eminence. He came of substantial farming stock in County Wicklow, and from 1784 to 1792 had trained for the

[41] Eliot to Graham, 16 Oct. 1844, Graham Papers; Yore to Slattery, 13 Nov. 1845, Slattery Papers.
[42] M. Tierney, 'Catalogue of letters relating to the Queen's Colleges 1845-50, in the papers of Archbishop M. Slattery', *Collectanea Hibernica*, No. 9 (1966), pp. 83-120.
[43] Cullen to Kirby, 28 Jan. 1853, Kirby Papers.
[44] Newman to the Oratorians, 23 Feb. 1845, *Letters and Diaries*, xvi. 54.
[45] There is no full-scale published life of Murray. See, however, W. Meagher, *Notice on the life and character of His Grace Most Rev. Dr. Murray...with historical and biographical notes* (1853); K. B. Nowlan, 'Daniel Murray', *New Catholic Encyclopedia*, x. 86.

priesthood at Salamanca where he was ordained in 1790. Appointed curate in Arklow, he had barely escaped death at the hands of the Antrim militia in their retreat from Vinegar Hill in 1798 and had been forced to flee to Dublin. In 1809, he was appointed coadjutor archbishop to Dr Troy, archbishop of Dublin, where he gradually took over most of the running of the diocese and was appointed archbishop on the death of Troy in 1823. In Murray the trait that struck most contemporaries was his mildness. Doyle, who worked in close cooperation with him, called him 'an angel of a man'.[46] Dr William Walsh, bishop of Halifax, Nova Scotia, reporting to Cullen on a controversy during which Murray had been bitterly abused, commented that although there was exacerbation of feeling on all sides, 'from this I must ever except the good Dr Murray. He was as calm ... and discreet as ever.'[47] A succession of lords-lieutenant—Anglesey, Normanby, Heytesbury, Bessborough, and Clarendon—worked easily with him. Stanley remarked that there was 'no milder man to all appearance'.[48] Lord John Russell praised him in the House of Commons as 'distinguished for his moderation of opinion',[49] while for Clarendon he was 'a model of a bishop'.[50] J. P. Kennedy, who resigned from the Board of National Education because of differences with other commissioners, stated that with Murray 'I could go on forever'.[51] Thomas Hyde Villiers, who visited Ireland in 1828 to study the situation there, told Greville that 'Murray is a very clever man, but not so ambitious as Doyle'.[52] His fellow-clerics, too, even when they disagreed with him, still retained affection and esteem for him.[53] He was, however, not a forceful personality and there was a suggestion that he lacked firmness in dealing with abuses. When Doyle remonstrated with him on this point,

[46] Fitzpatrick, *Doyle*, ii. 374.

[47] Walsh to Cullen, 18 Jan. 1845, Cullen Papers; see pp. 216-17.

[48] Gladstone's memorandum, 9 Dec. 1837. MSS 44777, ff. 40-51, cited in W. E. Gladstone, *Prime Ministers' Papers*, ed. J. Brooke and M. Sorensen (1972), ii. 88.

[49] *Hansard*, lxxx. 1248, 2 June 1845.

[50] Clarendon to Russell, 10 Aug. 1847, Clarendon Papers.

[51] Kennedy to Thomas Spring Rice, 12 Dec. 1838, Monteagle Papers, National Library of Ireland, cited in D. H. Akenson, *The Irish Education Experiment: the National System of Education in the nineteenth century* (1970), p. 131.

[52] C. Greville, *The Greville Memoirs, A journal of the Reigns of King George IV, King William IV and Queen Victoria*, ed. H. Reeve (1913), i. 226, 20 Dec. 1828.

[53] Cooper to Cullen, 22, 25 Sept. 1844, Cullen Papers.

Murray gave him the disarming reply that 'it was difficult to know the exact point where clemency should cease and severity begin.'[54] Other critics, like O'Connell, feared that he was over-trusting in his dealings with the government, and he undoubtedly had a deep-rooted respect for legal authority.

His caution and circumspection were well known. Sir Dominic Corrigan, visiting physician to Maynooth College, described an important interview he had with some bishops; Crolly and Denvir took an active part but 'Dr Murray with his characteristic caution said little'.[55] So careful was he in what he said and wrote that a Jesuit contemporary, John Lynch, described him as 'a most cautious man who never gave a direct answer when he could possibly avoid it'.[56] Peace-loving and unwilling to hurt others, he was described by Pusey as 'apologetic' and ecumenically minded.[57] When building the pro-Cathedral, he refused to take the commanding site now occupied by the General Post Office in O'Connell Street lest he offended Protestant susceptibilities, and for the same reason he asked the Cistercians to cancel the public ceremony they planned in honour of their first foundation in Ireland since the Reformation.[58] The moderate line Murray pursued was not always appreciated. A bitter dispute arose between Dr MacHale and Dr O'Finan, bishop of Killala, and the Congregation of Propaganda asked Murray to investigate the affair. When Murray unwillingly accepted the task, he was blamed by both parties. O'Finan reproached him for reporting to Propaganda that it was inadvisable that he return to his diocese, while MacHale was picqued, according to Murray, because he was told 'that I was less adverse than he would wish to poor Dr O'Finan'.[59] If Murray appeared to be less forceful than some would have

---

[54] Fitzpatrick, *Doyle*, ii. 375.

[55] Corrigan to Redington, n.d. 1847, Clarendon Papers. Sir Dominic Corrigan (1802–80); Sir Thomas Redington (1815-62), MP for Dundalk; Under-secretary for Ireland, 1846.

[56] Fitzpatrick, *Doyle*, i. 244.

[57] Pusey to Newman, 9 Aug. 1841, H. P. Liddon, *Life of Edward Bouverie Pusey* ... (1894), ii. 246-7.

[58] M. Ronan, 'Archbishop Murray, 1766-1852', *IER*, lxxvii (1952), 243; K. J. Walsh, *Dom Vincent of Mount Melleray* (1962), pp. 190-1.

[59] O'Finan to Murray, 11 Mar. 1839; Murray to O'Finan, 28 Mar. 1839, Murray Papers; Murray to Cullen, 4 Apr. 1839, Cullen Papers.

liked, he was not timid—as his public stand on such questions as the veto in 1816, the national education system, the Bequests Act, and the Ecclesiastical Titles Act proved. On the Queen's Colleges issue he was to show such tenacity that his opponents accused him of stubborness.

Pastorally, he accomplished much. At the time of his consecration, Dublin possessed only one decent-sized church; by the year of his death in 1852, no less than ninety-seven new churches had been built.[60] He welcomed the newly re-established Jesuits and the recently founded order of Christian Brothers and encouraged the foundation of the Irish Vincentian Fathers.[61] His greatest pastoral achievement was probably his work in connection with the institution of three orders of nuns—the Irish Sisters of Charity, the Sisters of Loreto, and the Sisters of Mercy—for the care of the poor and sick and for work in education.[62] By 1844, his diocese contained a quarter of all the regular clergy and convents in Ireland. With their help a number of orphanages and asylums and a large Catholic hospital were also built.[63] He was mission-minded, establishing in 1838 the first Irish branch of the Association for the Propagation of the Faith and assisting Fr John Hand to found All Hallows College for the provision of priests for the English-speaking world.[64] The education of the poor was a major concern because in Dublin, at the beginning of his episcopate, there were only three Catholic schools. Murray began discussions with the government with a view to obtaining 'some general system of education in the advantages of which our Roman Catholic poor could freely participate', and in 1826 he established his own Education Society.[65] When the national system

[60] Meagher, *Murray,* pp. 9-10, 146*.

[61] Meagher, *Murray,* pp. 34, 40-2; J. D. Fitzpatrick, *Edmund Rice, founder... of the Brothers of the Christian Schools ...* (1945), pp. 173, 179-82, 197-8, 239-42, 250-1, 317-18, 336.

[62] For the Sisters of Loreto and the Sisters of Charity, Murray saw to their training, bought the property they needed and supported them throughout his life. His role in connection with the Sisters of Mercy was less direct. S. Atkinson, *Mary Aikenhead; her life, her work and her friends* (1879); A Loreto Sister, *Joyful Mother of Children: Mother Frances Teresa Ball* (1961); R. Burke Savage, *Catherine McAuley: the first Sister of Mercy* (1955).

[63] *Catholic Directory,* 1845, pp. 227-43.

[64] Meagher, *Murray,* pp. 42-4.

[65] Murray to Goulburn, 22 April. 1824; Goulburn to Murray, 18, 27 May 1824, Murray Papers.

of education was established in 1831, he became one of its most diligent commissioners and by his death there were 220 schools in Dublin acceptable to Catholics. His correspondence with Frances Ball and Mary Aikenhead reveals him as a spiritual guide of deep faith, gentle firmness, and understanding. His pastoral letters, particularly that on the 'First Appearance of the Cholera' (1832), show his practical concern for the poor, and in 1845 he introduced the Society of Saint Vincent de Paul to visit and help them.

An enduring achievement was the reorganization of the church in his diocese. In July 1831 Murray and his suffragans, Doyle, Kinsella, and Keating, after preliminary meetings between themselves, held four separate diocesan synods and drew up statutes for the Dublin province.[66] His own diocese was efficiently organized. Politically, Murray was essentially a moderate; the excesses of the French Revolution and the rebellion of 1798 had left such an impression on him that he feared that popular movements such as the Repeal agitation would entail widespread bloodshed and would tumble down both throne and altar, as he put it, 'in one common ruin'.[67] Clerical intervention in secular and radical politics was repugnant to him, and he courageously opposed it. He was, none the less, patriotic, and Sheil reports him as exclaiming dramatically at a public meeting in the pro-Cathedral in Dublin that 'the contemplation of the wrongs of my country makes my soul burn within me!'[68] But such an outburst was not characteristic of him; he was perhaps more devoted to the church for whose cause he was ready to fight, as both Stanley and Russell implied and as his stand on the Ecclesiastical Titles Bill later bore witness.[69] He had a realistic grasp of politics and had little patience for those 'fools who became quite suspicious of every kind of mischief, if we come at all into contact with people

[66] Statuta Diocesana per provinciam Dublinensem observanda ... (1831); Meagher, *Murray*, pp. 128-31.

[67] Murray to Clarendon, 6 Jan. 1848, Clarendon Papers; cf. Murray to Propaganda, 13 Dec. 1845, Murray Papers.

[68] R. L. Sheil, *Sketches legal and political*, ed. M. W. Savage (1855), ii. 191. Sheil gives no date for Murray's outburst but it probably preceded the Relief Act of 1829.

[69] Gladstone's memorandum, 9 Dec. 1837, Add. MSS 44777, ff. 40-51, cited in Gladstone, *Prime Ministers' Papers,* ii. 88; *Hansard*, lxxx. 1247-8, 2 June 1845, Russell.

in power'.[70] Even before succeeding Troy as archbishop of Dublin, he had been involved in important negotiations concerning the veto, Emancipation, and Maynooth College. With Dr Richard Whately, the Anglican archbishop of Dublin, he agreed to become one of the commissioners on the inquiry into the Poor Law in 1833. In 1835, he had become the unlikely target of a fierce no-popery campaign carried on throughout Britain by the Revd Robert J. McGhee and the Revd Mortimer O'Sullivan. Murray defended his church with dignity and humour, writing directly to the prime minister, Lord Melbourne, and making a noble appeal to the English people's sense of fair play.[71] By 1844, however, Murray was in his seventy-sixth year and he tended to place most of the day-to-day burdens of administration on the shoulders of a very devoted and efficient administrator, Archdeacon John Hamilton.[72]

Murray's willingness to work with the Irish administration, especially over education, was at the root of the trouble that arose between him and the archbishop of Tuam, John Mac-Hale.[73] MacHale (1791-1881) was one of the most influential men in Ireland—and one of the most controversial—from the 1820s until his death in 1881. Dr McGrath has described well the influences that helped to shape this formidable man:

As a child, John MacHale had seen the French troops marching from Killala to Castlebar, and had followed to the grave the corpse of his parish priest, summarily hanged for having harboured some officers of the invading force. His early education was received at the local 'hedge-school' and at the 'classical academy' at Castlebar, schools which carried on the tradition of a century of struggle for freedom of religion. His theological studies were pursued at Maynooth, and he was the first Irish prelate since the Reformation to be wholly educated in Ireland. His diocese contained some of the wildest and poorest parts of the country, and was the scene of the most ruthless incidents of the land war and of the most shameless efforts of the proselytising societies. Every circumstance, therefore, tended to develop his nationalist leanings ...[74]

[70] Murray to Slattery, 30 July 1844, Slattery Papers.

[71] Meagher, *Murray,* pp. 170-95.

[72] John Hamilton (*c.* 1800-62).

[73] B. O'Reilly, *John MacHale, Archbishop of Tuam: his life, times and correspondence,* 2 vols. (1890) is the standard biography.

[74] F. McGrath, *Newman's university: idea and reality* (1951), p. 92.

Immediately after his ordination in 1814 he was appointed lecturer in dogmatic theology at Maynooth and in 1820 he succeeded to the chair. It was while lecturing in Maynooth that he commenced his long series of public letters denouncing what he saw as abuses in church and state, from Bible Societies and the Kildare Place Society to the government's neglect of the poor. If his pen rivalled Doyle's in eloquence and power, he lacked the latter's balance and was too prone to rush into print. He was a cultural nationalist who spoke the Irish language by preference and in it wrote several works.[75] Deeply influenced by the sufferings of the people in the west of Ireland, he felt called to champion their rights.[76] O'Connell called him the 'Lion of the West' (or 'the Lion of the Fold of Judah'); Archbishop Crolly once ruefully remarked that O'Connell could have more aptly called him 'the Tiger of the tribe of Dan'.[77] There was no denying the Lion's courage and more than one person received a severe mauling from him. His suffragan, Dr O'Finan, crossed him and, despite an appeal to Rome, was forced to retire from the diocese. During this episode Stanley, at the informal discussion in Peel's house, paid a handsome tribute to MacHale's power: on its being mentioned that the pope was supporting Dr O'Finan against MacHale, he remarked that 'if the Pope comes into collision with Dr MacHale in Ireland I'll back Dr MacHale'.[78] Heytesbury, in the midst of sharp conflict with MacHale in 1844, regarded him as the only Irish bishop with courage.[79] Later, John Henry Newman was not alone in fearing to cross him.[80] MacHale's fearless courage was apparent when the commissioners inquiring into Maynooth in 1826 rebuked him for publicly criticizing the Established Church, contrary to the

[75] He was responsible for awakening a life-long interest in the Irish language in Fr Peadar Ó Laoghaire, the creator of modern Irish prose and a central figure in the Gaelic Revival at the turn of the century; P. Ó Laoghaire, *Mo Sgéal Féin* (1915), pp. 92-4; *My Own Story,* translated by Sheila O Sullivan (1973), pp. 53-5.

[76] Travellers' accounts and contemporary investigations show that the people of Connaught were by far the poorest in Ireland; T. W. Freeman, *Pre-Famine Ireland, a study in historical geography* (1957), pp. 242-68.

[77] Diary of James Donnelly for 1852, Donnelly Papers, Clogher Diocesan Archives. James Donnelly (1823-93), bishop of Clogher, 1864-93.

[78] Gladstone's memorandum, 9 Dec. 1837, Add. MSS 44777, ff. 40-51, cited in Gladstone, *Prime Ministers' Papers,* ii. 88, 9 Dec. 1837.

[79] Heytesbury to Graham, 3 Dec. 1844, Graham Papers.

[80] Newman to St John, 21 Feb. 1854, 26 June 1856, *Letters and Diaries,* xvi. 50; xvii. 298.

rules of the college. He yielded nothing, claiming that 'I was only using the privileges of a British subject' and demanding why, when others were permitted to attack his church, he should not be permitted to reply.[81] When he left his professorship to become coadjutor bishop of Killala in 1825, perhaps because of the violation of the rule concerning public writings, he did not receive the customary vote of thanks from the college.

There was, however, a negative side to MacHale's courage: all accounts converge to show that he was a most difficult man to work with. Archbishop Healy, one of his successors in the see of Tuam and author of the official history of Maynooth College, said of him that he was always in opposition, while Mgr D'Alton, the historian of Tuam, described him as 'ready to differ from anybody, and ready to attack anybody'.[82] Canon Ulick Bourke, an intimate friend, wrote that his 'unwillingness to co-operate, of which O'Connell had complained more than once previous to the Repeal movement, became a settled state of mental conviction.'[83] On more than one occasion his fellow-bishops complained of his intractability.[84] Cullen, with whom he had been on terms of friendship for many years, complained to Pius IX, to the Congregation of Propaganda and to his friend, Kirby, then rector of the Irish College in Rome, of MacHale's unruly nature: 'The sole obstacle to perfect harmony in the episcopal body is Mgr the archbishop of Tuam, who cannot resign himself to thinking like his colleagues, and who even changes his own opinions when they come to be adopted by others, so as to remain always in opposition.'[85] A few months later Cullen asserted that MacHale 'loves to find himself in opposition to the others', and there is a touch of humour and more than a little truth in Dr Dixon's description of MacHale as 'His Holiness's Opposition in the Irish episcopal body'.[86]

[81] *Eighth report of the Commissioners of Irish Education: Roman Catholic College of Maynooth, PP 1826-7*, xiii. 829-31.

[82] J. Healy, *Maynooth College: its centenary history, 1795-1895* (1895), p. 453; D'Alton, *Tuam*, p. 49.

[83] U. J. Bourke, *The life and times of the Most. Rev. John MacHale, Archbishop of Tuam* (1882), p. 141.

[84] See p. 61.

[85] Cullen to Propaganda 26 May, 1854, Acta vol. 336, Propaganda Fide Archives, cited in J. H. Whyte, 'Political Problems, 1850-1860', P. J. Corish, ed. *A history of Irish Catholicism*, vol. v (1967), pt. 2 and 3, p. 5.

[86] Dixon to Kirby, 24 Mar. 1859, Kirby Papers, cited in E. R. Norman, *The Catholic Church and Ireland in the Age of Rebellion, 1859-1873* (1965), p. 12.

Despite his *frondeur*-like activities and the divisiveness that he introduced into his dioceses of Killala and Tuam and among his fellow-bishops, MacHale was an outstanding leader of men. No other bishop of his time received the same admiring loyalty from his faithful nor the same constant support of the bishops of his province. Murray lamented to Clarendon that:

as long as MacHale perseveres in his present course of political and spiritual agitation the Church will go from bad to worse, but if he were to take up the cause of order and subordination and to behave decently like any other Christian Bishop all the rest of the Prelates would follow. The moderate ones because it would fall in with their wishes and the turbulent ones because he exercises an absolute control over them ...[87]

Clarendon believed that even Murray and the 'well affected bishops' were 'as much intimidated by MacHale and Co as ever the Tipperary farmers were by the Whiteboys.'[88] When in Rome in 1831-2, he impressed both the conservative Pope Gregory XVI and the Liberal Catholic leaders, La Mennais, Lacordaire, and Montalembert, those 'pilgrims of God and liberty' who had come in a vain attempt to win the pope to their views. Thereafter the Liberal Catholics followed MacHale's career with keen interest.[89] On the way home, he visited Munich where he impressed the historian Ignaz Döllinger, the central figure in an important group of young German Catholic intellectuals. Later Döllinger, writing to La Mennais to commend him on his submission to the papal condemnation of Liberal Catholicism, bitterly lamented that their own churches had no bishop of MacHale's calibre: 'cet excellent homme nous a fait sentir encore plus amèrement ce qui nous manque: des évêques qui aient l'érudition, le noble courage et l'esprit d'indépendence d'un prélat irlandais.'[90] In 1834, MacHale's name came to the fore as a successor to the archbishop of Tuam. 'Anybody but him' was Melbourne's alarmed reaction, and the government immediately took energetic diplomatic steps to block MacHale's appointment.[91] Palmerston's efforts in Rome won over Cardinal

---

[87] Clarendon to Russell, 21 Dec. 1847, Clarendon Papers.

[88] Clarendon to Russell, 28 Jan. 1848, ibid.

[89] W. J. Roe, *Lamennais and England; the reception of Lamennais' religious ideas in England in the nineteenth century* (1966), p. 190.

[90] Döllinger to Lamennais, 12 Oct. 1832, G. Goyau, ed. *Le Porte-Feuille de Lamennais, 1818-1836* (1930), p. 109.

[91] Greville, *Journal*, iii. 215-16, 27 June 1835; Broderick, *Holy See*, pp. 84-99.

Bernetti, the secretary for state, and other influential members of the curia, but, by August, Charles Justin MacCarthy, who was in the English college in Rome, was able to report delightedly to his friend La Mennais, that 'le Pape pour cette fois, tint ferme et malgré les accusations de libéralisme qui pleuvaient de toutes parts, confirma la nomination.'[92] The favourable impression MacHale had made on Gregory stood him in good stead, apparently, for the pope was reluctant to accept the criticisms made of him. Furthermore, so many of the Irish bishops supported MacHale that Gregory felt that if he appointed anyone else it would appear that he had been swayed by the English government.[93]

Murray was one of the bishops who, in reply to a query from Rome about MacHale, strongly supported his candidature. Questioned on MacHale's alleged involvement in politics he gave an interesting assessment of the matter:

cum de his rebus politicis scriberet stilum aliquando suum nimis, ut opinor, accuisse. Meminisse tamen oportet pauperibus circumdatum esse egestate et miseria tabescentibus: et si in hujusmodi miseriae causas acrius quam Ipse vellem animadverterit, id pietate erga pauperes suae tribuendum esse puto et zelo quo flagrabat Religionis, quamvis ultra metas prudentiae, ut quidem automabant, paulisper forte progresse. Attamen illum a civilibus commotionibus omnino abhorere certo certius est.[94]

The comments of Murray, a man so different from MacHale in temperament and outlook, have the ring of truth. MacHale's province of Connaught was the poorest in the country. Ninety-six per cent of the population was Catholic, yet it was the object of a determined and partially successful Evangelical Protestant mission which envenomed religious feelings.[95] The echoes of

[92] MacCarthy to Lamennais, 11 Aug. 1834, E. Forgues, *Lettres inédites de Lamennais à Montalembert* (1898), pp. 329-30.

[93] Wiseman to MacHale, 25 Aug. 1834, cited in O'Reilly, *MacHale*, i. 246; Cullen to MacHale, 28 Feb. 1835, ibid., i. 248; Aubin to Seymour, 1 Aug. 1834, FO 170/25, cited in Broderick, *Holy See*, p. 93. Nicholas Wiseman (1802-65), rector of the English College in Rome, cardinal archbishop of Westminster, 1850-65; for Paul Cullen, rector of the Irish College in Rome, see p. 62; George Seymour (1797-1880) was the English Resident Minister at Florence; Thomas Aubin (d. 1844) was attaché at Florence but permanently resident at Rome from 1832 to 1844. His letter quotes extensively from Bernetti's account of his own audience with the pope.

[94] Murray to Pedicini, 16 Aug. 1834, SC Irlanda, vol. 28, ff. 211-12, Propaganda Fide Archives. For translations of documents, see Appendix p. 359. ff.

[95] D. Bowen, *Souperism: myth or reality? a study of Catholics and Protestants during the Great Famine* (1970), pp. 88-106.

the conflict reached Parliament in 1835, and fears were expressed for the safety of the missionaries and their flock exposed to the violent reactions of the Catholics.[96] Later, when news of the mission's successes reached Rome, an alarmed curia sought explanations from MacHale on the losses to the church.[97] These events contributed to make MacHale, already a difficult character, much less tolerant of the establishment in church and state than his more urbane colleague, the archbishop of Dublin. Pastorally, Connaught was not as well provided for as Dublin, largely because it had not the same resources as the metropolis but partly, too, because MacHale—forever suspicious of the intentions of the government—neglected to use even the funds he could have obtained.[98] Politically, MacHale was O'Connell's staunchest and most important clerical supporter, and O'Connell's anxiety to keep his support was shown in 1838 when imploring him to join the Precursor Society: 'perhaps the fate of Ireland depends on your decision'.[99] MacHale did not fail him either then or during the Repeal movement, and the 'dreaded name of John of Tuam' was always a force to be reckoned with in both secular and ecclesiastical politics. O'Connell's respect for him was more than political, for he trusted him in family matters too.[100] MacHale was a complex character, revered by some, hated by others. Clarendon, after meeting him and finding him surprisingly quiet-spoken and reasonable, formed the opinion that 'he is a vain, turbulent, ambitious man but not a bad one'.[101] Optimistically, Clarendon entered into correspondence with the archbishop. 'I have had a shot at the Lion (of Judah) in his den', he told Russell, adding patronizingly: 'If I could assist MacHale in relieving the people of Tuam ... and could continue to communicate confidentially

---

[96] *Hansard*, xxviii. 1203-5, 25 June 1835, Bishop of Exeter.

[97] Bowen, *Souperism*, p. 142.

[98] The table (see p. 33) shows how poorly Connaught was provided for; although in comparison with the Dublin province, its population was greater and more scattered, it had fewer diocesan priests, regular clergy, convents and colleges. There were only 44 national schools in the province compared with 112 in the Dublin province.

[99] O'Connell to MacHale, 6 Sept. 1838, W. J. Fitzpatrick, *Correspondence of Daniel O'Connell, the Liberator* (1888), ii. 147-8.

[100] O'Connell to his daughter Betsey, 28 June 1839, ibid., ii. 187-9.

[101] Clarendon to Russell, 26 Oct; Clarendon to Lansdowne, 26 Oct. 1847, Clarendon Papers.

with him I should not despair of making him an instrument of good, for his vanity is unbounded and with that one might guide his equally unbounded ambition into a right course'.[102] The Lion was not so easily managed, however, and before long Clarendon came to the conclusion that he was more difficult than even Dr Phillpotts, the crusty bishop of Exeter.[103]

Murray and MacHale—the two most influential men in the hierarchy—represented well two different traditions. Murray stood for the older, more conservative and more accommodating tradition, though he was not a time-server and co-operated only if he thought that this would serve the church's long-term interests. MacHale was more dynamic and headstrong, strongly nationalist, deeply involved in public affairs, secular politics, and theological controversy, representing a new, aggressive clerical tradition which had shown its strength in the Emancipation campaign. Both traditions could draw upon the nature of the Irish political movements led by O'Connell, who showed during his career that he could co-operate with British parties and governments or that he could confront and oppose them. Murray had been trained in pre-Revolutionary Spain; MacHale in nineteenth-century Maynooth.

In view of the prominent part played by bishops in public affairs, an impression might emerge of a completely politically-minded hierarchy. Such a picture would be superficial. The great majority of bishops were churchmen rather than demagogues, involved in pastoral rather than political activity, with priorities quite different from those of the laity. The private record of their annual meetings and of the decisions taken there show that they were chiefly concerned with the reorganization of church discipline in such matters as the administration of the sacraments, selection of bishops and the regulation of the amounts payable by the laity in dues and stipends.[104] Their seminaries, too, whether in Ireland, Paris, Rome, or Belgium, and the provision of priests for Catholics throughout the empire took much of their attention. They pressed for schools free from

---

[102] Clarendon to Russell, 10 Dec. 1847, ibid.
[103] Clarendon to Russell, 7 Jan. 1848, ibid.
[104] Meetings of the Irish Bishops, DDA.

proselytism, freedom of worship for Catholic soldiers and Catholic education for their children, legal provision for the poor, and help for famine-victims. The merits of the national education system were closely debated by them, and there was, too, an oft-repeated condemnation of any attempt by the government to pay the clergy. The only reference to politics in these records was the unanimous direction to their clergy, in 1834, to remain aloof from them. The correspondence of such bishops as Murray, Slattery, and McNally shows a predominant concern for daily administration, clerical discipline, the state of religion among the faithful, financial questions, land for churches, and liturgical matters. The less frequent correspondence with the Congregation of Propaganda, besides providing general accounts of the state of the dioceses, is concerned with liturgical and religious problems and includes a good admixture of domestic grievances and disputes. Educational problems, together with the vexed and related question of proselytism, figure prominently in the bishops' dealings with one another and with both the government and the Roman curia. The bishops, then, were essentially pastors of the flock. They were also keen reformers. A promising beginning had been made at their annual meeting in 1829—no doubt under the exciting stimulus of Catholic Emancipation—when they had identified some of the problems most needing attention. In the 1830s and 1840s many bishops, acting individually and in diocesan and provincial synods, introduced long over-due reforms. Their zeal impressed informed observers such as Clarendon, who admitted to Lord Minto in 1848: 'Indeed I think that among our own bishops we should find it difficult to match such men as Dr Crolly, Murray, Denvir, McGettigan, Haley [*sic*], Egan, Kennedy, Ryan and others for their unostentatious piety and the intense zeal with which they labour for the welfare of their flocks.'[105]

It is more difficult to generalize about the 2,400 priests, for conditions varied greatly from diocese to diocese. Observers, including some who opposed them on other grounds, extolled their pastoral zeal particularly during the cholera outbreak of

---

[105] Meetings of the Irish Bishops, 5 Feb. 1829; Clarendon to Minto, 9 Feb. 1848, Clarendon Papers, Letterbook 2.

1832.[106] Clarendon, while severely critical of their involvement in nationalist politics, paid them the following tribute: 'I don't believe that any clergy in Europe work harder or undergo greater privations with more patience and good will.'[107] In general, the bishops were satisfied with the manner in which their priests were fulfilling their ministry. Bishop Sugrue of Kerry reported officially to Rome in 1822: 'De qualitatibus ecclesiasticorum favorabiliter loqui possum, aliqui sunt piissimi, laborosi et zelo pleni, per multi assiduitate et predicatione placent...'[108] Murray, in his report to Rome in 1835, painted a glowing picture of the zeal and probity of his clergy: 'id maxime mihi solatio est clerum scilicet mihi immerenti et pene inutili subditum Religionis zelo alte esse imbutum, honestis moribus praeditum (?), predicatione Verbi Domini aliisque Officii sui operibus assidue deditum adeo ut multi A-Catholicorum grege, Deo favente, gremio Sanctae Matris Ecclesiae quotidie resti-tuantur.'[109] Slattery wrote in the same vein of his clergy: 'tam in Sacramentorum administratione quam in Verbi Dei praedi-catione, quisquam pro suo posse cum laudabiliter assiduitate laborant ... Pastores ... sunt zelo fervidi et vineam Domini assidue colunt, nec aliquod inter eos existit scandalum quod remedio potiori indigeat. E contra graves sunt et bonis moribus imbuti.'[110] In Clogher, the reforming bishop, McNally, reported in 1853 that he was well satisfied with the zeal, good-behaviour, and generosity of his clergy although he did uncover some cases of drunkenness, immorality, and neglect of duty.[111] Such abuses existed elsewhere as the files of Propaganda and synodal decrees indicate.[112] Clerical indiscipline was also a problem. In some dioceses, priests belonging to families which traditionally

[106] Sir Richard Musgrave, *Hansard,* vii. 647, 27 Sept. 1831; Revd Thomas Guthrie, Minister of the Free church of Scotland, at a meeting to protest against the Maynooth Grant, 1 May 1845; A. S. Thelwall, *Proceedings of the Anti-Maynooth Conference of 1845...* (1845), pp. 194-5.

[107] Clarendon to Minto, 9 Feb. 1848, Clarendon Papers.

[108] K. O'Shea, 'Three early nineteenth century diocesan reports', *Kerry Arch. Soc. Jn.,* x (1977), 75.

[109] Murray, Relatio Status 1835, Murray Papers, DDA.

[110] Slattery, Relatio Status 1845, Slattery Papers, 1845.

[111] McNally, Relatio Status 1853, Italian translation, Kirby Papers, 1853, Irish College Archives.

[112] E. Larkin, 'The Devotional Revolution in Ireland, 1850-75', *AHR,* lxvii (1972), 625-30.

filled the ranks of the clergy, asserted a claim to certain parishes, even enlisting the physical support of the faithful in successful attempts to eject the bishop's nominee from the parish church.[113] This abuse was prevalent enough in Ulster to warrant inclusion among the reserved censures drawn up by the synods of the Armagh province in 1834 and 1835 which decreed a suspension against priests 'qui laicis consilium aut favorem praebuerint ad obstruendas fores ecclesiae contra parochum aut vicarium legitime constitutum, aut eos impulerint ad subtrahenda ab eis consueta stipendia.'[114] Occasionally, too, the older priests felt obliged to defend their traditional rights against the reforming zeal of the bishop as he sought to create new parishes at the expense of older ones or when he appeared to apportion too much of their authority or revenues to the assistant priests or to restrict overmuch demands for fees.[115] Many of those difficulties had their roots in practices which had survived from an earlier age and from the disturbed state of the church during the penal days, when the links between priest and parishioner were closer than the bond between priest and bishop. Uncertainty, too, existed as regards the roles of bishops, parish priests, chapters, assistant priests, and regular clergy. Over recent decades the bishops had taken determined and successful action to establish more discipline, as the reforming legislation of the synods in the 1830s and 1840s shows.

If the problem of clerical discipline was a priority for the bishops, a more general complaint against the priests was that they were exacting in the collection of their dues. In 1834, the Reverend David Croly, a Cork priest who conformed to the Established church, in a detailed description of clerical finances, complained that the priests endeavoured to enforce their demands for money 'by the dint of terror'. Having abandoned the simpler style of living of former times, 'the country Priest now copes with the country Squire, keeps sporting dogs, controls elections, presides at political clubs and sits "cheek by jowl" at public dinners and public assemblies with Peers of the land...'[116] Leith Ritchie, who travelled in Ireland in 1838,

---

[113] McNally to Cullen, 13 July 1844, Cullen Papers.

[114] *Statuta dioecesana in dioecesi Derriensi observanda et a RR^{mo.} Petro M'Laughlin, episcopo Derriensi in sua synodo dioecesana edita et promulgata 1834* (1891), p. 57.

[115] Cf. memorandum of Clogher parish priests 1835, Clogher Diocesan Archives.

[116] D. Croly, *An essay religious and political on ecclesiastical finance as regards the Roman Catholic church in Ireland,* (1834), pp. 27, 30.

reported a conversation with a labourer who described the priests as 'a griping, close-fisted set', adding that 'if we are slow in coming forward, he [the priest] calls out our names from the altar and tells us that the labourer being worthy of his hire, if we do not pay him he will not work'.[117] In 1843, Fr James Maher, parish priest of Carlow-Graigue, complained bitterly to his nephew, Dr Paul Cullen, that the demands of the priests had multiplied: 'dues, dues is the perpetual cry, the constant Sunday theme of some, the altar is occupied for an hour every Sunday, for the transactions of the Priests and oats and turf, and all the arrears of Baptisms and Unctions'.[118] Francis O'Neill, a Waterford priest working in Plymouth shortly after the Famine, told Kirby that the priests in Ireland were accused of demanding money for the sacraments and acknowledged that 'this is no false charge against them for all whoever had any experience even in our own Diocese ... will acknowledge that too much cannot be said against it'.[119] Croly and Ritchie were hostile witnesses and Maher was a contro-versialist who habitually painted situations in sombre colours, but there is some corroborative evidence for the allegations. The hierarchy's own committee on church discipline, composed of one bishop from each province, had reported back to their own body in 1829 that 'some priests show unwillingness to administer Extreme Unction without previous remuneration'.[120] How widespread this abuse was the committee did not say: the implication is that it was not common. Nevertheless, the bishops forbade priests to receive dues during the hearing of confessions (a common feature of the stations) and resolved 'that any clergyman withholding his ministry on the score of not receiving his usual dues, be punished by his ordinary'.[121] It has been claimed that 'the seriousness of the problem of clerical avarice *vis-à-vis* the faithful ... was certainly reflected in early nineteenth-century Ireland in the need of the bishops of the province of

[117] L. Ritchie, *Ireland, picturesque and romantic* (1838), pp. 104-5.
[118] Maher to Cullen, 21 Feb. 1843, Cullen Papers, cited in E. Larkin, 'Economic Growth, Capital Investment, and the Roman Catholic Church in Nineteenth-Century Ireland', *AHR*, lxxii (1966-7), 859.
[119] Francis O'Neill to Kirby, 31 July 1853, Kirby Papers, cited in Larkin, 'Devotional Revolution', p. 649.
[120] Meetings of the Irish Bishops, 11 Feb. 1829, DDA.
[121] Ibid.

Dublin to set up by statute a uniform tariff for clerical dues at the diocesan synods in the summer of 1831'.[122] Certainly the diocesan synods held during this period were at pains to fix the amount of 'dues' or fees which the priests should require of the faithful, but this establishment of uniform tariffs was not new.[123] Indeed, the Munster synod of 1828 merely re-enacted the tariffs prescribed by the synod of 1808, which in turn had contented itself with updating the scale fixed in 1775.[124] The bishops of Limerick, Robert Lacy and Denis Conway, had regulated mass stipends and fees early in the eighteenth century.[125]

As the clergy was totally dependent on these fees for its support, it is necessary to examine the matter further.[126] MacHale and Higgins summed up the church's outlay between 1817 and 1847 as follows:

Building of churches	£3,000,000
Parochial Houses	100,000
Convents for nuns	240,000
Monasteries for monks	200,000
Colleges	200,000
Schools for the poor	200,000
Maintenance of the clergy	18,000,000
	£21,940,000[127]

The impressive figure of eighteen million pounds which is given for the maintenance of the clergy—which works out approximately at an average salary of £260 per annum—may well be too high.[128] Doyle put the general average of a bishop's income at between £450 and £500 per annum; Archbishop Curtis placed it between £500 and £600 per annum but thought that it occasionally reached £1,000.[129] Since a bishop's income, however, was derived from the revenue of his mensal parishes and

[122] Larkin, 'Devotional Revolution', p. 632.

[123] See pp. 35-6.

[124] *Monita Pastoralia*, pp. 66-7.

[125] *Statuta et constitutiones diocesis Limericensis* (1842), p. i.

[126] For a general view, see J. A. Murphy, 'The Support of the Catholic Clergy in Ireland, 1750-1850', *Hist. Studies*, V (1965), 103-21.

[127] 'Brevi Rilievi sopra il sistema d'insegnamento misto ...', SC Irlanda, xxx, ff. 182-3, 35, Propaganda Fide Archives; cited in E. Larkin, 'Economic Growth', p. 587.

[128] Larkin, 'Economic Growth', pp. 857-8.

[129] *Minutes of Evidence on the State of Ireland. PP 1825*, ix. 230, 255.

Table 2

The Catholic Church in Ireland in 1845[a]

Dioceses	Parish priests	Curates	Churches	Convents of nuns	Monasteries or Christian Schools	Regular Clergy	Catholic population in 1834
Archd. Armagh	51	67	126	2	...	10	309,564
Derry	35	52	88	...	...	...	196,614
Clogher	36	60	78	...	...	...	260,241
Raphoe	25	29	48	...	...	...	145,385
Down and Connor	38	25	82	...	...	...	154,029
Kilmore	40	47	90	...	...	...	240,593
Ardagh	39	51	68	...	1	4	195,056
Meath	67	74	142	4	...	16	377,562
Dromore	16	20	36	1	...	...	76,275
Total in Armagh	347	425	758	7	1	30	1,955,319
Archd. Dublin	47	126	122	26	2	50	391,006
Kildare and Leighlin	45	73	112	11	...	5	290,038
Ossory	33	58	94	4	...	15	209,848
Ferns	35	59	100	6	...	15	172,789
Total in Dublin	160	316	428	47	2	85	1,063,681
Archd. Cashel and Emly	45	64	90	1	4	10	296,667
Cork	33	46	84	6	2	22	303,984
Killaloe	51	68	120	1	2	3	359,585
Kerry	44	44	93	8	2	2	297,131
Limerick	42	57	83	3	4	12	246,302
Waterford	36	70	76	10	4	14	253,091
Cloyne and Ross	54	84	113	...	2	2	436,627
Total in Cashel	305	433	659	29	20	65	2,229,553
Archd. Tuam	60	72	113	1	7	...	411,467
Clonfert	20	21	44	1	...	2	119,082
Achonry	22	22	43	...	...	...	108,835
Elphin	41	51	81	...	...	4	309,761
Kilmacduagh and Kilfenora[b]	18	16	36	1	2	...	81,642
Galway	14	11	16	5	...	14	56,503
Killala	21	18	40	...	...	...	136,383
Total in Tuam	196	211	378	8	9	20	1,187,507
	1,008	1,385	2,218	91	42	200	6,436,060

[a] The sources for this table are W. J. Battersby, *The complete Catholic Directory* (1846), p. 332, and Public Instruction Report, 1835.

[b] Kilfenora, though united to Kilmacduagh in 1750, was part of the province of Cashel.

an annual contribution of £2 or more from the priests (often
only the parish priests), it was not of the same pressing concern
for the faithful as the support of the priests of their own parish.
The income of parishes varied considerably. In the province of
Armagh, according to Curtis's testimony before the Commission on the State of Ireland in 1825, there was 'no parish
that is worth less than £100 per year, from that to £120, perhaps
£130'.[130] Archbishop Kelly testified that in the province of Tuam
there were some parish priests 'who have between themselves
and their coadjutors £150'.[131] Doyle, who had gone to the
trouble of eliciting returns from each of his parishes five years
earlier, reported to the same Commission that although a few
parishes had an income of over £200 and three had an income
of £500, the great majority had between £100 and £200.[132] In
1832 Doyle told the House of Lords Committee on Tithes that
'the different unions throughout the diocese produced at an
average ... £300 a year' out of which one or more assistant
priests had to be paid.[133] John Leslie Foster, MP for Louth,
who often advised Peel on Irish affairs and was regarded by
Catholics as an able and well-informed adversary, had also
taken the trouble to make investigations. He told the 1825
Commission that 'it is a question which I have asked everywhere ... in no instance has a priest less than £80 a year. I
consider £200 is considerably above average ... If I were obliged
to name an average ... I should say that at present it was about
£150 a year, but less than £200.'[134] Ten years later Beaumont
accepted Doyle's figure of £300 for the parish; Tocqueville,
too, after careful inquiries throughout the country, was satisfied
that £300 was the average amount for a parish of which £120 or
£150 went to the parish priest; Croly thought that 'scarcely
any parish yields four hundred per annum and many a parish
does not yield one third of that amount'.[135] The curates, or

[130] Ibid., p. 256.

[131] Ibid., pp. 366-7.

[132] Ibid., p. 231.

[133] *First and Second Report from the Select Committee, Lords, on Tithes in Ireland, 1831-2*,
xxii. 277.

[134] *Minutes of Evidence taken before the Select Committee, Lords, appointed to inquire into the
State of Ireland ...*, *PP 1825*, ix. 66.

[135] Beaumont, *L'Irlande*, ii. 290; Tocqueville, *Journeys*, p. 174; Croly, *An essay*,
pp. 29-30.

assistant priests, who were considerably more numerous than the parish priests, were far worse off. A curate's income was set, according to Doyle, at one-third of the total parish income; if there was a second curate it was further reduced.[136] This arrangement applied only when the curate lived apart from the parish priest. If he lived with the parish priest, which was generally the case, he would receive only a quarter of the parish income. In the 1830s some synods adopted this division of parish revenue and generally improved the miserable lot of the curate, but in many parishes he still received no more than £10 or £20 in addition to his keep and the maintenance of his horse. Fr Patrick Larkin, parish priest of Moyne, Co. Tipperary, reported with evident satisfaction to his archbishop: 'I give my curate £20 a year and every mass that may occur.'[137] In view of their poverty it is not surprising to find some curates in the Dublin diocese squabbling over petty fees and emoluments.

Stole fees (offerings made at marriages, baptisms, funerals, and similar functions), Christmas and Easter dues, and, to a lesser extent, mass-stipends constituted the parish clergy's usual sources of income. The scale of stole fees varied but provincial synods took care to regulate it strictly. In 1817 the Connaught bishops ordained that: 'Pro matrimonio, Aureum, praeter collectas voluntarias aliquibus in locis fieri solitas. Ubi vero hae collectae non fiunt, liceat Parocho earum loco, praeter aureum exigere quinque solidos Anglicanos [*sic*] ... Literis [*sic*] testimonialibus in matrimonium quinque solidos Anglicanos'.[138] The Munster bishops in 1828 provided that 'the sum of one Guinea may henceforth be required as a general marriage fee and ... no more ... under penalty of suspension *ipso facto* ... yet whereas there are many among the lower classes...unable ... to make a tender of that sum, our Clergy will not require it ... but will thankfully accept of a half-a-guinea, or less.' Certificates of freedom to contract marriage outside the parish

[136] *Minutes of Evidence on the State of Ireland, PP 1825,* ix. 231.

[137] Larkin's Visitation Report to Archbishop Slattery, June 1842; Slattery Papers. Cf. similar reports of parish priests to Slattery: McDonnell to Slattery, 28 Nov. 1840; T. Mahony to Slattery, 14 Aug. 1849, Slattery Papers.

[138] *Acta, decreta et ordinata in Concilio Provinciali habito Tuamae sub ... Oliverio Kelly, Archiepiscopo Tuamensi ... Ejusque Suffrageneis, diebus 6ta, 7ma et 8va Mensis Maii, Anno Domini 1817* (1817), p. 17.

were to cost no more than five shillings, 'sub poena suspensionis ipso facto'.[139] It was twice as expensive to marry in the Dublin province where, in 1831, the bishops jointly fixed the fees as follows: 'Post celebratum Baptismum, quinque solidi solvantur; post solemnizatum Matrimonium, quadraginta solidi; Testimonio libertatis ad Matrimonium contrahendum dato, solidi decem; pro missis privati stipendium sit duo solidi ...' For poorer parishioners the scale was lower: 2s. 6d. for baptism, £1 for marriage and 5s. for letters of freedom.[140] Nothing at all was expected from the very poor.[141] The bishops of the province of Armagh met in 1834, but apart from warnings against avarice left the regulating of fees to local custom.[142] In this province, as in the province of Connaught, the 'collectae voluntariae' or offerings made by the congregation on the day of the function, constituted, in many parishes, an important, if variable, part of the income from fees. Information on Christmas and Easter dues is more sparse. Both the individual and total amounts varied considerably. The schoolmaster, J. O'Callaghan, of Knockaderry, Co. Limerick, noted in his diary the amounts of the priest's collection at Christmas over a number of years: in 1826 it was £43; in 1828, £48.10s.; in 1829, £41 and in 1837, £45.15s.[143] The voluntary system of support for the clergy often led to unseemly wrangling and even to open protest, for it imposed a heavy burden on an impoverished people, but Dr Kelly, the archbishop of Tuam, no doubt judged correctly when he claimed before the House of Lords Committee in 1825 that: 'However much the people may have complained, I think they would prefer, notwithstanding, to support their own clergy, to seeing them paid by the State.'[144] Since the priests often dined with their faithful, who made it a point of honour to

---

[139] *Statuta Synodalia pro unitis diocesibus Cassel. et Imelac ...* (1810), pp. 125-6.

[140] *Statuta diocesana*, pp. 165-74.

[141] *Minutes of Evidence on the State of Ireland, PP 1825*, ix. 230.

[142] *Statuta dioecesana in archdioecesi Ardmachensi observanda et a Romo. Thoma Kelly ... in sua synodo dioecesani edita et promulgata; Hebdomeda 3a mensis Aug. AD 1834* (1834), pp. 91.7.

[143] Diary of J. O'Callaghan, entries for Christmas 1826, 1828, 1829, 1837. The diary is an unpublished MS in the possession of Mr Robert Cussen, Kinelarty, Newcastle West, Co. Limerick.

[144] *Reports from the Select Committee appointed to inquire into the State of Ireland ... PP 1825*, viii. 260.

entertain them generously, especially during the frequent Stations, this hospitality, taken with the financial support they received, provided them with a moderately respectable style of life. Their standard of living varied from province to province and from parish to parish and there was, as we have seen, a considerable difference between the resources of a parish priest and those of his curate. The pressing needs of the great multitude of poor could absorb whatever surplus a zealous pastor might have.[145] Taking the evidence as a whole, it would appear that the priests were hard-working, and that while the curates were miserably poor, the parish priests, although far from wealthy, could live tolerably well. They were not altogether immune from faults common enough in a clergy totally dependent on the voluntary offerings of their flock, who, despite the burden it imposed, preferred to support them themselves rather than see them maintained by the state. The relationship between priests and people was close: according to Thomas Kelly, the secretary to the Commissioners for Education, the Catholic clergy, in contrast to the clergy of the Established church, 'kept up a perpetual domestic visitation through every part of the parish'.[146] To millions of the faithful the local priest was the church. Because this relationship between priest and people gave rise to much angry criticism, it must now be briefly examined.

Critics accused the priest of exercising a kind of spiritual intimidation on the people because, as Nassau Senior wrote in 1844, he was 'a pastor armed with such all-powerful weapons as confession, penance and absolution'.[147] The priest's influence, however, was more subtle than that accusation implied. Indeed, the ultra-Protestants and the government, victims of their own illusions in attributing excessive power to the clergy, unconsciously increased both its influence and pretensions. That power was certainly a reality. The faithful, reflecting the existing Catholic theology of the priesthood as evidenced by Lacordaire in France or by Henry Manning later in England, looked upon the priest as 'the Lord's anointed'; and both they

[145] E. Dechy, *Voyage: Irlande en 1846 et 1847* (1847), p. 171; T. P. O'Neill, 'The Catholic Church and Relief of the Poor, 1815-45', *Archiv. Hib.*, xxxi (1973), 132-45.

[146] *Report from the Select Committee appointed to inquire into the progress and operation of the new plan of education in Ireland PP 1837*, ix. 225.

[147] Nassau Senior, 'Ireland in 1843', *Edinburgh Rev.*, lxxix (1844), 215.

and the clergy themselves constantly referred to his 'sacred character'. Apart from his highly respected celibacy, his role at mass, in the confessional, and in the administration of the last rites gave the priest a place apart in the eyes of a deeply religious people. The fact that he was often the only educated Catholic in the local community enhanced his prestige but cast him too, willy-nilly, into the role of the community's spokesman. History had played a vital part. During the penal times, priests and people were thrown together in a struggle for survival, and this unity in adversity survived the end of the persecutions. The recent agitation for Catholic Emancipation had strengthened those bonds. Baptist Noel, no friend of the Catholic priests, admitted in his account of his tour in 1836 that 'a persecuted and sympathising priesthood had been the object of almost idolatrous veneration'.[148] In 1835, Tocqueville expressed his astonishment at the 'unbelievable unity between the Irish clergy and the Catholic population'. He believed that the reason for this unity was 'not only that the clergy are paid by the people but because all the upper classes are Protestants and enemies'.[149] Beaumont made the point that 'l'Irlande ayant été en même temps attaquée dans sa liberté et dans son culte, la religion et la patrie se sont mêlées dans l'âme de l'Irlandais, et se sont devenues pour lui une seule chose.' As a result the Irish clergy, in contrast to clergy elsewhere—who were confined to a purely spiritual role—'a sur le peuple la double authorité, et il la possède seul'.[150] Writing from a different angle, the Franciscan, Fr Michael Brenan, was eloquent on the 'tender and powerful ties of unionship'; during the persecutions, the priests never forsook the people who, in their turn, never forgot this fidelity.[151] Despite Brenan's fulsomeness, this attitude is one that emerges in the public statements and, more interestingly, in the private correspondence of the clergy. Beaumont, too, remarked on the same close ties between priest and people.[152]

[148] B. W. Noel, *Notes on a short tour through the midland counties of Ireland in the summer of 1836* ... (1837), p. 81; Baptist Noel (1798-1873), minister at St Johns, Bedford Row, London; a leading evangelical.

[149] Tocqueville, *Journeys*, p. 136.

[150] Beaumont, *L'Irlande*, ii. 36-7, 47.

[151] M. J. Brenan, *Ecclesiastical History of Ireland* ... (1840), p. 665.

[152] Beaumont, *L'Irlande*, ii. 39.

Perhaps the most striking account of the close links between priest and people is Tocqueville's narrative of his two-day stay in a village near Tuam. As he accompanied the priest on his rounds he was struck by the warmth of affection between him and his flock. From the little village child who led him to the priest's house and up the stair to his room, to the dying peasant and his family whom the priest visited at the end of his long round of visits, the people showed an affection for the priest that was deep and respectful if simple. Later, when rejecting Tocqueville's argument for a state salary for the clergy, the priest could make the following remarkable claim:

You have seen, Sir, how the village looks on me, ... they have reason to love me, for I love them too. They have confidence in me and I in them. Every man in a way regards me as one of his brothers, as the eldest of the family. How does this arise, Sir? Because the people and I have need of each other all the time. The people gives the fruit of its labours liberally to me, and I give them my time, my care and my entire soul. I can do nothing without them, and without me they would succumb under the weight of their sorrows. Between us there is a ceaseless exchange of feelings of affection.[153]

A more critical explanation was provided by Clarendon in a detailed memorandum to Russell in 1847:

...an Irishman loves his religion and the Ministers of his Church, not so much for their own sake and his own spiritual welfare, as because he is deeply impressed with the idea that they are national. Nor is this to be wondered at if we bear in mind the enormous weight of oppression ... and ... civil persecution which a steadfast adherence to their religion has entailed upon the Roman Catholics of Ireland. The spirit of nationality burns strongly in an Irishman's breast, and the priests encourage the political feelings with which he regards his religion, not only because they themselves are animated by the same feelings, but because they are thereby able to acquire and maintain influence over their flocks.[154]

Clarendon's memorandum, which was intended as a brief for Minto in the latter's effort to secure papal condemnation of clerical involvement in politics, was accurate enough in asserting that the Irishman saw his religion and priests as 'national', but to allege that that was the main or sole reason for his attachment to his religion was an oversimplification. Clarendon

---

[153] Tocqueville, *Journeys*, pp. 160-73, esp. 171-2.
[154] Clarendon to Russell, 1 Oct. 1847, Palmerston Papers, cited in F. Curato ed. *Gran Bretagna e Italia nei documenti della missione Minto* (1970), i. 81.

further overstated his case when he went on to claim that 'the spiritual power of the priest depends upon his political uniformity with the people'. Another hostile and well informed observer, Maria Edgeworth, criticizing Sydney Smith's suggestion of paying the Catholic clergy as too facile a solution to the problem of clerical involvement in popular politics, commented acutely that he did not take into account 'that the priests love power as other men do—as well as money—and that their love of power over their flocks cannot easily be bought off'.[155]

The literature of the period affords further insight into the relationship between clergy and people although, in accordance with the political outlook of the writer, it alternately depicts the priest as tyrant or hero. An attachment to his flock and an advanced ecumenical spirit are the priestly traits most evident in William Parnell's interesting novel, *Maurice and Berghetta,* with a dedication, incidentally, to the priests of Ireland 'on whom the civilization and subordination of the lower orders in Ireland depend'—in itself an acknowledgement of the influence of the priests.[156] In Anthony Trollope's novel, *The MacDermots of Ballycloran,* the priests appeared to mix well with their parishioners and to be treated respectfully but without obsequiousness.[157] The Banims' *Father Connell* is the ideal type of the dedicated country priest who devotes himself to his flock. The final heroic scene describes his attempt to save the life of his erring sheep, Edmond, and the account is attributed to the archbishop of Dublin:

Father Connell had reached Dublin, about 8 o'clock that morning but in a very feverish, shattered and exhausted state ... he had immediately called on his old friend the archbishop ... almost on the instant, the writer was thus obliged perforce to accompany him to the vice-regal lodge, ... and finally ... Father Connell, while in the act of presenting on his knees, to the Lord Lieutenant, the memorial in Edmond's favour, had fainted, and very shortly afterwards, died.[158]

---

[155] Maria Edgeworth to Richard Butler, 3 Apr. 1845, cited in M. Hurst, *Maria Edgeworth and the public scene; intellect, fine feeling and landlordism in the age of reform* (1969), p. 144.

[156] W. Parnell, *Maurice and Berghetta, or the priest of Rahery* (1819), pp. v-vi; 347-51.

[157] A. Trollope, *The MacDermots of Ballycloran,* 3 vols. (1847), i. 65-73; see pp. 245-6.

[158] J. and M. Banim, *Father Connell,* 3 vols. (1842), iii. 269, 298-99.

This theme is elaborated by John Banim in his poem, 'Soggarth Aroon', in which he gives classical expression to the intimate bond between peasant and priest:

Who, in the winter night
Soggarth Aroon,
When the cold blast did bite,
Soggarth Aroon,
Came to my cabin-door
And on my earthen-flure,
Knelt by me sick, and poor,
Soggarth Aroon?[159]

Thomas Moore's moving lyric, 'The Irish peasant to his mistress', extols the loyalty of the peasant to his church despite the allurements of the Established church:

Thro' grief and thro' danger thy smile hath cheered my way
Till hope seem'd to bud from each thorn that around me lay
Yes, slave as I was, in thy arms my spirit felt free
And bless'd even the sorrows that made me more dear to thee ...
Thy rival was honour'd, while thou wert wrong'd and scorn'd
Thy crown was of briers, while gold her brows adorn'd;
She woo'd me to temples, while thou lay'st hid in caves
Her friends were all masters, while thine, alas! were slaves.[160]

In Charles Lever's novel, *The Confessions of Harry Lorrequer*, the demagogue-cleric who threatens his flock with 'the terrors of his church' to further a political cause makes a brief appearance.[161] William Carleton, author of *Traits and Stories of the Irish Peasantry* and of many novels, was close to the people he depicts, and although his writings are often highly critical of the clergy (he was employed by a stridently anti-Catholic newspaper), his realistic insight into the peasant society of pre-Famine Ireland has scarcely been equalled. The themes of clerical cunning and greed, of peasant obsequiousness and superstition fill many of his pages, and yet priest and peasant are shown as closely and warmly bound together. At Shane Fadh's wedding it is the priests who with flailing whips save the wedding feast from degenerating into a faction fight, and Fr Corrigan, adding spiritual threats to physical efforts, commands the rival families

[159] C. M. Collins, *Celtic Irish Songs and Song-Writers* ... (1885), pp. 325-6.
[160] T. Moore, *Poetical Works* (1845) p. 182.
[161] C. Lever, *The Confessions of Harry Lorrequer* (1839).

'in the name of the Catholic Church and the Blessed Virgin Mary to stop this instant, if you don't wish me ... to turn you into stocks and stones where you stand'. If they do not shake hands and promise never to fight again, he threatens to ex-communicate them; on the ringleaders he imposes the severe pilgrimage of Lough Derg as a penance. After an evening's joviality in which the priests took their full share, the bride's mother slipped two fat fowl into the friar's pocket, and Shane dropped two bottles of whiskey into the other 'so that his Reverence was well balanced any how'.[162]

The Gaelic literature, from which an intimate picture of the relationship between priest and people might be expected, does not explicitly set out to describe it. The general impression it conveys is that harmony was the normal relationship but that the laity drew a clear distinction between religious and secular affairs.[163] A friendly relationship, almost one of camaraderie, is evinced in the unique diary of Humphrey O'Sullivan who recounts with evident relish the pleasant evenings spent with the priests: 'Four of us dined with Father James Hennebry ... We had a boiled leg of mutton ... a roast goose ... port wine and punch ... tea and sweet Irish songs and spent the night till eleven o'clock merry, happy, light-hearted, joyous, pleasant and gay'.[164] Mutual friendship and respect mingled with a certain independence is the attitude found in many of the poets who, moreover, had a distinctive tradition of their own to uphold. Seán Ó Braonáin, a Kerry poet of the period, reproved the critic of the clergy as 'a senseless heretic', defended the denunciation from the altar of a fellow-poet for associating with the 'Calvinist' minister and praised a priest in extravagant, poetical terms for his interest in learning and his priestly qualities.[165] Diarmuid O'Shea, another Kerry poet, sharply

[162] W. Carleton, 'Shane Fadh's Wedding', *Traits and Stories of the Irish Peasantry* (1865), i. 67-9; 82. cf. 'The Lough Derg Pilgrim' ibid. i. 236-70; 'The Station', ibid. 145-80; 'Going to Maynooth', ibid. ii. 97-187. The *Traits* were originally published mainly between 1828 and 1834.

[163] J. A. Murphy, 'Priests and People in modern Irish history', *Christus Rex*, xxiii (1969), 234-59.

[164] A. Ó Súilleabháin, *Cín Lae Amhlaoibh*, ed. T. de Bhaldraithe (1970); *Cinnlae Amhlaoibh Uí Shúilleabháin; the diary of Humphrey O'Sullivan*, ed. M. McGrath (1928-9), ii. 13, entry for 12 Sept. 1828. Cf. entry for 28 Sept. 1828. Humphrey O'Sullivan (1780-1836) was a Kilkenny linen draper; his diary covers the period 1827-35.

[165] P. de Brún, *Filíocht Sheáin Uí Bhraonáin*, (1972), pp. 93, 91, 111-13. Seán O Braonáin (? 1790 - ? 1850).

rebukes one priest for his churlishness and bad temper, contrasting him with other kindly alms-giving priests.[166] In a rather unusual incident a priest in the Limerick area summons three Gaelic poets to rhyme the minister of the New Reformation out of the parish.[167] One of the best-known poets of the period, Anthony Raftery, the blind Connaught rhymester, in a pious mood, engages in a long friendly banter with the dean who has imposed on him the difficult penance of climbing Croagh Patrick and making the gruelling Lough Derg pilgrimage nine times, pleading with him not to be severe but to recall Christ's words in Galilee: 'whose sins you shall forgive they are forgiven.'[168] The reverence of Art Mac Bionaid, the last of the Armagh poets, for the priest is never in question. He denounces those who attack Fr Callaghan, praises Fr Duffy for his piety, knowledge, and generosity and bitterly laments the defection and marriage of Fr Butler who, although he had for his spouse the Morning Star, the Help of Sinners and the Queen of Virgins, has abandoned her for Miss Duff.[169]

Folk-lore endowed the priest with thaumaturgical powers in areas bordering on the spiritual. His 'power' protects the land of a Protestant who sheltered him; he curses, with effect, the landlord who evicted a tenant, while those who curse him or receive him badly are dogged with misfortune. As one story begins: 'Old thorns and old priests should be left alone; there's a power in the pair of them if they want to use it'.[170] While the evidence we have seen is not exhaustive, the pattern of the people's attitude to the clergy emerges as one that was reverential in religious matters and friendly, even indulgent, in social relations. Often, however, the poet maintained an independence and the faithful a certain distance from the priest. His spiritual role and his commanding position in

[166] S. Ó Súilleabháin, *Diarmuid na Bolgaighe agus a chomhursain* (1937), p. 98. He wrote several other poems praising the priests; cf. ibid, pp. 10, 20. Diarmuid Ó Seaghda (? 1760 - ? 1847).

[167] M. Seoighe, *Cois Maighe na gCaor,* (1965), pp. 106-12.

[168] D. de hÍde, *Abhráin agus dánta an Reachtabhraigh* ... (1969), pp. 236-9; Antoin Ó Reachtabhra (1784-?1835).

[169] A. Mac Bionaid, *Dánta*, ed. T. Ó Fiaich and L. Ó Caithnia (1979), pp. 27, 62-3, 50. Art Mac Bionaid (1793-1879).

[170] P. Ó Héalaí, 'Cumhacht an tSagairt sa Bhéaloideas', *Léachtaí Cholm Cille VIII; ár nDúchas Creidimh* (1977), ed. P. Ó Fiannachta, pp. 109-31.

the parish—which he would sometimes exploit—bred among the faithful not merely respect but often fear and a reluctance to cross his path.

In matters that touched on politics and money the people were potentially and often actually independent, drawing a clear distinction between the 'sacred character' of the priest and the man. O'Connell had insisted before a Select Committee in 1825 that 'there is not anything like a blind submission of the Catholics to their clergy, not at all'.[171] Lord Clare told Lord Francis Leveson Gower, the chief secretary in 1828, that 'the people neither obey the magistrates nor their priests when they act in opposition to their wishes'.[172] In evidence to the Select Committee on Tithes in 1837, James Christopher, a Kilkenny lawyer, said that the clergy complained 'that they cannot speak to their flocks on the subject of tithes without endangering their own influence'; and the county resident magistrate, Joseph Green, asserted that the people took the advice of priests when they told them not to pay tithes but rejected it when they told them to pay.[173] Major George Brown, chief magistrate of police in County Clare, reported that when some priests tried to stop the agitation against tithes, 'the people threatened that if they did, they would not pay them their dues'.[174] This was no idle threat, as the evidence of the resident magistrate of police for Tipperary, Mr Gerald Fitzgerald, showed: 'the parish priest of Powerstown ... had recommended his parishioners to pay tithe as long as it was legal, and his curate gave different advice; the result has been that the parishioners have determined to pay those dues which they formerly paid to the parish priest to the coadjutor.'[175]

This independent attitude in political and economic matters in no way implied a lack of religious fervour. It has recently been argued that the pre-Famine generation of Irish were non-practising Catholics, 'if indeed they were Catholics at all'.[176]

[171] *State of Ireland Report, PP 1825*, viii. 81.

[172] Clare to Lord Francis Leveson Gower, 22 Sept. 1828, cited in Murphy, 'Priests and People' p. 248.

[173] *Reports from the Select Committee, Commons, on Tithes in Ireland, PP 1831-2*, xxi. 41, 44.

[174] *Reports from the Select Committee, Lords, on Tithes in Ireland, PP 1831-2*, xxii. 132.

[175] Ibid., pp. 14-15.

[176] E. Larkin, 'The Devotional Revolution in Ireland, 1850-75', *AHR*, lxxvii (1972), 651.

Such a conclusion is not borne out by the evidence of the many visitors to Ireland during the period. Count Charles de Montalembert, visiting Ireland in 1831, wrote in moving terms of the faith and devotion of the people kneeling in the mud and rain to hear mass: 'Je ne me figure en effet de plus vénérable que la foi du peuple irlandais.'[177] Tocqueville appears to have accepted the account of the faith of the people which the parish priest of Newton-Pratt, Co. Mayo gave him in 1835: 'the people have a strong and living enthusiasm for religion. In this parish, with more than ten thousand Catholics, I know only one adult who does not confess.'[178] In Castlebar, the chief constable (whom Tocqueville believed to be an Orangeman) informed him that the people were deeply attached to their faith: '"Take our goods, but do not touch our beliefs", this is the cry which echoes a thousand times among the agricultural population of Ireland.'[179] Beaumont simply notes that 'Le peuple irlandais est dans son église.'[180] James Johnston, a widely travelled physician and author of several successful books on medicine, remarked in his account of his tour in Ireland in 1843 that 'In no country have I ever observed the *people* more zealous and sincere in their religious devotions than the Catholics of Ireland. If the chapel be full, you will see them on their knees round the doors exposed to the winds and rains.'[181] In 1844 Johann Kohl, a German traveller, commented: 'the Irish are the most genuine Roman Catholics in the world.'[182] The French traveller, Édouard Dechy, who was in Ireland in 1846 and 1847, gives a description of a mass which echoes Montalembert: 'La messe est toujours accompagnée d'un sermon, qui se fait souvent en langue irlandaise ... au milieu du recueillement le plus profond. Les paroissiens sont nombreux, viennent de loin; la foule se presse dans l'église, s'étend dans le cimitière, prie avec ardeur'.[183]

This attachment to their creed clearly emerges from the brief reports which the priests of the parishes made to the archbishop

[177] C. de Montalembert, *Avenir,* 18 Jan. 1831.

[178] Tocqueville, *Journeys*, p. 191.

[179] Ibid., p. 192.   [180] Beaumont, *L'Irlande*, ii. 38.

[181] J. Johnston, *A tour in Ireland, with meditations and reflexions* (1844), p. 120.

[182] J. G. Kohl, *Travels in Ireland* (1844), p. 107.

[183] Dechy, *Voyage,* p. 191; W. M. Thackeray conveys a similar impression: *Irish Sketch-book* (1843), pp. 40-1, 110.

of Dublin between 1830 and 1846. (These reports are in the form of printed schedules which the parish priest and his curates had to fill in, sign, and present to the bishop before the episcopal visitation of the parish took place. Among the questions required to be answered were the number of communicants and the number of adults who did not approach the sacraments at Easter-time. In addition to the schedule, the parish priest was required to give in writing the names of the most obstinate absentees from their Easter duties, the names of public sinners, with some account of the nature of their misdemeanours, and a list of all public abuses such as illegal combinations, quarrelling, violation of the Lord's day, wakes, Sunday dances, etc. This schedule was introduced into many dioceses in the 1830s and a copy is appended to most of the diocesan statutes published at this time. It was not always welcomed by the parish priests; cf. the comments of the Clogher priests, undated and unsigned mss in the Clogher Diocesan Papers. The date is almost certainly 1835 or 1836.) Although some priests may have been motivated by a desire to present their parishes in a favourable light, the striking similarity in the evidence from one hundred and forty-five reports covering forty-four parishes means that it cannot be lightly dismissed. The parishes were all rural, in counties Dublin, Kildare, and Wicklow. With few exceptions the pastors were well satisfied with the faith and practice of their flock. Notorious sinners, such as unbelievers, drunkards, and libertines are mentioned, often by name, and comprise a minimal percentage of the population. In Arklow, Co. Wicklow, the parish priest reported in 1843 that of the seven thousand adult Catholics, only ten neglected their Easter duty. For the bishop's information he listed scandalous and atheist members of his flock, who numbered six: two were impure, one a drunkard, another would not go to mass, another would not go to confession, and the sixth had married outside the church. In Sandyford, Co. Dublin, the parish priest reported that there were 'about a dozen of habitual absentees' from the Easter duty.[184] From Castledermot, Co. Kildare, the parish priest reported that among the eight thousand Catholics 'there is no particular

[184] Schedule for the parish of Arklow, Sandyford, and Glencullen, 1843, Murray Papers 1843, DDA.

abuse ... nor are there any obstinate absentees'.[185] This favourable impression is confirmed by such visitation reports as have
survived in the archdiocese of Cashel for the same period.[186]
From Moyne the parish priest reported to Dr Slattery that he
had no refractories. In Loughmore only one absented himself
from the sacraments. From Drangan it was reported that all go
to confession and four to five hundred go to monthly communion. The situation was much the same in the neighbouring
parish of Killenaule; up to six hundred or more went to communion on the first and third Sundays and there were 'but few
who habitually absent themselves from their Easter duty'. In
New Inn however, the parish priest complained that 'eighty
heads of families' absented themselves from Easter duties. Of
the town of Cashel itself the dean reported that 'the great body
of the faithful go to Communion twice a year. There are about
fifty absentees, mostly of the town, very few from the country,
from the Easter duty.'[187] In almost all these parishes lay confraternities flourished, particularly those of the Sacred Heart,
the Blessed Virgin, and the Blessed Sacrament. What is surprising in all those reports is the high number of weekly and
monthly communicants at a time when frequent communion
had not received the warm encouragement it was later to receive
from Pius IX and Pius X.

Attendance at Sunday mass was much less regular than it
was to become in the twentieth century, as the figures given in
the Report of the Commissioners of Public Instruction in 1834
indicate.[188] The very variable percentages (from 30 per cent
upwards) which can be deduced from this report is no proof,
however, that the people were not devout. The report does not
appear to take account of those who were under-age and those
over-age nor of those who remained at home to mind younger
children. Many people, too, did not attend Sunday mass because
they had neither proper clothing nor shoes; sometimes they did
not attend because the parish church was too distant or too

[185] Schedule for the parish of Castledermot, 1840, Murray Papers, 1840, DDA.
[186] These reports are similar in form to those of the archdiocese of Dublin but fewer
of them have survived. They are to be found in the Slattery Papers.
[187] Schedules for the parishes of Moyne, Loughmore, Drangan, Killenaule, New
Inn and Cashel; Slattery Papers, 1845.
[188] First Report of the Commissioners of Public Instruction, Ireland, PP 1835, xxxiii.

dilapidated and small. The commission of 1834 was informed that there was but one chapel in the village of Oughterard 'in a district of about twenty-five miles long'.[189] Ten years earlier Fr Michael Collins, parish priest of Skibbereen, Co. Cork, had told the Select Committee investigating the Disturbances in Ireland, that his chapel was 'in such a state that he was in constant fear of an accident'. Furthermore, it was 'so small that half the congregation stayed away—the old, the infirm and the delicate—rather than be in the open air'.[190] The 'stations', by providing for the celebration of the sacraments in farmhouses in different parts of the parish, gave more people the opportunity of attending mass and receiving the sacraments than the attendance at the parish church would appear to indicate. These considerations apart, attendance at Sunday mass in this era immediately post-dating the Penal Laws, had not become the criterion of the practising Catholic it was later to become with the tighter organization of the church in the second half of the nineteenth century.[191] Even then it was not uncommon for a considerable proportion of the people to absent themselves from Sunday mass.

Older religious practices—patterns, pilgrimages, holy wells, wakes, and even stations—were under attack, as a reforming church, in common with Tridentine catholicism everywhere, strove to exert discipline over popular forms of piety, fearful lest the superstitions and excessive festivity of many of those practices prevail over their religious aspects and lead, as they sometimes did, to abuses.[192] In their place the church promoted a piety that was instructional and individualist based largely

---

[189] Ibid., p. 895.

[190] *Minutes of Evidence taken before the Select Committee appointed to inquire into the Disturbances in Ireland...PP 1825,* vii. 359.

[191] Larkin, 'Devotional Revolution' pp. 644-5; D. W. Miller, 'Irish Catholicism and the Great Famine', *Journal of Social History,* ix (1975-6), 81-98.

[192] A. Dupront, 'La religion populaire dans l'histoire de l'Europe occidentale', *Revue d'histoire de l'Eglise de France,* lxiv (1978), 185-202. The bishops decided at their meeting on 11 Feb. 1829 'that pilgrimages to wells be totally abolished'; Meetings of the Irish Bishops, DDA. The archbishop of Cashel declared the Patron of Doneskeagh as suppressed for ever; *Statuta Cassel.,* pp. 230-1; the diocesan statutes of the province of Armagh condemned 'lusus inhonesti' at wakes; *Statuta Ardmachensi,* p. 98. The Armagh bishops, on 2 Feb. 1838, passed resolutions regulating pilgrimages to Lough Derg, the oldest and most famous of Irish pilgrimage centres; Bishop Browne (Kilmore) to Bishop Kernan, 20 Mar. 1838, Kernan Papers, Clogher Diocesan Archives.

upon the printed prayer book and catechism. The Irish towns which had seen, in the course of the eighteenth century, the emergence of a wealthy Catholic middle class, witnessed also a remarkable development in the publication of Catholic apologetic and devotional literature.[193] By 1824 Doyle was able to exult over 'the vast variety of moral and historical tracts which were daily issuing from the Catholic press'.[194] Three years later Doyle, with the approval of the other bishops, founded the Irish Catholic Society for the Diffusion of Useful Knowledge which came to be known as the Catholic Book Society.[195] To bring its publications within the reach of all the faithful the bishops vigorously promoted lending libraries in the parishes, and one of the questions on the schedule that the parish priest had to fill up for the bishop's visitation concerned the number of volumes in the parish library.[196] 'Garden of the Soul Catholics' was a term applied to many English Catholics of this period, but as Dr Wall has pointed out, the popularity in the Irish booksellers' lists of Richard Challoner's prayer book, with its individualist, meditative, and instructional approach, indicates that the term could be equally applied to many Irish Catholics, at least to those living in urban conditions.[197]

The education provided by the national system created a growing market for this devotional literature in English based on the spirituality of the towns which, together with the importation of newer devotions from the continent, was to form the basis on which the devotional life of the nineteenth century was to develop. Already the familiar devotions of the twentieth-century Irish church were in evidence in the cities and large

---

[193] M. Wall, 'The rise of a Catholic middle class in eighteenth-century Ireland', *IHS*, xi (1958), 91-115; T. Wall, *The sign of Dr Hay's head* ... (1958), pp. 41-90, 109-16; M. V. Ronan, *An Apostle of Catholic Dublin: Father Henry Young* (1944), pp. 47-52; 147-81.

[194] J. Doyle, *A letter ... on the education of the poor* ... (1824), p. 6.

[195] T. Wall, 'Catholic Periodicals of the Past', *IER*, fifth series, ci (1964), 289-303.

[196] *Statuta Diocesana*, p. xii.

[197] Wall, *Dr Hay's head*, p. 76; Richard Challoner (1691-1781), vicar-apostolic for the London district; author of popular books of devotion including *The Garden of the Soul or a manual of spiritual exercises and instructions* ... (1740). For an analysis of the devotional characteristics of the *Garden of the Soul* see J. Bossy, *The English Catholic Community, 1507-1850* (1975), pp. 364-77.

towns.[198] Closely connected with devotions, the direct catechizing of their poorly instructed flock constituted a high priority
for the bishops, and since the beginning of the century they had
shown a tendency to standardize the many catechisms in use.[199]
Confraternities for teaching christian doctrine, in existence
since 1788, played an increasingly important role. New congregations of teaching sisters and brothers involved themselves
in this work and the clergy readily availed themselves of the
wide opportunities for catechizing in the new national schools.
Yet, although perhaps as much as half of the total Catholic
population used Irish as a first language, printed devotional
literature in that language, apart from catechisms, was meagre
and often suspected of being the work of proselytizing agen-
cies.[200] An extraordinarily rich oral tradition of religious poetry,
narrative and prayer together with extensive copying of favourite authors, compensated to some extent for this scarcity.[201]
Although some priests preached in Irish and some bishops like
MacHale, Egan and Murphy encouraged the use of the language
by their clergy, it appears that the English-speaking districts
(and probably Leinster) were being better catered for than the
rest of the country. In a revealing remark, Bishop Doyle told
the Select Committee on Tithes that 'the discipline in my
diocese you may take as a pattern of what prevails now in the
province of Dublin, and pretty much like that which prevails
in Munster and Connaught. In the North, where Catholics are
still in a depressed state, the discipline, I believe is considerably

---

[198] In 1844, Dublin had the following devotions: Bona Mors confraternity, devotions
to the Sacred Heart of Jesus and the Immaculate Heart of Mary, novenas for the
principal feasts of the Blessed Virgin, novena in honour of St. Francis Xavier,
Exposition of the Blessed Sacrament, Stations of the Cross and Devotions in honour
of the Three Hours agony on Good Friday; *Catholic Directory*, 1845, pp. 396. Similar
devotions existed in Waterford; ibid., 1836, p. 13. Some of them were associated with
the friaries, others, like the rapidly growing devotion to the Sacred Heart, had come
more recently from France and Italy.

[199] P. Wallace, 'Irish Catechesis—the heritage from James Butler II, Archbishop
of Cashel 1774-1791', (Catholic University of America, Ph.D. thesis 1975), pp. 105-11.

[200] An exception was the *Pious Miscellany* of Tadhg Gaedhealach Ó Súilliobháin,
a collection of religious verse which reached its 14th edition in 1832. Tadhg Ó Súilliobháin or Timothy O'Sullivan (1715-95), a wandering Munster poet.

[201] P. Ó Fiannachta, ed. *Léachtaí Cholm Cille VII: ár ndúchas creidimh* (1977);
D. Ó Laoghaire, *Ár bpaidreacha dúchais* (1975). This recent collection of Irish prayers
shows the richness of the tradition.

different.'[202] Differences in religious discipline and practice existed between the four provinces and between city and country, for the reforms of the Counter-Reformation were slower in penetrating the west and north of the country than the east. Nevertheless, the evidence available indicates that, taken as a whole, the pre-Famine Catholics were not lacking in fervour nor their pastors in zeal.

Apart from instruction given during the administration of the sacraments, much of the catechizing was carried out by priests and lay teachers in the parish or national schools. If, however, the rapidly increasing population was to achieve a deeper understanding of its faith, more catechizing and evangelizing were necessary than the church was able to provide. The number of priests available was inadequate. Fr Collins told the Select Committee on Disturbances that the number attending religious duties had fallen because of the inability of the overworked clergy to give instructions on Sunday or to catechize the children.[203] Murray, too, complained that 'they [the priests] are obliged to shorten the time [in confession] allotted to each, on account of the great number they have to attend to, and the comparatively small number of clergy'.[204] McNally told Cullen that the conditions normally required for gaining the Jubilee—the confession of one's sins—could be fulfilled only with great difficulty because the clergy were overworked and they had no religious or order priests to help them.[205] When the bishops petitioned for an increased grant for the national seminary at Maynooth, the recurring theme in their case was the insufficient number of priests.[206] The complaint was justified: in 1834 there were 2,156 parish clergy for a Catholic population of 6,436,060 or one priest to every 2,985 Catholics. This ratio not only compared unfavourably with the ratio in France (1:847) which the French hierarchy regarded as unsatisfactory, and with the proportion within the Established church in Ireland (approximately 1:408), but represented a

---

[202] *First and Second Reports from the Select Committee, Lords, on Tithes in Ireland, PP 1831-2,* xxii. 278.

[203] *Minutes of Evidence, Select Committee on Disturbances, PP 1825,* vii. 357.

[204] Ibid., p. 653.

[205] McNally to Cullen, 3 Jan. 1846, McNally Papers, Clogher Diocesan Papers.

[206] See p. 249.

serious deterioration when matched against demographic movements.[207] Table 2 (p. 33), representing the organization of the church in 1845, reveals sharp regional disparities. The Dublin dioceses and some Armagh dioceses were better supplied with priests and churches than those of the west, from Raphoe to Kerry. The table indicates that there was, in broad terms, one priest for every church. These figures make no allowance for elderly, sick, and otherwise incapacitated priests. The death rate was high: in the dioceses of Kerry and Clogher twenty-eight priests died in 1817, most of them from typhus, contracted while ministering to the sick.[208] The regular clergy, who might have provided pastoral support, had declined steadily in numbers from over 700 in 1742 to a mere 200 in 1845.[209] Nuns and brothers, although showing a remarkable increase since the beginning of the century, were relatively few in number and unevenly distributed. There were ninety-one convents of nuns and forty-two monasteries of brothers. While the northern and western dioceses were poorly provided for (seven of them not possessing a single religious house), Dublin, on the other hand, showed a concentration of religious houses: the division reflected broadly the economic situation. The over-all picture makes it strikingly clear that the number of clergy and religious was completely inadequate for the rapidly increasing population.

A tangible sign of the people's attachment to their faith was the amazing number of new churches built during the period between Emancipation and the Famine which so impressed

[207] In the mid-eighteenth century when the Catholic population was less than three million, the ratio was much more favourable. Dr Seán Connolly, in his 'Catholicism and Social Discipline in Pre-Famine Ireland' (New University of Ulster, D.Phil thesis, 1977), pp. 80-8 and Table I, calculates the ratio in 1731 as 1:1,587 and in 1800 as 1:2,676. Cf. J. Brady and P. J. Corish, 'The Church under the Penal Code', P. J. Corish, ed., *A history of Irish Catholicism* (1971), vol. 4, pt. ii, pp. 1, 40-1; and H. Fenning, *The Undoing of the Friars of Ireland: a study of the novitiate question in the eighteenth century* (1972), pp. 40-1. The 1851 census for England and Wales showed that there was a minister of the Established church for every 1,035 persons; M. A. Crowther, *Church embattled: religious controversy in mid-Victorian England* (1970), p. 219.

[208] *Eighth report of the Commissioners of Irish Education: Roman Catholic College of Maynooth, PP 1826-7*, xxiii. 59.

[209] See Fenning, *The Friars*, passim, esp. pp. 154-236, for the reasons for this decline. The figure of 200 for 1845 is probably an underestimate; the returns sent to the editor of the *Catholic Directory* were not complete.

visitors. In 1844 Kohl, remarking on the number of new churches in almost every large town, commented that 'In many parts of Ireland the Catholic churches are now beginning to tower over those of "the establishment" ... and all over the country the Irish Catholics are vying with the English Protestants in the zeal with which they build new churches and repair old ones.'[210] The diarist Charles Greville reported that 'the zeal and the increased wealth of the Catholics have been employed not only in building and repairing chapels but in constructing some very magnificent churches.'[211] Thackeray spoke of 'the many handsome cathedrals for their [the Catholics'] worship which have been built of late years in this country by the noble contributions of the poor man's penny and by the untiring energies and sacrifices of the clergy.'[212] Six major churches in Dublin, and cathedrals in Tuam, Ennis, Killarney, Armagh, Ballina, and Longford were completed or begun during this period. Even the poorer dioceses built many churches. The diocese of Elphin reported that 'twenty-six slated chapels have been erected since 1825', and Achonry diocese claimed that new chapels had been built in every parish in the ten years from 1831 to 1841.[213] The vicar-general of Killaloe illustrated the progress made since the beginning of the century: 'When forty-six years ago, I returned to this country ... there were not in this county [Clare] three slated chapels, and now there remains very little more than that number not replaced by very handsome edifices.'[214] The *Catholic Directory* claimed in 1844 that 'within the last thirty years, nine hundred Catholic churches have been built or restored in Ireland'.[215] The faithful often contributed their labour free, an outstanding example being the building in 1832 of the first Cistercian monastery since the Reformation, at Mount Melleray in Co. Waterford.[216] In general it can be said that the number of churches that had been built since 1829, often on land provided by Protestant landlords, had gone far to transform the external image of the church.[217]

[210] Kohl, *Travels,* pp. 110, 125.
[211] [C. C. F. Greville], *Past and present policy of England toward Ireland* (1845), p. 291.
[212] Thackeray, *Irish Sketch Book,* pp. 40-1.   [215] *Catholic Directory,* 1844, p. 305.
[213] *Catholic Directory,* 1842, pp. 322, 320.   [216] Walsh, *Dom Vincent,* pp. 156-66.
[214] Ibid., p. 306.   [217] Greville, *Past and Present Policy,* p. 291.

A further sign of the vitality of the church was the relatively flourishing state of its seminaries and religious congregations. The number of students in the national seminary at Maynooth had risen from 391 in 1826 to 438 in 1844. Although the older orders had not recovered from the decline that set in during the eighteenth century, the period witnessed the activities of several charismatic leaders whose social and educational work was to endure. Chief among them must be reckoned Edmund Rice (1762-1844), founder of the Christian Brothers whose numbers increased from 45 in 1831 to 105 in 1844; Mary Aikenhead (1787-1858), foundress of the Sisters of Charity; Catherine McAuley (1778-1841), foundress of the Sisters of Mercy; and Frances Ball (1794-1861), foundress of the Sisters of Loreto. Together with the Presentation Nuns, founded in 1775, their congregations were to control most of the education of Irish Catholic youth for the next century. On a different level, the recently founded Congregation of Irish Vincentians had launched their first 'mission' in 1842. They visited a parish for a period of weeks and provided the faithful with instructions, sermons, and spiritual exercises.[218] This new approach to evangelization was to prove highly successful and to exercise a powerful influence on the devotional life of the people. An even more striking, if less enduring, transformation had come from the work of the Cork Capuchin friar, Fr Theobald Mathew (1790-1856), whose temperance movement had by 1844 made an astonishing impact on the country, cost the exchequer almost one million pounds in lost revenues, and claimed more than three million adherents. Lord John Russell called it a 'moral miracle', and Kohl commented: 'It may be questioned whether history can present a parallel to this great moral revolution, or whether any ever acquired so great and bright a name in so short a time'.[219] Catholics were interested, too, in the wider church beyond the United Kingdom. The establishment of All Hallows College in Dublin to provide priests for English-speaking Catholics throughout the world was but a symptom of a more widespread movement. The establishment

---

[218] E. J. Cullen, *The origin and development of the Irish Vincentians*, 1833-1933 (1933), p. 45; M. Purcell, *The Story of the Vincentians* (1973), pp. 109-18.

[219] Cited in E. R. Norman, *A history of modern Ireland* (1971), pp. 74-5; Kohl, *Ireland*, p. 54.

of the Association for the Propagation of the Faith in Dublin in 1838 involved the laity in the work of the missions and before long the Irish branch of the Association was sending £7,000 a year to the general fund in Lyons, an amount which compared favourably with that provided by every other country in Europe except France.[220] The phenomenon of Irish bishops and clergy ruling the Catholic church throughout the English-speaking world was beginning to emerge.[221]

The increasingly desperate poverty of so many of its faithful constituted a pressing problem for the church which they supported with their pittances and, in turn, depended on for help in time of need. Religious congregations, like the Sisters of Charity, and a plethora of benevolent societies of all denominations attempted to succour the poor, but the amount they could accomplish was limited in extent and mainly confined to the towns. The priests constituted the only class in constant contact with the poor, and their normally generous efforts to help them strengthened the bond between people and clergy.[222] Dechy reported in 1846: 'On a vu de ces prêtres porter l'amour de leur prochain jusqu'à vendre leur habillement pour secourir les pauvres.'[223] Doyle and Murray pressed for an adequate provision for the poor, and Murray had become one of the Poor Law commissioners. MacHale, Higgins, Maginn, and other bishops denounced the government's neglect of the poor, and the bitterness at the failure of the Appropriation clause in the Church Temporalities Bill of 1833 and subsequently was due to disappointment that the Established church's surplus revenues would not be used to relieve distress. It cannot be claimed, however, that the church had worked out a coherent social policy; in view of its limited resources and the contemporary understanding of its role, it would perhaps be wrong to expect one. Mostly poor and badly educated, the faithful, although generally kind, hospitable, and of chaste morals, were often ill-disciplined and violent. Despite denunciations by

[220] *Catholic Directory*, 1845, p. 203; 1846, p. 235.

[221] P. Corish ed. *A history of Irish Catholicism* (1970-71), vi. parts 2-6.

[222] T. P. O'Neill, 'The Catholic Church and the Relief of the Poor, 1815-45', *Archiv. Hib.*, xxxi (1973), 132-45.

[223] Dechy, *Voyage*, p. 193; cf Beaumont, *L'Irlande*, ii. 39; Tocqueville, *Journeys*, pp. 170-1, 185-9.

bishops and politicians alike, the secret societies, although on the wane, still existed and often produced outrages and murders. Faction-fighting was not uncommon, although Fr Mathew's Temperance movement was bidding fair to wipe out drunkenness, one of the major sources of disorderly behaviour.

Next to the stark poverty of the cottiers, what struck most observers was the deep division in Irish society running largely along religious lines. In 1844, Greville commented that 'Ireland is the only country in the world in which a condition of social and political disorganisation prevails, growing out of or closely connected with religious animosities.'[224] Kohl, too, discovered that there were separate Protestant and Catholic stage-coaches and separate inns and hotels.[225] Fitzgerald, the president of the Catholic seminary at Carlow, when he visited Tocqueville at an inn kept by Protestants, remarked that 'when they saw me coming in to visit you, they were extremely surprised'.[226] In Kilkenny, a Protestant barrister told Tocqueville that 'you cannot conceive the distance that holds these two groups apart', assuring him that he had only once dined in the house of a Catholic and that was by accident.[227] Thomas Wyse, commenting on the request of Lord Mount Cashel to the home secretary to prevent a 'Popish bridge' being erected at Youghal, commented humorously that 'balls, dinners, dances, and dresses, like bridges and hotels, and for aught I know rivers, were divided into Popish or Protestant.'[228] The underlying distrust between the two religions had recently erupted into a bitter polemical war with the launching, mainly by Irish Anglican Evangelicals, of a vigorous effort to convert the Catholics to Protestantism. This 'New Reformation', as it was called, is usually dated from the provocative charge of the Evangelical archbishop of Dublin, William Magee when, in 1822, he described the Catholics as possessing a 'church, without what *we* can properly call a religion' and 'blindly enslaved to a supposed infallible ecclesiastical authority'.[229]

[224] Greville, *Past and Present,* pp. 270-1.
[225] Kohl, *Travels,* p. 190.
[226] Tocqueville, *Journeys,* p. 134.
[227] Ibid., p. 151.
[228] T. Wyse, *Historical sketch of the late Catholic Association of Ireland (1829),* p. 224.
[229] W. Magee, *A charge delivered at his primary visitation* ... (1822), p. 22.

Enthusiastic missionaries of the New Reformation vigorously preached the gospel in villages and at fairs throughout Ireland, and distributed an enormous number of bibles, gospels, prayer books, and religious tracts, a number of them in the Irish language.[230] Numerous societies dedicated themselves to the education of the children of the poor in schools and orphanages. The Catholic clergy saw this missionary endeavour as proselytism and, led by Doyle and MacHale, hit back vigorously. The result was bitter polemical warfare and a further polarization of the communities, Doyle himself attributing the hardening of his own views 'to this new reformation' which he accused of speaking 'all manner of evil things of the Catholic clergy and people.'[231]

Doyle believed that the whole frame of society was disorganized and attributed this condition not merely to the inequality of the law but 'still more immediately [to] the incessant collision and conflict of religious opinions'.[232] Ecumenical himself in outlook, he had proposed in 1824 the reunion of the Anglican and Roman Catholic communions claiming, somewhat optimistically, that on most points 'there is no essential difference between Catholics and Protestants; the existing diversity of opinion arises, in most cases, from certain forms of words ... or from ignorance or misconceptions which ancient prejudice and illwill produce and strengthen.'[233] Although the proposal (which Murray, too, had supported) had proved abortive, Doyle declared a few years later that 'every Catholic should say ... to every Protestant, every liberator ... to every Orangeman, every Priest to every Parson, "jungamus dexteras"'.[234] Murray in 1835 addressed the

---

[230] The number of religious books distributed was spectacular. In 1837 Baptist Noel gave the following list: 'The Tract Society has issued a vast amount of religious tracts and books. The Hibernian Bible Society, since its commencement in 1806, has issued 314,899 Bibles, 466,812 Testaments. The Sunday School Society, by the help of the British and Foreign Bible Society, has distributed 95,417 Bibles, 397,558 Testaments... In the past year the Irish Society has distributed 569 Bibles, 1,615 Testaments; and within the same period, the London Hibernian Society has distributed 3,117 Bibles, 22,976 Testaments, making with those distributed by them in former years, a total of 369,868 Bibles and Testaments.' Noel, *Tour*, p. 386.

[231] *Select Committee. Tithes, PP 1831-2*, xxi. 388-9; xxii. 100.

[232] J. Doyle, *Letter to Robertson* [sic] *esq. M.P. on a union of the Catholic and Protestant Churches* (1824), p. 1.

[233] Ibid., pp. 1-8; Fitzpatrick, *Doyle*, i. 320-37; ii. 514-22.

[234] Fitzpatrick, *Doyle*, ii. 2.

Protestants of Great Britain as 'beloved fellow-Christians ... lovers of justice ... you whose honourable reverence for truth forms such a prominent feature in your character.'[235] Relations between individual church leaders were often cordial. In Limerick Dr Ryan and Dr John Jebb, the Catholic and Anglican bishops respectively, were on friendly terms, and similar relationships existed in Ulster between Crolly and Dr Henry Montgomery, moderator of the Presbyterian Synod, and in Dublin between Murray and Dr Richard Whately, the Anglican archbishop.[236] In recent years, however, distrust between Protestants and Catholics had increased. Anglicans felt under attack from Radicals in Parliament and a resurgent Catholicism. In Ulster, the more liberal-minded Unitarians were losing ground to the orthodox and more anti-Roman Presbyterians lead by Henry Cooke.[237] The 'New Reformation' and the activities of Protestant missionary societies had sharpened Catholic fears of proselytism. The use of schools for inculcating the doctrines of the Established church had been common enough since the eighteenth century and had thwarted previous attempts to provide education for the majority of the children of the kingdom. Doyle, in the course of his impressive testimony before the House of Lords investigating the State of Ireland in 1825, when asked to what he attributed the opposition which had arisen to the education of Catholic children with other children, had replied categorically: 'Exclusively to the efforts which have been made by persons differing from us in religion to interfere directly or indirectly with the faith of Roman Catholics.'[238] O'Connell complained that the Catholic children of north Dublin were 'a prey to the baleful and destructive influence of nearly forty fanatical and proselytizing establishments'.[239] A significant improvement came in 1831 when the Whig government established the national system of

[235] Meagher, Murray, p. 170.

[236] John Jebb (1775-1833), bishop of Limerick, Ardfert, and Aghadoe, 1823; Henry Montgomery (1788-1865), moderator of the Presbyterian synod of Ulster, 1829; a Unitarian.

[237] Henry Cooke (1788-1868), leader of the orthodox Presbyterians who finally excluded Unitarian ministers from the general synod of Ulster.

[238] *Minutes of evidence on the State of Ireland, PP 1825*, ix. 244.

[239] O'Connell to Hickey, 15 Dec. 1827, D. O'Connell, *Correspondence 1824-1828*, iii. 366 ed. M. R. O'Connell (1974).

education.[240] Towards the end of the 1830s, however, concern began to be voiced that even this new system might be used for proselytism. As this issue was to cause the first major split in the ranks of the bishops and to lie at the root of later difficulties, it will be necessary to treat of it in some detail.[241]

Unlike the Established church and the Dissenters, the Catholics had welcomed the national system for, though they would have preferred a separate system, the bishops, after ten years of negotiation, were realistic enough to see that the new system with its safeguards against proselytism was as much as they could hope to obtain. In 1838, however, MacHale denounced both the government's control over the Board of National Education and the alleged latitudinarian content of the religious text-books sanctioned for use in the classrooms, notably Whately's *Lessons on the Truth of Christianity*, seeing in them a threat to the faith of the children. His public attacks on the Board eventually drew a rebuttal from Murray and sparked off a three-year controversy between the two archbishops. In a letter to Dr Paul Cullen, rector of the Irish College in Rome and general agent of the Irish bishops, Murray made a measured case for the system:

Whoever is acquainted with ... the difficulty we have had in procuring the present system, the utter hopelessness of obtaining aid from Parliament for anything better, the dangers of allowing the education funds to go back to the exclusive management of Protestants, the experience which the Catholics have had of the beneficial effects of the system which they have seen for the last seven years working under their eyes without the least interference with their religion and the consequent hold which it has obtained upon their minds ... must be convinced that any attempt ... to upset ... the present system...would ultimately fail, after having ... inflicted a wound upon religion from which it would not for a long time recover.[242]

[240] The national system provided for the joint education of Catholics and Protestants. It did not interfere with the religious beliefs of any of the children and gave facilities for instruction in their own creed. I. Murphy, 'Primary Education', *A history of Irish Catholicism*, ed. P. J. Corish, vol. V, fasc. 6, pp. 1-52.

[241] The most complete account of this dissension is E. Larkin, 'The quarrel among the Catholic hierarchy over the National system of education in Ireland, 1838-41', *The Celtic Cross* (1964), pp. 121-44.

[242] Murray to Cullen, 13 Mar. 1839, Cullen Papers. Paul Cullen (1803-78); rector of the Irish College, Rome, 1832; archbishop of Armagh, 1849; archbishop of Dublin, 1850; cardinal 1866. The essential work on him is P. Mac Suibhne, *Paul Cullen and his contemporaries with their letters*, 5 vols. (Naas, 1961-77). See also E. R. Norman, *The Catholic Church and Ireland in the age of rebellion, 1859-1873* (1965); Larkin, *Catholic Church in Ireland.*

Murray's realistic approach is fully apparent in this assessment of the situation. With Doyle and the other three archbishops, he had striven hard in the 1820s to obtain a scheme as acceptable as the national education system, judging correctly that Parliament would not give the Catholics their own system. Furthermore, experience had shown that there was little danger to Catholic children in the schools as they were being run. For him the wonder was that: 'we have been able to obtain funds for building up so good a system; and it can only be exceeded by that other still greater wonder that Catholic hands are so busily at work to pull it down'.[243] Murray showed himself more practical than MacHale, for the government had rejected the demands of even the Established church for a separate grant. On the question of textbooks, however, MacHale had a better case than Murray cared to admit. Bishops Egan, Blake, Browne, and Crolly, although favourable to the system as a whole, had misgivings regarding them, and from Rome, Dr Nicholson, a friend of Murray, reported after a conversation with Cardinal Fransoni, the prefect of the Congregation of Propaganda, that 'the books, the eternal books were, and are still, a stumbling block in our way'.[244]

The year 1838 was marked by repeated clashes in the press between MacHale and Murray. In January 1839, the hierarchy made a valiant effort to resolve its difficulties at its meeting in Dublin, where twenty-two of the twenty-five bishops present gave their individual assessment of the national system.[245] All the Connaught bishops along with Higgins, Cantwell, and Keating condemned the system whereas the other sixteen, including the archbishops of Armagh, Cashel, and Dublin, gave it their support. The line of demarcation between the two groups was by no means absolute, for several of those who supported MacHale had mixed feelings on the matter. Ably

[243] Murray to Cullen, 20 Apr. 1839, Cullen Papers.
[244] Nicholson to Hamilton, 18 May 1841, Hamilton Papers, DDA; Francis Joseph Nicholson (1803-55); Discalced Carmelite friar; ordained 1829; coadjutor archbishop of Corfu, 1846; archbishop of Corfu, 1852. Nicholson, who spent much of his time in Paris and Rome, worked hard to forward Murray's case on the issues of national education and the Bequests Act. On the question of the Academic Colleges he acted as confidant of the Russell administration. Giacomo Fransoni (1775-1856); cardinal, 1826; prefect of Propaganda, 1834.
[245] Meetings of the Irish Bishops, 23 Jan. 1839, DDA.

seconded by Higgins, he succeeded, however, in having the final decision transferred to Rome, but only at the cost of further straining episcopal unity. Browne complained that the bishops could have settled the question themselves without taking it to Rome, while Ryan spoke of 'unnecessary alarms' and suspected political as much as religious considerations.[246] Crolly criticized MacHale's 'unwise and obstinate conduct'.[247] Kinsella, on the other hand, organized support for Murray; and Slattery, who blamed MacHale for splitting the bishops, successfully canvassed all the Munster bishops.[248] Murray was determined to stand his ground, not hesitating to underscore the inconsistencies of some of his opponents who, though they denounced the system, were busily accepting its schools in their dioceses.[249] He warned Cullen in measured terms that:

if the Holy See thinks proper, in opposition to the declared judgement of the great majority of our bishops, to interfere with our present system, it will assuredly incur the responsibility of handing over the education of our poor ... to ... the greatest enemies of our religion.[250]

Two factors favoured MacHale's party: the presence in Rome of Cantwell and Higgins and, even more important, the support furnished by Cullen. Fearful of proselytism and detecting theological errors in the textbooks, Cullen used his influence in Roman circles to have the system condemned, and his vice-president, Tobias Kirby, a pious and zealous priest less circumspect in expressing his opinions, warmly supported him.[251] In July 1839, the Congregation, removed from the realities of Irish Catholic difficulties and impressed both by MacHale's thoroughly Catholic approach and Cullen's ultramontane support for it, decided to condemn the national system. The bishops in the majority were taken aback. Crolly was bitterly

---

[246] Browne to Cullen, 14 Mar., 13 Apr., 10 Sept., 19 Nov. 1839, Ryan to Cullen, 28 Sept.1840, Cullen Papers.

[247] Crolly to Cullen, 4 Feb. 1839, ibid.

[248] Kinsella to Slattery, 3 June, 7 Dec; Ryan to Slattery, 17 May; Foran to Slattery, 17 May; Murphy to Slattery, 17 May; Egan to Slattery, 18 May; Crotty to Slattery, 20 May; Kennedy to Slattery, 20 May 1840, Slattery Papers.

[249] Murray to Cullen, 24 Feb. 1840, Cullen Papers.

[250] Murray to Cullen, 20 Apr. 1839, ibid.

[251] Tobias Kirby (1804-95); vice-rector of the Irish College, 1836; rector, 1850-91; archbishop of Ephesus, 1885. He was a close friend of Cullen.

annoyed, particularly when David Richard Pigot, MP for
Clonmel and solicitor-general for Ireland, told him that Cullen
had been 'the principal tool employed for the destruction of the
system'.[252] Nicholas Wiseman, the rector of the English College
in Rome, also informed Crolly that Cullen had not acted
honestly in the affair, and the primate wanted to drop him as
the bishops' agent in Rome.[253] Murray was not prepared even
yet to accept defeat. The Congregation's decision had not been
ratified by the pope and Murray exerted his influence to have
the matter reopened. This time Murray sent his own official
agents to Rome. He also warned Cullen gently but firmly:

> I lately saw a letter addressed to the Government by one of their Diplomatic
> Agents ... which stated that nothing could be decided ... until the arrival of
> Dr MacHale's deputy; but that, all through he had a most efficient one in
> the President of the Irish College. I need not say how galling this intelligence
> would be to the great majority of the Irish Prelates, if they could place the
> slightest reliance on a piece of information, which for many reasons they
> could not possibly anticipate.[254]

Cullen's role in Irish church affairs was of special importance
because of his key position in Rome. He was born in county
Kildare into a well-to-do farming family with a strong nationalist tradition, and was educated for the priesthood at Carlow
and Rome, his father refusing a free place for him at Maynooth
because he disliked his son's taking the oath of allegiance and
refused to have any of his sons accept the king's money.[255] After
a brilliant career at Rome, he was ordained in 1829 and became
professor of Greek and Oriental languages in the College of
Propaganda with responsibility also for the Polyglot press. In
1832 he became rector of the newly re-established Irish College.
Well respected in Roman circles for his ability and piety, he
used his influence to counteract government pressure against
nationalist agitation and to co-ordinate and stiffen resistance to
it among the bishops at home. Nationalist in politics and ultramontane in ecclesiastical outlook, his sympathies lay with
O'Connell and MacHale. His position as agent for the Irish
bishops increased his influence. Dr Charles Russell, a reliable

[252] Crolly to Murray, 5 July, 1839, Murray Papers.
[253] Crolly to Murray, 4 Aug. 1839, ibid.
[254] Murray to Cullen, 28 Feb. 1840, Cullen Papers.
[255] Mac Suibhne, *Cullen*, i. 7.

if friendly witness, reported in 1843 that 'everyone to whom I speak tells me that he [the pope] will not refuse Dr Cullen anything he asks'.[256] Nicholson referred sarcastically to him as 'the Pope of Ireland'.[257] During this period of his career, Cullen had little first-hand knowledge of Ireland—for he had lived in Rome since the age of seventeen—but he maintained a wide and regular correspondence with many Irish clerics, and the warm hospitality he showed to those who visited the Irish College won him many friends among them.

What effect Murray's warning had on Cullen it is difficult to say, but when he visited Ireland in 1840, he undertook, at the request of the secretary of the Congregation of Propaganda, an inquiry into the national system. He was pleasantly surprised. 'I have seen a good number of schools', he informed Fransoni, 'and I have noticed they could not be more Catholic than they are.'[258] He strongly urged that matters be allowed to remain as they were.[259] Six months later, in January 1841, Propaganda, after considering evidence from both Murray's and MacHale's agents, came to that very decision. It neither condemned nor approved the system but left the matter to the judgement of each bishop for his own diocese, recommending, however, certain safeguards particularly as regards the textbooks.[260] Murray had won, but the dispute, for all its external settlement, left wounds that never quite healed. Murray, whose effectiveness as guardian of Catholic interests on the National Board had been challenged, was affronted and spoke of the 'apparent double-dealing' of MacHale's supporters. He felt too that they would show the hierarchy in a harmful light since the government would see them as 'utterly factious'.[261] Murray's anxiety that the church should project an acceptable

---

[256] C. W. Russell to ——, 2 Jan. 1843; Russell to Denvir, 3 Mar. 1843, *Irish Monthly*, xxi (1893), 413-19. Charles William Russell (1812-80), professor of Humanity at Maynooth College, 1835-45; professor of Ecclesiastical History, 1845-57; president of Maynooth College, 1857-80; frequent contributor to the *Dublin Review;* friend of John Henry Newman.

[257] Nicholson to Hamilton, 15, 23 June 1845, Hamilton Papers, DDA.

[258] Cullen to Fransoni, 7 Aug. 1840, Mac Suibhne, *Cullen,* i. 230.

[259] Cullen to Propaganda, 13 Sept. 1840, ibid., pp. 231-5.

[260] Murphy, 'Primary Education', pp. 17-18.

[261] Murray to Cullen, 28 Feb. 1840, Cullen Papers.

image emerges clearly—and not for the first time.[262] He had kept the majority of the bishops with him. On the other hand, a substantial minority had formed behind MacHale who, distrustful of the establishment in church and state, had become concerned that Murray, living in the capital and serving as a member of a government board, should prove too amenable to the influence of Dublin Castle and over-trustful of the intentions of the Protestant commissioners such as Dr Whately. Murray's victory was, in the event, to prove a temporary and precarious one. The question of the immunity of State education from proselytism was to recur, and Catholic education remained a major and unsettled issue between the state and the church for the rest of the century.

Another concern of Irish Catholics, by no means unconnected with the first, was for the independence of their church. From the time of the relief acts in the late eighteenth century, the state, acknowledging that Catholicism was not to be easily rooted out, considered more than once the advisability of providing salaries for the priests with a view to gaining control over them and of removing their dependence on the peasants. Prior to Emancipation, the attitude of the bishops (and of O'Connell) to a state pension for the clergy was ambivalent. After 1829, however, they firmly opposed it. Kinsella told Tocqueville in 1835 that he went to London explicitly to counteract one such effort. The reason he gave for the bishops' opposition was that it would destroy the union between priest and people: 'If we received money from the State they [the people] would regard us as officials of the State, and when we advised them to respect law and order they would say "That is what they are paid for".'[263] Wherever Tocqueville raised this question the clergy gave him a similar reply.[264] Beaumont admitted that the opposition to such a project, which he personally favoured, would come from the Catholic clergy.[265] Nevertheless, after Emancipation many saw the clergy as too indepen-

---

[262] Murray to Cullen, 24 Dec. 1838, ibid., where Murray fears that a decision to exclude the *Scripture Lessons* used in the schools would make Catholics 'a laughing stock for the Protestants and embarrass exceedingly the Catholic population of the country'.

[263] Tocqueville, *Journeys*, p. 145.

[264] Ibid., pp. 145, 172, 174, 54, 133.

[265] Beaumont, *L'Irlande*, ii. 175.

dent of the state and too dependent on the people, and proposals abounded to bring them more under state control by this
'golden link'. Anglesey, Holland, Littleton, and Grey discussed
it in 1832. When it was spoken of openly in 1837, the bishops
at their annual meeting expressed their 'unalterable determination to resist, by every means in our power, a measure so
fraught with mischief to the independence and purity of the
Catholic religion in Ireland'.[266] Higgins, who was in Rome,
raised the matter with the pope, assuring him passionately that
every bishop in Ireland would 'beg his bread throughout any
diocese rather than ever receive a pension'. To this plea, the
pope replied warmly, 'You are right, you are right; do you all
oppose it and I will support you.'[267] In 1841 the question flared
up again with the publication of Lord Alvanley's pamphlet *The
state of Ireland considered,* and Lord Clifford's reply.[268] Alarmed,
the bishops took their precautions against such a scheme,
resolving at their meeting on 10 November: 'that ... Dr Murray
be requested to call a Special General Meeting of the Prelates
of all Ireland, in case he shall have clear proof, or well-grounded
apprehensions, that the odious and alarming scheme for a state
provision for the Catholic Clergy ... be contemplated by the
Government ...'[269] O'Connell and the laity were even more
hostile than the clergy to such schemes, seeing them as insidious
attempts to control what was for them an independent and a
national institution.

From the evidence available, it appears that, despite un-
resolved problems, the church had made considerable progress
since Emancipation, and the picture that emerges of it by 1844
is that of a lively, fervent, self-confident institution with a sure
hold on the loyalty of the faithful and increasingly conscious
of its role in Irish public life. The number of churches and
convents springing up throughout the country was the most
obvious sign of its development. Education financed by the

---

[266] Meetings of the Irish Bishops, 10-13 Jan. 1837, DDA.

[267] Nicholson to Hamilton, 1 Feb. 1837, Hamilton Papers, DDA.

[268] Alvanley, Lord [William Arden], *The state of Ireland considered* (1841). The
author was the second Baron Alvanley (1789-1849). H. C. Clifford, *Letters addressed to
the Right Hon. Lord Alvanley on his pamphlet entitled 'The state of Ireland considered'* (1841);
Hugh Charles Clifford, seventh Lord Clifford of Chudleigh (1790-1858).

[269] Bishops' resolution, 10 Nov. 1841, Meetings of the Irish Bishops, DDA.

state and yet free from proselytism had come, for the first time, within the reach of hundreds of thousands of Catholic children. Religious orders were providing some social services, catechetical instruction and, specifically, Catholic education. The church had preserved its freedom from any kind of direct control by the state. It had a full complement of bishops, whose selection was regulated after 1829 by a Roman decree, following consultation between the hierarchy and the Curia; their annual meetings gave a coherent character to the policies they pursued. Diocesan reorganization was under way and, although much depended on the zeal of the individual bishop, provincial synods had prepared the ground for further progress. The most urgent problem for church leaders, painfully aware of the needs of their rapidly expanding and impoverished flock, was how to provide and train more priests.

Priests, too, constituted a major problem for upholders of the established order in church and state, but for different reasons. Fear of 'an irresponsible power' was the motive advanced by Alvanley and other supporters of the scheme of pensioning the clergy. Certainly, the Irish clergy was in a very independent position. The penal laws and the denial of recognition to the Catholic Church in Ireland had an unexpected result: by 1830 the Irish Church was less dependent on the state than any church in Europe. Efforts to nominate the bishops, to pay the clergy and to control the education of priests had all failed. The resulting unique position of independence could, and did, tend towards the establishment of a free church in a free state. Understandably, however, it appeared to its critics as a state within a state, ruled by a powerful and privileged caste, responsible to no one and using spiritual intimidation on their flocks to achieve political ends. Peel's criticism of the clergy was chiefly concerned with this political activity. It was with bitter rhetoric that he addressed his cabinet in 1844:

Who summoned the meeting at Clontarf—the first meeting that we were able to suppress from its own inherent illegality? A confederacy of some twenty or thirty priests. They signed the first requisition for the meeting at Clontarf and to that requisition not one lay name was attached.

He went on to speculate how instructive it would be 'to know how many of these priests received their education at Maynooth'.[270] The involvement of the clergy in politics must now be examined.

---

[270] Peel's cabinet memorandum, Add. MSS 40540, ff. 50-1. No date is given on the memorandum, but as Gladstone was studying it on 28 Feb. it is probably of that date or of 27 Feb; W. E. Gladstone, *Diaries,* ed. M. R. D. Foot and H. C. G. Matthew (1974), iii. 330, 28 Feb. 1844.

2

THE IRISH CLERGY AND POLITICS;
OFFICIAL DISQUIET AND ROMAN RESERVE

In 1830, the hierarchy issued a lavish statement of Catholic gratitude for Emancipation. In it the bishops made clear their intention of withdrawing totally from involvement in public affairs: 'We find ourselves discharged from a duty which necessity alone allied to our ministry ... a duty which we have gladly relinquished in the fervent hope that by us or our successors it may not be resumed.'[1] Yet a decade later, clerical involvement in politics had become so marked that Peel determined on a sustained and politically perilous attempt to silence or placate the clergy. Before embarking on a positive programme of reconciliation, Peel's government decided to approach the Holy See with a view to obtaining a public Roman condemnation of the political involvement of the clergy. This political move was to have repercussions in Westminster and in Vienna, no less than in Rome and in Ireland.

The movement which forced Emancipation on Wellington's government and through Parliament, incorporating as it did all sections of the Catholic community, had shown Catholics their strength. Yet if in retrospect this great movement marked the formal arrival of the political power of the clergy, the bishops were undoubtedly sincere in expressing their intention to abstain from politics, and they attempted to enforce this policy on their clergy. In 1831, the bishops of the Dublin province, and in 1834, the entire hierarchy, pledged themselves to tell their priests 'to avoid in future any allusion at their Altars to political subjects, and carefully to refrain from connecting themselves with political clubs—acting as chairman or secretaries at political meetings—or moving or seconding resolutions on such occasions'.[2]

---

[1] *Dublin Evening Post,* 16 Feb. 1830.
[2] Meetings of the Irish Bishops, 28 Jan. 1834, DDA; Broderick, *Holy See*, pp. 58-61.

The times were not conducive to clerical disengagement from politics. Emancipation had not proved the boon it had been held out to be.[3] Discontent was rife. The need for some provision for the poor, the problem of tithes and the Protestant evangelical. missions (especially in Achill and Dingle) were issues that kept Doyle, MacHale, and other clerics active in public affairs and, given their position in the community and the difficulty of separating religion from politics, their involvement is not surprising.[4] The long drawn-out political battles over Appropriation in the 1830s kept mutual hostility alive. The general election of 1835 saw many allegations of clerical intervention, Dr Phillpotts dating the renewed political involvement of the bishops from this contest.[5] Egan had intervened on behalf of O'Connell's candidate in Kerry, while Dr Edward Nolan, who had succeeded Doyle as bishop of Kildare and Leighlin, urged the peasants in his diocese to support popular candidates.[6] In 1836, during the debate on municipal reform, Stanley alleged that there were 'abundant proofs of the influence of the Catholic clergy and that they exercised influence for the furtherance of political designs peculiar to the Catholics'[7], while Graham appealed to England not to give up Irish Protestants as 'an easy prey to the fury of the demagogue, the vengeance of the priest, or the madness of the people'.[8] Lyndhurst denounced the priesthood as 'the most formidable engine of political power...ever wielded in any country'.[9] These complaints need cautious evaluation; they came from men who were moved (to greater or lesser degrees) by political prejudice but who were sincere defenders of the Established church at a time when anti-Catholicism was on the upsurge in England. It is clear, however, that the clergy were keenly interested, to say the least, in the political state of the country. At a dinner at

[3] Tocqueville, *Journeys,* p. 132; W. McCullagh Torrens, *Memoirs of ... Richard Lalor Sheil* (1855), ii. 221-2.

[4] Fitzpatrick, *Doyle,* ii. 215, 228-9, 230-1; Doyle gave at some length his reasons for involvement in public affairs when questioned before the Select Committees on Tithes; *PP 1831-32,* xxi. 308-9; xxxii. 100.

[5] *Hansard,* xli. 1298-9, 27 March. 1838.

[6] G. L. Lyne, 'Intimidation and the Kerry Election of 1835', *Journal of Kerry Archaeological and Historical Society,* iv (1971), 87-8; *Annual Register,* 1835, p. 15.

[7] *Hansard,* xxxii. 93, 8 Mar. 1836.

[8] Ibid., col. 65, 8 Mar. 1836.

[9] Ibid., col. 1132, 18 Apr. 1836.

Kilkenny in 1836, attended by an archbishop, other bishops and many priests, Tocqueville found the clergy very much on the side of the people and commented that they were 'as much leaders of a Party as representatives of the Church'.[10] Beaumont was of opinion that the priests ruled Ireland, under O'Connell.[11] A few of them, certainly, such as John Sheehan of Waterford, John Miley of Dublin, and Michael Burke of Clonmel, played significant roles in nationalist politics.[12] Most of the specific allegations, however, concerned clerical intervention in elections, and even on this score there were no prosecutions for electoral intimidation. Dr Whyte has shown that the clergy's success was due to their organizational ability at elections, which rivalled that of the landlords.[13] On the whole, it would appear that while the Whigs were secure in power, the clergy as a whole were not deeply or permanently involved in any political movement.[14] With the advent of a new Conservative government and with O'Connell's change in tactics, this situation was to change dramatically.

The formation of Peel's government in 1841 was the culmination of a steady growth in the Conservative party's success after 1837, particularly in England. This government was exceptionally experienced in Irish affairs—five of its members had been chief secretaries, one a viceroy. Peel particularly, although lacking in sympathy with its inhabitants, had an excellent knowledge of Ireland from an official point of view. At the age of twenty-four, in 1812, he had been appointed chief secretary and remained in the post until 1818. As home secretary from 1822 to 1830, he was much concerned with Irish affairs. They had left their mark on him: the Emancipation issue had blown up in his face, damaged his career, and left lasting doubts in the minds of the Ultras of his party as to his reliability.

[10] Tocqueville, *Journeys*, p. 130.

[11] Beaumont, *L'Irlande*, ii. 36-47.

[12] John Sheehan (d. 1854) parish priest, St. Patrick's Waterford 1828-54. John Miley (1785-1861) close friend of O'Connell; rector of the Irish College, Paris, 1849; parish priest of Bray, Co. Wicklow, 1859. Michael Burke (d. 1866), parish priest, St Peter and Paul's, Clonmel; vicar-general of diocese of Waterford.

[13] J. H. Whyte, 'The influence of the Catholic Clergy on Elections in Nineteenth Century Ireland', EHR, lxxv (1960), 239-59.

[14] On clerical involvement in politics in the 1830s see Macintyre, *The Liberator*, pp. 111-17.

Again, Irish affairs had played a significant part in bringing down his first ministry in 1835. It was a tribute to his stature that he was able to change his position on the Catholic issue, and there is no reason to doubt his full acceptance of the implications of the Emancipation Act. With thirty years' experience, his views on Ireland had matured, and in 1837 he remarked that England had failed to solve the Catholic question in both Ireland and Canada.[15] In August 1841, on the eve of his coming into power, when deploring gratuitous insults to Irish Catholic feelings, he declared that if he could not retain power 'except by encouraging and favouring such feelings, I say at once, that the day on which I relinquish power rather than defer to such feelings, will be ten times a prouder one, than the day on which I obtained it.'[16]

Sincere though this protestation of impartiality was, Peel's own use of Irish and Catholic issues to serve the purposes of opposition during Melbourne's second administration created difficulties for its effective later implementation. His position between 1835 and 1841 had its difficulties, particularly in view of the attitude of the House of Lords and of Wellington, and he had not always restrained, or been able to restrain, his followers. This political opportunism was to leave him open to the taunts of the Whigs.[17] It merited, too, the deep-rooted suspicion of the Irish, for many of whom Peel remained, in Disraeli's striking description of 1845, 'the same individual whose bleak shade fell on the sunshine of your hopes for more than a quarter of a century'.[18] Peel's choice of ministers, which included Lyndhurst, Stanley, Wellington, Graham, Buckingham, Hardinge, Ripon, Goulburn, and Knatchbull—all of whom had at one time or another, shown hostility to Irish Catholic claims—tended to deepen that suspicion. It was his Irish appointments, however, that were awaited with most interest in Ireland.

[15] Gladstone's memorandum, 9 Dec. 1837, Add. MSS 44777, ff. 40-51, Gladstone, *Prime Ministers' Papers*, ii. 88.

[16] *Hansard,* lix. 428-9, 27 Aug. 1841.

[17] W. Nassau Senior, 'Ireland in 1843', *Edinburgh Rev.*, lxxix (1844), 232-48; *Hansard,* lxxix. 646-58, 11 Apr. 1845, T. B. Macaulay.

[18] *Hansard,* lxxix, 567, 11 Apr. 1845.

Peel, as Russell remarked, had no Drummond to send to
Ireland, but from his own Irish experience he was aware of the
necessity of choosing carefully.[19] Lord De Grey became lord
lieutenant and Lord Eliot chief secretary.[20] Peel professed to
see in these appointments guarantees of his policy of administering impartial justice to Ireland, and Russell, the leader of
the opposition, welcomed De Grey's and, particularly, Eliot's
appointment.[21] As it turned out, however, Peel had blundered
badly, not least in his choice of lord lieutenant. De Grey did
not want the position and had repeatedly said so earlier and
again as late as May 1841.[22] His wife, a sister of Lord Ennis-
killen, a leading Orange peer, had warned Peel that her Orange
connection would be an insuperable objection.[23] It would have
been better for Peel if he had heeded these appeals, for De Grey
was to prove difficult to manage and openly identified himself
with the High Tory party. Of even more consequence were his
repeated clashes with his chief secretary, Lord Eliot.

Eliot was a liberal-minded conservative who, during the
Municipal Corporations debate in 1839, had denounced the
Reverend Thresham Gregg for describing the Catholic religion
as idolatrous; as a result he was himself criticized by the ultra-
Protestant press.[24] When Peel appointed him chief secretary,
the *Dublin Evening Mail,* voicing Irish Tory suspicions, warned
Eliot 'that no trucking with democracy will go down here'.[25]
Eliot had his own remedies for Ireland even before going there,
one of which, it is important to note, was the potentially explosive one of increasing the grant to Maynooth College.[26]

---

[19] Russell to Palmerston, 19 Aug. 1843, Palmerston Papers, cited by J. Prest,
Lord John Russell (1972), p. 193.

[20] Thomas Philip, Earl De Grey (1781-1859); 1st lord of the admiralty 1834; Edward
Granville Eliot, (1798-1877); 3rd earl of St Germans, 1845; lord lieutenant of Ireland,
1853-5.

[21] The other important appointments were: Sir Edward Sugden as lord chancellor,
Edward Lucas, under-secretary, Francis Blackburne, attorney-general, Joseph
Devonsher Jackson, solicitor-general and Abraham Brewster, law adviser at Dublin
Castle. Lucas, Jackson, and Brewster were regarded with suspicion by Catholics. For
Peel's, Russell's and O'Connell's comments on the appointments, see *Hansard,* lix.
554, 526-7, 591, 17 Sept. 1841.

[22] Gash, *Peel,* p. 394; De Grey to Peel, 18 May 1841, Add. MSS 40477, f.3.

[23] Lady De Grey to Peel, [n.d. circa 8 May 1839] Parker, *Peel,* ii. 389.

[24] Eliot to Gregg, 23 July 1839, St Germans Papers, Port Eliot.

[25] *Pilot,* 8, 29 Sept; *Dublin Evening Mail,* 10, 20, 27 Sept. 1841.

[26] Graham to Peel, 1 Dec. 1841, Add. MSS 40446, ff. 162-5.

When he came to Ireland, he established good relations with the Catholic bishops, raised the possibility of tenant right and wholeheartedly supported the national system of education. His friendliness with the bishops provoked complaints from the Irish Tories, and Graham was annoyed with him in 1841 for raising such difficult issues as Maynooth and tenant right.[27] The educational question gave rise to lasting discord between Eliot and the rest of the Irish administration and the Established church.[28] As a result the House of Commons was treated to the unusual spectacle of an open disagreement on the floor of the house between Eliot and the solicitor-general, Serjeant Jackson, who strongly opposed the national system of education.[29] Jackson was an Irish Tory whose appointment had been opposed by the queen on the ground that he was attached to 'the very violent Orange party'.[30] In 1835, he had introduced petitions against the Maynooth grant alleging that 'the clergymen educated at Maynooth by the public bounty ... turned their chapels into political arenas, and used their pulpits as rostra.'[31]

De Grey's chief supporter within his executive, however, was Edward Lucas, the under-secretary. An Irish protestant landlord and an able administrator, he held his conservative views so strongly that he was prepared to abandon the government at its most critical hour, in June 1843, rather than consent to the appointment to a junior post of a person whom he regarded as a Whig.[32] His position was so strong that, although Peel and Graham regarded his conduct as shabby, De Grey forced them to give way.[33] The other important figure in the Irish administration was the chancellor, Sir Edward Sugden, who, although an excellent lawyer, seriously embarrassed the government and drove moderates into O'Connell's camp by his ill-judged dismissal of the Repeal magistrates in May 1843.[34]

[27] J. E. Devereux to Cabinet, 28 Oct. 1843, Derby Papers, Box 12/5; Graham to Peel, 1 Dec. 1841, Add. MSS 40446, ff. 162-5.

[28] Eliot to Peel, 4 June 1842, Add. MSS 40480, ff. 76-8; Nowlan, *Repeal,* pp. 27-30.

[29] *Hansard,* lxv. 208-16, 15 July 1842.

[30] Victoria to Peel, 25, 26 Oct. 1841, Royal Archives A/11/66.

[31] *Hansard,* xxviii. 896, 19 June 1835.

[32] McCaffrey, *O'Connell,* p. 162.

[33] De Grey to Peel, 8 June, 1843, Add. MSS 40478, ff. 67-9; Nowlan, *Repeal,* p. 47.

[34] Peel to Sugden, 1 June 1843, Parker, *Peel,* iii. 51-2; Nowlan, *Repeal,* pp. 46-7.

Taken as a whole the Irish administration had little or no *esprit de corps*. Eliot, whom observers like Greville saw as too weak, complained of not being consulted and finally recommended that the chief secretaryship be abolished.[35] De Grey made damning comments on almost every member of his own administration.[36] Graham expressed the fear in 1843 that the administration was not asleep but dead, and Disraeli jibed at the 'weakest executive in the world'.[37] For his unfortunate choice of officials in 1841 Peel paid a heavy price, and not merely because both he and Graham had to spend much of their time deciding trivial matters and composing quarrels. On the vital question of education, Peel was at first inclined to yield to the Established church's claim for a subsidy for Anglican activities in education such as had existed prior to the setting-up of the national system. Eliot and Anthony Blake (the lay Catholic commissioner on the national board) pleaded with him not to yield.[38] It became likely that both the Protestant and Catholic archbishops of Dublin would resign if the national system were weakened: Whately disliked denominational education, while Murray was struggling desperately to reverse the MacHale-inspired condemnation of the system by the Congregation of Propaganda. Peel, wisely advised by Graham, decided to maintain the status quo and thus to demonstrate that the government was not wedded to a high church policy.[39] Again, Catholics alleged that they were excluded from official patronage and administration—a complaint echoed by Russell and which Peel himself recognized as well founded, as he frankly explained to Croker:

They [the Protestants] have had pretty nearly a complete monopoly of every good thing that this Government have had...to dispose of. Take political office, take judicial office, ordinary civil service, representative peerage, honorary

---

[35] Eliot to Peel, 12 Dec. 1842, Add. MSS 40480, ff. 200-5.

[36] De Grey to Peel, 8 June 1843, Add. MSS 40478, ff. 67-8.

[37] Graham to Peel, 5 Sept. 1843, Add. MSS 40449, ff. 23-6; *Hansard*, lxxii. 1016, 16 Feb. 1844.

[38] Eliot to Peel, 4 June 1842, Add. MSS 40480, ff. 76-8; Blake to Wellesley, 20 Sept. 1841, Add. MSS 37313, ff. 75-7, Wellesley Papers; Blake to Peel, 3 Feb. 1842, Add. MSS 40501, ff. 257-9. For Blake's career, see pp. 136-7.

[39] R. B. McDowell, *Public opinion and government policy in Ireland, 1801-46* (1952), pp. 206-7.

distinctions, legal appointments ... notwithstanding the nominal equality of civil privileges by statute, the practical result is that the Roman Catholics gain little by it.[40]

With an Irish administration weighted towards conservatism, at discord within itself and resolutely excluding Catholics from any crown patronage, it was difficult for Peel to live up to his promise of providing a government that Catholics could regard as impartial.

One important factor that made it difficult for Peel to achieve much in Ireland was the hostility, partly political and partly personal, between him and O'Connell, the leader with whom millions of Irishmen identified. To O'Connell even the prospect of a Tory government was a disaster, and before 1841, in the light of the Whigs' increasingly precarious hold on power, he had turned again to popular agitation. The support of the Catholic clergy was of prime importance to him, and by his persistent appeals and clever tactics he played a major part in bringing the clergy back into politics. In 1838, when he established the Precursor Society, he made clear the importance he attached to their support: 'the public mind must be excited, and it is most fortunate for the end contemplated that a more fitting or powerful auxiliary no political party was ever blessed with than the Irish people have attached to them in the persons of the Catholic clergy.'[41] Although this statement is consistent with his tendency to flatter the clergy and to extol the links between them and the people, it also represented a basic feature of his political outlook. He was successful in winning for his Precursor Society not merely many of the priests but a considerable number of bishops, including Crotty, Haly, Browne of Galway, Foran, Keating, and Kennedy.[42] Perhaps the most remarkable expression of support he received was that of Archbishop Crolly, who justified his support in impressive terms:

I feel as a Christian prelate, I should be zealous in my anxiety to place before you not only the divine precepts of religion, but the best standards in politics ... The archbishops and bishops of Ireland ... all feel, as I do, that the time has come when every man in Ireland, whether wearing the clerical character or not, should stand forward to demand long retarded justice.[43]

[40] Peel to Croker, 17 Dec. 1844, Parker, *Peel*, iii. 130-1.
[41] *Pilot,* 12 Nov. 1838.   [42] Broderick, *Holy See*, pp. 109-11.
[43] *Pilot,* 28 Jan. 1839.

Crolly did not intend to follow O'Connell beyond 'the bounds of justice', but his statement shows how far some of the bishops were prepared to go in supporting the demands for 'justice for Ireland', and contrasted strikingly with their passivity, for example, before the Emancipation campaign. In so far as O'Connell had dropped all mention of Repeal from the programme, it could be argued that they were seeking social reforms rather than constitutional changes and that the state of the country justified their action. His lifelong opposition to violence as a means to achieve political goals and his repeated condemnation of secret societies attracted a clergy conscious of the social and political aspirations of their flocks. Political feelings apart, they were unwilling to abandon the great Catholic leader.

O'Connell's ability to mobilize clerical support was shown at the beginning of the new Repeal agitation in 1840. With the imminence of the Conservatives' return to power, he set up the Repeal Association and begged for MacHale's help, telling him, with some exaggeration that 'the fate of Catholic Ireland is now in your hands'.[44] This help was freely forthcoming, and the first great Repeal meeting was held at Castlebar in Mayo on 26 July 1840. Both MacHale and Browne of Galway publicly joined the Repeal Association in August, and Cantwell, Blake, Foran, Higgins, and Feeny soon followed their example.[45]

O'Connell's success in winning over the bishops was, however, by no means complete. Denvir of Down and Connor, although a Repealer, refused to take a lead in the movement, 'while the Primate and some of the senior Prelates are undecided'.[46] Slattery coyly pleaded that he was 'a retiring person'.[47] Egan of Kerry told O'Connell that although 'the Irish people are not done justice by our British Parliament', as a 'puny politician' himself he did not see his way clearly enough and was unwilling to commit himself. He added significantly that many 'are deterred from joining the Repeal Association

---

[44] O'Connell to MacHale, 6 Sept. 1838, *O'Connell Corr.*, pp. 147-8.

[45] Broderick, *Holy See*, pp. 112-22.

[46] C. Gavan Duffy to O'Connell, 18 Oct. 1840, *Irish Monthly*, xv (1887), 600.

[47] O'Connell to Slattery, 17 Jan; Slattery to O'Connell, 19 Jan. 1841, Slattery Papers.

through fear of a revolution'.[48] This fear was most strongly felt by Murray, who saw more clearly than most the limits of moral force as a weapon. A letter to Hamilton, his vicar-general, throws abundant light on his predicament:

The rent will probably flow in plentifully but what will the non-Repealers do? Will their subscription to the Rent identify them with the repeal agitation? It appears to me as certain as that the sun is now in the firmament that repeal can never be carried without such a convulsion as the great majority of its present supporters could not contemplate without horror. I know that Dr Yore will not agree with me in this opinion but I have as yet heard no argument which supplied the least ground for believing that I can ever change it.[49]

Murray's dilemma was real. He could not abandon the Liberator by churlishly refusing the rent, yet he plainly did not believe in the feasibility of Repeal and feared that the agitation would bring a replica of the French Revolution and the rebellion of 1798.

Crolly, too, who had only two years earlier strongly supported the Precursor movement, opposed the Repeal agitation, though he was unwilling to come out publicly against it. He told Murray, who had apparently urged him to oppose the agitation or to use his influence with the bishops, that

I have so often vexed Mr O'Connell by my opposition to his injudicious and unfortunate Repeal agitation that I am sure he would pay very little attention to anything that I could say to him on that subject. The late atrocious manifesto published by the English Protestants, the intolerant menaces of our Irish Conservatives and the indignation of the persecuted Catholics afford at present a favourable occasion for exciting the people of Ireland to call for a domestic parliament. I hope that I have succeeded in guarding my clergy against that desperate and dangerous infatuation. But I could not promise myself any further success by applying to any of the prelates who have rashly given encouragement to Mr O'Connell, contributing to support him in his deplorable undertaking. If I would venture to solicit support to stop the Repeal agitation, whilst larger contributions are received for that purpose, my motives might be represented in such a manner as would expose me to the odium of many misguided poor Catholics.[50]

[48] Egan to O'Connell, 28 Sept. 1840, O'Connell Papers, property of Maurice R. O'Connell.
[49] Murray to Hamilton, 3 Oct. 1840, Murray Papers; William Yore (1781-1864), parish priest of Arran Quay Church, Dublin, and vicar-general.
[50] Crolly to Murray, 22 Aug. 1841, Murray Papers. The 'atrocious manifesto' to which Crolly referred was probably the address issued by the Protestant Association at its meeting at Exeter Hall on 6 Aug., in which it denounced 'the Popish priests

Crolly's letter illustrates the dilemma of those moderates who, aggrieved at the intolerance of the ultra-Tories, could neither drop O'Connell nor bring themselves to agitate for Repeal. Crolly was too prudent a man to risk unpopularity and merely hoped that agitation would die down. Although he was not the man to give a steady lead to the hierarchy, he feared that he would not be listened to even if he had tried.

O'Connell expressed disappointment at the meagre results of his appeal, and complained to Higgins that 'some of our prelates are neutral on Repeal, and there is at least one [Murray or Crolly?] who is actively opposed.'[51] The intervention of the Roman curia requesting Crolly to dissuade priests and bishops from participating in politics may well have been the reason why Crolly and others were slow to support O'Connell's new venture. It is true that Crolly had defended the clergy, but the warning from Rome may have achieved its aim. Then, too, many bishops, who would readily unite with O'Connell in demanding much-needed reforms, shrank back from such a radical demand as the repeal of the Union, sceptical of its feasibility and concerned at the agitation which it involved. Despite his expression of disappointment O'Connell received considerable support from the clergy, and his complaint to Higgins may have been merely a plea for more intensive campaigning on his part.

O'Connell was also alert to any attempt to use Rome to block his attempt to gain clerical support. Both MacHale and he had been concerned at the activity of some English Catholic gentlemen at Rome, who represented the movement as extreme.[52] When early in 1842 Charles Acton, an Englishman, was proclaimed cardinal, O'Connell wrote to Cullen repudiating Acton's description of the Irish as 'British' and expressing his anxiety at the presence in Rome of Lord Shrewsbury, who was an 'anti-Repealer'. He warned Cullen that Irish Catholics were very much alive to any interference with their temporal

---

as being in too many cases ... political incendiaries who abuse the power which superstition has given them over the minds of their benighted flocks in order to incite them to the commission of any crimes which may further their own factious ends'; *The Times*, 7 Aug. 1841.

[51] O'Connell to Higgins, 10 Apr. 1841, NLI, MSS 11489.
[52] MacHale to Clifford, 13 Dec. 1841, MacHale, *Letters*, pp. 542-57.

concerns 'which are legitimately within the province of the laity as well as of the clergy'. On the question of Repeal, his earnest hope was that 'his Holiness will not interfere with any of the Irish Catholic clergy or suffer them to be interfered with'. Then, in a remarkable statement, he outlined the heads of a memorial which he intended, if necessary, to put to the pope to prove to him that Repeal would be of such benefit to Catholicity that 'I am prevented from presenting it in its true colours to the British people lest it should have its effect of increasing their hostility to that measure'. He then advanced sixteen reasons why Repeal would favour the church. The Protestants, he alleged, were 'political Protestants, that is Protestants by reason ... of political power being almost entirely confided in them'. If the Union were repealed, 'the great mass of the Protestant community would with little delay melt into the overwhelming majority of the Irish nation'. Repeal 'would free the Catholic people ... from the burden of supporting the use-less Protestant Church', and 'would at once disengage the Church lands from the hands to which they have been unjustly transferred by means of the so-called Reformation.' Catholics would then be able to endow their own clergy and provide an adequate number of priests. Catholics, too, would be able to participate 'on strictly Catholic principles and subject to the regulations of the Irish Episcopal Synod', either in Trinity College or in a new university. These were but some of the blessings which O'Connell believed would result for the church from the repeal of the Union.[53]

This remarkable document would have powerfully reinforced the fears of Protestants as to the effect of a repeal of the Union achieved by a nationalist-Catholic popular movement: they would become a vanishing minority in a state where a well-endowed Catholic church would play a predominant role. It shows, too, the lengths which O'Connell was prepared to go to keep the Catholic clergy on his side and to forestall any Roman prohibition. Undoubtedly, in keeping with his character, O'Connell, the advocate, was using the plea best calculated to win his case with the pope, the Roman curia and the Catholic clergy. Furthermore, behind his humble, reverential language

[53] O'Connell to Cullen, 9 May 1842, Cullen Papers.

lay an implied threat that he would brook no interference in civil matters from Rome or from the hierarchy at home. This was typical of an attitude consistently held since the time of the Veto affair, when he had abused Quarantotti, Pius VII's acting vice-prefect, and threatened the Irish clergy that if they bowed to the 'Dagon' of Dublin Castle, they would be deserted by the people and 'would preach to still thinner numbers than attend in Munster or Connaught the reverend gentlemen of the Established Church.'[54]

Despite his efforts, O'Connell's Repeal movement made so little headway up to 1843 that both Peel and the lord lieutenant felt they could treat it with contempt.[55] *The Times* concluded with satisfaction that 'the game is up for the old man', and *Blackwood's Magazine* commented gleefully: 'Poor old soul, his cuckoo cry of Repeal grows feebler and feebler; yet he must keep it up, or starve.'[56] Then with dramatic and frightening suddeness, in the spring of 1843, the movement burst into life and within weeks appeared to pose a most serious threat to the integrity of the empire. While the Repeal rent swelled and people from all classes joined the movement, the frightening phenomenon of monster meetings throughout the country, attended by hundreds of thousands of enthusiastic but orderly demonstrators caused consternation in the Dublin administration. De Grey, abandoning his nonchalant attitude to Repeal, begged Peel to take strong and immediate action to deal with the crisis: 'Let whatever you do be strong enough ... Let no morbid sensibility or mawkish apprehension of invading the Constitution ... be allowed to weigh.'[57] The Catholic clergy were prominent on the Repeal platforms and no Repeal banquet was complete without a rousing speech from a priest or bishop. Clergy who hitherto had held back, joined the movement. Bishop Kennedy, declaring himself content with O'Connell's moderation in seeking only a subordinate parliament, publicly proclaimed his support and called on all his clergy to follow suit.[58] Some bishops tried to remain aloof. Murphy of

[54] Speech at meeting of Irish Catholic Board, 24 Jan. 1815, cited in MacDonagh, 'Politicization', p. 40.
[55] Peel to De Grey, 2 Jan. 1842, Add. MSS 40477, ff. 137-8.
[56] *The Times*, 28 Mar. 1842; *Blackwood's Magazine,* liii (1843), 141-2.
[57] De Grey to Peel, 6 May 1843, Add. MSS 40478, ff. 39-44.
[58] *Nation*, 18 Mar. 1843.

Cork told O'Connell that: 'It is not my habit to interfere in political matters; after forty-six years devoted to the quiet exercise of my priestly and episcopal functions it only remains for me to invoke the God of Wisdom to enlighten the minds of the governing and the governed.'[59] His neighbour, Crotty, perceptively commented that he was 'not altogether so sanguine as to the belief that the Repeal of the Union would prove a panacea for all our sufferings'. He was willing, however, 'to go the full length with Mr O'Connell in every measure agreeable to the law of God and of our country'.[60] Kinsella, too, refused to take part in the Repeal banquet despite pressure from some of his clergy.[61] The participation of the bishops, however, became the focus of comment with Dr Higgins's sensational announcement at the Repeal meeting in Mullingar, Co. Westmeath, on 14 May: 'I have reason to believe, I may add, I know, that every Catholic bishop in Ireland, without an exception, is an ardent Repealer ... I know that virtually you all have reason to believe that the bishops of Ireland were Repealers, but I have now again formally to announce to you that they all declared themselves as such.' O'Connell, who was sitting next to him, exclaimed 'this is the best news I ever heard. Let Bobby Peel hear that.'[62] This sensational speech coincided with, indeed perhaps provoked, an official investigation into the whole question of the Repeal agitation and of clerical involvement in it.

De Grey had already alarmed the cabinet by his reports of the remarkable upsurge of the Repeal agitation.[63] To secure precise information, Colonel Duncan McGregor, inspector general of the constabulary, sent, on 15 May, a highly confidential and detailed questionnaire to the county inspectors of constabulary. On 17 May, the under-secretary sent a similar document to all the resident magistrates in the country. The replies of thirty-eight inspectors and fifty-seven magistrates,

---

[59] *Nation*, 27 May. 1843; K. B. Nowlan, 'The Catholic clergy and Irish politics in the eighteen thirties and forties', *Hist. Studies*, ix (1974), 119-35; M. Murphy, 'Repeal, popular politics and the Catholic clergy of Cork', *Cork. Hist. Soc. Jn.*, lxxxii (1977), 39-48.

[60] *Nation*, 27 May 1843.

[61] Kinsella to Murray, 4 June 1843, Murray Papers.

[62] *Morning Chronicle*, 17-18 May 1843.

[63] McCaffrey, *Repeal*, pp. 59-60.

which were printed for the cabinet, constitute a remarkably full and hitherto unexamined source for assessing the state of the Repeal movement and the religious and clerical influences at work in it.[64] A vital question in the document was whether the advocacy of Repeal had lately received an additional impulse, and from what causes. Almost every reply reported a remarkable upsurge. Some attributed this to the depression, unemployment and the Poor Law; others to O'Connell's successful agitation, the Repeal debates in the corporations and the propaganda of the newspapers. The most constantly recurring factor was the priests' advocacy of Repeal. The reply of a Kilkenny magistrate is typical of many: 'Undoubtedly the advocacy of the Repeal has latterly received very great additional impulse, from the active part which the Roman Catholic clergy have taken, with the exertions of the Repeal Wardens of each district under the stimulus of Mr O'Connell.'[65]

A further question was: 'Are the Roman Catholic clergy generally in favour of the Movement, and what measures do they adopt, either at the altar or elsewhere, to influence the people?' The replies were that they favoured Repeal 'generally' in Kerry and Antrim, 'to a man' in Cork and Roscommon, and that, in Mayo and Galway, in fact, they were the 'mainspring' and the 'principals' of the movement. They influenced the people but did not normally use the altars for that purpose. From Kildare, the magistrate reported that 'the Roman Catholic clergy are, with few exceptions, advocates for Repeal and endeavour (and effectively) to influence the people by harranguing them at the meetings.'[66] From Belfast, the resident magistrate reported: 'that the...clergy are favourable to the

---

[64] These important papers were consulted by the present writer in the Derby. Papers, Box 34. They are apparently unavailable elsewhere. Marked secret and confidential, the questionnaires and replies were printed as four separate documents: (i) *Circular addressed by order of the Irish Government to the County Inspectors of the Constabulary Force, with several answers received from those officers;* (ii) *Questions addressed by order of the Government to the County Inspectors of the Constabulary Force with a precis of the answers received from those officers 1843;* (iii) *Circular addressed by order of the Irish Government to the stipendiary magistrates in Ireland with several answers received from those officers;* (iv) *Questions addressed by order of the government to the Stipendiary Magistrates in Ireland with the precis of the answers received from those magistrates 1843.* There were no reports given for Dublin city, Londonderry had no stipendiary magistrate.

[65] Magistrates' replies, pp. 7-8.

[66] Magistrates' replies, pp. 3-5.

movement I have little doubt'.[67] In Armagh, it was found that the clergy advanced Repeal 'by their attendance at the Repeal meetings, the dinners, their speeches'.[68] A magistrate for Mayo, Pierce Barron, a Catholic, reported that 'the ... clergy are almost all in favour of the movement, particularly the curates', though he added that 'a few of the old parish priests ... are adverse to the agitation'.[69] From Nenagh, in Tipperary, Major Priestly reported that he had heard of only one priest who was not a Repealer and that he was assured that a priest had threatened to excommunicate any person who would not join the movement.[70] On the whole, the north was more muted. From Ballymena, in Antrim, the county inspector reported that if any Repeal meeting were attempted the Protestant population would put it down. Nevertheless, he was convinced that the priests' feelings 'are as strong on the subject as their brother clergymen in the South of Ireland'.[71] One of the most penetrating reports was from J. K. Kernan, resident magistrate for Sligo and nephew of the Catholic bishop of Clogher, who claimed to be well informed of the clergy's views. He reported that:

The Roman Catholic clergy are very generally in favour ... There are certainly many exceptions, particularly amongst the old clergy and the parish priests. The great supporters of the agitation among this body, and the most dangerous members of the Roman Catholic priesthood are those young men who, within the last five or six years, have left the Catholic Seminary of Maynooth, and are now scattered about the country parishes as curates. I am informed that more than two or three instances have occurred, where parish priests have most reluctantly joined the Repeal Association, because they were threatened by their curates to be held up to the scorn of their parishoners ...

He went on to recommend that the government pension the clergy, adding the significant comment that to do so would be 'the certain means of crushing every species of agitation in the country. Sever the Catholic clergy from the agitators and agitation must cease.'[72] Such direct endowment of the clergy was politically impossible, but Kernan's view of the Maynooth-trained

[67] Ibid., pp. 29-30.
[68] Ibid., p. 34.
[69] Ibid., pp. 55-7.
[70] Ibid., pp. 92-4.
[71] Inspectors' replies pp. 21-2.
[72] Magistrates' replies, pp. 63-5.

clergy was to be accurately reflected in the attitudes of Peel and his colleagues.

The reports also give the attitude of several of the bishops. The Armagh county inspector attributed the 'passive' attitude of the priests in that county 'to the expressed sentiments of the ... Archbishop here [Crolly], who seems to have been hitherto unfavourable to Repeal'.[73] Crolly's colleague and friend, Denvir, bishop of Down and Connor, was, however, observed coming out of the Repeal assembly room in Belfast.[74] In Donegal, McGettigan was reported as declaring that the time had not yet arrived for his clergy in the north to take a leading part in the cause of Repeal.[75] He would not allow his clergy to speak on the matter in the chapels.[76] In Cavan, all the clergy except the bishop, Browne of Kilmore, were favourable; he was, the magistrate believed, 'inimical to it on the ground that he thinks it could not be obtained, but he allows his clergy to think as they please.'[77] Higgins of Ardagh and Cantwell of Meath had no such reservations. From Mohill in Leitrim, the magistrate reported that 'letters from ... Higgins were read from the altars ... urging the attendance of the people at the Repeal meeting', but to attend 'without sticks, and to observe sobriety'.[78] In Meath, Cantwell's public adhesion to Repeal persuaded the few priests opposing it to come over to the movement.[79] The only bishop in the Dublin province mentioned in the report from that region was Haly of Kildare and Leighlin. The inspectors from Kilkenny and Carlow reported that he was almost alone in not coming out in favour of Repeal, but the magistrate from Kilkenny expected that he would join the movement.[80] In Munster, Ryan was also reported as being the only one of the Limerick clergy not in favour of Repeal.[81] By contrast, his neighbour, Kennedy of Killaloe, instructed all his priests to use their utmost exertions in the cause of Repeal.[82]

[73] Inspectors' replies, pp. 22-3.
[74] Magistrates' replies, pp. 29-30.
[75] Ibid., pp. 35-6.
[76] Inspectors' replies, pp. 24-5.
[77] Magistrates' replies, pp. 53-4.
[78] Ibid., pp. 54-5.
[79] Ibid., pp. 19-23.
[80] Inspectors' replies, pp. 1-2; 2-3.
[81] Magistrates' replies, pp. 82-4.
[82] Inspectors' replies, pp. 42-4.

It was not possible to ascertain the views of Egan, bishop of Kerry.[83] In Connaught, MacHale's influence came in for more than one mention.[84] Feeny, too, bishop of Killala, had presided at a Repeal meeting as early as 19 February 1843, where the principal speakers were his priests.[85]

The government was concerned that the Repealers might tamper with members of the police. In general, inspectors reported no such tampering but the inspector for Longford echoed the fears of some when he declared: 'I have no doubt, however, that the priests have the ear and confidence of the great majority of the Roman Catholic members of the force ... [S]hould any ... crisis arise ... the Roman Catholic policemen would, almost to a man, be guided by the secret instructions and influence of the priests.'[86] Another interesting feature (which cannot now be dealt with in detail) was the connection between Repeal and the Temperance movement. Undoubtedly, the Repealers made so much use of the local Temperance societies, in order to reinforce the peaceful nature of their campaign, that almost all the replies reported that the members of the Temperance societies were all repealers. A few reports accused the priests of using the organization of the Temperance movement in order to forward Repeal.

What these reports show more clearly than any other source is not merely the almost complete commitment of the priests to Repeal but the vital dependence of the movement on their support. It was the priests and in some instances bishops who called it into being and maintained it in the parishes. They were described as 'the very spring and essence of it', 'the great main spring which at present works the machinery to the extent it has arrived at'.[87] Without them the movement would collapse. It must of course be remembered in any assessment of these reports that they came from officials entrusted with the maintenance of law and order, men who in politics and religion were generally opposed to the nationalist clergy. The religion and political views of many of the magistrates are listed: a mere handful were Catholics and only one showed Repeal sympathies.

[83] Magistrates' replies, pp. 75-6.   [84] Ibid., pp. 50, 51-2, 55-7.
[85] Ibid., pp. 57-9.   [86] Inspectors' replies, pp. 7-9.
[87] W. S. Tracey (RM Limerick), Magistrates' replies, pp. 84-7; B. Warburton (RM Galway), ibid., pp. 46-8.

A number of the reports end with strong appeals to the government to crush the movement. It is probable, too, that both magistrates and inspectors had discussed the Repeal movement among themselves beforehand. Nevertheless, although the evidence can be termed hostile, it cannot on that score be dismissed. The convergence of almost a hundred reports is too striking and, taken as a whole, they have the ring of truth about them.

The priests were prominent at the famous meeting in Mallow, Co. Cork, on Sunday 11 June when O'Connell, in launching his rousing 'Mallow Defiance' to the applause of an enthusiastic multitude, prefixed it with the claim that the cabinet was meeting in emergency session to take measures against the Repeal movement.[88] He was uncannily correct. An alarmed cabinet had met once again on 8 June to consider the banning of the monster meetings, Wellington pressing for such a measure and even Peel favouring such a course, although he feared that such legislation 'would leave untouched the root of them which is the organisation of the Roman Catholic priests'.[89] An emergency meeting was arranged for Sunday, 11 June, and Gladstone, who had earlier criticized O'Connell's willingness to transact parliamentary business on the Lord's Day, now noted sententiously in his diary that 'the nature of the emergency seemed to me to justify the interruption of the Christian rest'.[90] The nature of this emergency was the consideration of the reports of the magistrates and inspectors which had just arrived from Dublin Castle.[91] The cabinet, in Peel's own words, gave 'close and anxious attention to the state of Ireland' but finally rejected the two proposals before it, one of which would ban discussion of Repeal, the other of which would ban the monster meetings. The first appeared too extreme a measure but the second, as Peel told an anxious lord lieutenant, would be ineffective for the Repealers would still hold meetings after mass on Sunday 'without public notice, by means of that organization

    [88] *Freeman's Journal*, 14 June 1843.

    [89] Gladstone's memorandum, 8-10 June 1843, Add. MSS 44819, ff. 99-100, Gladstone, *Prime Ministers' Papers*, ii. 204-6.

    [90] Gladstone's memoranda, 18 May 1841, Add. MSS 44777, ff. 74-6; 7 June 1841, Add. MSS 44819, ff. 63-4; 11-17 June 1843, Add. MSS 44819, ff. 100-2, Gladstone, *Prime Ministers' Papers*, ii. 140, 146, 205-6.

    [91] Eliot to Graham, 8 June 1843, Graham Papers.

which Religion when allied with Politics easily presents'.[92] The reports had convinced the cabinet that the clergy constituted the real source of the movement's strength. Peel told the Knight of Kerry of his alarm at the clergy's role.[93] Stanley, a cool and shrewd observer, expressed his similar fears: 'one of the most formidable features of the present movement is the religious character which it is rapidly assuming, partly, from the exertions of the priests, partly from the skill with which O'Connell has enlisted among his Repealers the Temperance Bands.'[94] Graham flamboyantly decribed the movement as 'a religious struggle directed by the Roman Catholic hierarchy and priesthood'.[95] De Grey was convinced that 'every priest is a drill sergeant and every chapel an orderly room'.[96] He gave Peel his version of how the present situation had come about: 'I firmly believe that O'Connell began the excitement of the question, as a *financial* measure—the ardent and universal co-operation of the priests, founded upon their hopes, intentions and prospects of subverting the Established Church, has now made it a religious question.'[97] De Grey's estimate of O'Connell's original intentions was far too narrow, and he was scarcely correct in seeing the main thrust of the movement at the height of the Repeal Year as the subversion of the Established church. The Catholic clergy would no doubt have been glad to see their church prevail and many of them cast envious eyes on the rich livings of the Established church, but apart from O'Connell's remarkable letter to Cullen there is scant evidence to support the assertion that they contemplated the destruction of their rivals. The Repeal movement was not, as De Grey believed, primarily 'a religious question', but one in which political, religious, and social motives were inextricable. The government, however, was now convinced—and with good reason— that the clergy's role in the movement was central; the key question, as Peel saw it, was how to deal with their organization rather than with the actual monster meetings.

[92] Peel to De Grey, 12 June 1843, Add. MSS 40478, ff. 79-84.
[93] Peel to Knight of Kerry, 24 June 1843, Add. MSS 40478, f. 95.
[94] Stanley to Carew, 14 June 1843, Derby Papers, Box 174/2.
[95] Graham to Stanley, 16 July 1843, Graham Papers.
[96] De Grey to Graham, 12 June 1843, Graham Papers.
[97] De Grey to Peel, 17 June 1843, Add. MSS 40478, f. 88.

While these disturbing reports were coming in from magistrates and inspectors, Higgins' Mullingar speech was rever-
berating throughout the United Kingdom. Lord Beaumont, a
Catholic peer, denounced it as the most disgraceful statement
ever uttered, a sentiment in which the Earl of Wicklow and
Lord Brougham concurred.[98] Higgins, feeling that he had gone
too far, explained that he opposed separation from England
and claimed that 'I have done more for the last fourteen years
to allay angry feelings, maintain peace and resignation among
the people under the most revolting oppression than the whole
of their [the peers] noble body in Ireland.'[99] The peers were
mainly concerned with Higgins's attack on themselves; the
government was more worried by his startling claim that all
the bishops had declared themselves repealers.[100] Sugden,
however, was able to assure Graham that Murray had contacted
Crolly and Slattery and he hoped that the three archbishops
would 'publicly disavow Dr Higgins'.[101] Graham remained
pessimistic and, in his dramatic fashion, lamented that 'the
reign of Terror has commenced in Ireland and a declaration of
attachment to British connection is regarded as a national
crime and a personal disgrace.'[102]

Graham's fears proved justified. A disappointed Sugden
reported that 'Dr Slattery *affects* to treat the declaration ... as
unworthy of notice' and that no reply had come from Crolly.[103]
Less than two years earlier Crolly had labelled Repeal 'a
desperate and dangerous infatuation',[104] but now motives of
prudence prevailed, for no protest came from him. Murray had
indeed been shocked by Higgins' speech. At first he refused to
credit the reports but on being convinced of their accuracy, he
complained to his vicar-general, Hamilton, of Higgins' 'out-
rageous breach of courtesy towards his episcopal brethren'.[105]

---

[98] *Hansard,* lxix. 752-3, 23 May 1843.

[99] *Morning Chronicle,* 27 May 1843.

[100] T. B. C. Smith to Graham, 18 May; Sugden to Graham, 21 May; De Grey to
Graham, 24 May 1843, Graham Papers.

[101] Sugden to Graham, 22, 23, 24 May 1843, ibid.

[102] Graham to Sugden, 25 May 1843, ibid.

[103] Sugden to Graham, 24 May 1843, ibid.

[104] Crolly to Murray, 22 Aug. 1841, Murray Papers.

[105] Murray to Hamilton, 18 May 1843, Hamilton Papers, DDA.

Nine days after the speech, when no support was forthcoming from the other archbishops, he publicly disavowed Higgins' claim in an open letter to his clergy:

You must have read with extreme surprise a statement ... intimating that all the Catholic bishops had ... thrown themselves, as ardent Repealers, into the great political movement which is now agitating the country ... I have taken no part whatever in that movement; and ... in no instance did I give any human being the slightest reason to suppose that I have. In January, 1834, I concurred in the resolution unanimously passed at our...meeting, recommending our clergy to abstain ... from taking any prominent part in proceedings of a merely political character. To the spirit of that resolution I strictly adhere ...[106]

Although Graham lamented that the letter was limited to a disclaimer on Murray's own part, yet the archbishop's action, with its recall of the hierarchy's resolution of 1834, was courageous at a time when in Graham's own words, 'a reign of Terror' prevailed. Murray soon found that he stood alone. No other bishop spoke out, as Bishop Kinsella regretfully wrote, for although Bishop Haly wrote a letter endorsing Murray's attitude, he would not publish it.[107] Murray then turned to Cullen in Rome, hoping that some help might be forthcoming from the Holy See. 'Could anything', he asked, 'be prudently done there to restrain us somewhat more within the sphere of our own immediate duties?'[108] He was asking the wrong man; Cullen was of one mind with MacHale and Higgins, corresponded with them on the subject, and put about the impression that the pope viewed the Repeal movement benevolently. Fr Maher could write enthusiastically to Cullen a few months later that 'the bishops who are not with the movement say nothing in opposition. The clergy follow the same prudent policy. But the great majority of the body [i.e. the clergy] are in the cause, heart and soul.'[109]

Murray's efforts to steer his own clergy clear of politics were not successful. When O'Connell held the monster meeting on the hill of Tara on 15 August 1843, the archbishop was mortified to see the names of two of the priests from his own parish among

[106] *Dublin Evening Post,* 23 May 1843.
[107] Kinsella to Murray, 4 June 1843, Murray Papers.
[108] Murray to Cullen, 29 May 1843, cited in Broderick, *Holy See,* pp. 135-6.
[109] Maher to Cullen, 25 Aug. 1843, Murray Papers.

the list of those present. He complained to Hamilton that whatever might be these priests' private opinions, the Tara meeting was not the place for them to be. Fr Peter Cooper, one of the priests in question, explained that he had remained 'on the outskirts of the crowd ... studiously avoiding to appear with any degree of prominence in the scene further than was necessary to satisfy the curiosity that brought me there.' Cooper placed himself in Murray's hands, adding however, that 'by this I do not mean in the least to compromise ... whatever private feelings I may entertain'.[110] A minor ecclesiastic like Cooper, trying to remain undetected on the outskirts of the crowd, could scarcely feel much guilt when one of the most impressive sights of that memorable meeting on the hill of Tara was the two bishops, McLaughlin and Cantwell, advancing together through the applauding multitudes to take their places on the platform with O'Connell.[111] Murray, with his customary kindness to his subordinates, took no further action, and Cooper remained to plague him in future controversies.

The Clontarf meeting promised to outdo even the Tara meeting. Murray was in an awkward position: Clontarf was only two or three miles from his residence. Knowing that political activity was going on among the clergy in preparation for the meeting, he wrote a note of admonition to one of his senior priests, Fr Carey: 'A report has reached me that the Theological Conference over which you preside has been converted under your guidance into a kind of political club,...I beg further to express a hope that the circular addressed to the clergy of the Conference as to their conduct next Sunday has not had your concurrence.'[112] The Sunday was 8 October 1843, the day

---

[110] Cooper to Murray, 28 Aug. 1843, Murray Papers. Peter Cooper (1800-52), b. Dublin; educated Maynooth; ordained 1822; curate, St. Audeon's 1823-34; pro-Cathedral 1834-52; prebendary; wrote articles on education and on relations of church and state; published *The Anglican Church, the creature and slave of the State, being a refutation of certain Puseyite claims* ... (London 1844); secretary of the synod of Thurles, and secretary of the Catholic University committee. Newman, to whom he rendered valuable services, called him 'a kind, zealous, disinterested friend to me'. He was noted for his charity to the poor.

[111] A. Cogan, *The ecclesiastical history of the diocese of Meath* ... (1837-74), iii. 507-8.

[112] Murray to Carey, 3 Oct. 1843, Murray Papers; this was probably Fr James Carey, vicar-forane and parish priest of Swords from 1806-59; he was a Dominican friar.

appointed for the Clontarf meeting. Murray's efforts to prevent clerical participation in the preparation of this meeting failed utterly. The requisition for the meeting was signed by twenty-four priests of Fingal (North Dublin), including two vicars forane, and eight parish priests.[113] Fr Carey was the first to sign. Another signatory, Fr Peter Tyrell, parish priest of Lusk, was later indicted with O'Connell. The meeting was of course never held, and the reinforcements which Wellington had dispatched from England were never needed. But on that same evening, a strong military force was deployed outside Murray's pro-Cathedral. Murray's comment to Hamilton is illustrative of his feelings:

The array of military force that paraded so ostentatiously before our church on Sunday evening, seems to have been intended as an indication that our clergy are objects of peculiar suspicion (can we wonder at it?) and that in case of an outbreak, they would be amongst the first victims to be aimed at. I long foresaw, and it required no spirit of prophecy to do so, that if the agitation were persisted in the whole power of England would as far as necessary be employed to crush it, but I was ridiculed as over-timorous (or something worse) and the dream of moral influence as able to accomplish everything was clung to, in opposition to the plainest dictates of common-sense. I was quite as much alive as any of the agitators to the benefits which a domestic Legislature would be capable, if peacefully obtained, of conferring on the country; but I trembled to think on the effects of a struggle to obtain it by means of physical force. All doubt on the subject has now vanished. England has announced its determination to encounter all the calamities of civil war rather than submit to the monster evil of a repeal of the Union; and but for the prudence evinced by our poor people ... the shores of Clontarf would be again steeped in torrents of blood ...

Then, in a direct reference to the political involvement of the clergy, Murray added that if a civil war should break out, how bitter ought to be the regrets of 'those ministers of the religion of peace who had lent the influence of their sacred character to prepare the way for such a catastrophe'.[114] He was keenly sensitive to the criticisms of timidity and of lack of patriotism that he knew were being circulated about him for his failure to support the Repeal movement. Although he himself appreciated the advantages of a Dublin-based parliament he was too realistic and his insight into English attitudes to Repeal was too clear to

[113] The original requisition is in the Murray Papers.
[114] Murray to Hamilton, 13 Oct. 1843, Hamilton Papers, DDA.

believe that it was feasible. Unlike most other Irishmen, he had seen the real limits of moral force as a weapon: its effectiveness was strictly related to English limits of political tolerance. These latter had now unequivocally been reached.

By this time, O'Connell had attracted universal attention. Leading American politicians, including Robert Tyler, son of the President of the United States, spoke on Repeal platforms in the United States, while the President himself, John Tyler, came out strongly in its favour, declaring categorically that on Repeal he was 'no halfway man' and hoping that it would come soon. American dollars poured in to boost the rent.[115] From France, Alexandre Ledru-Rollin, a leading Radical, went so far as to promise military aid if the government should suppress the movement and O'Connell was forced to persuade him not to come to Ireland at the height of the agitation.[116] From Austria, Lord William Russell told his brother, Lord John, that 'there is not a pastor in the remotest village ... who is not occupied with O'Connell, whose first question is not about O'Connell'.[117] In Vienna itself, the English ambassador reported with alarm a general sympathy for O'Connell's movement.[118] In December 1844 Cavour noted the absorbing interest O'Connell's movement held for European politicians, both radical and conservative: 'The present singular condition of Ireland has excited the attention of all in Europe who are interested in politics'.[119]

Of more immediate importance to the bishops and priests involved in the Repeal movement was the attitude of the Holy See. Loyalty to the pope was a characteristic mark of the Irish church. Stanley tempered his praise of Archbishop Murray's 'mildness' with the comment that 'let any occasion arise on which he [Murray] can support the Pope against the King, and he will do so to the uttermost'.[120] England had no diplomatic

[115] McCaffrey, O'Connell, pp. 71-2.

[116] Ibid., pp. 75-6.

[117] Lord William Russell to Lord John Russell, 10 July 1843, Russell Papers, PRO, 30/22/4c, ff. 85-6.

[118] See p. 98.

[119] C. de Cavour, Considerations on the present and future prospects of Ireland (1845), pp. 1 and 4.

[120] Gladstone's memorandum, 9 Dec. 1837, Add. MSS 44777, ff. 40-51, Gladstone, Prime Ministers' Papers, ii. 88.

relations with the pope, but from the time of the French Revolution, when both England and the Holy See had been united against a common enemy, there existed a strong temptation for any government, Whig or Tory, to seek papal help when dealing with Irish Catholics. Patrick Curtis, archbishop of Armagh from 1819 to 1832, had been appointed, it was reliably believed, at the request of Wellington. In 1825 Lord Burghersh, English ambassador to Tuscany, told Canning that 'the court of Rome see, with dissatisfaction, the unruly spirit at various times shown even against itself by the Catholic Clergy of Ireland', and that it would co-operate with the government in achieving a settlement which would include payment of the clergy and a say for the government in the nomination of bishops.[121] In the 1830s, the Whigs had exercised what amounted to an unofficial veto on Irish episcopal appointments until the pope became restive at their unceasing demands and, as we have seen, appointed MacHale as archbishop of Tuam.[122] A direct Roman check on the political activities of the clergy, however, could now have had serious repercussions. In 1839 Cardinal Giacomo Fransoni, prefect of the Congregation of Propaganda, had rebuked MacHale for his speeches at political banquets: 'Optarem videlicet vehementer non modo ut nulla ratione politicarum controversiarum sis participes, verum etiam ut palam in coetu, vel conventu quolibet ab ea loquendi ratione te contineas, quae politicis controversiis te deditum esse significaret.'[123] MacHale, replying that he had always urged obedience to religious and civil authorities, explained that toasts such as 'To the people, the source of all legitimate power' and 'civil and religious liberty for the whole world' had not the same Jacobin overtones in Ireland that they had on the continent.[124] Fransoni also complained to the primate of

---

[121] Burghersh to Canning, 2 Apr. 1825, FO 79/44, cited in G. Mooney, 'British Diplomatic Relations with the Holy See, 1793-1830', *Recusant History,* xiv (1978), pp. 202-3, 209.

[122] Broderick, *Holy See,* pp. 66-108; see pp. 24-5.

[123] Fransoni to MacHale, 26 Feb. 1839, Lettere e Decreti, 1839, vol. 321, ff. 155-6, Propaganda Fide Archives. Cited in Broderick, *Repeal,* p. 101. Giacomo Fransoni (1775-1856), nuncio to Portugal, 1827; cardinal 1826; prefect of Propaganda 1834-56.

[124] MacHale to Fransoni, 25 Mar. 1839, Acta 1839, vol. 202, ff. 256-7, cited in Broderick, *Repeal,* pp. 105-6.

bishops' speeches at civic banquets, but Crolly replied that unless the clergy joined the laity in the struggle for their religious and civil liberties, the people would suffer and a division between people and clergy would ensue. He emphasized that 'the greatest prudence is necessary lest we offend a faithful people by an unexpected separation from them.'[125] Crolly's reply provides a striking example of the different way in which the bishops in Ireland and the curia in Rome saw this problem.

Despite Fransoni's rebuke, MacHale's position was strong in Rome. Fr Ennis, Murray's agent on the education question, reported that MacHale was regarded as the 'champion of papal rights and church privilege'.[126] Lambruschini was reported to be on his side.[127] Lord Clifford, one of a group of influential English Catholics living in Rome, recounted an unusual incident during the controversy concerning the education issue in 1839. He and Lord Shrewsbury went to Lambruschini to support Murray's position as against MacHale's. When Shrewsbury called MacHale a radical, Nicholson reported:

Upon which Lambruschini sneeringly said Dr MacHale a Radical indeed. Lord Clifford said he could hold out no longer and immediately detailed a speech of Dr MacHale's at a dinner in Galway to prove it. Notwithstanding this interview, Lord Clifford says, the Cardinal continued in favour of Dr MacHale's views... It was reported ... that some of the underlings said in reference to Lord Shrewsbury's interference ... ne sutor ultra crepidam.[128]

When, four years later, at the time of Higgins's sensational Mullingar speech, Clifford complained that 'the designs of the MacHale party ... have been unblushingly *supported* by the Ministers of His Holiness with too much success', he named Lambruschini as being largely responsible. Clifford applauded Murray's moderate stand and condemned equally Higgins' outburst and Beaumont's rejoinder.[129] It is surprising, how-

---

[125] Crolly to Fransoni, 27 Apr., 1839, cited in Broderick, *Holy See*, pp. 103-8.

[126] Ennis to Slattery, 14 Jan. 1840, Slattery Papers.

[127] Luigi Lambruschini (1776-1854) entered Barnabite order; cardinal 1831; secretary of state 1836. He persuaded both French and Austrians to vacate the papal states in 1838. He was a strong candidate for the papacy in 1846.

[128] Nicholson to Hamilton, 19 Sept. 1839; Hamilton Papers, DDA.

[129] Clifford to Murray, 24 May 1843, Murray Papers.

ever, to find him quoting Lambruschini as supporting Mac-Hale, for the cardinal was conservative in outlook and, while nuncio at Paris, had looked askance at the 'liberal' views of Doyle, remarking, after the Clare election, that while Ireland tended to free herself politically from England, she also, unfortunately, tended to free herself religiously from Rome.[130]

Whether or not, as Clifford believed, Lambruschini supported MacHale, his friend, Prince Metternich, looked on events in Ireland with some alarm. He saw O'Connell as a radical in the same mould as the Belgian and Polish Catholics, and the clergy as masking pure revolutionary calls for liberalism under the guise of religious freedom. He did, however, believe that the Catholics were not fairly treated, and in 1839 suggested to the English government that they restore to the Catholic clergy the temporal goods of which they had been despoiled. Simultaneously, he wanted the pope to denounce the Irish agitation which he regarded as a political movement in the guise of religion. Not surprisingly his naïve suggestions had no effect.[131] Four years later, at height of the Repeal movement, he asked the curia to discourage the clergy from taking part. Lambruschini told him that the Holy See disapproved of the conduct of some of the bishops in Ireland and promised to submit the whole matter to the pope.[132]

The reigning pope was the seventy-eight year-old Gregory XVI, a holy monk who devoted tireless energy towards the spread of christianity in non-christian lands.[133] During the Revolution, he had been expelled from Rome for his opposition to the French. Later experiences in Italy did nothing to change his anti-revolutionary ideas, and he naturally turned for support to Metternich, the upholder of legitimacy in Europe. Gregory had told the Poles to obey their legitimate rulers and had condemned La Mennais' Liberal Catholicism. His own government was legitimist and conservative in outlook and did little to bring in much needed reforms into the papal states. Gregory had some

---

[130] L. M. Manzini, *II Cardinale Luigi Lambruschini* (1960), pp. 152-3.

[131] Broderick, *Holy See,* pp. 165-6.

[132] D'Ohms to Metternich, 1 July 1843, copy, FO 7/313, cited in Broderick, *Holy See,* p. 170. D'Ohms was the Austrian chargé d'affaires in Rome.

[133] Bartolomeo Alberto (Mauro) Cappellari (1765-1846) entered Camaldolese monastery 1783; cardinal, 1826: pope, 1831.

knowledge of Irish affairs; he had been prefect of Propaganda and had, in 1829, issued the regulations for the election of Irish bishops. The bishops sent reports regularly to Rome and many of them visited him and discussed Irish affairs with him. In 1837, he was reported by Nicholson as remarking to Higgins that O'Connell 'only looks for equal laws and equal justice and he is right'.[134] During the Repeal movement, Cullen and Kirby, who had ready access to him, made sure that he was kept informed. They generally reported him as sympathetic to their point of view.[135] By this time, Gregory, who during the French Revolution had bravely asserted the independence of the church in a work entitled *Il Trionfo della Santa Sede*, had reason to beware of erastianism in many states. In Prussia, he took a stand in defence of the archbishop of Cologne, Klemens Droste zu Vischering, who had been imprisoned by the Prussian government. Towards the tsar, too, he had come to adopt a resolute attitude, and in July 1842 issued an *allocutio* condemning the oppression of Catholics by the Russian government. The problems of the church in these two countries were on his mind when he told Cullen that same year that he feared for religion if the British government were allowed to interfere at all in ecclesiastical affairs.[136]

When O'Connell's letter to Cullen[137] arrived in May, Cullen was probably on his way to Ireland. The vice-rector, Kirby, took up the question of Repeal with the pope without apparently mentioning O'Connell's memorial. When Gregory, more realistic than his interlocutor, expressed his fear that Repeal was unobtainable, Kirby replied that:

if the people adhered to him [O'Connell], he would most certainly succeed. The Clergy, I said, already approved, and several of the Bishops. I said this for the purpose of giving him an opportunity of reprehending such an act on the part of the Bishops and Clergy, and yet no breath of such reprehension ... escaped him. He expressed in the kindest way the conviction of Mr. O'Connell's virtues, and merits and especially of his love for religion, and wisdom in guiding the poor oppressed people of Ireland thro' such difficulties without the violation of the laws of the land ... His whole discourse was that of one

---

[134] Nicholson to Hamilton, 1 Feb. 1837, Hamilton Papers, DDA.
[135] Mac Suibhne, *Cullen*, i. 238-41; 263; iii. 27.
[136] Cullen to Murray, 19 Feb. 1842, Cullen Papers, DDA.
[137] See pp. 78-80.

who by no means disapproved of the legitimate and peaceful struggles of Mr. O'Connell, the Irish Bishops and Clergy in the assertion of the rights of their oppressed country by such means.[138]

From other inquiries, too, Kirby came to the conclusion that there was no ground for suspecting papal action against Repeal. Kirby may have drawn too much from the pope's informal conversation, but he was a reliable, if sometimes naïve, witness. Gregory, while regarding Repeal as difficult of achievement, had no intention of condemning O'Connell or his clerical supporters as long as they did not go too far. Probably, as the English ambassador reported of Metternich, the arch-enemy of popular movements, he saw in O'Connell's campaign the struggle of his church against oppressive Protestantism.[139]

A year later when the Repeal movement was at its height and the clergy deeply involved, some indication of the pope's attitude can be gleaned from comments from Rome. Cullen told Murray that

The Pope does not wish to interfere at all with the Irish clergy at present ... he said that the clergymen who have taken part in it should recollect that they have to preach 'Jesum Christum et hunc crucifixum'. However, he added, I would not condemn them, as in certain occasions, it is necessary to be on the spot, and to know all the circumstances of the case before you can say whether the thing is right or wrong.[140]

Cullen's statement is supported by Fr Charles Russell, a trustworthy witness, who told Murray that at his leave-taking audience with the pope on 2 July 1843: 'He spoke with great feeling of the affairs of Ireland and said that the present proceedings were certainly not illegal and could hardly be matter for surprise. "Basta se non si ecceda" was his concluding observation.'[141] The pope did not here refer directly to clerical involvement, but these two statements, taken together with Kirby's earlier comments, indicate a relatively favourable attitude and a tacit acceptance of some clerical involvement.

---

[138] Kirby to Cullen, 16 June 1842, cited in Broderick, *Holy See*, pp. 167-8.

[139] See p. 98. Two months later Kirby reported that the pope was annoyed with O'Connell, but this annoyance does not appear to be connected with the Repeal movement; it may have been linked with Gregory's attitude towards the situation in Poland; Kirby to Cullen, 10 Aug. 1842, ibid., p. 168.

[140] Cullen to Murray, 11 July 1843, Murray Papers.

[141] Russell to Murray, 3 Aug. 1843, ibid.

Such an attitude on the part of the representative of a highly conservative state who, as spiritual head of the Catholic church discountenanced clerical involvement in secular affairs, is surprising. Behind it lay an understandable reluctance to become involved in affairs concerning which he did not feel fully informed and a prudent willingness to leave matters to those on the spot. The pope felt, too, that the grievances of the Irish Catholics were substantial. From his contact with the cardinals, Cullen was able to supply another reason for Roman reserve on the issue: 'They appear to think it would not be safe to interfere where such vast numbers of clergymen and several bishops have taken up the question with such ardour'.[142] The cautious Roman curia had no intention of risking a schism in Ireland in order to help the English government in its embarrassment.

Nothing, then, came of Metternich's intervention. Indeed, the English ambassador in Vienna, Sir Robert Gordon, brother of Lord Aberdeen, the foreign secretary, appears to have had doubts regarding Metternich's own attitude to the Repeal movement. In June 1843, he wrote: ' ... the Repeal agitation is not the less viewed with intense interest by him [Metternich] and all Roman Catholic parties abroad as being a struggle for the ascendancy of their religion.' He added sourly that: 'O'Connell is universally looked upon as a Saint and a Martyr. The sooner he is made the last, the better.'[143]

Whatever Metternich's personal opinions were, events now involved him in Irish affairs. Those same events were also largely responsible for embroiling Graham, as home secretary, in an affair that cast much bitterness over his political life—the charge of having opened the correspondence of Italian revolutionaries, such as Mazzini, and passing on information to the Austrian government. The origin of his involvement in the Post Office affair was traced by Graham to contacts he had with Count Neumann, the Austrian ambassador in London, late in 1843. Dr Donajgrodzki, in his stimulating study of Graham at the Home Office, makes the point that even the most recent and detailed account of the Post Office affair (by F. B. Smith) is not able to establish the circumstances in which

---

[142] Cullen to Murray, 11 July 1843, Murray Papers.
[143] Gordon to Aberdeen, 13 June 1843, Add. MSS 43211 (2nd part), f. 311.

Neumann contacted Graham.[144] Dr Donajgrodzki suspects that in addition to Neumann's letter to Graham of 21 November which Smith cites as the origin of the move to trace Mazzini, a meeting took place between the two men. He notes, too, the discrepancy in the dates, for Graham referred to an interview with Neumann 'in the month I think, of October, 1843', and suggests that Graham was mistaken about the date. It is possible to shed some light on the two problems raised by Dr Donajgrodzki—the circumstances of Neumann's contacting Graham and the unsatisfactory chronology. Dr Donajgrodzki is right in suspecting that besides Neumann's letter of 21 November, a meeting took place between him and the home secretary. Two such meetings can be traced. Graham was not mistaken about the date, however, for the meetings did take place in October, and this early date adds special importance to the unusual, and hitherto unsuspected, context in which the affair originated.

In October, the Duc de Bordeaux, the Bourbon pretender to the French throne, visited England.[145] Peel and Graham saw his visit as an Austrian and Prussian counter-move to the meeting of the queen and Louis Philippe at Château d'Eu a few weeks earlier. To complicate matters, they feared that the Catholics would persuade the duke, an ardent Catholic, to visit Ireland, where they would use him, as Peel put it, 'as a lever, by which they might extort assistance from Louis Philippe'.[146] Bordeaux, whom O'Connell had lauded to the skies, had attended a Catholic service in Edinburgh, called on Lord Shrewsbury, the leading Catholic peer and did indeed contemplate such a visit.[147] What most disturbed the ministers was the timing of this visit, coinciding as it would with a peculiarly sensitive situation in Ireland. In the same month of October the Repeal agitation had reached its climax when the government finally confronted O'Connell, banned the monster meeting planned for Clontarf on 8 October, and a week later arrested the leaders. Despite its initial success the government

---

[144] A. F. Donajgrodzki, 'Sir James Graham at the Home Office', *Hist. Jn.*, xx (1977), 114-19; F. B. Smith, 'British Post Office Espionage, 1844', *Historical Studies*, xiv (1969-71), 189-203.

[145] The Duc de Bordeaux (1820-83) was more generally known as the Comte de Chambord.

[146] Peel to Graham, 18 Oct; Graham to Peel, 19 Oct. 1843, Graham Papers.

[147] Ibid.

could not rule out the possibility of grave civil disturbances, and shiploads of troops had been sent to Dublin, Cork, and Limerick. A visit, at this juncture, of the Catholic Bourbon pretender to a restless Ireland, noted for its francophile sentiments, would constitute further embarrassment for a government not yet sure of the course events might take. It was an unexpected stroke of luck for the anxious home secretary when, on 19 October, Neumann came to see him on a completely different matter.

Political discontent had long been rife in some Italian states, including the badly-governed papal states, fomented by Italian exiles from the havens of English and French territories. Under pressure from Lambruschini, Metternich had agreed to make representations to both these governments, and the object of Neumann's unexpected visit, as Graham reported to Peel, was that 'we should use our authority at Malta to prevent the Press of that Island being converted into an engine of attack on our neighbours.' Another grievance raised by Neumann came closer to home:

He complained also of an Italian paper published in London until lately by a refugee of the name of Mazzini, which had been circulated throughout Italy and which suggests the plan of armed Banditti acting simultaneously on various different points; and he asserts that the recent disturbance in the 'Legacies' or Papal territories, are to be traced to the suggestions contained in this paper.

As Neumann began to leave Graham raised the matter of Bordeaux's projected visit to Ireland, remarking that the English government would regard it as an unfriendly act. Neumann asserted that he had already told the duke as much but that the latter, although admitting that his intention of visiting Ireland had been given up for the present (*'pour le moment'*), remained non-committal.[148] Graham and Peel were quite dissatisfied with this interview, Graham remaining convinced of connivance on the part of Austria and Prussia.[149] A week later, however, Neumann returned, this time with a promise that Bordeaux would not visit Ireland but requesting in return a declaration that the revolutionary press in Malta would be regarded with

[148] Graham to Peel, 19 Oct. 1843, ibid.
[149] Ibid; Peel to Graham, 20 Oct. 1843, ibid.

disfavour by the British government. Graham was willing enough to enter into such an arrangement.[150] Irish affairs thus contributed to lead him into that tangled web of international intrigue involving a French pretender, Italian revolutionaries, and Austrian and papal diplomats, allowing his parliamentary opponents to cast public scorn on this most un-English act of opening private correspondence and to pin on him the responsibility for the death of those heroes of the Risorgimento, the Bandiera brothers.

A few days after Neumann's first visit, De Grey urged the government to ask the Holy See to control the political activities of the Irish clergy, and Graham and Peel placed the matter before Aberdeen.[151] When, a short while later, Metternich requested the English ambassador to have the Malta sedition suppressed, Gordon widened the issue by demanding a *quid pro quo* from the papal government:

At the time, I could not help enquiring from Prince Metternich whether when the Papal government were asking for the interference of the British Authority to suppress the sedition that came from Malta, he did not think it might appear to that government to be fitting on their part and in like manner to exercise their authority toward suppressing the preaching of sedition by their priesthood in Ireland, by which the Repeal movement was so notoriously instigated.[152]

He had a lively interview with Altieri, the papal nuncio at Vienna, which the latter described in some detail to Lambruschini:

Il bello poi era che il med ᵐᵒ [medesimo] fuocoso Tory, pretendeva che sifatta misura dovesse esser compensata dalla pubblica e severa reprimanda, che, secondo lui è obbligo del S. Padre di lanciare contro il clero cattolico d'Irlanda onde interdirgli di sostenere … l'agitazione … per la Revoca dell'Unione.

Apart from demanding a *quid pro quo* in the shape of a public reprimand, Gordon was not above using bullying language to Altieri: 'Nel calore del suo discorso, si dimenticò al segno di dire che il Papa non si crede obbligato a repprimere la *ribellione* degl' Irlandesi, il Governo Britannico non si stimerà neppur

---

[150] Graham to Stanley, 27 Oct. 1843, ibid.

[151] De Grey to Graham, 20 Oct. 1843; Graham to Peel, 30 Oct; Graham to De Grey, 30 Oct; Peel to Graham, 1 Nov. 1843, Graham Papers.

[152] Gordon to Foreign Office, 15 Nov. 1843, FO 7/311, PRO.

tenuto a negare assistenza ai Bolognesi, qualora l'invocassero in appoggio de' loro reclami.' A threat to assist the Bolognese rebels was strong language for England to use. Altieri's caustic comment to Lambruschini was: 'Simili spropositi possono dare un'idea delle passioni che dominano il Gabinetto Inglese ed i suoi agenti.'[153]

The English demands, however, could not be brushed aside by calling them 'spropositi'. Aberdeen told the Austrian minister in London that from the Holy See's silence it would be deduced 'che il Papa non vuol dar torto ai nemici del governo Inglese'. Metternich, no doubt still smarting from the change in English foreign policy which the Château d'Eu visit appeared to indicate, complained to Altieri of the unreliability of the 'Pseudo Thorys' [sic]. On the Irish question, he seized the occasion to attach much of the blame to the government, telling Gordon (whom he classed as an obstinate Tory) that: 'non tutto il torto sia dalla parte degli oppressi ma che molto ne ha il Governo col non accordare spontaneamente ai medesimi ciò che lor compete per guistizia ed equità.' Gordon coldly replied that the government could do no more for the Irish. Metternich's rejoinder was that neither could the pope do more than he had done, and was doing, to maintain peace and submission among the Irish Catholics. Metternich's defence of the papal conduct pleased Altieri, but he pointed out to Lambruschini that the chancellor had gone too far:

mentre il Sigʳ Prpe [Principe] assicura il governo Britannico dell'impegno con cui il Santo Padre riprova le tendenze rivoluzionarie de'Cattolici Irlandesi, si permette forse più del dovere di far credere che la condotta del Sigʳ O'Connell, e de'suoi partigiani, sia in tutte le sue parti giudicata biasimevole agli occhi del Capo della Chiesa, ed abbia perciò incorso la più severa Sua condanna.[154]

Whatever their attitude to clerical involvement in the Repeal agitation, the Roman diplomats had no intention of condemning O'Connell and his supporters.

Peel, however, was delighted with Gordon's initiative and decided to follow it up by collecting 'a nosegay' of the speeches

---

[153] Altieri to Lambruschini, 5 Nov. 1843, Archivio dalla Nunziatura di Vienna, Vol. 280F, ff. 198-208, Archivio Segreto Vaticano. The dispatch is marked 'riservatissimo'. Ludovico Altieri (1805-67), titular bishop of Ephesus, apostolic nuncio to Austria, 1836; cardinal, 1840.

[154] Altieri to Lambruschini, 15 Nov. 1843, ibid., ff. 212-13.

and writings of the clergy to send to the pope. 'If we cannot regale his Holiness with the Bouquet, let Metternich have it.'[155] Graham specified for De Grey the type of bouquet he desired: 'The speech of Dr. Higgins, his letter on the duties of a soldier, some of the reported addresses from the altar ... and some of Dr. MacHale's after dinner harangues will provide materials for a highly scented nosegay such as the Malta press can never equal.'[156] The colonial office now instructed the Maltese government to check the revolutionaries; and Aberdeen, at Peel's request, sought reciprocal papal action against the Irish clergy. He told Gordon to point out that the activities of the Irish clergy were 'not only disgraceful to religion, but are dangerous to other thrones as well as that of England'. The government was seeking to increase the pressure by widening the terms of the argument. The papal condemnation of the Irish clergy would have to be public. 'It seems imperatively to demand', Aberdeen wrote, 'the public and unequivocal reprobation of the Holy See.'[157] Metternich, on receiving the dossier, promised Gordon to do his best to procure such 'a public and unequivocal reprobation'.[158]

Lambruschini wasted no time in examining the dossiers forwarded to him. His reply was a carefully written memorandum, a promemoria, a copy of which was sent to Metternich early in February 1844. It gave nothing away and skilfully analysed the weaknesses in the case submitted. Lambruschini first contested the English government's suggestion that the Irish and Maltese agitations were similar. The former involved loyal constitutionalists, the latter notorious anarchists. The movement in Ireland was an 'agitazione popolare', the Maltese 'le congiure dei refugiati'. The Irish professed loyalty to the queen and intended to use only constitutional means in their effort to modify constitutional relations between two parts of the empire. All European governments were aware of the methods and the anarchical aims of the Italian conspirators in Malta. Lambruschini divided the dossier of priests' sermons

[155] Peel to Graham, 27 Nov. 1843, Add. MSS 40449, ff. 233-4.
[156] Graham to De Grey, 29 Nov. 1843, Graham Papers.
[157] Aberdeen to Gordon, 30 Dec. 1843, Add. MSS 43211 (2nd Part) f. 378.
[158] Gordon to Aberdeen, 2 Jan. 1844, Add. MSS 43157, f. 24.

into two parts. The first consisted of reports of sermons from
the altar taken down by government agents, and he felt it
permissible to hope that these were not always exact: 'quantunque sia lecito sperare che la relazione di discorsi non scritti, ma
improvvisati con passione, e con un opposta passione ascoltati,
non sia riuscita sempre esatta.' Further, even if the priests were
guilty of all the charges brought against them, the Holy See
would have to follow the due process of church law: having
learned the names of the accused priests, it must inform them
of the charges brought against them and permit them to defend
themselves. Even then one could not condemn the mass of the
Irish clergy for the faults of a few. Going on to the cuttings
from *The Pilot*, Lambruschini saw their tone as different from
the reports of the sermons. The natural meaning of what they
contained was, in his view, that the Irish clergy actually abstained *en masse* from political agitation and that they preached
loyalty to the queen and the constitution. If the Holy See
reproved priests for not respecting the constituted authority,
they could reply that the very text of the discourses of which
they were accused was their best defence. If the Holy See told
them it was illegal to set themselves up as judges of the fundamental laws of the kingdom, they could further reply that the
Holy See's task was to preach Catholic moral doctrine and not
to judge what was or was not in conformity with the constitution
of the country. The authors of these speeches boasted that it
was they who held the people back from violence and rebellion—
a claim no one challenged. If the Holy See condemned them
publicly, they could reply that if they had not mixed with the
people and supported their movement, they would not have
retained the authority to stop the greater excesses of rebellion
and anarchy. The Holy See ventured to hope that those sentiments were the honest intentions of the clerical orators, even if
some were carried away by the emotional atmosphere of the
monster meetings.

On the question of curbing their activities, Lambruschini
pointed out that whereas the government in Malta had the
power to enforce the law of the land, the Holy See had no such
power in Ireland. The only means at its disposal were instructions and advice, instruments which had to be used with care
lest their edge be blunted:

Ora inerendo a questa considerazione che il Santo Padre non può non riguardare come un canone indeclinabile della prudenza dirrettiva del suo pastoral ministero, si riconoscerà facilmente che una pubblica riprovazione della condotta del Clero d'Irlanda sarebbe per la parte della S. Sede, nelle attuali circostanze, una misura non ben calcolata.[159]

The public condemnation that the government sought was something that Rome would not give. Since this was the declared aim of the English negotiations, it must be concluded that they proved fruitless. Professor Gash's account of the matter tends to obscure this important fact.[160] An impression is conveyed that Peel extracted political profit from the situation, and having regaled his Holiness and Metternich with 'a nosegay' of treasonable clerical speeches, lectured them on the disgrace which those clerics were bringing to religion and the danger which they brought to thrones. On the contrary, Lambruschini got what he wanted—a check on the Maltese agitators—whereas he refused to grant what the English government sought—a public and unequivocal condemnation of the activities of the Irish clergy. Neither Gordon's reaction nor the reaction he ascribed to Metternich support the view that Peel's government gained any tangible diplomatic or political benefit. Gordon reported that 'Prince Metternich has received a reply from the Papal government... and I regret to say that it is so vague and unsatisfactory that His Highness has not thought proper to give me a copy of it to be transmitted to your lordship.'[161] Altieri, who had shown some sympathy towards O'Connell, was pleased, hoping that Lambruschini's letter would preclude for the future 'le vie dirette e indirette delle quali si servì il Governo Britannico per ottenere che la Santa Sede aggiungesse alla di lui forza materiale l'autorevolissima efficacia della sua voce per soffocare i reclami degli oppressi ed infelici Irlandesi.'[162] Metternich undertook to urge Rome to issue paternal addresses to the Irish clergy as they are in the habit of sending through the Bishops in Hungary' to priests of liberal political views. In

---

[159] Promemoria from Lambruschini to Metternich, Feb. 1844, copy enclosed in letter from Lambruschini to Altieri, 10 Feb. 1844, Nunziatura di Vienna, vol. 281Q ff. 203-7; Archivio Segreto Vaticano; Broderick, *Holy See*, pp. 229-31.

[160] Gash, *Peel,* p. 415.

[161] Gordon to Aberdeen, 19 Feb. 1844, Add. MSS 43221, f. 83.

[162] Altieri to Lambruschini, 8 Mar. 1844, Archivio della Nunziatura di Vienna, Vol. 280G, f. 47, Archivio Segreto Vaticano.

reality, however, Metternich was claiming as his own initiative
what Lambruschini had promised in the document which
Gordon did not see, for while refusing a public reprimand, the
cardinal undertook to use moral influence with the Irish clergy.
Accordingly, he sent a copy of his memorandum to Fransoni
together with some of the newspaper clippings, explaining to
him that there would be no public condemnation of the clergy
but merely some fatherly admonition, and that this was a matter
for the Congregation of Propaganda.[163]

This document gives an interesting insight into Lambruschini's outlook on the situation of the Irish church. The
analysis, coming from the conservative first minister of one of
the most conservative regimes in Europe, shows considerable
effort to understand the complexities of the Irish situation, a
keen realization of the limits of the Holy See's power and a
sensitivity to possible reactions in Ireland. The pope, who had
the final decision, had also no intention of condemning the
Irish clergy. Cullen, writing while Lambruschini's reply was
still undelivered, reported: 'He is still much attached to Ireland
and inquires most anxiously about Repeal. The English government made an attempt to get him to write to the Irish Bishops
to desist from taking part in that movement. But he declined to
do so alleging that those who were on the spot must best know
what was to be done in so difficult a question.'[164] Cullen, who
undoubtedly used his own position to counter government
moves, reported a month after the promemoria was issued that
'many attempts are daily made to get him [the pope] to take up
the English views against Ireland but he is always the same.'[165]

The government's efforts to use Rome to influence the
Catholic Church in Ireland had failed. Rome did not like
clerical involvement in politics and was no friend of democracy.
Nevertheless, it put no trust in the altruism of secular governments, and the Cologne affair and the tsar's persecutions were
not forgotten. Its reaction was in line with its customary
prudence. Moreover, through the Irish College, the O'Connel-

---

[163] Lambruschini to prefect of Propaganda, 10 Feb. 1844, SC Irlanda, dal 1843-6,
vol. 28, ff. 199-210, Propaganda Fide Archives.

[164] Cullen to MacHale, 4 Jan. 1844, Mac Suibhne, *Cullen*, i. 246-7.

[165] Cullen to MacHale, 12 Mar. 1844, ibid., i. 247.

lite clergy had its own lines of communication with the Holy See and was able effectively to counter government pressure.

Almost a year after the English government's request to Rome, the Congregation of Propaganda sent a private letter to Crolly asking him to admonish any clergy engaged in political activity.[166] This response was both belated and inadequate. Aberdeen had made it clear that nothing less than a public condemnation would be effective: ' ... the abuse of their sacred functions by the Roman Catholic priesthood in Ireland ... will scarcely be affected by the private circulation of pastoral letters... it seems imperatively to demand the public and unequivocal reprobation of the Holy See.'[167] On the other hand, the Roman government had reason to be well pleased with the assistance given by England in curbing the Italian conspirators. Aberdeen, who in December 1843 had curbed their activities, again promised Neumann 'to do something more in Malta' and also to keep an eye on the Carbonari in England.[168] On 1 March 1844, Graham, possibly at Aberdeen's instigation, issued a warrant for Mazzini's letters to be opened. They were forwarded to the Foreign Office where a digest of their contents was taken to Neumann.[169] It is not surprising that in April Metternich expressed his cordial thanks for the valuable assistance given by Her Majesty's government in tracing and denouncing the plans of some conspirators who, it was believed, 'meditated an attack on Rome itself'.[170] On 14 June Thomas Duncombe, the Radical member for Finsbury, denounced Graham for opening the letters of Mazzini and others, thereby introducing the 'odious spy system of foreign countries' ill-suited to the 'free air of a free country'.[171] Returning to the attack on 24 June, Duncombe cited a letter from Mazzini which contained an extract from the *Milan Gazette* of 20 April claiming that 'the English Cabinet had addressed to that of Vienna promises extremely satisfactory concerning the agitation prevailing in Italy, and especially in the territory of the Pope.' 'But what',

[166] See p. 155.
[167] Aberdeen to Gordon, 30 Dec. 1843, Add. MSS 43211 (2nd part), f. 378.
[168] Aberdeen to Graham, 2 Jan. 1844, ibid. ff. 378-80.
[169] Donajgrodzki, 'Graham' p. 115.
[170] Gordon's despatch to the Foreign Office, 2 Apr. 1844, Add. MSS 43157, ff. 26-7.
[171] *Hansard,* lxxv. 895, 899, 14 June; 1264, 24 June 1844.

demanded an irate Duncombe, 'had they to do with the Pope? They had no diplomatic relations with the Pope. And yet they were told by Mr Mazzini that they opened his letters to gratify the Pope.'[172] For almost a year the attacks in and out of Parliament dragged on, further injuring the reputation of the already unpopular home secretary. Thus, his attempt to obtain public papal condemnation of the political activity of the Irish clergy had not merely failed to achieve its stated aim but had involved Graham in the most damaging incident of his public career. As he feared in later life, 'he would only be remembered as the Home Secretary who opened Mazzini's letters'.[173]

By this time, the 'Year of Repeal', as O'Connell had confidently called 1843, had come and gone. If he had failed to achieve Repeal, however, he had brought the Irish question to the centre of English politics; and his efforts to win over the Irish clergy had been so successful that Murray alone had had the courage to disavow the claim that all the bishops were repealers. The secret investigation into the Repeal movement in May showed the government that the clergy was at the heart of the movement, findings which were confirmed by the reports of the sermons and speeches and by the signing by the Dublin priests of the requisition for the Clontarf meeting. Peel, fearing that this union between O'Connell and the clergy might eventually result in the dismemberment of the Empire, made the breaking up of this 'powerful combination' the cornerstone of his Irish policy.[174] 'Sever the clergy from the agitators, and agitation must cease' had been the positive advice of the magistrate Kernan, and this was now Peel's own view. His first move had been an attempt to elicit from Rome a public condemnation of the political activities of the clergy, but despite Metternich's support and the use of the Maltese agitation as a bargaining counter, it had failed. Other means would have to be found.

Even as Cullen was remarking on the pope's stand on Irish affairs, a surprised Altieri was reporting to Lambruschini on changes in English attitudes. Gordon had visited him and discussed the Irish question with him:

---

[172] Ibid. 1267-8, 24 June 1844.
[173] Cited in J. T. Ward, *Sir James Graham* (1967), p. 306.
[174] See pp. 120-1.

discorrendomi della condanna di O'Connell, mi fece intendere che si questi insieme al clero Cattolico d'Irlanda ... inveci di eccitare una sollevazione illegale ed irragionevole volesse rinunziare all' idea della Revoca dell'Unione, ... e si contentasse di esporre i gravami, di cui si lamenta il popolo Irlandese, facile sarebbe il render loro la dovuta guistizia, giacchè non negava che abbiano ragione di reclamarla in parecchi punti, sopra tutto ne' pesi che supportano in vantaggio della Chiesa Anglicana.

Altieri added cynically that such a confession, 'nella bocca di chi sempre ripeteva che il suo Governo non dovea, ne voleva far nulla per gl'Irlandesi', showed that the government now felt forced to adopt a milder attitude.[175] Gordon's remarks indicated that the Repeal agitation had brought a new realization to the English government of the pressing need to remedy Irish grievances, particularly those concerning religion. If Peel had been content with seeking strong, impartial government up to this point, the Repeal movement showed that more was necessary. Altieri's surmises proved correct. By the early spring of 1844, the government was evolving a new policy of conciliation towards Ireland.

---

[175] Altieri to Lambruschini, 8 Mar. 1844, Archivio della Nunziatura di Vienna, vol. 280 G, f. 47, no. 1892, Archivio Segreto Vaticano.

3

THE GENESIS OF THE
GOVERNMENT'S PROGRAMME AND THE
CHARITABLE BEQUESTS ACT, 1844

The sympathy of European countries and of America brought some consolation to Repealers. Of far greater significance, however, was the increase in friendly interest among English politicians in the unhappy state of Ireland. Fr Maher wrote to Cullen in Rome that 'even Tory England herself is beginning to admit that we are aggrieved and ought to be conciliated'.[1] 'Our Irish movement has at least this merit that it has roused the English nation from slumber', O'Connell told Lord Campbell in September 1843: 'Our grievances are beginning to be admitted by all parties ... to be afflicting'.[2] The mismanagement, if not unfairness of his trial in January 1844, won O'Connell widespread sympathy among Whigs and Liberals. Gavan Duffy noted that when O'Connell attended meetings in London, Manchester, and Liverpool, in the early spring of 1844, 'in each town, as if they were moved by a common impulse or schooled by a common prompter, the aim of the meetings was such concessions to Ireland, as would render repeal of the Union unnecessary'.[3]

Within the Conservative party, too, Peel had already turned his mind to conciliation and by February 1844 was to lay before the cabinet a full programme of Irish reforms. The first of those was to be the reform of the law governing charitable bequests. Extraordinary though it may now appear, this comparatively minor and innocent measure aroused furious reaction in Ireland, provoked serious divisions within the Catholic community and became a crucial test of Peel's ability to launch a successful and conciliatory programme of reforms.

---

[1] Maher to Cullen, Aug. 1843, Murray Papers.
[2] O'Connell to Campbell, 9 Sept. 1843, *O'Connell Corr.*, ii. 308-9.
[3] C. Gavan Duffy, *Young Ireland: a fragment of Irish History 1840-50* (1880), p. 459.

From May to August, in the debates on the Arms Bill and on Smith O'Brien's motion on Irish discontent, Whigs, Liberals, and Radicals made clear their profound dissatisfaction with the government for the alarming state to which, they alleged, it had reduced Ireland. Prominent among the measures they called for was a fairer treatment of the church of the majority. Russell and the Irish members discountenanced payment of the Irish clergy; Palmerston, reviving an idea of O'Connell's, suggested instead that the voluntary endowment of the clergy be facilitated.[4] Neither the debates nor the solemn remonstrance of the Irish Liberals against 'the fatal policy which has alienated from your Government and your institutions the minds of a large portion of our fellow countrymen', had any visible effect on the government's conduct.[5] The agitation, however, had forced the government to reconsider its policies. A few days after the important cabinet meeting of 11 June 1843, Peel urged Graham to '*look out*' for suitable Catholics for office: 'we must discard that favourite doctrine of Dublin Castle "You cannot conciliate your enemies, therefore give everything to the most zealous of your friends".'[6] Although Graham joined Peel in urging the lord lieutenant to avoid 'an unbroken series of appointments of an exclusive and high Protestant character', they pleaded in vain: De Grey remained convinced that 'conciliation is a chimera'.[7] When they pressed for the appointment of John Howley, a Catholic, as third serjeant-at-law, De Grey remained adamant.[8] Peel then drew up a letter and took the unusual step of passing it on for endorsement to Graham, Stanley, and Sugden before sending it to De Grey. In it he insisted that 'considerations of policy and also of justice demand a *liberal* and indulgent estimate of the claims on the favour of the Crown of such Roman Catholics as abstain from political agitation.' The law had taught the Protestant to consider himself in a superior class and to expect a monopoly of the

---

[4] *Hansard*, lxx. 1069-70, 12 July 1843.

[5] Macintyre, *Liberator*, pp. 274-5.

[6] Peel to Graham, 16 June 1843, Parker, *Peel*, iii. 53-4.

[7] Graham to De Grey, 10 July 1843, Graham Papers; De Grey to Peel, 18 Aug. 1843, Parker, *Peel*, iii. 56.

[8] Peel to De Grey, 24 July 1843, Add. MSS 40478, ff. 119-20. The three serjeants-at-law had precedence over other barristers except the attorney-general and solicitor-general.

favours of the crown. The policy of the law had changed, and they ought not to allow the effect of the preceding policy to remain in full force. Otherwise, he asked,

what motive can we hold out to the well-affected Roman Catholic to abjure agitation ... if the avenue to ... legitimate distinction be in point of fact closed to him...? Every avenue to popular favour is opened and if every avenue to Royal favour be closed, we have done nothing by the removal of disabilities but organise a force of mischievous demagogues.[9]

Under the united pressure of the ministers, De Grey reluctantly gave way and appointed Howley. In the following months, Peel and Graham pressed for fairer treatment for Catholic doctors and police.[10] Peel's limited initiative was successful, and Catholics, including O'Connell, were gratified by the promotion of some of their co-religionists. It was only after the proclamation of the Clontarf meeting and the arrest of O'Connell that the government felt free to contemplate more adequate reforms.

Credit for translating this feeling into action must go not merely to Peel but to Eliot and Graham. After the victory over O'Connell, Eliot returned to the reforms he had been urging for so long and this time with more success, for now both Graham and Peel agreed with him that it was time for healing measures, Peel remarking that 'mere force ... will do nothing as a permanent remedy'.[11] Graham assured Eliot that he would consider: 'any measures ... which you may suggest, not excluding the reconstruction of Maynooth with an enlarged grant and a scheme for the payment in some shape or other of the Roman Catholic clergy.'[12] Eliot, heartened by this promise, undertook to acquire further information.[13] He visited Leinster and Munster and concluded that it was the younger clergy who were engaged in agitation.[14] By January 1844, he was able to put detailed suggestions to Graham on two main points: pro-

[9] Peel to De Grey, 22 August. 1843, Add.MSS 40478, ff. 160-6.

[10] Parker, Peel to Graham, 31 Aug. 1843 *Peel*, iii. 61; Peel to Eliot, 6 Oct. 1843, Add. MSS 40480, ff. 260-1.

[11] Eliot to Graham, 16 Oct. 1843, Graham Papers; Peel to Graham, 19 Oct. 1843, Add. MSS 40449, f. 105.

[12] Graham to Eliot, 20 Oct. 1843, Graham Papers.

[13] Eliot to Graham, 24 Oct. 1844, ibid.

[14] Eliot to Graham, 15 Nov. 1843. Graham Papers; Lady Jemima Cornwallis Diary, 1843, St. Germans Archives, Port Eliot.

vision for the clergy and the improvement of Maynooth College. The former, he argued, was an essential reform if the clergy were not to remain dependent on the masses, but he recognized the difficulties facing direct state provision: 'If the Cabinet comes to the conclusion that the experiment would be too hazardous ... they would ... do well to consider the suggestion of Lord Palmerston that individuals should be enabled to give lands to a certain extent as glebes to the Roman Catholic clergy.' On Maynooth, Eliot concluded that the case for improving the college was overwhelming. His basic criticism turned on the meanness of the government's subsidy; he insisted that 'for benefits so grudgingly and sparsely doled out, the inmates cannot feel any great gratitude to the State and they consequently go forth bound to the State by no tie either of interest or affection.' Assuming as a basic principle that the priests, because of their power for good and evil, must be won over, Eliot recommended that they should be made 'comfortable' while in Maynooth, their professors better paid and bursaries provided for more able students which would have the effect of attaching them to the state. As the Protestant objection was to the principle rather than to the amount, he argued that an increased grant would not materially strengthen the opposition. This dangerously naïve view, which was later adopted by Peel, was not to be borne out. Eliot finally proposed, as a sop to anti-Maynooth feeling, that the trustees' control be tightened and that they should be required to report annually.[15]

Impressed by this communication, Graham told a surprised Eliot: 'I showed your letter...to Sir Robert Peel and he and I agreed it was expedient to circulate it for the consideration of the cabinet and I took this step yesterday ... The last two suggestions ... have long occupied my thoughts and appear to me well worthy of the most deliberate consideration.'[16] After discussing the matter further with Eliot in London, Graham, at the cabinet meeting on the queen's speech, raised the possibility of conceding an increased grant to Maynooth and some indirect endowment of the Catholic clergy.[17] In his account of

[15] Eliot to Graham, 8 Jan. 1844, Graham Papers.
[16] Graham to Eliot, 12 Jan. 1844, ibid.
[17] Gladstone's memorandum, 29 Jan. 1844, Add. MSS 44777, ff. 115-18, Gladstone, *Prime Ministers' Papers*, ii. 229.

the government's new policy, Professor Gash conveys the impression that the whole initiative was Peel's.[18] He omits all mention of Eliot's letter which contains the main points of Peel's memorandum of 11 February, the document which officially inaugurated the new policy of concessions. Eliot's letter was known to cabinet ministers for over a month before this, and Graham had raised those same points a fortnight before Peel issued his memorandum. Further, since Eliot had pressed these same reforms, in season and out of season, for over three years and despite discouragements, his contribution deserves recognition. Later, Graham, who had been critical of him, was to pay him the handsome, if belated, tribute of having prepared the ground for the policy of reforms: 'You have contributed much to bring affairs to the point where a better policy may be adopted ... by a steady adherence to your own sound and generous sentiments, amidst the clamour of much abuse and the strong pressure of adverse influence.'[19]

It had become increasingly urgent that the government should evolve and pursue a coherent and constructive programme of Irish policies because the Opposition was concentrating its energies on the critical situation in Ireland. When Nassau Senior prepared to write a full-length article on Ireland in 1843, the problem was discussed by the Whig leaders—Russell, Macaulay, and Lord Jeffrey (along with Sydney Smith). Senior's *'cheval de bataille'*, he told Napier, was provision for the priests.[20] The Whig leaders, although theoretically in favour of such a measure, doubted its feasibility. Macaulay feared that: 'Against such a measure there are all the zealots of the High Church, and all the zealots of the Low Church; the Bishop of Exeter and Hugh Macneile; Oxford and Exeter Hall; ... all the English Dissenters; all Scotland; all Ireland ... '[21] Russell felt that unless the feelings, pride, and ambition of the Irish people were satisfied, offers to pay the clergy would be regarded as a bribe.[22]

[18] Gash, *Peel,* pp. 415-19.

[19] Graham to St. Germans, 10 Feb. 1845, St. Germans Archives, Port Eliot; see also Graham to St. Germans, 19 Apr. 1845, ibid.

[20] Senior to Napier, 14 Nov. 1843, cited in S. Leon Levy, *Nassau W. Senior, 1780-1864* (1970), p. 136.

[21] Macaulay to Napier, 25 Nov. 1843, G. O. Trevelyan, *The life and letters of Lord Macaulay* (1890), p. 444.

[22] Russell to Napier, 1 Dec. 1843, cited in Levy, *Senior,* pp. 137-8.

Convinced that the Tories had nullified the Emancipation Act since Catholics were still as effectively, and more invidiously, excluded from office as before 1829, he had come to the view that 'Peel and the good government of Ireland appears to be a contradiction in terms', alleging privately that every month of Tory government was making it more difficult 'to restore that sweet sleep in which Irish agitation slumbered from 1835 to 1842'.[23] Russell wanted a positive programme and told Pigot and Lansdowne that the party should be prepared, when Parliament met, to state what course they advised to meet the perils which hung over Ireland.[24] Charles Buller, the Radical member for Liskeard, sought O'Connell's views on the measures necessary.

In his reply of 16 January, O'Connell outlined what he believed would conciliate many: religious equality, fairer franchises, and improvement of the tenant's position by such measures as fixity of tenure and. taxes on absentee landlords.[25] Despite O'Connell's scathing remarks to Buller on Lord John's anti-Popish and anti-Irish bias, his proposals impressed the Whigs, Clarendon considering them as moderate and worthy of attention, Buller remarking to O'Connell that the great question was that of establishing 'entire religious equality' in Ireland.[26] Shortly afterwards some fifty Irish Whigs, including the Duke of Leinster, Lords Charlemont, Clanricarde, Talbot, and Meath, Thomas Redington, Anthony Blake, and Thomas Wyse, adopted a petition demanding 'healing measures' for Ireland. The Irish Whig members decided to go over to Westminster for 13 February, 'on which day', Eliot reported, 'they seem to expect an Irish debate'.[27] His information was correct, for on that day Russell set in motion a full-scale debate on the state of Ireland.

This marathon debate, which lasted a full nine days, marked a new approach to Irish problems, Greville seeing in it 'the

[23] Russell to Lansdowne, 19 July; 18 Nov; 9 Oct. 1843, G. P. Gooch (ed.), *The later correspondence of Lord John Russell, 1840-1878* (1925), i. 64-5;69.
[24] Russell to Lansdowne, 31 Oct., 1843, Gooch, *Russell*, i. 67.
[25] O'Connell to Buller, 9 Jan. 1844, Russell Papers, PRO, 30/22/4c, ff. 132-7.
[26] Clarendon to Russell, 25 Jan. 1844, Gooch, *Later correspondence*, i. 69; Buller to O'Connell, 16 Jan 1844, O'Connell papers, NLI, MSS 13649.
[27] Eliot to Graham, 19 Jan. 1844, Graham Papers.

starting point of a new Catholic question'.[28] Russell gave the cue to his party with a forceful speech on the theme that 'Ireland is occupied not governed', while Macaulay brilliantly exposed the Tories' error of using Ireland for opposition purposes during Melbourne's administration and thus fomenting religious hatred.[29] Disraeli summarized the bafflement experienced by statesmen at the intractable nature of the Irish problem: 'One says it was a physical question; another, a spiritual. Now, it is the absence of the aristocracy, then the absence of railroads. It was the Pope one day, potatoes the next.' Then in one brilliant summary, he gave his own perceptive analysis: 'a starving population, an absentee aristocracy, and an alien Church, and, in addition, the weakest executive in the world. That was the Irish question.'[30]

Although Lord John's motion was defeated, the debate marked a significant turning-point. Both in Parliament and outside it, the necessity of reform for Ireland was now generally admitted. O'Connell expressed his delight that 'popular sentiment out of the House declares itself strongly in favour of Ireland and that the debate in Parliament 'was going on very favourably'[31] Greville, commenting on the debate, remarked:

... it is impossible not to be struck with the very remarkable change in the tone and temper in which the Irish discussion was then carried on, and still more with the altered state of opinion which now prevails in society on this topic. It is difficult to meet with any one in or out of Parliament who does not admit that *something must be done*, and the whole of the minority of 226, with no inconsiderable portion of the majority ... not only avowed this conviction, but appeared ... impressed with the necessity of laying the foundation of a real and permanent union between the two countries. Much difference of opinion prevails as to ... what the people of England could be brought to consent, and what the people of Ireland would be content to receive. But even those ... opposed to any change in ... Church property, admit that ... the Catholics must be satisfied.[32]

This general feeling provided the context for Peel's new policies. Part of Peel's genius was his constructive use of his colleagues' work. On 11 February, he circulated to the cabinet a memo-

[28] Greville, *Journal*, 17 Feb. 1844, v. 162-3.
[29] Russell, *Hansard*, lxxii, 684, 13 Feb. 1844; Macaulay ibid., 1169-94, 19 Feb. 1844.
[30] Disraeli, ibid., 1016, 16 Feb. 1844.
[31] O'Connell to Fitzpatrick, *Correspondence*, 20 Feb. 1844, ii. 319.
[32] Greville, *Past and Present Policy*, pp. vi-vii.

randum on the fundamental issues of Irish reform, in which he restated Eliot's suggestions, but prefixed to it his own commitment to 'the great principle of maintaining intact the Established Church'.[33] In advising concessions, he dwelt on the imperial argument: the position in which they stood towards Ireland, in the event of war, made it very desirable that they should well consider what they could do voluntarily in the hope of improving its condition. His immediate aim was 'to detach ... from the ranks of those who cannot be reclaimed or conciliated, all those who are not yet committed to violent counsels, and are friendly to the connection between the two countries.' The cabinet discussed the memorandum on 12 and 13 February. The question of indirect endowment caused no difficulty, but Gladstone and Goulburn protested against an increase in the Maynooth grant.[34] In view of this difference of opinion, it was decided to avoid all mention of Maynooth in the debate. At the end of the first week of debate, when the ministers had heard able speeches from Russell, Disraeli, and Howick, Peel sent his colleagues a second memorandum. He reminded them how similar the situation now was to that in 1793 and 1800 when reforms had been forced on the government. He then discussed the means at their disposal for meeting the present threat:

we cannot hope to pass coercion bills. If we did pass them could we execute them, could we execute them through any other instrumentality than that of the known and recognised law - that is Trial by Jury? What I fear is that that instrument would break in our hands ... I know not what remedy there can be for such an evil as this but the detaching from the ranks of Repeal, agitation, and disaffection a considerable portion of the respectable and influential Roman Catholic population...

The threat of the Repeal movement had galvanized the government into action and, as Peel realized, the options open to it were limited. Better concede reforms with good grace than risk a repetition of the situation of 1829. Peel therefore made further suggestions to his colleagues. These included some reforms of the Established church and the abolition of ministers' money; further municipal reform; and improved educational facilities for Catholics by opening up Trinity College

[33] Peel, cabinet memorandum, 11 Feb. 1844, Add. MSS 40540, ff. 19-25.
[34] Gladstone's memorandum, 13 Feb. 1844, Add. MSS 44777, ff. 119-26, Gladstone, *Prime Ministers' Papers*, ii. 232-4.

and providing new academical colleges.[35] Owing to the opposition of Stanley, Gladstone, and others, Peel was forced to drop those proposals which seemed to impinge on the position or property of the Established church. Stanley advised Peel that 'the promotion of Catholic ecclesiastical (combined with civil) education should be the point at which we should endeavour to meet the wishes of the Roman Catholics.'[36] When Graham went a step further and spoke of 'a Roman Catholic education both for the intending priests and others', Gladstone again protested, and Peel watered down the proposition.[37]

Winding up the debate in the Commons on 23 February, Peel had only one new reform to offer: indirect endowment by a reform of the law of charities. The other measures to which the government pledged itself were the Commission on the relations between landlord and tenant, equality of franchise between Great Britain and Ireland, and a rather vague promise of a system of academical education for classes higher than those educated in national schools. With the debate out of the way Peel circulated to his cabinet a third memorandum on Irish reform. While recommending that the franchise, endowment, and education questions should receive immediate consideration, he expressed his conviction that the proposals on education were insufficient and that a commission of inquiry into Maynooth, which would consider the possibility of combined academical education for clergy and laity and the extension of Trinity College, should be set up. The time was right for Irish reforms, he believed, for the debate had gone favourably, their friends favoured kind legislation for Ireland, O'Connell had been beaten, and there was a temporary lull in Ireland. This was the 'crisis in the affairs of Ireland which must be taken at the flood' now, if ever there was to be a prospect of detaching moderate Catholics from Repeal. Returning to the argument of imperial security, Peel asked 'what an inducement there is both to France and the United States to presume on the State of Ireland'. Finally, no doubt with a view to winning over Gladstone and the churchmen among his colleagues, Peel

[35] Peel, cabinet memorandum, 17 Feb. 1844, Add. MSS 40540, ff. 230-37.

[36] Stanley to Peel, 18 Feb. 1844, Derby Papers, Box 174/2.

[37] Gladstone's memorandum, 27 Feb. 1844, Add. MSS 44777, ff. 127-8, Gladstone, *Prime Ministers' Papers*, ii. 235-6.

stated: 'we are resolved on maintaining at any hazard the Church of Ireland in all its rights ... The voluntary proposal by us of that which we can consent to ... will be much more creditable to the government and of ten fold more advantage in Ireland than the reluctant acquiescence hereafter in the proposals of our opponents.'[38] At the cabinet meeting of 2 March all members, except Gladstone, accepted Peel's view, and the way was now open for implementing the new reform programme for Ireland.

As Gash points out, in these three Irish papers in February 1844 Peel had exposed both the essence and detail of his whole future policy.[39] He managed his party well, showing consideration for his colleagues' views, marshalling every cogent argument to press his case, and achieving a remarkable consensus. For Gladstone's and the churchmens' benefit, he emphasized his commitment to the church, contrasting it with what would happen if the opposition came to power. Since by his timely establishment of the Ecclesiastical Commission in 1835 he had accomplished more than many churchmen to strengthen the church in England, his comment as he left the room after the second cabinet—a comment underlined by an anxious Gladstone in his own account—struck a statesmanlike note that impressed his colleagues: 'Depend on it, the attack upon the Church of Ireland can only be staved off by liberal concession.'[40] Imperial security was a further argument which he used to impress on his colleagues the need for conciliating Ireland (and there is evidence that this argument weighed heavily with him).[41] What is striking, however, is that he concerned himself with religious reform. Beaumont, who watched Irish affairs closely and was strongly convinced that religious reform took priority over all others, realized how difficult, if not impossible, it would be for a Tory government to propose it and believed that Peel would have to take a different line: 'le ministère tory ... tentera probablement de préférence les réformes sociales et politiques, et s'il les veut efficaces, sera

[38] Peel, cabinet memorandum, [28] Feb. 1844, Add. MSS 40540, ff. 40-55.
[39] Gash, *Peel,* p. 240.
[40] Gladstone's memorandum, 27 Feb. 1844, Add. MSS 44777, f. 128, Gladstone, *Prime Ministers' Papers,* ii. 236.
[41] *Hansard,* lxxix. 1040-1, 18 Apr. 1845.

tenu de les faire d'autant plus larges, qu'il n'y aura rien mêlé de relatif a l'église.'[42] The determining consideration, however, that spurred Peel into action and shaped the type of reform he was to offer was alarm at the alliance between clergy and repealers.

The reports of the magistrates and police in June 1843 had convinced him that the priests were the mainstay of Repeal and that they could not be touched either by banning meetings or ineffective prosecutions. Again and again he expressed his fear at this powerful combination.[43] The recurrent theme of his memoranda in February 1844 is the necessity of detaching the moderate clergy from the ranks of Repeal. When he appointed Lord Heytesbury as lord lieutenant in July 1844 with a view to carrying through his reform programme, he briefed him on 'the absolute necessity ... of disuniting, by the fair legitimate means of a just, kind and conciliatory policy, the Roman Catholic body and thus breaking up a sullen and formidable *confederacy* against the British connexion.'[44] Hard-pressed in parliament to defend the increased grant to Maynooth,when taunts of inconsistency were daily thrown in his face by Whig and Tory alike, when Disraeli denounced him as the 'parliamentary middleman' who 'bamboozles one party and plunders the other' and Macaulay scornfully announced to him that his day of reckoning had arrived at last, Peel revealed the reasons for all his reform measures for Ireland:

our motives for introducing this measure are these. In 1843, there was a formidable excitement in Ireland ... There was a universal feeling at that time that you ought not merely rely on applications of force ... that ... you must break up in some way or other, that formidable confederacy which exists in that country against ... the British connexion. I do not believe you can break it up by force ... You can do much to break it up by acting in a spirit of kindness, forebearance, and generosity.[45]

Even later, when O'Connell's movement was clearly on the wane, Peel retained this preoccupation with the danger a combination between the Catholic religion and popular move-

---

[42] Beaumont, *L'Irlande,* i. liii; Preface to the 6th edition; *État de la question d'Irlande en 1844.*
[43] Peel to Knight of Kerry, 24 June 1843, Add MSS, 40478, f. 95.
[44] Peel to Heytesbury, 8 Aug. 1844, Add. MSS, 40479, 23-30.
[45] *Hansard,* lxxix. 1026-7, 1040, 18 Apr. 1845.

ments constituted in Ireland. In a revealing statement to Lord Lincoln, when the latter became chief secretary in 1846, he noted gravely that 'the spirit of Popery and its alliance with democratic feelings and Institutions will constitute a very formidable combination against the Peace of Ireland, and the maintenance of cordial union with this country.'[46]

It is scarcely surprising, then, that Peel's reform programme of 1844 was geared primarily towards the Irish clergy and had as its immediate objective the hiving-off of clerical support from O'Connell. It would be unjust, however, to see his programme as having merely this negative aim, important though it appeared to him for the good government of the country. After the shock of O'Connell's successful national movement, he realized that a positive approach was necessary. 'It is clear', he told Graham immediately after the arrest of O'Connell, 'that mere force, however necessary the application of it, will do nothing as a permanent remedy for the social evils of that country.'[47] Although the outcry at the unfair nature of O'Connell's trial and the clamour of political opponents put pressure on Peel to take more positive action towards Ireland, it was his own political insight that brought home to him the necessity for concessions.[48] He now bent his considerable administrative skills to achieving as much reform as his own party would be persuaded to accept. In the outcome, he went well beyond the limits to which they were prepared to go.

Peel laid great and shrewd stress on the timing of reforms. To Parliament, he could justify his conversion to reforms on the ground that he had first maintained law and order by his victory over O'Connell and that the concessions were made from a position of strength and not extorted from fear of agitation. A difficulty arose here. Timing that was perfect in Westminster might not necessarily be so in Ireland; the humiliation of the great Irish leader did not create a favourable atmosphere for the acceptance of concessions. This difficulty brings out the weakness in Peel's reform plan, for it was evolved in a setting very different from that of the people it was

[46] Peel to Lincoln, [n.d.] Mar. 1846, Newcastle MSS.
[47] Peel to Graham, 19 Oct. 1843, Add. MSS 40449, ff. 105-6.
[48] Gash, *Peel*, pp. 411-16.

intended to help. In the absence of Irish advisers who understood the feelings of the majority, his plan could be interpreted as a solution imposed from without and from above. Peel and many of his cabinet had had some experience in Irish affairs and made use of whatever information was available, but they had not the same relatively direct access to Irish public opinion as the Whigs enjoyed. Leaving the Devon Commission to investigate the land question and postponing temporarily the education reforms while differences within the cabinet over Maynooth were being worked out, the government decided that voluntary endowment would be the first reform.

In 1764, the Irish Parliament had set up a committee to inquire into bequests left for charity and, before its own dissolution in 1801, established a board to administer them.[49] Although the board did good work in discovering charities, its procedure was costly and wasteful.[50] Proceedings dragged on for years as in the case of Judith Ruth of Mullingar, where 'the costs were nearly double the amount of what was ultimately recovered'.[51] Despite the fact that the vast majority of bequests was Catholic, fifteen years after the Emancipation Act only one of the board's fifty members was a Catholic. As the board, composed mainly of Protestant clergymen, had overextensive discretionary or *cy-près* powers, Catholics were chary of making bequests. (*Cy-près* is the application of a charitable donation to a purpose as near as possible to the original purpose when that original purpose has failed.) Although the Committee on Miscellaneous Estimates in 1829 recommended a reform and O'Connell included it in his programme in 1830, nothing was done.[52] Other unsuccessful efforts were made in 1834 and 1838, but the hierarchy, needing money urgently, was not content to let the matter rest. The church was not able to meet the needs of the growing number of poor as well as her own educational and building programmes. Bequests would bridge the gap between expenditure and income, but these would not be forthcoming as long as Catholics feared that the

---

[49] 40 Geo. III. c. 75 (Ir).

[50] Walsh, *O'Connell*, pp. 6, 10*-13*.

[51] *Education in Ireland, Select Committee Report, PP 1836*, xiii. 77-8.

[52] *Irish Miscellaneous Estimates, Select Committee Report, PP 1829*, iv. 155-60.

Charities board migh divert them to non-Catholic purposes.[53] The sums involved were considerable. In July 1844, Wharncliffe informed the House of Lords that: 'one Roman Catholic bishop ... had in trust ... one bequest of £55,000, and another of £35,000. Since the beginning of this year there had been bequeathed altogether for charitable purposes in Ireland above £30,000, of which £6,253 was for Protestant purposes and £23,477 for Roman Catholic uses.'[54] It was not surprising that the bishops petitioned the chief secretary, Morpeth, in 1840 to include Catholic ecclesiastics on the board. Nothing, however, came of their memorial.[55] In March 1844, however, O'Connell brought in a bill, with the blessing of the hierarchy, which aimed at solving the question of the perpetuity of bequests to the church by constituting every Catholic bishop 'a body politic and corporate' with perpetual succession. This would avoid the troublesome intervention of trustees.[56] This device of a *corporation sole* was the simplest and most equitable way of dealing with Protestant and Catholic charities, but it would have meant placing the Catholic hierarchy on the same footing as the bishops of the Established church, and this was unacceptable to Graham and the government.[57] Ten weeks later O'Connell was in Richmond Jail and his bill was dropped —a fact that played a considerable part in sharpening the controversy that ensued.

The way was clear for the government's bill. Early in April, Graham instructed the Irish attorney general, Thomas Berry Cusack Smith, to draft a bequests bill that would satisfy the Catholics but avoid recognition of their hierarchy.[58] Three months later, on 18 June 1844, Lord Wharncliffe introduced the government measure, entitled the 'Charitable Donations

[53] J. D. Fitzpatrick, *Edmund Rice, founder ... of the Brothers of the Christian Schools ...* (1945), pp. 227-9, gives cases of bequests lost to the Brothers.

[54] *Hansard,* lxxvi. 907, 16 July 1844.

[55] The memorial was incorporated by Murray in his pastoral letter 'to the ... clergy and faithful of the diocese of Dublin', *Freeman's Journal*, 26 Dec. 1844. An undated draft in Murray's handwriting is to be found in a file containing letters of Archbishops Troy and Murray, 1809-23, DDA.

[56] *Hansard,* lxxiii, 531; 4 Mar. 1845, lxxiii, 839-40; 11 Mar. 1845; see Walsh, *O'Connell,* pp. 17, 101.

[57] Graham to Peel, 7 Apr. 1844. Add. MSS 40449 ff. 394-7.

[58] Graham to Peel, 3 April 1844, Add. MSS 40449, ff. 374-5; Graham to Peel, 5 Apr. 1844, Add. MSS 40449, ff. 380-2.

and Bequests for Roman Catholic Ministers (Ireland)' Bill. A new board was to be set up consisting of ten nominated members—of whom five were to be Catholic—and three *ex-officio* members. The board's functions were to be similar to those of the old board, with the notable exception that the much-criticized *cy-près* powers were withheld from it. Clause 15 contained the main provisions and permitted donors to vest property in the new commissioners to hold in perpetual succession 'in trust for building ... any Place of Worship of Persons Professing the Roman Catholic Religion, or in trust for any ... Person in Holy Orders of the Church of Rome officiating in a district ... or for building a Residence for his and their Use.' A proviso laid down that the bill could not be construed as repealing the sections in the 1829 Relief Act which made bequests to religious orders illegal. The measure was a great improvement on existing legislation. The inclusion of Catholics as commissioners and the elimination of *cy-près* powers were intended to restore Catholic confidence in the board. Although the method of securing a trust in perpetuity was neither as simple nor as satisfactory as O'Connell's plan, the bill did make it possible to avoid the troublesome, costly, and often risky method of private trusteeship and so faciliated private endowment of the Catholic church.

The bill was favourably received, on the whole, in both Houses of Parliament, although Lord Hatherton and the Marquess of Clanricarde expressed regret that the government had not adopted O'Connell's simpler and more effective bill. Lord Beaumont, however, attacked O'Connell's bill and made the following remarkable claim:

He had ... had communications on the subject with parties that he considered higher authority on the matter than even the Catholic Clergy of Ireland themselves; and he could say distinctly that, with the present relations between this country and Rome, it was not the desire of any higher parties that anything should be done tending to establish the Catholic Clergy of Ireland as corporations, having power of controlling funds left for religious purposes... without any control of them either by state or by the foreign power by which they were influenced, namely the Papal See.[59]

---

[59] *Hansard*, lxxvi., 94-5, 28 June 1844.

It was generally thought that Beaumont was claiming some communication with the Holy See. Such a claim was scarcely credible. It was not substantiated when challenged and served only to create suspicion and exacerbate feelings.

From Catholic members, the main complaint was one of lack of consultation. As Sheil pointed out, 'no reason had been offered for not consulting a single Roman Catholic Prelate upon a Bill which related to property held for ecclesiastical purposes'.[60] Such consultation would have avoided some of the blemishes in the measure. The government, however, showed a readiness to accept amendments. It was specified that when questions concerning the Catholic church arose, they would be submitted to the Catholic commissioners who would give a certificate of the facts to the board on which it would then act. The term 'minister', as referring to Catholic clergy, was dropped because Catholics disliked its Calvinist overtones. Graham, under criticism from the Catholic members and on Eliot's prompting, went further and brought in an amendment of some constitutional moment.[61] Clause 15 now referred to the beneficiaries of bequests as, 'any archbishop or bishop or other person in Holy Orders of the Church of Rome'. Although the territorial titles of the bishops were ommitted, the clause was a real recognition of the bishops' spiritual functions, and went far towards inserting the Roman church into the constitution. This limited recognition was as far as Peel and Graham could go while maintaining the position of the Established church. They now felt that they could ignore further criticisms of the bill, attributing them (as Peel acidly told the queen) to a desire to 'prefer the grievance to the remedy'.[62] Indeed criticism in Parliament had so weakened that Robert Dillon Browne was alone in his opposition to the third reading.[63] During that summer, too, Peel had repealed a number of obsolete penal laws against the Catholics and now, pleased with the easy passage of the Bequests bill through Parliament, he turned

---

[60] Ibid., 1528, 29 July 1844.

[61] Ibid., 1658-60, 1 Aug. 1844; Eliot to Graham, 23 June 1844, Graham Papers.

[62] Peel to the queen, 30 July 1844, Royal Archives, A16/112.

[63] *Hansard*, lxxvi. 1780-1, 5 Aug. 1844. Dillon Browne was MP for Mayo and, allegedly, under the influence of MacHale.

towards the implementation of this first part of his Irish reform policy.

From a strictly official point of view, prospects for implementing such a policy had taken a decisive turn for the better. De Grey remained unenthusiastic about the new concessions. He still opposed the government's education policy, and Graham had to remind him sharply that 'we must not put croziers in the hands of Bishops to be used as instruments for pulling down what we seek to uphold.'[64] In June 1844, however, De Grey retired on the grounds of ill-health, the nationalist press alleging that Peel had got rid of him for his opposition to the educational policy. Peel now appointed Lord Heytesbury, an experienced diplomat, as lord lieutenant, a change well timed in view of the reform policy.[65] Indeed, the new policy could not have been implemented without such a change. Heytesbury worked well with Eliot, and harmony was restored within the Irish administration. A career diplomat, Heytesbury also proved the willing instrument and able administrator of the policies to which Peel and Graham now devoted increasing attention. The prime minister and his home secretary together constituted a formidable combination, and it is a tribute to the importance attached to the new Irish policy that the two most powerful men in the cabinet devoted such attention to it.

Sir James Graham, the minister with chief responsibility for Ireland, was an able, extremely hard-working home secretary, but his high-handed manner and aloofness made him inept at handling people.[66] By 1844 he was most unpopular, not least, as we have seen, because of his part in the letter-opening affair. With respect to Irish problems, he had supported Catholic Emancipation, but had resigned from Grey's government in 1834 over the Appropriation issue, telling Bentinck that he could accept no compromise since 'the maintenance of the Protestant Establishment in Ireland is necessary for the preservation of the Union'.[67] On the same grounds he fiercely attacked

---

[64] Graham to De Grey, 26 Feb. 1844, Graham Papers.

[65] William A'Court (1779-1860), ambassador to Portugal 1824-7; created 1st Baron Heytesbury 1828; lord lieutenant, July 1844 - July 1846.

[66] A. P. Donajgrodzki, 'Sir James Graham at the Home Office', *Hist. Jn.*, xx (1977), 97-120.

[67] Graham to Bentinck, 12 June 1834, cited in Ward, *Graham*, p. 137.

the Irish Corporations Bill in 1836, an action which his bio-grapher, McCullagh Torrens, regarded as his most lamentable error.[68] His reaction to Irish problems tended to be hasty and extreme. At the height of the Repeal movement, he had told De Grey that 'if it come to a struggle, we must call on the Protest-ant Yeomanry of the North and place arms in their hands.'[69] Later, however, along with Peel, he opposed Wellington's pressure to act in this way.[70] In Parliament, too, he rashly declared that 'conciliation has been carried to its utmost limits in Ireland'.[71] This unfortunate statement was one his opponents never allowed him to forget. Yet, he regretted his hasty words and, two years later, claimed that his actions had been better than his words.[72]

This claim was not groundless. From the autumn of 1843, he played a major role in formulating the government's new policy of conciliation. Irish evils, he believed, were the result of 'the bankrupt condition of the landlords and the severance of the religion of the people from all connection with the State.'[73] To him is due the credit for setting up the Devon commission, potentially a major contribution to the solution of the problem. The commission's work was necessarily long-term, and in the meantime he encouraged Eliot to produce his plans. He piloted the Charitable Bequests Bill through the House of Commons in a conciliatory manner and he was now prepared to put the necessary administrative effort into planning and carrying out the entire programme of concessions. The constant stream of letters between him and the Irish government over the next few years showed an increasingly intelligent grasp of the Irish situation. Although he exploded in angry frustration at Irish behaviour on occasions, he was prepared to accept Heytesbury's and Eliot's evaluations.[74] Indeed, the loyalty and encouragement

[68] Cited in Ward, *Graham,* p. 153.

[69] Graham to De Grey, 20 May 1843, Graham Papers.

[70] McCaffrey, *O'Connell,* p. 151.

[71] *Hansard,* lxx. 52, 16 June 1843.

[72] Ibid., lxxix. 920-1, 17 April. 1845.

[73] Graham to Peel, 2 Sept. 1843, Graham Papers.

[74] To strengthen his own position and to reassure his co-religionists, Murray published in the press an official assurance concerning the treatment of the regular clergy and, later, a further assurance that no negotiations for a concordat were afoot. In both cases Graham was severely critical of Murray's action. See p. 201.

he showed to the Irish government during this period was in striking contrast to his reaction towards officials in England.[75] Graham hoped that the government's first conciliatory measure —the Charitable Bequests Bill—would go part of the way towards opening up lines of communication with at least some of the Catholics. He told Heytesbury, within a few days of the latter's arrival in Ireland, that 'the patronage under this Bill and the arrangement and discussion that must precede the settlement of any scheme of Roman Catholic collegiate education will necessarily place us in advantageous terms in communication with the Roman Catholic hierarchy and the better portion of their nobility.[76]

Peel, too, sent Heytesbury his own instructions which shed interesting light on how he now believed that Ireland should be administered. Impartiality was the key, he insisted, for it was the only way to win the Catholics from O'Connell and from the domination of the clergy: 'I do not despair of weaning from the cause of Repeal the great body of wealthy and intelligent Roman Catholics by the steady manifestation of a desire to act with impartiality ... One of the consequences of this maybe... the refusal...of the Laity to submit to an intolerable spiritual domination in political matters.'[77] A week later, he decisively rejected the prevailing Tory attitude in Ireland:

The cry ... has been for a century past, and I doubt not now is 'the Protestants are the friends of the British Connexion; reliance can be placed on them' ... All this means 'continue to us the monopoly of favour and confidence which before 1829 the Law secured to us. Consider the members of the Church as the garrison of Ireland and govern Ireland on the garrison principle'. The answer is that the system is unjust, is dangerous but above all is utterly impracticable.[78]

Peel and Graham now decided that three of the Catholics on the new board set up by the Charitable Bequests Act should be ecclesiastics.[79] This move, which was suggested by Lord Hatherton to calm Catholic fears that lay commissioners would interfere in matters of church discipline, was to prove crucial;

[75] Donajgrodzki, 'Graham', pp. 108-10.
[76] Graham to Heytesbury, 4 Aug. 1844, Graham Papers.
[77] Peel to Heytesbury, 1 Aug. 1844, Add. MSS 40479, ff. 15-18.
[78] Peel to Heytesbury, 8 Aug. 1844, ibid., ff. 23-30.
[79] Graham to Heytesbury, 4 Aug. 1844, Graham Papers.

it committed the government to finding three bishops who would consent to become commissioners. The first step was to contact Dr Murray. Peel resolved that he should be addressed as 'Most Reverend Archbishop Murray', for although he saw this acknowledgement of his title as an important constitutional step, he felt that 'we must not withold a recognition which the law has expressly sanctioned'.[80]

If Peel and Graham believed that their first reform would be accepted as a measure of conciliation, they miscalculated Irish Catholic opinion.[81] In the summer of 1844, the Catholics were in no mood to be conciliated. The first reports of the bill were published in newspapers carrying mourning columns and a permanent banner headline entitled 'Remember 30 May 1844',—the day O'Connell had been jailed. 'Justice has not been done to me' were O'Connell's words from the dock; nationalist Ireland identified with him and smarted from the affront. *The Sun* summed up the state of opinion with a quotation from *The Pilot*, asserting that 'the imprisonment of O'Connell had infused into the hearts of the Irish ... a deep brooding hatred to England'.[82] Against this background it was not surprising that the reaction to the bill was hostile. The moderate *Dublin Evening Post* called it 'the first essay of Her Majesty's Ministers to place the Catholic clergy under the control of the State', and, a week later, asked: 'what else could be expected from the Ministry now in power—from Lord Lyndhurst, whose denunciation of the Irish Catholics, and their clergy as "aliens" in religion, as well as in language and blood, is forcibly revived by this Tory attempt to legislate *for* the Catholic Clergy.'[83] *The Pilot*, O'Connell's paper, published a two-column criticism of the bill, calling Peel's administration 'a trickster as well as a tyrant government'.[84] Lord Beaumont's claim to speak with some higher authority caused fierce resentment. Frederick

---

[80] Peel to Graham, 21 Aug. 1844, Add. MSS 40450, ff. 105-6.

[81] The fullest accounts of the ensuing controversy are those of W. J. Walsh, 'The Board of Charitable Donations and Bequests', *IER*, 3rd series, xiv (1895), 875-94, 971-6; *O'Connell, Archbishop Murray and the Board of Charitable Bequests ...* (Dublin n.d.) Walsh was archbishop of Dublin 1885-1921, and a member of the Bequests Commission.

[82] *Pilot*, 1 July 1844.

[83] *Dublin Evening Post*, 29 June, 2 July 1844.

[84] *Pilot*, 1 July 1844.

Lucas, founder and editor of the influential and hard-hitting Catholic weekly, the *Tablet*, scoffed at 'the bearer of the secret dissent of the Holy See from the universal wish, on an Irish Church question, of the Irish clergy', and ridiculed the idea of 'the Pope appealing from Archbishop Murray to Lord Beaumont'.[85] MacHale also entered the field. Brushing aside the 'strange effusions' of this 'parliamentary proxy of the Holy See', he attacked the bill as 'surpassing, in its odious provisions, the worse enactments of penal times and developing a maturity of wicked refinement in legislation which the more clumsy artificers of the anti-Catholic code would in vain attempt to rival.' This reaction was grossly excessive but another criticism was well founded. Why, he demanded, were not the Catholic bishops or lawyers asked for their opinion on a matter that affected the eight million Irish Catholics?[86]

Although the amendments made to the bill satisfied most of the Irish members—the *Dublin Evening Post* admitting that the act was much less obnoxious in its final form[87]—the addition of a new clause (16) was to have the opposite effect. As this clause became the centre of controversy, its history is worth detailing. With a view to avoiding abuses of undue pressure on the dying, Graham had instructed Smith, the Irish attorney-general, to include a three-month restriction on bequests.[88] Smith, accordingly, included in clause 15 a proviso that no bequest under the act be valid unless executed and registered three months before the testator's death. Knowing that the restriction was new to Ireland and anticipating Catholic opposition, he carefully limited the restriction to bequests entrusted to the new board.[89] This left it free for Catholics to make bequests without restriction, as before, provided they did not entrust them to the Board. What happened next is not quite clear. According to Smith, a Catholic peer suggested that the restriction be made applicable

[85] *Tablet*, 6, 13 July 1844; Frederick Lucas (1812-55), friend of John Stuart Mill and Thomas Carlyle; called to the Bar, 1835; convert to Catholicism, 1839; founded the *Tablet*, 1840; founder of the Tenant League in Ireland, 1850; E. Lucas, *The life of Frederick Lucas, M.P.* (1886).

[86] MacHale to Peel, 2 July 1844, *Pilot*, 5 July 1844.

[87] *Dublin Evening Post*, 10 Aug. 1844.

[88] Graham to Peel, 5 Apr. 1844, Add. MSS 40449, ff. 380-3.

[89] Smith to Heytesbury, 11 Sept. 1844, Graham Papers.

to every religious denomination.[90] In order to meet the peer's wishes, and because the privilege in clause 15 entrusting bequests to the new commissioners was intended to facilitate Catholic endowment and was, therefore, confined to Catholics, the three-month proviso was struck out and erected into a separate clause—16—which then read: 'And be it enacted, that after the Commencement of this act no Donation, Devise or Bequest for pious ... Uses in Ireland shall be valid ... unless the Deed, Will, or other Instrument ... shall be duly executed Three Calendar Months ... before the Death of the Person executing the same.' The result was that the Georgian Mortmain Act was, for the first time, extended to bequests in Ireland, irrespective of whether the bequests were for the endowment of the Catholic clergy or for charity in general, and regardless of whether or not they were entrusted to the new board.[91] It was an unfortunate addition in that the new clause was quite extraneous to the intention of the act, which was to facilitate endowment of the Catholic church. Peel had stated when proposing the measure to his cabinet that he was well aware that it was 'tantamount to a relaxation of the statute of mortmain', but that 'the state of Ireland made such relaxation necessary'.[92] Instead of relaxing the statute of mortmain, the act extended its provisions in Ireland.

Even before the proviso became of general application, MacHale had complained that 'it would go to forbid the restitution of plundered property, and would consign the death-bed penitent to all the horrors of despair.'[93] Murray, however, saw the

----

[90] Ibid.

[91] The Mortmain Act of 1736 (9 Geo. II. cap. 36) made void gifts of land for charitable purposes if made by will and made void similar gifts if made by deed unless the deed was executed twelve months before the donor's death. It was an act of the British Parliament and did not apply to Ireland. Sugden, the Irish lord chancellor, may well have played a part in introducing the provisions of this act into the Bequests Bill of 1844. On 25 Nov. 1841, in the case of The Incorporated Society in Dublin for promoting English Protestant Schools in Ireland v. The Right Hon. John Richards, Sugden declared that he would be glad if the law on charities in the two countries were still further assimilated 'by extending to this country the provisions of the 9 G.2, c. 36, to which there is no corresponding statute in this country'. *Irish Equity Reports* ... iv (1842), p. 214. O'Connell claimed to have thwarted his efforts to bring in legislation to this purpose; Walsh, *O'Connell,* pp. 30*-2*, 85.

[92] Cabinet memorandum, 11 Feb. 1844, Add. MSS 40540, ff. 19-25.

[93] MacHale to Peel, 2 July 1844, *Pilot,* 5 July 1844.

bill as a distinct improvement, and told Slattery that 'Dr Mac-Hale's description of the bill is an evident misstatement of the purport of it.'[94] When Fr Cooper drew attention to the unfavourable change brought about by the new clause, Murray was taken aback and immediately protested to Eliot that

the change which has been made in the original bill by the introduction of the 16th clause ... will entirely rob it of the popularity to which it would be otherwise so well entitled. Nothing will reconcile the Catholics of Ireland to this clause. It wholly changes the character of the bill and will cause it to be considered not as a boon but as establishing a new and grievous penal law.[95]

Although Eliot pleaded that the provision, since it applied to all religions, was not aimed at the Catholics, Murray was not satisfied, and informed Slattery and Crolly that 'should it receive the Royal Sanction in its present state, I at least would not be one of the five commissioners to execute that law'.[96] The extension of the limitation from bequests for church endowment to all charitable bequests was unacceptable to him.[97] Despite Murray's rebuff to Eliot, Peel and Graham urged Heytesbury to contact Murray immediately.[98] The lord lieutenant, already alarmed at the attacks of MacHale and the press, was afraid that 'our best card will be lost if we lose Dr Murray', but he was at a loss how to contact him. Fortune favoured him. As he was composing a plaintive letter to Peel bewailing the 'thundering' of MacHale, the abuse which Conciliation Hall was showering on the act and the general lack of moral courage, a deputation which included the Protestant and Catholic archbishops of Dublin arrived at the Vice-Regal Lodge, according to Heytesbury, 'in the same carriage'. Seizing the opportunity, he persuaded Murray to return in a few days time to talk over the act with him.[99]

On that same day, another important event took place that influenced the course of the debate. From Richmond Jail,

[94] Murray to Slattery, 30 July 1844, Slattery Papers.

[95] Murray to Eliot, 9 Aug. 1844, (draft) Murray Papers.

[96] Murray to Slattery, 9 August 1844; Crolly to Murray, 14 Aug. 1844, Murray Papers.

[97] Murray, To the ... clergy and people of ... Dublin, *Freeman's Journal*, 26 Dec. 1844.

[98] Peel to Graham, 21 Aug., 1844, Add. MSS 40450, ff. 105-6; Graham to Heytesbury, 24 Aug., 1844, Graham Papers.

[99] Heytesbury to Peel, 24 Aug., 1844, Add. MSS 40479 ff. 37-40.

O'Connell issued his professional opinion on the act in reply to a query submitted by Dr Cantwell, bishop of Meath. The act, he asserted, would injure the doctrines, discipline, and constitution of the church and bring all bequests, existing and future, into the 'greedy grasp' of the Commissioners. Although critical of clause 16, O'Connell, however, astutely pointed out a means of evading it: 'the mode of proceeding is to grant or bequeath, not the land, but a sum of money chargeable on the land for the intended charitable purpose.'[100] This solution to Clause 16 was just what Murray wanted. Although he rejected O'Connell's other objections to the act, he gladly accepted his opinion on this clause, and, having checked it with Anthony Blake, he dropped his opposition.[101]

On 27 August, the day after O'Connell's opinion appeared in the *Pilot*, Heytesbury and Murray met in the Vice-Regal Lodge. It was a historic meeting because it was the first occasion on which the lord lieutenant met one of the chief representatives of the Catholic church to discuss the government's new policy, and from his point of view not merely the fact of the meeting but the manner in which it passed off was a success. Murray acknowledged the good intention of the government and took exception to clause 16 alone, for it imposed new restrictions totally unacceptable to the Catholics. He brought a legal interpretation—strangely similar to O'Connell's—which Blake had prepared for him and which concluded that although the law invalidated the bequeathing of land within three months of a testator's death, it did not invalidate the charging of real estate with money payments even up to the total value of the land. If the government could confirm the accuracy of this interpretation, Murray promised to waive his other objections. Heytesbury, impressed by Murray's conciliatory attitude and anxious to succeed in his first mission in Ireland, referred the matter to London.[102] Graham and Peel, further removed from the Irish scene, were unsympathetic. Graham condemned Blake's interpretation as mere evasion.[103] Peel, referring evidently to Blake,

[100] *Pilot*, 26 Aug. 1844.

[101] Murray to Slattery, 30 Aug. 1844. Slattery papers; Crolly to Murray, 29 Aug., 1844, Letter-book, 1823-48, Murray Papers.

[102] Heytesbury to Peel, 27 Aug. 1844, Add. MSS 40479, ff. 45-8; Heytesbury to Graham, 3 Sept. 1844, Graham Papers.

[103] Graham to Peel, 2 Sept. 1844, Add. MSS 40450, ff. 118-21.

and possibly to Murray, scorned 'their tortuous ways of which others would be ashamed'.[104] He promised Graham that he would stand firm lest Murray boast that he had exacted changes as the condition of serving on the commission, and expressed the belief that some of the lay Catholics welcomed the limitation on death-bed bequests. If Blake's interpretation was to prove the correct one, however, Peel thought that they should not exclude it.[105]

Events in Ireland overtook the government. MacHale, satisfied by O'Connell's opinion that his own opposition to the act had the support of the leading lawyer and politician of the land, took a step that was to have far-reaching consequences. To forestall any secret agreement with the government, he and Bishops Cantwell and McGettigan met at Coffey's Hotel in Dominick Street, Dublin, on 26 August, and drew up a protest against the act and warned bishops who might contemplate becoming commissioners that they would be interfering in the spiritual jurisdiction of other bishops.[106] They circulated the protest to the bishops for their signatures and for those of their clergy.

Murray, who lived within a mile of Coffey's Hotel, received his copy of the protest through the post, and in a letter to Slattery, he did not conceal his indignation:

The manifesto from Coffey's Hotel, reached me, as it did your Grace, *by post*. I had not the honour of seeing any of the distinguished members of the Junta since their arrival in Dublin. I did not, therefore, think I was bound to sign a document, about which it would have been so very easy to ascertain my opinion if it was thought to be of any value, and accordingly I took no notice of it.[107]

A note of personal hostility is evident in his letter, understandable enough in view of the cavalier way in which he had been treated and the background of disagreement on the national education and Repeal issues. The primate, Crolly, reacted similarly, refusing to sign the protest and criticizing the three signatories for expecting the other bishops tamely to follow

[104] Peel to Graham, 30 Aug. 1844, Graham Papers.

[105] Peel to Heytesbury, 5 Sept. 1844, Add. MSS 40479, ff. 57-60.

[106] Charitable Bequests folder, 26 Aug. 1844, Murray Papers, DDA; *Pilot,* 23 Sept. 1844.

[107] Murray to Slattery, 30 Aug. 1844, Slattery Papers.

their example.[108] It remained to be seen whether this circular would attract any support from the other bishops and clergy, or whether MacHale's gamble would fail. The government knew nothing about this protest circulating to the bishops and priests of the country, and, at that moment, it was facing graver threats to its Irish policies.

With growing alarm, Graham noted that the law lords seemed likely to reverse O'Connell's conviction and complained to Peel that the whole Irish policy 'which I had contemplated and to the completion of which I had ventured to look forward with hope is likely to be subverted and turned into confusion by the judgement in the Lords.'[109] When on 6 September O'Connell's sentence was reversed, the sensation was considerable. O'Connell's triumphal parade through the heart of Dublin and the tremendous celebrations throughout the country showed that he still enjoyed overwhelming national support. It was not the enthusiasm of the masses that was the government's chief worry. Police spies reported seditious harangues by the priests from the altar, and as far away as Rome the clergy triumphantly hailed O'Connell's release.[110] The celebrations in Dublin caused more alarm. To the government's chagrin, Murray presided at a solemn pontifical mass with Te Deum in his own cathedral where the sermon was preached by Fr John Miley, a well-known friend of O'Connell, who represented his release as a miracle from heaven. Graham was furious, regarding Murray's presence as an act of 'culpable weakness, if not of duplicity.'[111] Yet he urged Heytesbury not to allow negotiations with him to be broken off easily. It was better, he reflected, not to leave the archbishop exclusively to O'Connell. As he pompously put it, it should be indicated to Murray that the door of Dublin Castle was not yet barred to him: 'I fear that he will not have the courage to beard the Lion who is now at large and roaring fearfully but still we must endeavour to bring him to terms and to bend him to our purpose'.[112] To maintain their hold on Murray, it would be necessary to meet his difficulties

[108] Crolly to Murray, 29 Aug. 1844, Letter-book, 1823-48, Murray Papers.
[109] Graham to Peel, 2 Sept. 1844, Add. MSS 40450, ff. 118-19.
[110] Graham to Wellington, 2 Oct. 1844, Graham Papers.
[111] Graham to Heytesbury, 13 Sept. 1844, ibid.
[112] Graham to Heytesbury, 11 Sept. 1844, ibid.

concerning clause 16. As Blake had suggested a solution, Peel and Graham, despite their previously expressed scorn for his 'tortuous ways', now decided that he sould be consulted.[113] Thus an elusive but central figure in Irish affairs again assumed the familiar role of unofficial Catholic adviser to the government.

From the time that the Marquess Wellesley had brought him to Dublin in 1821, the solicitor, Anthony Blake, second son of Martin Blake of Holly Park, Co. Galway, had played such an important part in Irish politics that some called him the virtual ruler of the country, while others attributed every change that took place to his influence.[114] Exaggerated though these assertions were, there was no doubting Blake's influence. Madden thought him the best informed person on the state of Ireland and added: 'No other man of either party knows more of the government of Ireland than Mr Blake. He is not merely himself possessed of natural acuteness and discernment, but he has the advantage of constant and unrestrained intercourse with the very greatest personages that have influenced the politics of Ireland.'[115] This was certainly true. In 1823 Wellesley made him chief remembrancer of the Court of Exchequer—an extraordinary appointment in view of Blake's Catholicism. His influence extended to both Goulburn, the chief secretary, and Lord Plunket, the Irish chancellor.[116] O'Connell, who saw it as 'very fortunate' that Blake should be at the vice-regal court, regarded him as a friend whom he could consult.[117] Blake's influence with successive lord lieutenants was so great that he was known as 'the backstairs Viceroy', Sheil confirming that he was consulted upon measures and upon men and was 'a

[113] Graham to Heytesbury, 11 Sept. 1845, Graham Papers.
[114] *Dublin Evening Post*, 13 Nov. 1845. Anthony Richard Blake (1786-1849). The only (brief) account of his career is in R. L. Sheil, *Sketches legal and political* (1855), i. 368-71.
[115] D. O. Madden, *Ireland and Its Rulers*, ii. 196-7.
[116] Lady Gregory, ed. *Mr Gregory's letter-box, 1813-30* (1894), p. 187; Greville, *Journal*, 11 Jan. 1829, i. 234.
[117] O'Connell to Maurice O'Connell, 5 Jan. 1822; 19 June 1823, O'Connell, *Correspondence of O'Connell*, ii. 347, 147, 489. Although Blake opposed Repeal, O'Connell was using him as an intermediary as late as 1843, according to Greville, *Journal*, 10 Sept. 1843, v. 130.

puller of wires in the political puppet show'.[118] When Anglesey became lord lieutenant, Blake became a member of his private cabinet.[119] When Mulgrave (later Lord Normanby) became lord lieutenant, Blake retained his influence, and in 1836 Morpeth, the chief secretary, insisted on making him a privy councillor.[120] His advice and evidence were sought on all the great topics of the day. He was commissioner on the Education Inquiry from 1824 to 1827 and on the Poor Law Inquiry in 1833. He gave evidence before Committees on the State of Ireland (1825), Tithes (1831-2), Education in Ireland (1835), and Mortmain (1844). After the Inquiry into Maynooth in 1826, he submitted a plan to Wellesley for the reform of the College.[121] During the Anglesey administration, he sought to bring Whately and Doyle together on the tithes question and helped to work out a plan acceptable to Anglesey.[122] The Poor Law Commission's report owed much to Blake, and Morpeth, on behalf of the cabinet, commissioned him in 1836 to draw up a bill on the basis of the report.[123] Education was his main interest, and he was in contact with the Catholic bishops, particularly Doyle and Murray. His work may well have formed the basis of the national education system in 1831, and he certainly played a part in persuading a reluctant Stanley to introduce the system.[124] His interest in education, particularly in the national system, remained a lifelong commitment.[125] He became one of the most active and influential commissioners and worked well with both Whately and Murray.[126] He claimed

[118] Sheil, *Sketches,* i. 368-71; Gregory, *Letter-Box,* p. 187.

[119] Cloncurry, *Personal Recollections of the Life and Times, extracts from the correspondence of Valentine, Lord Cloncurry* (1849), p. 332.

[120] Blake to Wellesley, 31 Dec. 1836, Add. MSS 37310, ff. 411-13, Wellesley Papers; Normanby to Blake, 29 Nov. 1844, Blake Papers.

[121] Heytesbury to Graham, 16 Oct. 1844, Graham Papers.

[122] Blake to Doyle, 12 Dec. 1831, Fitzpatrick, *Doyle,* ii. 325; Anglesey to Cloncurry, 27 Apr. 1834, Cloncurry, *Personal Recollections,* p. 367.

[123] Morpeth to Russell, 27 Sept., 5 Oct. 1836, Russell Papers, PRO, 30/22/2C; Morpeth to Blake, 15 Apr. 1836, Blake Papers.

[124] Cloncurry, *Recollections,* p. 390; Anglesey to Grey, 21 Mar. 1831, PRO (Northern Ireland), T 1068-4, cited in Akenson, *Education Experiment,* p. 111.

[125] Blake left a large legacy to the funds of the national schools; Sheil, *Sketches,* i. 371. His work as a commissioner was unpaid, yet he drew up many of the reports, distributed Catholic bibles free to the Catholic teachers and prepared a harmony of the gospels for use in all classes.

[126] Akenson, *Education Experiment,* p. 128.

that the national system alone could extinguish 'sectarian bile' by uniting young persons of all creeds in the same schools and by teaching them to regard each other as fellow-students and fellow-Christians.[127]

His other public interest was the relationship between church and state.[128] In 1828, he had argued for some 'domestic control' of the church.[129] This statement and his support of the veto caused some Catholics to suspect him of erastianism.[130] In politics, he wanted the Union 'cemented and secured' and had his own four-point plan to achieve this: establishment of diplomatic relations with the Vatican; propitiation of the clergy and the religious feelings of the people; provision for the poor, and an extension of the franchise. Without such measures, he feared that 'the government will continue to want in Ireland, the true, natural, legitimate proofs of authority'; the longing for separation would grow and lead to ultimate disaster both for Ireland and the Empire.[131] Blake's brilliance and charm made people suspicious of him. In the 1820s, he was labelled 'dangerous' by many Protestants, but not all could resist his fascinating influence.[132] Greville in 1833 spoke of him as 'a dangerous, Jesuitical fellow', but came later to seek and value his advice on Ireland.[133] Henry Lambert found him so 'extremely guarded and diplomatically laconic' that he could not divine his political views, while Sheil described him as shrewd and ingenious.[134] Heytesbury was warned by both Graham and political advisers in Dublin of his astuteness.[135] Some Catholics, too, feared him for similar reasons. Cooper spoke

---

[127] Blake to Peel, 3 Feb. 1842, Add. MSS, 40-501, ff. 257-9.

[128] Blake's library contained the works of the Fathers (Athanasius, Ambrose, Augustine, Tertullian) most concerned with the relations between church and state. *Catalogue ... from the library of Rt. Hon. Anthony R. Blake* (1849).

[129] A. R. Blake, *Thoughts upon the Catholic question*, (1828), p. 73.

[130] Lucas, *Lucas*, i. 176; MacHale to Peel, 24 Jan. 1845, MacHale, *The Letters of the Most Rev. John MacHale...* (1847), pp. 590-1; O'Reilly, *MacHale*, i. 448-9.

[131] Blake to Wellesley, 10 Sept. 1841, Add. MSS 37313 (Wellesley Papers), ff. 70-4.

[132] Gregory, *Letter-box*, pp. 187, 193.

[133] Greville, *Journal*, 10 Sept. 1833, ii. 415; Normanby to Blake, 29 Nov. 1844, Blake Papers. Greville cited Blake often as an authority in his work, *Past and Present Policy in Ireland* (1844).

[134] Lambert to Cloncurry, 3 June 1834, Cloncurry, *Recollections*, p. 461; Sheil, *Sketches*, i. 368-71.

[135] Graham to Heytesbury, 11 Sept. 1844, Graham Papers.

of him as 'one of the most plausible intriguers that ever stood in shoe leather'.[136] MacHale's assertion that he was 'the pliant and dexterous follower of every successive administration', although a tribute to Blake's resilience, did not take account of the part Blake played in moulding the policies of these administrations and disposing them towards a more favourable treatment of his co-religionists.[137] Blake was a Liberal in politics, and when the Tories came to power it appeared that his influence had come to an end. Before long, however, Dr Grey feared, with some reason, 'that Blake had got the ear of Eliot'.[138]

On the bequests issue he was early in the field. According to Murray, he drew up the bill which O'Connell presented in March 1844 to establish the Catholic bishops as a corporation sole, a solution he again put forward before the Select Committee on Mortmain in July 1844; he also wrote to Graham on modifications in the bill then passing through parliament.[139] His role during the rest of the parliamentary discussions is typically difficult to establish, but Cooper, a hostile critic, alleged that he

made over to London, and in his own characteristic way, wrote to 'his friend, Dr Murray', whose opinion, he not only previously knew, *but himself formed* and showing the letter about privately in answer approving the bill in all save the *three month* clause, changed the whole tone of the opposition into the weak, washy thing it became, half despair, half approbation.[140]

Cooper's account is plausible enough (although he disliked all that Blake stood for). The tactics which he attributed to Blake were similar to those which the latter had used on other occasions. When Heytesbury, following Graham's advice, invited him to see him, he too fell victim to Blake's charm: 'Nothing could be more satisfactory than the assurance he gave me of his earnest desire to smooth away all difficulties.' Blake revealed his political colours when agreeing with Heytesbury 'that we should have nothing to do with repealers and agitators'. They should consider the new board as 'a bond of union between the

[136] Cooper to Cullen, 22 Sept. 1844, Cullen Papers.
[137] MacHale to Peel, 24 Jan. 1845, *Letters*, p. 590.
[138] De Grey to Graham, 29 May 1842, Graham Papers.
[139] *Report from the Select Committee on Mortmain together with minutes of Evidence, PP 1844*, x. 177; Graham to Eliot, 6 July 1844, Graham Papers.
[140] Cooper to Cullen, 22 Sept. 1844, Cullen Papers.

Catholic Body and the executive'. Blake promised that nothing would be wanting on his part to induce Murray to cooperate. Blake, although at first unwilling, even agreed to become a commissioner himself on learning that Murray wished him to join the board.[141]

Despite Graham's pessimism, the government's plan was making progress, and the O'Connell banquet on 19 September (to which Murray merely sent a message of goodwill) was more than counterbalanced by a second visit paid to Heytesbury by the archbishop.[142] The law officers had meantime reported that although Blake's interpretation was not the one intended by Parliament, it was almost certainly the correct one, and Heytesbury assured Murray that the government would stand by it.[143] Murray, then, at Heytesbury's request, named acceptable Catholic commissioners, undertaking to contact the episcopal ones himself. All appeared settled, and Peel and Graham congratulated Heytesbury on the success of this first step in their Irish reform programme, Graham jubilantly commenting that 'it will go far to divide the Roman Catholic body and to establish amicable relations between the State and the sound portion of the Roman Catholic hierarchy and priesthood.'[144]

Graham's complacency was shattered by urgent news from Heytesbury which crossed with his own letter in the post.[145] On the morning of 21 September, the *Freeman's Journal* published the protest which MacHale had drawn up a month earlier. It now bore the signatures of an archbishop, twelve bishops, the administrator of a vacant see (appointed its bishop a few days later), seven hundred clergy, and many of the regular clergy. Other signatures continued to flow in, including the prestigious names of Cullen and Kirby, rector and vice-rector respectively of the Irish College in Rome. Although most of the bishops were from Connaught, bishops representing all four provinces had signed.

[141] Heytesbury to Graham, 17 Sept. 1844, Graham Papers.
[142] Heytesbury to Graham, 20 Sept. 1844, ibid.
[143] Smith to Heytesbury, 11 Sept. 1844; Heytesbury to Graham, 13 Sept. 1844, and enclosures, ibid; Peel to Graham, 9 Sept. 1844, Add. MSS 40450, ff. 150-1.
[144] Graham to Heytesbury, 22 Sept. 1844, Graham Papers.
[145] Heytesbury to Graham, 21 Sept. 1844, ibid.

The protest condemned not merely the mortmain implications of clause 16 but other sections too. Clause 15 laid down
that: 'nothing herein shall be construed to render lawful any
Donation ... in favour of any Religious Order ... prohibited by
an Act passed in the Tenth Year of King George the Fourth ...
or ... in favour of any Member...thereof.' Since some of the
commissioners would be Catholics, perhaps bishops, this
clause, the protest argued, would bind them to assist in putting
the penal clauses of the Emancipation Act into effect against
the regular clergy. Clause 6 stated that religious questions
arising within the commission should be referred to committees
of Protestants or Catholics, according as to whether the matter
was Protestant or Catholic: 'the Consideration of all Charitable
Donations ... in which any Question shall arise ... concerning
the Usages or Discipline of the Church of Rome, shall be
referred to a Committee ... consisting of those Commissioners
who profess the Roman Catholic Religion.' Although this
seemed a reasonable provision, the effect, the protesters alleged,
was to make commissioners who might be laymen, with 'neither
practical religion nor faith', the judges in matters of Catholic
discipline. The protest ended by uncovering what, it claimed,
were the real intentions of the government:

If the Board is to be composed of Bishops ... we must regard the novel project
of selecting Ministerial Favourites from the hierarchy as most calculated, at
once, to create division in our body ... and to ... destroy the confidence of
our faithful people who ... cannot fail of being alarmed at seeing them accept
place and patronage under the crown.[146]

Bitter though this final comment appeared, it was not groundless. If the government favoured some bishops, divisions within
the hierarchy might well follow, and a laity, resentful at
O'Connell's imprisonment, viewed with suspicion any collaboration of the bishops with the government. The sections
which the protest criticized could be read to bear the construc-
tions placed on them, but that such were not the intentions of
the government in introducing the measure had been shown by
their readiness to accept amendments. Distrust of the government was the root of the problem. The protest transformed
the subsequent history of the controversy. Because of its divisive

[146] *Freeman's Journal*, 21 Sept. 1844.

origin, its violent tone, and its undoubted success, it polarized attitudes within the hierarchy. By stating the case so strongly and so publicly and by antagonizing the archbishop of Dublin, MacHale may well have prevented a compromise solution that would have been acceptable to all.

Murray, who had earlier affected to ignore the manifesto, could no longer remain untouched by a protest signed by so many of his colleagues. Blake, who believed that MacHale and Higgins, though not O'Connell, were responsible, described the archbishop as 'exceedingly nervous' as a result of the protest. It now remained to be seen what effect it would have on the two prelates whom Murray was trying to induce to join him on the new board.[147] He had written to Haly assuring him that the act was not the unmixed evil its opponents made it out to be and that, under proper management, it could be turned to good account. Haly, normally a supporter of Murray, his metropolitan, had been impressed by O'Connell's opinion, but he now accepted Murray's assurances and criticized the protesters: 'the same clamour was raised against the ... system of National Education and with one or two exceptions, by the same individuals.' The protest had scared him, however, and, even before ending the letter, he had second thoughts. Underlining his words carefully, he begged Murray to wait to see if the storm would blow over: '*Perhaps it would seem better to your Grace not to act on this letter for a few days in order to see what influence this protest would have on the public mind. In its present exalted state* it may naturally be expected that current of feeling will run with violence against the bill.'[148] The following day a worried Haly again wrote to Murray to say that he would come to Dublin to see him on the matter.[149] The second bishop contacted by Murray was Crolly, and in view of his pleas to Murray to support the act, it seemed a mere matter of form to get his assent. Murray was both surprised and disappointed when a severely shaken primate warned him that it was not prudent for either of them to place themselves in opposition to 'Mr O'Connell, [and] a majority of the bishops and clergy'. He pointed out

[147] Heytesbury to Graham, 22 Sept. 1844, Graham Papers.
[148] Haly to Murray, 23 Sept. 1844; 24 Sept. 1844, Murray Papers.
[149] Haly to Murray, 24 Sept. 1844, Murray Papers.

that the protesters had put forward plausible reasons and incontrovertible facts: the exclusion of the regular clergy from the benefit of the act, clause 16, and possible Protestant interference with the bishops' authority. There lurked too, the dread 'that this measure may eventually prepare the way for a pension to the Catholic clergy'. Then, too, he feared that MacHale might take the matter further:

the prelates who have concocted the protest will forward it with the signatures of nearly all the clergy to Rome and ... the superiors of the regular clergy will endeavour to have it sanctioned by the Sacred Congregation ... The Catholic commissioners will be charged with the crime of executing a penal law against their brethren.

The result would be that the Catholic commissioners would lose the confidence of the clergy and people of Ireland, and 'the public press will exhibit them as the enemies of their religion and their country'.[150]

Blake, whose plea Crolly had also rejected, now urged Heytesbury to see Murray and Crolly, adding, however, that the 'chief exertions should be made at Rome, for which place Dr MacHale's emissaries were already *en route*'. He asked Heytesbury to hold over the appointment of commissioners until after the bishops' meeting. Heytesbury refused on the grounds that the Bequests Act was the first of a series of measures for Catholic relief, and they would accomplish nothing 'if we were to be paralysed at our first step ... by a refusal on the part of the leaders of the Catholic body to cooperate with us.'[151] Heytesbury, although disappointed, was determined not to abandon the field.[152] Graham voiced his anger against the 'protesting malcontents' and resolved to expose Murray and the secret negotiations in order to vindicate the good intentions of the government and to reveal the 'factiousness' of the bishops.[153] Although Peel shared his exasperation, he remained cooler and more hopeful.[154] Much now depended on Murray's reaction. Blake spoke of 'the state of nervous excitement into which Dr Murray was thrown by these proceedings, and his

[150] Crolly to Murray, 23 Sept. 1844, Murray Papers.
[151] Heytesbury to Graham, 24 Sept. 1844, Graham Papers.
[152] Heytesbury to Graham, 21, 22, 24 Sept., ibid.
[153] Graham to Peel, 24 Sept. 1844, Add. MSS 40450, ff. 180-1.
[154] Peel to Graham, 25 Sept. 1844, Add. MSS 40450, ff. 189-91.

embarrassment how to act or what to decide.' His 'nervous state' was, Blake added, much increased by finding that several priests of his own diocese had signed the protest—a fact which proved 'that Dr MacHale was gaining ground upon him'.[155] Some, like Cooper and Fr Mathew Flanagan, the parish priest of Francis Street, had gone further and had publicly condemned the act which their archbishop supported.[156]

Murray now faced a difficult choice. If he, like Crolly, withdrew his support it would mean the failure of the government's reform measure; general boycott by the bishops and clergy would effectively frustrate the new law. Such a move would have far-reaching consequences. It is difficult to see how the further Catholic reforms of the government—Maynooth and academical education—could have been successfully introduced without some degree of established co-operation from the clergy. Peel's and Graham's cherished plan of creating or strengthening a moderate party, to wean away support from O'Connell, would receive a fatal blow. If, on the other hand, Murray continued his support, the probable consequences had been spelt out by Crolly: the majority of the bishops, O'Connell, and the regular clergy would oppose him; they would appeal to Rome to have the law condemned; Murray would lose the confidence of clergy and people and would be denounced by the popular press as the enemy of faith and fatherland. Disunity, the great crime in the eyes of Catholics, would spread throughout the church in Ireland.

Murray, believing the act, although bungled, to be a good one, had already committed himself on the general principle, and had asked for and received assurances from the government on the most offending clause. It would have been wiser, as Cooper acutely observed, to say that such approval was his own opinion and that the other bishops should be consulted.[157] Having made a commitment, however, he was reluctant to withdraw, even without the knowledge that Peel and Graham were contemplating making his secret negotiations public. At

---

[155] Heytesbury to Graham, 24 Sept. 1844, PRO FO 43/48.

[156] *Tablet*, 24, 31 Aug. 1844; Mathew Flanagan (d. 1856), born in Smithfield, Dublin; educated at Maynooth; curate at Saint Catherine's, Meath Street; parish priest of Saint Nicholas' Without, Francis Street.

[157] Cooper to Cullen, 2 Oct. 1844, Cullen Papers.

that moment came the protest to complicate matters further and, in Murray's view, it was its publication that made unified action impossible.[158] The personal affront he felt at the manner of its composition no doubt influenced his decision to ignore the protest. There was another characteristic in Murray's general attitude that was not shared by all his fellow-Catholics. Like his friend Doyle, he had a deep respect for the enactments of Parliament as the law of the land, whereas many of his fellow-countrymen, active for so long in agitation, believed in protesting and campaigning in order to wrest a better deal from the government. Murray's previous achievement on the national education issue in turning defeat into victory, his scorn for the dubious way in which the bishops' signatures to the protest had been obtained and the high esteem in which the majority of bishops had always held him gave him reason to believe that he could again carry them with him and, if need be, deflect a Roman condemnation. One of the difficulties of the situation was that the bishops met only once a year, and there was no formal way in which he could consult the other bishops except by the unsatisfactory means of writing. In his own diocese, he had in his council, according to Cooper, 'no clergyman of independent thought ... they are echoes and no more'.[159] Professional jealously may have influenced this judgement, but Cooper was probably right in further alleging that Murray's principal adviser was Blake, with whom he had worked for so long on the national education commission.[160] It was Blake who now urged the lord lieutenant to see Murray again, and the meeting took place on 25 September.

Murray, to Heytesbury's delight, was 'in a much stouter frame of mind' than he had expected, revealed to him the way the protest had been contrived, his own indignation with MacHale, and promised his continuing support. Murray was hopeful, too, about winning over Crolly and Haly, assuring Heytesbury that many bishops were favourable and that the laity were so 'almost to a man'.[161] Murray was over-sanguine, or ill-informed. No layman came out in favour of the act, and

[158] Murray to Cullen, 1 Oct. 1844, ibid.
[159] Cooper to Cullen, 2 Oct. 1844, ibid.
[160] Cooper to Cullen, 25 Sept. 1844, ibid.
[161] Heytesbury to Graham, 25 Sept. 1844, Graham Papers.

Crolly refused to budge. With an admirable respect for episcopal solidarity, he told Murray of his unwillingness 'to oppose the majority of my brethren ... even when my own private opinion differs from that which they agree in holding.' As he asked Murray, 'if the majority of our brethren would be dissatisfied with us what good could we accomplish?'[162] Crolly, concerned about the unity of the church and his responsibility as primate, was also afraid of opposing both MacHale and O'Connell. Heytesbury, who had his own domestic problems (Lady Heytesbury was dying), was left in a 'perplexing position' by Crolly's refusal. Eliot's return to Dublin came as a relief to him.[163] During the fortnight of Lady Heytesbury's final illness, Eliot managed the negotiations; and the good relations he had built up with Blake, Murray, and Crolly stood him in good stead. On the morning after his arrival, Eliot met Heytesbury and Blake to plan their next move.[164]

Blake had composed a letter answering satisfactorily the three objections found in the protest. He explained clause 16 on the general policy lines of mortmain. He contended that the religious orders were left exactly as they were before the act. Finally, he claimed that there would be no interference in church affairs, for the duties of the board were to be purely administrative.[165] Inspired probably by Murray, he rendered the government an even greater service. He told the ministers of the 1840 memorial, in which the bishops had asked for far less than was now being offered them, and even told them that the memorial had been filed away in the archives of the Board of Charitable Bequests. Eliot confessed to Graham that had not Murray and Blake 'told us where the document was we should have remained in ignorance of its existence.'[166] The document delighted the government. Graham saw it as proof of the factious nature of the opposition.[167] Peel used it as an illustration of the motives which induced the prelates to denounce a useful law

[162] Crolly to Murray, 28 Sept. 1844, Murray Papers.

[163] Heytesbury to Graham, 27 Sept. 1844, Graham Papers.

[164] Eliot to Graham, 29 Sept. 1844, ibid.

[165] Blake to Heytesbury, 27 Sept. 1844, Add. MSS 40450, ff. 209-10.

[166] Eliot to Graham, 3 Oct. 1844, Add. MSS 40450, ff. 223-5.

[167] Graham to Peel, 5 Oct. 1844; Add. MSS 40450, ff. 231-2, Peel to Graham, 4 Oct. 1844, Add. MSS 40450, ff. 229-30; Peel to Aberdeen, 4 Oct. 1844, Add. MSS 40454, ff. 274-5.

favourable to their church—'a good test of the real character of their present conscientious scruples', as he remarked sarcastically.[168]

Blake now advised that Eliot, since he was friendly with Crolly, should write to the latter using Blake's arguments and should remind him of the 1840 memorial.[169] Eliot's explanations almost convinced Crolly that the protesters' objections were founded on misconceptions, but he prudently refused to join the board, asking instead that the appointments be deferred until after the bishops' meeting in November.[170] Eliot, after consulting Murray and Blake, advised acceding to this request and Graham, reversing Heytesbury's earlier decision, agreed to it lest negotiation be endangered. Eliot informed Crolly that the government would defer the appointments, reaffirmed his pledge concerning religious orders and gave the law officers' opinion that a will charging lands to their full value with charitable bequests would be valid, even if made within three months of the testator's death.[171] Crolly, while accepting Eliot's assurances graciously, now raised some further minor difficulties.[172] In this state of balance the negotiations rested.

If the news from Armagh was unsatisfactory, the news from Cashel was even more so. In a letter to Slattery which sheds light on his own outlook, Murray argued that the bishops should try to get the best bargain they could and that the act, though imperfect, met most of the demands of the 1840 memorial. Since it was merely the first part of a whole programme of reform, particularly in education, in which the church was deeply concerned, it would be folly, he believed, to rebuff the government at this stage: 'If the bishops turn away from them [the government] there is no knowing what course they may adopt.'[173] This realistic approach to the relations between church and state was rejected by Slattery, who instead expressed surprise that Murray, who in August had opposed the act, should now support it.[174] Another influential bishop, Kinsella,

[168] Peel to Heytesbury, 4 Oct. 1844, Add. MSS 40479, ff. 82-3.
[169] Heytesbury to Graham, 29 Sept. 1844, Add. MSS 40450 ff. 207-8; Eliot to Graham, 29 Sept. 1844, Graham Papers; Eliot to Crolly, 30 Sept. 1844, ibid.
[170] Crolly to Eliot, 4 Oct. 1844, ibid.
[171] Eliot to Crolly, 12 Oct. 1844, ibid.
[172] Crolly to Eliot, 14 Oct. 1844, ibid.
[173] Murray to Slattery, 1 Oct. 1844, Slattery Papers.
[174] Murray to Slattery, 1, 3, 5 Oct. 1844, ibid.

took a moderate line but, as on the Repeal question, he refused to commit himself. In a letter to Murray, which the archbishop communicated to Eliot, Kinsella admitted that although the act might have been better, it did much more than the hierarchy had requested in the 1840 memorial. He would not scruple to become a commissioner, but he thought himself bound to defer to the decision of a large majority of the bishops. He trusted, however, that a fair description of the act would remove the bishops' objections, some of whom, he was convinced, had never even read it. Crolly, Kinsella complained, was a 'waverer', this not being the first time he had so hesitated. Kinsella, however, had little sympathy for the government. It had no great right to expect to find the bishops favourably disposed towards the act, for it had not even consulted them on it beforehand whereas it was standard practice to consult the leading persons on a measure that was to affect them.[175] Kinsella's letter strikes an affirmative note. The act, although not perfect, was a good one, and the main mistakes of the government arose from lack of consultation. This, then, was the situation in the middle of October. The government was desperately anxious to implement the act, for failure to do so would have meant a humiliation at the hands of the repealers, and would entail difficulties for their whole reform policy. Murray had stood firm despite the agitation. Haly had agreed half-heartedly to act with Murray, but since he was leaving the country, this was of little help. MacHale had gained a majority of bishops and clergy to his side. Crolly and Kinsella were sitting on the fence. All looked forward with hopes and fears to the meeting of the bishops in November.

Meanwhile neither side remained inactive. The Reverend Thaddeus O'Malley wrote ably in favour of the act but he was unpopular with his fellow priests, and his was an isolated voice.[176] The nationalist and Catholic press, where the issue

[175] Eliot to Graham, 16 Oct. 1844, Graham Papers.

[176] *Freeman's Journal*, 23 Sept. 1844, Thaddeus O'Malley (1796-1877), b. Garryowen, Co. Cork; advocate of a Poor Law, national education, Federalism and later Home Rule. He had been twice suspended from his priestly duties. The government, despite Rome's disapproval, had appointed him rector of the university of Malta but dismissed him as unsuitable after a year. Because of his suspensions, his acceptance of the rectorship and his liberal views on education (he had defended the French Université in its conflict with the hierarchy), O'Malley was in bad odour with many Catholics both in Ireland and in Rome.

was fought out, was overwhelmingly opposed to the act. *The Freeman's Journal, The Pilot, The Tablet,* and the *Dublin Evening Post* published numerous articles, leaders, and letters in support of MacHale's position, and the protest gathered momentum as it was republished week after week with supplemental lists of clergy who adhered to it.[177] The struggle was already broadening on to an international plane. Murray's friend and agent, Dr Nicholson, wrote to him from Paris advising him to seek the support of Mgr Fornari, the nuncio.[178] Cullen wrote from Rome encouraging MacHale and congratulating Cooper for coming out publicly against the act.[179] Even more important steps were being taken. Late on the evening of 16 October, an envoy from Her Majesty's government arrived in Rome to put the whole matter before the Holy See.[180]

An appeal to Rome by the act's adherents was first mooted, not by the government but by Blake. He had already warned Heytesbury that MacHale and Higgins had probably written to Rome and that, to counteract them, the main efforts of the government should be in Rome. They should send William Petre, an English Catholic, to the Holy See. Nor should the government lose any time, for Blake feared that MacHale's emissaries were already *en route*.[181] The government took up his idea with alacrity. Graham urged Peel that if they were ever to communicate with the Holy See, this was an occasion when the Roman Catholic hierarchy was divided on a question, partly temporal, partly ecclesiastical, and when it sought Rome's intervention on grounds that misrepresented the nature of the law and the intentions of the government.[182] Graham did not know who Petre was, but insisted that if there was no agent at Rome, a special one should now be sent. Future relations with the moderates among the Irish Catholics might depend on the result. The foreign secretary, Lord Aberdeen, was accompanying the queen in Scotland, and Graham expected nothing to be

---

[177] *Pilot*, 18 Oct. 1844, contains a fifth supplemental list.
[178] Nicholson to Murray, 7 Oct. 1844, Nicholson Papers, DDA. Raffaele Fornari (1788-1854), nuncio in Brussels, prefect of the Congregation of Studies; cardinal 1850; nuncio in Paris.
[179] Cullen to MacHale, 11 Sept. 1844, cited in Walsh, *O'Connell*, pp. 25-26.
[180] Petre to Aberdeen, 19 Oct. 1844, FO 43/38.
[181] Heytesbury to Graham, 22, 24 Sept. 1844, Graham Papers.
[182] Graham to Peel, 26 Sept. 1844, Add. MSS 40450, ff. 184-7.

done for a week.[183] He reckoned without the energy of Peel who, impressed by the cogency of the case for action and accustomed to intervene in the conduct of foreign policy, immediately directed Lord Canning, Aberdeen's deputy, to despatch Petre to Rome, and pressed the Irish administration to supply him with a complete dossier: a copy of the act, Blake's letter commenting on the protest, some of Heytesbury's correspondence and the 1840 memorial.[184] Blake and Murray supplied other useful pieces of information which were duly passed on to Petre: that Cullen was a MacHaleite, that the Congregation of Propaganda was largely pro-MacHale, but that the most influential person on Anglo-Irish affairs was the English Cardinal Acton, who could be expected to support the government.[185] Petre was expected to receive support, too, from Dr Haly who, according to Eliot, had set off for Rome to represent Murray's case. The government was well satisfied. It would be Petre's mission to show Lambruschini the groundless nature of MacHale's complaints to the Holy See, and, in doing so, to reveal the factiousness of many of the Irish bishops.

Much had happened in the twelve months since O'Connell's arrest. The progress of the Repeal movement had spurred Peel to accept and evolve the religious reforms which Eliot had long advocated. The encouragement of voluntary endowment of the clergy was a suitable beginning, and the bill for the reform of the law governing bequests was drawn up in a conciliatory fashion. As MacHale's successful protest showed, however, strong opposition existed in Ireland to the new measure. This was, in part, due to real flaws in the act, in part also to the hostility created by O'Connell's imprisonment and to distrust of the government's intentions which were correctly seen as an attempt to break up the nationalist movement. Murray's support proved vital for the government and to retain it, Heytesbury had accepted a restrictive interpretation of the mortmain provisions of the act. The importance Peel attached to the act was shown by his readiness to accept Blake's advice of

[183] Ibid.; Graham to Heytesbury, 27 Sept. 1844, Graham Papers.
[184] Peel to Graham, 29 Sept. 1844, Add. MSS 40450, ff. 203-4; 3 Oct. 1844, Add. MSS 40450, ff. 219-20; Peel to Heytesbury, 29 Sept. 1844, Add. MSS 40479, ff. 75-6.
[185] Eliot to Graham, 7 Oct. 1844, Graham Papers.

an appeal to the Holy See although this was technically a breach of *Praemunire*. The Bequests Act was far more important than its provisions appeared to warrant. It was Peel's initial attempt to enter into a working relationship with the Catholic bishops. If it were successful, it would open the way for the rest of the programme of conciliation and weaken the massive clerical support for O'Connell. If it failed, the government would be seriously embarrassed; the measure would have been rejected by the very people it was intended to conciliate. Peel's administration in Ireland would still be trapped within its narrow High-Tory and Protestant limits.

4

ROME AND IRELAND: APPEALS
AND CONTROVERSY

The government's decision to counteract any appeal which
MacHale might make to Rome brought a new factor into the
controversy. It remained to be seen how Rome would react and
what effect its reaction would have in Ireland. Since the summer, Pope Gregory had been acquainted with the bequests
measure. When the bill was passing through the House of
Lords, Cullen, indignant at Beaumont's remarks, had gone
straight to the pope with a translation of the bill, his own
'Osservazioni' or comments on it and a copy of the *Tablet* of
6 July containing Lucas's criticisms of Beaumont. The pope
assured him 'that he had never been consulted and that if he
were he could never have approved such a measure.'[1] It is
unlikely, however, that he retained an active interest in the
matter over the summer months.

The next approach to the pope was an indirect one by Mac-
Hale. At the end of August, he sent Cullen a document (probably O'Connell's opinion) which he considered most important:
'Translated into Italian it will give his Holiness a clear idea of
the penal tendency of the measure ... he will have to strengthen
the weak and to determine the wavering.'[2] The 'weak' and the
'wavering' whom MacHale wanted the pope to strengthen and
determine were his old episcopal adversaries—Murray and
Crolly. MacHale had moved early and was not going to content
himself with half-measures. Meanwhile Kirby had expressed
alarm at the new act, and Murray wrote to reassure both Cullen
and Kirby hoping, no doubt, to counter any unfavourable
comment circulating in Rome. Amendments had been made in

---

[1] Cullen to Murray, 24 Oct. 1844, Murray Papers. Nicholson confirmed that the
pope, at this early stage, disapproved of the three-month clause: Nicholson to Murray,
7 Oct. 1844, Murray Papers.

[2] MacHale to Cullen, 31 Aug. 1844, Cullen Papers.

the bill, he explained, and more were expected; even if the new board was far from what could be wished, it was better than 'the wholly Protestant and bigoted Board' which had the power of altering Catholic bequests from the intentions of the testators.[3] Such was not Cullen's view, who congratulated Mac-Hale on declaring such decided war against the act: 'Ireland is now all united and we might dictate our own conditions. It would be horrible to submit quietly to such a bill.'

Cullen also congratulated Cooper on his stand against the act assuring him of the unfavourable opinion entertained in Rome on the matter.[4] Cooper now gave Cullen his own detailed analysis of the situation in Dublin, where 'the most influential and respected of the Irish Prelacy has committed himself upon this subject and is working heaven and earth to gain over, among his order, adherents'. He laid the blame squarely at Blake's door:

What would you have men do, when a prelate, whose name and deservedly from former merits, is a host in itself, signified his approval. The Members of Parliament are not to be blamed. But that evil genius—whose extreme vanity prompts him on all occasions to go behind the door, and whisper in the Great Man's ear and recommend himself by the display of his influence over an amiable bishop—he it is that has so infatuated the poor archbishop as to make him give under his hand an approbation of what if left to himself, I am persuaded Dr Murray would as soon put his hand in the fire as approve it.

From his position in the pro-cathedral in Dublin, Cooper was well placed to observe the movements of the archbishop, Blake and the government, and he suspected further moves by them: 'Blake ... is proceeding to Rome and was closeted on Friday morning last for hours with our Archbishop no doubt arranging their plans and rehearsing arguments for Cardinals etc. ... And one of the most plausible intriguers that ever stood in shoe leather is being sent over with that view.' Cooper warned Cullen that an effort would be made to win him over for 'it is said that much to your credit you came to the rescue on a former occasion [the national education controversy] renouncing your previous opinions because you found them erroneous.' Cooper, the priest who had naïvely explained to Murray that

---

[3] Murray to Cullen, 7 Sept. 1844, ibid.
[4] Cullen to MacHale, 11 Sept. 1844, ibid.

at the Tara meeting he had remained 'on the outskirts of the crowd', was right in suspecting an appeal to Rome. His criticisms of the Bequests Bill, although marred by a certain narrowness, presented a well-constructed case. His distrust of the government, his nationalist outlook, and his assertive Catholicism were typical of those of a large section of the clergy of the day. Lamenting that 'some infatuation had stolen over the sentinels of the sanctuary' he furnished his own explanation as to why so wise and prudent a man as Murray should allow himself to be 'hoodwinked': 'years and years ago I perceived this amiable weakness in Dr Murray, that once he comes to form a friendship for a man—particularly a layman—he can see in him but perfection.'[5] His criticism rings true. Murray's reliance on Blake's advice helps to explain his tenacious adhesion to the new act.

Higgins, who wanted no Roman interference on Repeal, now made a strong plea for papal intervention on the present issue:

... if the Pope does not at once issue an *order* to each bishop in Ireland forbidding him to correspond with the English government on matters affecting directly or indirectly the Religion of the country without first obtaining the concurrence and opinions of his brother prelates, the presumption, indiscretion and dangerous weakness of a *few*, will bring an open division among bishops, priests and people, will give a barbarous triumph to our enemies and utterly ruin religion.

Higgins claimed that this was the opinion of the vast majority of the priests and bishops.[6] Cullen needed little encouragement, and only awaited the pope's return from Castel Gandolfo to put the matter before him.[7] The contrast between the various attitudes is instructive. Murray, as in the educational issue, saw the act, although imperfect, as substantially good and was willing to try to make it work. MacHale and Higgins were not merely intent on defeating the measure but determined to use papal authority to end all collaboration between Murray and the government. Cooper, just as opposed to the act, was anxious to avoid hurting the archbishop whom he esteemed, and saw

[5] Cooper to Cullen, 22 Sept. 1844, ibid.
[6] Higgins to Cullen, 23 Sept. 1844, ibid.
[7] Cullen to MacHale, 3 Oct. 1844, ibid.

Blake as his evil genius. Cullen, further removed from the scene, was less concerned with the personalities involved but was fiercely opposed to English intervention in the affairs of the Irish church.

There now occurred an incident which may well have finally spurred Fransoni to come to grips with the problem bequeathed to him by Lambruschini—the political involvement of the Irish clergy. Early in October he learnt that the priests and students of the Irish College intended to celebrate O'Connell's liberation both in their chapel and in other parts of the college. While politely expressing his disbelief in such rumours, Fransoni warned Cullen that such demonstrations would displease the pope, 'cui sta molto a cuore che gli Ecclesiastici si astengano da prender parte nelle cose Politiche'.[8] Four days after this incident, Fransoni wrote to Crolly on the whole question of the political involvement of the clergy, basing his letter on the newspaper clippings supplied by Lambruschini eight months previously. Fransoni first recalled his earlier letter of 1839. If matters now stood as reported in the newspapers ('*si ita esset*'), clerics had said things in church and at the meetings and banquets which showed that they were far from strangers to party politics and worldly affairs. Crolly should admonish any clerics, particularly bishops, who might swerve from the church's traditional conduct of proclaiming only the gospel and of inculcating submission to the state in temporal affairs.[9] Fransoni's letter is stronger in form than the document of 1839, but it is not on the same intellectual level as Lambruschini's reply to Metternich. It prudently refrained from passing any judgement either on the Repeal movement or on the right of the laity to support it. Its generality, its failure to examine the details of the complicated Irish situation, and the hypothetical note which the words '*si ita esset*' introduced, left the rescript open to differing interpretations. Nevertheless, it was a clear reprimand to the politically involved clergy. As mail from Rome took about two weeks to reach Ireland, this letter reached

[8] Fransoni to Cullen, 11 Oct. 1844, Murray Papers.

[9] Fransoni to Crolly, 15 Oct. 1844, Lettere e decreti della Sacra Congregazione e Biglietti di Monsignor Segretario, 1844, vol. 331, ff. 794-5. Nicholson attributed the sending of this letter to the influence of Fornari; Nicholson to Murray, 10 Feb. 1845. There is no evidence to support this claim.

Crolly in Drogheda early in November. It was kept a closely guarded secret until the meeting of the bishops a fortnight later.

At the very time that Fransoni dispatched this letter to Crolly, Lambruschini received a letter from an agent of the English government concerning a new cause of complaint it had with the Irish bishops. The government was hampered in its dealings with Rome by the absence of a resident ambassador there. Thomas Aubin, attaché of the Legation in Florence who acted as the government's agent in Rome, had died in May 1844, and in July, Aberdeen received an application for the post from William Thomas Petre.[10] Petre, a member of a well-known Essex Catholic family, was accepted for the post, having convinced Stratford Canning of his intimate acquaintance with Lambruschini and others in the Roman Court. Petre had left England on 21 September 1844, intending to spend a week or ten days in Paris, to travel to Florence to present himself to the Legation there, and to proceed to Rome. Scarcely a week had passed when Canning, pressed by Peel, sent an urgent messenger, with directions on the bequests issue, to seek him out in Paris.[11] Not finding him there, the messenger hurried on to Florence, only to find that he had not arrived. Petre had been held up for three days in Avignon as the coaches were full; he finally hired a carriage down the Rhone valley to Marseilles, and arrived in Florence late on the night of 13 October.[12] There he found Canning's letter awaiting him. Petre wasted no time; he wrote to the cardinal secretary requesting an immediate interview, and, travelling on, arrived in Rome late on the night of 16 October.[13] When he saw Lambruschini on 19 October, his instructions, though not yet complete, were 'to induce the Roman authorities to pause before deciding upon the *ex parte* statement which will have been made known to them by Dr MacHale and his agents.'[14] To his surprise, the cardinal assured him that this was the first he had heard of

---

[10] Petre to Aberdeen, 15 July 1844, Add. MSS 43151, ff. 204-5. William Thomas Petre (1796-1858); attaché at Florence and agent at Rome, 1844-53; youngest son of George William Petre and Maria, daughter of Philip Howard of Corby.

[11] Canning to Petre, 1 Oct. 1844, FO 43/38.

[12] Petre to Canning, 14 Oct. 1844, ibid.

[13] Petre to Canning, 19 Oct. 1844, FO 43/38.

[14] Canning to Petre, 1 Oct. 1844, ibid.

either the act or the protest.[15] Petre asked for another interview within a few days, when he would have a communication of the utmost importance from Her Majesty's government, and Lambruschini agreed to receive him again on 21 October. At this second interview, Lambruschini was able to tell Petre that he had read vaguely about the Protest in the papers, but had forgotten the details. Those details Petre was eager to supply, since he now had the Foreign Office's dossier on the matter. Of these documents, Blake's letter again proved its worth, for the cardinal seemed impressed by it, and by the fact that most Catholic MPs had supported the passage of the act in Parliament. But he again assured Petre on his word 'as an honest man, da galantuomo', that no attempt had been made to influence the Holy See on the matter. 'Siamo vergini' he repeated, assuring Petre that since 1839 several pastoral letters inculcating peace had been sent to Ireland. The Holy See had considered the Irish question in depth, and feared that if they did anything else, they would 'embitter instead of softening the animosities of parties, and in the end perhaps produce a schism'. Then the cardinal surprised Petre by saying that 'His Holiness is more than the Propaganda and ... I am more than the Propaganda'—a statement he repeated. Petre had never alluded to the Propaganda, but evidently the cardinal was perplexed by the sincerity of the Foreign Office's conviction that MacHale had already taken the matter to Rome. The matter was one for Propaganda, he told Petre, and he may have felt that the Congregation had received MacHale's protest and was working behind the scenes. Perhaps he may have resented Propaganda's failure to take steps to implement his own request made eight months earlier. One detects some pique at the extensive powers of the Red Pope. (The cardinal prefect of Propaganda was called the 'Papa Rosso' because of the powers he enjoyed. He was in charge of all Catholics of the oriental rite and of Catholics in all countries where there was not a Catholic government. This sphere included Great Britain, Ireland, most of the German states, Holland, Scandinavia,

---

[15] Petre to Canning, 21 Oct. 1844, ibid. The lack of knowledge evinced by Lambruschini is strange, in view of Cullen's and Nicholson's assertions that the pope knew of the provisions of the bill before its enactment.

the United States, and mission countries. Although Lambruschini was the cardinal secretary of state, this office did not
give him pre-eminence over the prefects of the other congregations. The decisions of all the Congregations had to be
approved by the pope, who did not attend their meetings.) On
this enigmatic note, the second interview closed.[16]

If Lambruschini was anxious to find out what was going on
in the Propaganda, so was Petre. His next visit was to Cardinal
Acton, who, as a member of that Congregation and a loyal
subject of Her Majesty, would be able to tell him.[17] To his
astonishment, Acton reacted with the same surprised lack of
knowledge as Lambruschini. Acton had just returned to Rome,
so he made enquiries. When Petre returned, he assured him
that no steps had been taken by the protesting bishops to bring
their case before Rome and that the matter was not even on the
agenda of the meeting of Propaganda scheduled for 18 November.[18] Petre now settled down to a game of waiting and watching:
suspecting that MacHale's agents would arrive at any moment
and convinced that the curia was waiting their arrival and that
of Dr Murray's agent, he scrutinized all suspicious visitors
from Ireland. Finally, Dr Haly arrived, but when Petre hastened
to meet him to co-ordinate plans a further surprise was in store
for him, for it turned out that the bishop had come to Rome on
other matters.[19] Petre kept pressing for an immediate decision,
but as week followed week, he came to believe that the curia
was afraid to come to a decision until it knew the outcome of
the Irish bishops' annual meeting. 'The government here', he
confided to Canning, 'rather fear the Irish clergy, who themselves boast of their being cisalpine in their notions, that is, as
regards discipline.'[20] He paid a visit to the Irish College and

[16] Petre to Aberdeen, 21 Oct. 1844, FO 43/38; Petre to Conygham, 20 Oct. 1844,
FO 43/55.

[17] Charles Januarius Acton(1803-47) born Naples; educated at Westminster,
Magdalene College, Cambridge, and the Academia Ecclesiastica in Rome; secretary
to Lambruschini at the nunciature in Paris; secretary to the congregation of the
Regulars, 1831-42; cardinal, 1842.

[18] Petre to Canning, 23, 28, 29 Oct; 1 Nov. 1844, FO 43/38.

[19] Petre to Canning, 24 Nov. 1844, FO 43/38.

[20] Ibid. Petre's letters of 24, 28, 29, 30 Nov., 2, 5, 7, 8 Dec. were written on
continuous pages and dispatched together. They were received at the Foreign Office
on 19 Dec.

told them there, rather officiously, that he was the representative of the British crown in Rome and that 'he was engaged in most important negotiations, which would soon terminate in a regular treaty' from which the Catholic church would derive great benefit in all the British dominions.[21] Unknowingly, in his vanity he was sowing seeds of trouble.[22]

Behind the scenes, there was more activity than Petre suspected. Lambruschini had brought the matter before the pope, who instructed Acton to prepare a full report. By 8 November, Acton was able to give the secretary for state an ample dossier, complete with Italian translations, comprising Petre's documents, Cullen's 'Osservazioni' and the clauses in the 1829 Relief Act affecting the regular clergy. To these he had prefixed his own forty-page report. In this detailed report, Acton traced the history of the spoliation of the Catholic church in Ireland, the prohibition of its right to acquire property, the composition of the existing board for bequests, and its exorbitant powers of *cy-près*. He outlined the bishops' requests in their memorial of 1840 and showed how the government now claimed that they were meeting them. O'Connell's bill was far more generous, but Acton was realistic enough to doubt the likelihood of its being accepted, although he realized Catholic feeling on the matter:

È incerto se una proposizione di tale natura avrebbe potuto nei tempi presenti incontrare la maggioranza dei voti. Quello però che è certo si è che le speranze del Clero e dei Cattolici in Irlanda si accrebbero nell'aspettativa di vedere gli interessi della chiesa difesi nel Parlamento da un Oratore in cui riponevano la loro fiducia.

Then came O'Connell's trial and sentence, and Acton noted how ill-timed the government's action was: 'Il Ministero scelse, e bisogna confessarlo molto inopportunamente, l'epoca precisa in cui O'Connell era rinchiuso nel Castello di Dublino, per proporre il suo progetto di legge.'

This insensitivity as regards timing—an enduring weakness of Britain's Irish policies—sprang from an outlook which

[21] Cullen to Miley, 5 Dec. 1844, Cullen Papers.
[22] Petre, on an earlier occasion, told Conyngham of the Foreign Office that he would like to put on his uniform if presented to the pope, 'perhaps as attaché to the Legation'; Petre to Conyngham, 20 Oct. 1844, FO 43/55.

regarded the strict enforcement of law and order as the necessary preliminary to the granting of concessions. Acton explained
that the disadvantages of the new law were the three-month
clause, the position of the regular clergy, and the commissioners'
alleged powers of interference with the jurisdiction of the
bishops, but he also drew attention to a deeper problem: was
the new measure a snare to make the clergy dependent on the
state and to destroy the hierarchy's unity by favouring one
section as against the other? Still, in Acton's view, the measure
opened a way for the church to acquire property, and the
protesters were unrealistic in claiming that the government
would either alter the new law, or be unable to find substitute
commissioners if the bishops refused to go on the board. While
understanding the irritation of the protesters, Acton felt that
they were wrong to stir up the people; on the other hand, since
feelings were running high, it would be unwise to censure their
conduct. Significantly, he saw a parallel with the compromise
solution arrived at on the problem of the national schools.
Murray had been criticized on that occasion: 'L'effetto, però,
ha provato che la parte che hanno preso alcuni Prelati Cattolici
d'Irlanda nell'ingerenza delle dette scuole ha impedito che
cadessero esclusivamente nelle mani dei Protestanti, ed ha
servito per controbilanciare... i pericoli e gl'inconvenienti di
detto sistema'. Having made the point that Murray's policy
had been proved right in that earlier issue, Acton now recommended that his moderate line be again followed and that the
bishops take the places offered them on the new board:

...non vi può esser dubbio sulla espedienza della loro accettazione, che sarebbe
l'unico mezzo per riparare gl' inconvenienti che esistono da molto tempo, e
che la legge attuale non ha tolti, ma però assai diminuiti. Inoltre l'accettazione
d'impiego di Commissario per parte dei Vescovi non impedisce che la legge
non possa esser col tempo migliorata e resa più favorevole alla Chiesa.

Acton's practical conclusion was that the new law was an
improvement on the existing situation and there was nothing to
stop the bishops further improving it.[23] The report is impres-

---

[23] Acton to Lambruschini, 8 Nov. 1844, Archivio Storico, Sacra Congregazione
degli Affari Ecclesiastici Straordinari, Inghilterra, anno 1844, Pos. 46, fasc. 18,
piece 3, ff. 12-124. For a more complete description of this body of material, see
bibliography, p. 373. In future it will be cited as 'AA.EE.SS.'. For Cullen's 'Osservazioni', see p. 152.

sive both for its completeness and its accuracy. Acton was not blind to the government's underlying motives but believed that the church could extract some profit from a situation which he accepted as a *fait accompli*. Yet he understood well the strength of feeling in the country, and prudently advised the curia against condemning the majority of the bishops. Essentially, Acton's outlook was the same as that of Murray.

Acton's report quickly convinced Lambruschini that no time should be wasted before a meeting was held, and the secretary of his Congregation, Carlo Vizzardelli, set about preparing for one.[24] Vizzardelli was careful to invite Cardinal Bianchi, the prefect of the Congregation concerned with regular clergy.[25] Noting Acton's point about the parallel with the national education question, he discussed the matter with Brunelli, the secretary of Propaganda, and borrowed from him the file on that earlier controversy. To all this documentation, which he had printed and circulated, Vizzardelli added his own brief summary of the question. This included a useful scrap of information which he had just picked up from *L'Ami de la Religion*—that the Irish bishops were at that moment meeting in Dublin to discuss the whole question. At the end of his paper, Vizzardelli, in traditional style, formulated the two *dubbii* which the cardinals were expected to solve at the meeting:[26] 'se, e come convenga che si agisca per parte della Santa Sede in proposito della nuova Legge ...? cosa, e in che moda convenga rispondere al Governo Inglese ossia al Signor Petre?'

In the early afternoon of 24 November, seven cardinals— Lambruschini, Fransoni, Acton, Bianchi, Castracane, Polidori, and Mai—met in the secretary for state's office in the Palace of the Consulta on the Quirinal hill to resolve Vizzardelli's *dubbii*. They studied the background to the question and the success of the compromise solution on national education. One cardinal

[24] AA.EE.SS., fasc. 18, piece 5, ff. 8-11. Carlo Vizzardelli (1791-1851), secretary of AA.EE.SS., 1843; cardinal 1848 and prefect of the Congregation of Studies, 1848; mainly responsible for concordat with Tuscany, 1848-51.

[25] Vizzardelli to Bianchi, 20 Nov. 1844, AA.EE.SS., fasc. 19, piece 6, f. 8.

[26] Ibid., fasc. 18, piece 4, ff. 125-6; fasc. 19, piece 5, ff. 2-7. *L'Ami de la Religion* was a thrice-weekly Catholic paper published in Paris. It frequently contained accurate information on Ireland, and followed the bequests, Maynooth, and colleges questions closely.

asked for prior assurance from the government that the regular clergy would not be disadvantaged, and that Catholics would not have to involve themselves in Protestant trusts, or vice versa. Another cardinal, however, emphasized the desirability of not irritating England, since she could do great harm to the Catholic religion throughout her colonies. In general, opinion was suspicious of the whole thrust of the new law:

> prevalse in contrario un rifletto dedotto dalla indole primaria e dallo scopo della Legge in discorso, la quale tende in ultimo ad assoggettare al Governo Britannico le future temporalità della chiesa d'Irlanda e con ciò cominciare a togliere alla stessa chiesa quella indipendenza, che in mezzo alle passate persecuzioni, sempre ha essa conservata...

The lack of trust in the government's declared intentions which both Acton and the Congregation evinced is noteworthy; they feared that the government's motive was to destroy the independence of the Irish church. Roman prudence finally prevailed, and they decided not to take any definitive decision since they were not bound to do so and had not been consulted by the Irish hierarchy: 'quando niuno dei Vescovi Irlandesi avea su di esso fatto ricorso alla Sede non si conoscesse fin qui cosa essi stessi avesso [avessero] risoluto nella sopra indicata loro riunione in Dublino'. Although Lambruschini seemed in favour of informing *'dolcemente'* the bishops of their mistake, the meeting decided to defer doing so. To Vizzardelli's first *dubbio,* then, it was decided: 'Dilatta, cioé che per ora si debba differire di dare in proposito veruna instruzione ai Vescovi d'Irlanda'. As to the second dubbio it was decided to tell Petre that since the bishops had not consulted the Holy See, it would not be expedient to intervene but that if they did consult later the curia would counsel moderation:

> Respondendum, non expedire ut Sancta Sedes interveniat cum adhuc Episcopi eam non consuluerint: ceterum si deinde Episcopi scribant, Sancta Sedes dabit eisdem consilia pacifica = con intelligenza che questa riposta si concepisca nei termini i più ufficiosi; e si dia poi in scritto (senza firma) per non avventurarla alle alterazioni troppo facili nelle communicazioni verbali.[27]

This should have been the end of the discussion, but after the meeting two cardinals (possibly Lambruschini and Acton)

---

[27] Ibid., fasc. 21, piece 9, ff. 4-16. The account of the meeting is handwritten, with many erasures, and is not easy to decipher.

expressed reservations about the decision, or rather the lack of one. They had kept the English government waiting for months and now the reply was to be neither yes nor no; and they rightly pointed out that the government would see in it a ruse. The secretary was ordered to bring those observations to the attention of the pope when presenting the meeting's findings. The pope approved the findings, and Vizzardelli drew up a reply to Petre which Lambruschini, after papal approval of its contents, delivered to the special agent on 29 November 1844.[28] The letter thanked the government for the consideration it had shown to Catholics as evinced in the act. Some of the act's provisions, however, were not in keeping with canon law. On two important questions, the letter expressed the hope that the government would reassure the Irish bishops: that the religious orders would not suffer as a result of the law, and that the Protestant commissioners would not interfere with Catholic trusts. Drawing attention to the bishops' meeting on 12 November, Lambruschini told Petre that: 'Il risultato di questa loro deliberazione farà quindi conoscere se abbiano altri ragioni per cooperare o non cooperare alla esecuzione della legge.' Lambruschini was certainly not committing the Holy See overmuch. He did, however, reassure Petre that the Roman court had no communication with anyone but him, and when the agent anxiously enquired about the report that the pope had condemned the measure, the cardinal brushed this aside as no more than the 'usual babble of the newspapers'.[29]

In view of what we have seen, the success of the government's effort to win over the Holy See can now be better evaluated. The hitherto unutilized files of the Congregation for Extraordinary Ecclesiastical Affairs show how well informed the curia was on Irish affairs in general and on the implications of this apparently unimportant Bequests Act. Light is also thrown on the curia's method of decision-making. The carefulness of the examination, as borne out by the extent of the documentation and the comprehensiveness of the preparation, is impressive. It is also noteworthy that the cardinals' discussion focussed

[28] Ibid., ff. 13-15; piece 15 D. ii, ff. 99-100.
[29] Petre to Aberdeen, 29 Nov. 1844, FO 43/38.

on the central question of the liberty of the church in Ireland rather than on any immediate political gain. In deciding what course of action to follow, a prudent respect for Irish opinion was matched with a desire not to antagonize the English government. Although the decision was pragmatic, indeed evasive, reflecting the curia's customary caution, the government, nevertheless, had achieved its main object of preventing a Roman condemnation of the act, and had won instead a cautious approval of it. The protesting bishops had been shown in a factious light, but the Romans were more sympathetic to them than Graham would have hoped. Petre summed up accurately enough—if ungrammatically—what he thought would be the reaction of the Roman government:

> To disapprove of the protesting prelates nothing would I think ever induce this government nor would it support them in their opposition neither openly nor secretly; it knows and calculates how much is to be gained and, if consulted by the protesters, will recommend them to avoid strife among themselves, and to accept what has been given when not contrary to the canons of the church.[30]

When Petre's satisfactory dispatches were received by the government, so close had grown the relationship with Murray that Eliot asked Blake to take them to him.[31]

Murray needed some such encouragement, for events in Ireland had moved rapidly and dramatically since mid-October when Petre had begun his special mission. The success of the protest had shaken him, and he wrote to Cullen to counteract its possible effects in Rome. All it had achieved, he complained, was to proclaim to the world the disunity of the bishops. He left Cullen in no doubt as to his feelings on the deplorable manner in which the protest was concocted:

> ... if two or three bishops can, without imprudence, go into the diocese of another bishop, overlook the Ordinary, though residing almost next door and send circulars on a subject of general interest, to the absent bishops, calling on them, separately and without an opportunity of consulting with their brethren, to send answers, not to a bishop or a secretary of a bishop, but to a newspaper office for immediate publication, surely under such circumstances, union and general co-operation are not to be expected.

[30] Petre to Canning, 30 Nov. 1844, ibid.
[31] Eliot to Graham, 20 Dec. 1844, Graham Papers.

He was quick to underline the discrepancy between the opening words of the protest which read, 'having studied with attention the provisions of the act', and the well-known fact that many of the signatories had not had the opportunity to read the act. Brushing aside the usual criticisms of its provisions, Murray reminded Cullen of the 1840 memorial and added: 'Well, the government thought they were doing great things for us when they granted our request; but they did it in a bungling and unsatisfactory way, because they did not take the trouble of consulting us.' Even that lack of consultation he excused on the grounds that it might have involved difficult consultations with all religious bodies. Bungling though the government's effort was, Murray accepted its good intentions and, in any case, the act was now the law of the land.[32]

Before Cullen could comment on these explanations, his vice-rector, Kirby, made a public onslaught on the act, expressing the conviction that no Catholic could be found 'so vile, so perverse, and so dishonoured, as to join this horrid, this schismatical, this truly impious attempt to prostrate the liberties of the Church of God at the feet of its ancient and inveterate enemies.'[33] A fortnight later, Kirby wrote again warning that 'any Catholic who would attempt to perform the functions of the contemplated Charities Commission would render himself obnoxious to the severest penalties of the Church.'[34] Kirby used the superficial device of addressing both letters 'To the Lay Catholics who may be invited to act as members of the Charity Commission'. When Cullen made no attempt to disavow his vice-president, the usually mild-mannered Murray, in a rare outburst to Hamilton, bared his exasperation with both: 'Not one word about his distinguished vice-president. Has he no friend to beseech him to take some steps to save the character of his college from the disgrace that pious little fool is inflicting on it?'[35] Certainly, Kirby's 'startlingly strange lucubrations', as O'Malley unkindly described his comments, were a disappointment to some of the protesters. Edmund O'Reilly, professor of theology in Maynooth, a close friend of

[32] Murray to Cullen, 1 Oct. 1844, Cullen Papers.
[33] *Pilot*, 7 Oct. 1844.
[34] *Freeman's Journal*, 17 Oct. 1844.
[35] Murray to Hamilton, 20 Oct. 1844, Hamilton Papers, 1844, DDA.

Cullen and an opponent of the act, told Cullen that he 'did not meet any one who had a good word to say for *Kirby's letters* or himself as *connected with* them. They are treated as foolish productions.'[36] James Corr, a Dublin priest and friend of Kirby's, told him candidly that it would have been better if his letters had never appeared, since they 'seemed to me to be mere translation from some theological tract', and he suggested that Kirby had not read the bill.[37]

Cullen, however, was of the same mind as Kirby and was himself intent on winning over Murray. While accepting that the new board was an improvement on the old one, he argued that it infringed the rights of the bishops and might incur canonical censure. Then, counting on Murray's respect for the pope, he revealed his earlier action in translating the bill for Gregory, and the pope's assurance that he would never have approved of such a bill. Finally, Cullen placed the blame for the present *impasse* at the door of the government for deliberately omitting prior consultation. Now it was asking the bishops to rescue the act, even though in doing so they might shake their support among the people:

When such a storm had been raised, when such odium has been thrown on a measure, is it fair for the ministry to ask the Catholic prelates, whose powers and influence depend on the friendly feeling which passes between themselves and their flocks, to take on the task of carrying into effect so obnoxious an act and put public opinion at defiance?

Unity was Cullen's main plea, and he begged the bishops, if they were divided, to submit the case to the pope, hoping, no doubt, that Gregory would endorse the opinions he had put to him earlier.[38] Although Cullen put forward a number of canonical criticisms of the act, these showed a legalistic, indeed unrealistic, approach to the question; it was not to be expected that the English government should conform to all the niceties of canon law. His remarks about the lack of consultation had been the major ground of criticism since the bill had been first introduced into Parliament. His appeal for unity and for not

---

[36] E. J. O'Reilly to Cullen, 11 Dec. 1844, Cullen Papers; Edmund J. O'Reilly (1811-78), professor of dogmatic and moral theology at Maynooth College.

[37] James Corr to Kirby, 27 Jan. 1845, Kirby Papers.

[38] Cullen to Murray, 15, 20, 28 Oct. 1844, Murray Papers.

'scandalizing' the faithful is a moving one, but it did not con-
vince Murray whose only scruples, he told Cullen, were whether
bishops could with a safe conscience refuse office and thus
leave 'the treasury of the poor' in less trustworthy hands.[39]

Cullen's private pleas were strengthened by a public letter
from his uncle, Fr Maher. Writing from Rome, he made the
following amazing claim: 'The act is considered by all at Rome
as an infringement on the sacred rights of bishops ... destructive
of ecclesiastical discipline and a gross violation of natural rights.
There is no second opinion on the subject.'[40] Among a clergy
and people who looked so much to Rome for guidance in
spiritual matters, this claim was bound to make a deep impression. In view of the fact that the Holy See had given no
official opinion on the matter, it is difficult not to see it as other
than misleading. Certainly, to those who conscientiously
supported the act, this claim was calculated to bring doubt
and dismay. It could well have made Crolly waver again, and
cause other bishops to hesitate before taking on the united
opposition of popular opinion and Roman disapproval. For-
tunately for Murray, the letter, although written on 19 October,
did not appear in the press until 13 November, the second day
of the bishops' meeting. By that time, Crolly was able to produce his own more authoritative Roman document on clerical
political involvement, and all the participants were already
taking up positions on the bequests issue.

In the interval before the meeting the controversy grew more
violent. The Dublin correspondent of *The Times* remarked,
with some malicious glee, that in 'the want of some more
suitable field for the display of their ministerial avocations the
Roman Catholic clergy ... are ... engaged in a most unseemly,
if not disreputable, controversy respecting ... the Charitable
Bequests Bill.'[41] The *Freeman's Journal, The Pilot,* the *Dublin
Evening Post,* the *Monitor,* the *Tablet,* and the *Dublin Weekly
Register* all had regular articles and correspondence on the
subject, and the controversy spilled over into the *Morning
Chronicle* and *The Times.* The great mass of opinion expressed
was unfavourable to the act, and Murray's supporters were few

[39] Murray to Cullen, 31 Oct. 1844, Cullen Papers.
[40] *Pilot,* 13 Nov. 1844.
[41] *The Times,* 14 Nov. 1844.

in number. O'Malley had followed up his letters to the papers
by publishing a small pamphlet addressed to Crolly, which
reached a second edition in early November.[42] He argued the
matter very skilfully, pointing out the mistakes of O'Connell
and Cooper in their reading of the final text, but his support
was an embarrassment. Lucas in the *Tablet* made the point
strongly, indeed unfairly so:

THE REVEREND MR O'MALLEY HAS COME OUT IN ITS DEFENCE.
This move certainly cheers us ... He has tied about the neck of this Act the
millstone of his fame and no human help can save it from being drowned in
the depth of the sea ... If we were asked to state in the strongest and most
forcible manner the grounds of our hostility to this Act ... assuredly we know
not how we would fulfil it better than by saying shortly, that it is just such a
measure as the Rev. Mr O'Malley would approve.[43]

This was invective rather than argument, and it rebounded on
Lucas. O'Malley defended his reputation and called for
reasoned criticism, not personal abuse. A number of other
priests, some of whom were opposed to O'Malley, denounced
Lucas's unfair attack on the man and pointed out that O'Malley
was now an approved priest of the Dublin archdiocese, legitimately exercising his ministry there, whatever may have been
the so-called 'latitudinarian' opinions with which he had been
credited. Lucas withdrew, offered an ungracious apology, and
published an open letter to Murray asking him to decide the
reparation due.[44] Murray was annoyed at this clumsy effort
to embroil him. He told Hamilton that he had received a letter
from Lucas 'calling on me to give him for publication a letter,
either acquitting or condemning him for his attack on Mr
O'Malley. Does the man really think I am a fool? I will not
answer him.'[45]

Unfair though Lucas's comments were, there was some
ground for the suspicions entertained of O'Malley. A fortnight
after he published the second edition of his defence of the
Bequests Act, O'Malley wrote to Graham enquiring after the
job of secretary to the new board. Graham was pleased.
'Already', he commented with satisfaction, 'we have the priests

[42] *Charitable Bequests Act*, 4 Nov. 1844 (2nd edition), Murray Papers.
[43] *Tablet*, 5 Oct. 1844.
[44] *Tablet*, 12, 19 Oct. 1844.
[45] Murray to Hamilton, 20 Oct. 1844, Hamilton Papers, 1844, DDA.

soliciting favours and emoluments and looking to the Crown for the gratification of their hopes and ambitions.'[46] Graham and Heytesbury favoured appointing O'Malley, but when they consulted Murray, he demurred, considering him as not likely to add much to the popularity of the board. After consulting other bishops, Murray advised against the appointment since O'Malley was in bad odour at Rome.[47] The government then dropped O'Malley, but Graham told Heytesbury to offer him £200 out of the secret service money, and to convey to him 'that we were not unwilling to appoint him if the members of his own communion had not preferred another gentleman'.[48] The policy worked. O'Malley wrote again to Graham enclosing a note from Murray as a proof of how, 'by a trick', he had been deprived of the appointment. 'See what a bit of Roman Catholic patronage does in Ireland', Peel reflected, 'it obliges the man who gets it and engenders disunion between the disappointed and the Roman Catholic authorities who are supposed to influence the nomination.'[49] Graham was delighted that O'Malley 'acquits us of the "trick" but does not hesitate to accuse his ecclesiastical superiors', and echoing his leader's words, expressed the hope that this was 'the first fruits of a little State patronage for the first time conferred on the Roman Catholic clergy.'[50] O'Malley's complaints must be taken with reservations; a year earlier he had been convinced that he was wrongly deprived of the rectorship of the university of Malta.[51] Disappointed over the bequests board, O'Malley tried again, in Graham's words, 'to feather a nest for himself at Maynooth', and later again in the new colleges. His clear-sightedness so impressed Graham that he advised Heytesbury 'not to lose sight of Mr O'Malley and if from time to time he will consent to receive assistance from secret service money it ought not to be withheld.'[52] The episode reflects little credit on Graham; his

[46] Graham to Heytesbury, 19 Nov. 1844, Graham Papers.
[47] Heytesbury to Graham, 21, 24 Nov. 1844, ibid.
[48] Graham to Heytesbury 26 Nov. 1844, ibid.
[49] Peel to Graham, 18 Dec. 1844, Add. MSS 40450, ff. 412-13.
[50] Graham to Heytesbury, 19 Dec. 1844, Graham Papers.
[51] Stanley to O'Malley, 16 Jan., 1, 16 Feb, 6, 13 Mar., 4 Apr. 1843, Derby Papers, Box 175/2.
[52] Graham to Heytesbury, 13 Jan. 1845, Graham Papers. O'Malley refused to accept the secret service money.

readiness to use O'Malley was matched only by his inability to
realize how the appointment of an unpopular priest would
jeopardize the success of the government's policy of conciliating
the Catholics.

A new sharpness came into the controversy when another of
Murray's supporters, Fr Gregory Lynch, one of the curates at
Westland Row Church, wrote a letter to the *Freeman's Journal*
so violent that the editor refused to print it and it was published
instead in the *Dublin Monitor*. Lynch first castigated the 'Dominick Street conclave':

Who is there who had not heard of the coffee-room meeting? ... My witnesses
will be no other than the very Archbishop and the two or three other Prelates
whose bantling is the famous protest hatched and brought forth with all
honours in Coffey's hotel ... The venerable Archbishop of this diocese and
Primate of Ireland was not present, nor was he even invited to it, although
held at his own doors!!!

The protest was a 'popular delusion' and a 'monster'; some
names were forged, other signatories had not read the act, and
meddling ecclesiastics acting as 'jackalls' [*sic*] to bishops from
other dioceses went about extorting signatures. Lynch ended
up with swipes at Lucas, 'the slanderer of the Irish priest', and
at Kirby, 'the sub-prefect' of the Irish college.[53] This was hard
hitting indeed. William Walsh, bishop of Halifax, commented
humorously to Cullen that Lynch's 'virgin essay in the thorny
paths of newspaper theology is not much replete with maidenly
modesty', and hoped that the Lord would preserve both the
Irish church and Dr Kirby from 'this Lynch law'.[54] Cooper,
Lucas, and the bishops took no such light-hearted view of the
matter. Regardless of the fact that he was himself the chief
exponent of 'newspaper theology', MacHale warned that 'if
such persons are thus permitted to abuse the Prelates of Ireland
... uncensured by their superiors, you may soon expect to see
the venerable fabric of our National Church torn and the
stones of the sanctuary scattered over the land.'[55] Equally
appalled by Lynch's allegations of 'forgeries' and the savagery
of Lucas, Cooper appealed to Cullen for help against the
'cursed boons of an artful enemy' which were dividing the hier-

[53] *Dublin Monitor*, 25 Oct. 1844.
[54] Walsh to Cullen, 28 Oct. 1844, Cullen Papers.
[55] MacHale to Cullen, 26 Oct. 1844, ibid.

archy, and he gave his own interesting account of how those divisions originated:

Charity and unity of purpose or sentiment is gone from among our prelates since the unfortunate controversy on the Education Board. Faction and an ill-natured desire to thwart and overreach each other is ... the guiding principle of action among our superiors. But Dr. Murray leads one party among the bishops and Dr. MacHale leads another. And there they stand in front of each other like two hostile armies.

Mixed boards of Catholics and Protestants, which Cooper foresaw would come not merely for charities but also for Maynooth and the proposed colleges, were at the root of all the trouble, for their composition would be three-quarters Protestant and the rest 'milk and water Catholic':

There is a class of Catholic laymen here who are more to be dreaded in these questions than Protestants, and for this reason that their knowledge of our principles enables them to say what is the least amount of exemption from control and ecclesiastical freedom with which religion can contrive to hobble on—a contemptible cripple—to her end.

The person most blamed by Cooper among those 'milk and water Catholics' was Blake. He knew that Blake had been repeatedly closeted with the chief secretary, and what annoyed him most was that Blake was the friend and oracle of Dr Murray, who preferred his wishes to those of all the bishops and priests of Ireland: 'Think of a meddling ambitious layman having more influence through his episcopal friend than all the Irish church besides!' Cooper had earlier stigmatized MacHale's conduct during the national education question as haughty, imperious and over-bearing. This, in turn, generated sulking dislike in Murray. It was, however, galling to the other bishops that the affairs of the entire national church should be in the pocket of one prelate, or rather of one layman, 'a meddling, mischievous ambitious layman, choked with vanity and ever anxious to pare down the rights, privileges, and powers of the Church to the very lowest.' Cooper was aware of the importance of the gap between generations, and saw Murray's and Blake's policy as the 'timid, crouching policy of the last century'. He had been in favour of mixed boards during the national education dispute 'because it was then much', but he claimed, 'we have made giant strides in power since. The

Ministry *must* conciliate the Catholic church'. But though he believed that MacHale and his friends were right in the present dispute, he thought that their manner was wrong. 'How would Dr. MacHale like that three bishops should go to Tuam and from their conciliabulum there send him word through the penny post to follow in their track and send his submission to a public newspaper', Cooper indignantly asked.[56] His comments are not unjust. The division was between Catholics who supported compromise and cooperation with the government and those who saw such collaboration as weakness or betrayal. It was also true that Murray and those who thought like him were the last of a line of pre-Emancipation bishops in the mould of Troy and Curtis. The post-Emancipation bishops were in general to be far more uncompromising in their attitude to the government. Cooper's own support for an uncompromising stand on this issue did not blind him to MacHale's personal failings, failings which he was fair-minded enough to recognise as partly responsible for the dissension between the bishops.

The protest organized by MacHale had begun to produce a counter-reaction. As Eliot reported to Graham, a reaction had set in when it became known how it was drawn up: 'Dr Murray is much respected by them [the Catholics] and they are indignant at the manner in which he was treated by Dr. MacHale, and his friends.'[57] The Revd Paul Smithwick, a Dublin curate, publicly admitted that he had signed thinking that the protest had Murray's support; now he realized that it was drawn up in 'no friendly feeling' to Murray, and in defiance of courtesy, 'not to speak of the respect which his long and saintly career as head of the Irish church should demand from even an undisguised foe.'[58] From Maynooth, Edmund O'Reilly and Charles Russell remonstrated with Cullen for supporting it.[59] Russell added that he had every reason to believe that if the protest had not been published, there would not have been any difficulty in bringing the bishops to agree on a plan of objections to the bill which Murray meant to propose and a demand for a

[56] Cooper to Cullen, 2 Oct., 1844, ibid.
[57] Eliot to Graham, 12 Nov. 1844, Graham Papers.
[58] *The Times*, 14 Nov. 1844.
[59] O'Reilly to Cullen, 11 Dec. 1844; Russell to Cullen, 9 Nov. 1844, Cullen Papers.

modification of it. The protest had polarized the two tendencies within the church.

Although carefully following the controversy, the government, at this stage, was quietly awaiting news from Rome and the outcome of the bishops's meeting. The cabinet met on 19 and 22 November to discuss the questions of an increased grant to Maynooth College and of academical education for Ireland. The question of the Bequests Act, however, had to be brought to a successful conclusion before any firm steps could be taken on these further reforms and the government looked forward with anxiety to the coming meeting of the bishops. This meeting became the focal point for the hopes and fears of many parties in Ireland, Rome, and England. On Tuesday, 12 November, the bishops assembled in Murray's presbytery for what was to prove an eventful meeting. The accounts given by O'Reilly (MacHale's biographer), and by Lucas, on the one hand, and by Archbishop Walsh, Murray's vindicator, on the other, fail to provide an adequate description of what took place, and their summaries of the meeting's decision are not accurate. Lucas and O'Reilly claim that at the meeting a rescript from Rome was read. 'This rescript was adverse to the Act and favoured the opposition; and the Bishops were unanimous.'[60] Walsh, for his part, describes the rescript and the consequent unanimity as a 'fiction' and asserts: 'instead of protesting against the Act ... the bishops simply passed a Resolution in which, after referring to the difference of opinion to which the Act had given rise, they declared that each Bishop was *at perfect liberty* to act *according to the dictates of his own conscience* in reference to that measure.'[61] A Roman rescript was indeed read at the meeting, but this was Fransoni's letter to Crolly on the political involvement of the clergy. O'Reilly confused this rescript with Cullen's letter from Rome, then circulating, which claimed that opinion in Rome was opposed to the act. The bishops were unanimous in criticizing sections of the act, but O'Reilly is wrong when he claims that they were all adverse to the act in general. On the other hand, Walsh's assertion that the bishops simply passed a resolution leaving each one

---

[60] O'Reilly, *MacHale*, i. 572; Lucas, *Lucas*, i. 175.
[61] Walsh, 'Board of Bequests', *IER*, 3rd series, xiv (1895), 976; *O'Connell*, pp. 32-3.

free to support the act or to oppose it, is far too bland as an account of the meeting. The full story is more complex than either authority allows.

Twenty-two of the twenty-seven bishops were present.[62] Higgins and Crotty were ill, McNicholas and French were also absent. Haly, Cooper complained, 'seems to have purposely selected this moment for going to Rome'.[63] Early in the meeting (on Wednesday morning), Crolly produced his trump card—the letter from Fransoni. Anthony Blake (probably informed by Murray) reported to Heytesbury, that same evening, that the reading of the letter produced a 'very great sensation'. 'It is supposed', Heytesbury reported hopefully, 'it will induce many who were wavering, to abandon John of Tuam, and to rally around those of a moderate way of thinking.'[64] Heytesbury reckoned without the independent attitude of the bishops. The real sensation was not the production of the document but the fact that the unanimous resolution of the bishops accepting the document with 'respect, obedience and veneration' and pledging themselves 'to carry the Spirit thereof into effect', was proposed and seconded by Browne of Elphin and McNally, two of the most outspoken supporters of Repeal.[65] McNally, on the very next day, did not hesitate to write an open letter in favour of Repeal to the organizers of the Repeal banquet in Limerick; Browne, with MacHale, went straight from the bishops' meeting to speak at the same banquet.[66] Crolly's initiative had fallen flat, indeed it may have produced a further polarization of views if one is to judge from MacHale's account. It was, he claimed,

[a] document insidiously obtained for the purpose of crushing all discussion on this important, momentous, iniquitous act. It was a private letter addressed by the Cardinal-Prefect to the Primate containing vague complaints of some ecclesiastics and one or two bishops about intemperate speeches ... They were a repetition of the calumnies which our enemies often poured into the ears of the authorities and which, more than once, several of us have satisfactorily refuted. On this occasion it was evidently procured, nay extorted I am sure,

[62] *Pilot*, 15 Nov. 1844; *Dublin Monitor*, 15 Nov. 1844; *Nation*, 16 Nov. 1844.
[63] Cooper to Cullen, 18 Nov. 1844, Cullen Papers.
[64] Heytesbury to Graham, 13 Nov. 1844, Graham Papers.
[65] Meetings of the Irish bishops, 13 Nov. 1844, DDA.
[66] *Nation*, 23 Nov. 1844; see p. 180-1.

by a malicious and calumniating importunity for the purpose of awing the prelates ... The vague document has reference to neither time, place or person ...[67]

Although MacHale and his supporters were wrong in suspecting that Fransoni's letter was elicited for the purpose of stifling discussion on the bequests' issue, they were making it clear that they would brook no interference, even from Rome, with their own freedom of political action.

Blake of Dromore now attempted to read Cullen's letter giving some Roman views unfavourable to the Bequests Act, but Crolly ruled that this was contrary to the accepted procedure.[68] The protesters then tried to have Gregory Lynch condemned, and the minority countered by demanding that no bishop write on a matter thus pending until a synod be held. The protesters accepted but on condition that each bishop should pledge himself not to commit himself with the government on any question until he should have consulted the other members of the hierarchy. The result was stalemate, and both sides dropped their resolutions. By Thursday evening, Anthony Blake was forced to report that the bishops were equally divided, but that Crolly 'will throw his weight into Dr Murray's scale' and 'will read ... at the meeting the memorial of 1840'.[69] The debate became acrimonious and by Friday evening (15 November), Blake had to report regretfully that 'the noes (Mac-Haleites) will have it, but the ayes will not consider themselves bound by the decision.'[70] This last forecast was accurate, for MacHale obtained a clear majority of twelve to eight. To the twelve could be added three of the absentees (McNicholas, Higgins, and French) who had signed the protest. Slattery and McLaughlin, although they did not vote, were also opposed to the act. For practical purposes, the division then was seventeen bishops opposed to the act and eight in favour, subject to modifications, with two (Haly and Crotty) uncommitted.[71] A

[67] MacHale to Cullen, 17 Nov. 1844, Cullen Papers.
[68] Ibid; Blake to Cullen, 19 Nov. 1844, Cullen Papers.
[69] Eliot to Graham, 14 Nov. 1844, Graham Papers.
[70] Eliot to Graham, 15 Nov. 1844, ibid.
[71] *Nation*, 23 Nov. 1844. The list appears to be accurate, for the sentiments of all except Murphy, Crotty, and Haly can be verified elsewhere. Murphy usually supported Murray. Crotty appears to have been too infirm to travel (Crotty to Slattery, 17 Nov. 1845, Slattery Papers). According to Cooper, Haly usually sided with Murray,

comparison of the alignment of the bishops on this issue with their alignment on the national education problem four years earlier bring out several interesting points.[72] Crolly, Denvir, Kinsella, Murphy, Kennedy, Browne, and Ryan had supported Murray in 1839 and now four years later they supported him again. Five others who had supported him then—McGettigan, Blake, Egan, Slattery, and McLaughlin now took a different line (although the two latter abstained from voting). The new bishop of Clogher, Dr McNally, whose predecessor had supported Murray, supported MacHale. The division by province is also interesting. The seventeen bishops who opposed the act *in toto* were made up of seven from Tuam, six from Armagh, three from Cashel, and one from Dublin. The eight who accepted it, with modifications, comprised three from Armagh, three from Cashel, and two from Dublin.

Although MacHale had a majority, he had not won, for with a stubbornness again to be apparent in the colleges question, Murray and the minority refused to be bound by the majority —a fact of which MacHale bitterly complained when he wrote to Rome. Friday's discussions resulted in stalemate, and a final decision was postponed until after the archbishops had seen the lord lieutenant to ask for an increased grant for Maynooth College. At the meeting with Heytesbury and Eliot the following day, all went well until Heytesbury suggested changes concerning the trustees and visitors. When Murray agreed, a scene occurred which Heytesbury graphically described:

... up started John of Tuam and declared that he would consent to no alteration whatever and in saying so, he spoke in the names of the bishops assembled in convocation... I need not trouble you with any details of the amusing altercation that ensued between Drs. Murray and Crolly, on the one side, and Dr. MacHale, on the other, Dr. Slattery, the fourth Archbishop taking no part in the discussion though evidently leaning in favour of the former two ...[73]

---

but MacHale told Cullen that Haly had assured him that he was opposed to the measure, ever since he had read O'Connell's opinion. (MacHale to Cullen, 17 Nov. 1844, Cullen Papers). Haly's letter to Murray (see p. 142) showed him wavering and a later letter from the safe haven of Rome shows him as delighted to be released from his promise to serve on the board (Haly to Murray, 5 Dec. 1844, Murray Papers).

[72] Meetings of the Irish Bishops, 23 Jan. 1839, DDA.
[73] Heytesbury to Graham, 16 Nov. 1844, Graham Papers.

Although Heytesbury misjudged Slattery's attitude, the scene he described was an extraordinary one. The animosity that had been long building up between them had become so intense that even in the presence of the lord lieutenant and chief secretary, the bishops could no longer keep up the semblance of unity.

That evening a further meeting on the bequests issue was held, but this time some of the protesters were absent.[74] Crolly proposed and Egan seconded a resolution accepting the division of opinion as a fact: 'That as the prelates have taken different views of the new ... Act, it is the opinion of the meeting that every prelate be left at perfect liberty to act according to the dictates of his own conscience respecting that measure.'[75] Although the meeting made it clear that this resolution was not to be seen as approving the act in any way and stipulated that any bishop who felt opposed to the act could manifest his opposition to it in every legal, constitutional, and canonical way he pleased, the acceptance of the resolution was a tactical mistake on the part of the protesters, as Cooper noted bitterly.[76] That evening Blake sent an urgent note to Heytesbury to say that Crolly would act with Murray on the board.[77] The other bishop apparently recommended by Crolly was Kennedy of Killaloe, 'a very good and firm man'.[78] The split was complete and the protesters had suffered a setback. Cooper was crestfallen, while Lucas described the result as the 'triumph of the government over the Church in Ireland'.[79] In London, Graham was overjoyed at the division which the government's policy had already introduced within the ranks of the bishops and exulted with Heytesbury 'on the advantage of the position which we have ... won, when the heads of the Church, whose boasted strength is unity ... break out into unseemly conflict'. So pleased was he that he took the unusual step of forwarding Heytesbury's recent two letters to the queen remarking that

---

[74] Cantwell to O'Connell, *Pilot*, 15 Jan. 1845.
[75] Meetings of the Irish Bishops, 16 Nov. 1844, DDA.
[76] Cooper to Cullen, 20 Nov. 1844, Cullen Papers.
[77] Blake to Heytesbury, 16 Nov. 1844, Graham Papers.
[78] Heytesbury to Graham, 16 Nov. 1844, ibid.
[79] *Tablet*, 23 Nov. 1844.

the one which gives an account of the altercation between Roman Catholic Archbishops in the presence of the Lord Lieutenant is very curious. It proves to what an extent discord and disunion now prevail in the heart of the Roman Catholic hierarchy, whose strength has hitherto been their powerful combination and complete unity.[80]

The outcome was not as settled as Graham hoped. The angry protesters kept up a constant pressure. Letters poured in to Cullen asking him to use his influence in Rome to block the co-operation of the minority with the government.[81] MacHale complained bitterly not merely to Fransoni but directly to the pope of his colleagues' refusal to accept a majority verdict and of the division of the hierarchy.[82] A greater protagonist than MacHale now took up the cause. Towards the end of November, O'Connell, rested after the holiday in Derrynane, entered the controversy more actively than he had hitherto done.

Archbishop Walsh's study of the bequests controversy makes O'Connell the villain of the piece from beginning to end. His 'relentless opposition' as a political leader and as a leading lawyer is represented, in addition to the discontent in Ireland at his imprisonment, as the source of the bishops' and laity's opposition to the act.[83] A closer study of the episode shows that the chief opponents of the act were MacHale, Cantwell, Higgins, Cooper, and Cullen. Blake told Heytesbury that as regards the protest, he considered 'Dr MacHale and Dr Higgins to be at the bottom of the proceeding ... There was a strong political feeling in this matter, though he had reason to know that as far as O'Connell himself was concerned he was anxious to keep well with Dr Murray.'[84] This attitude of O'Connell is in keeping with the position he adopted during the national education controversy when, despite his dependence on Mac-Hale's support for his Precursor Society, he refused to be drawn into the controversy between the two archbishops, telling

---

[80] Graham to Heytesbury, 19 Nov. 1844; Graham to the Queen, 19 Nov. 1844, Graham Papers.

[81] Cooper to Cullen, 18 Nov., 20 Nov.; Battersby to Cullen, Nov.; 1844, Cullen Papers.

[82] MacHale to Fransoni, 25 Nov. 1844, SC Irlanda, vol. 28, ff. 347-9 Propaganda Fide Archives; MacHale to Pope Gregory, 25 Nov. 1844, Archivio Storico, AA. EE.SS. fasc. 21 piece 15B, ff. 91-2 (copy).

[83] Walsh, O'Connell, pp. 16-23.

[84] Heytesbury to Graham, 22 Sept. 1844, Graham Papers.

Fitzpatrick that 'I would rather cut off my right arm than show any disrespect to Dr Murray, a prelate who above all living men, I venerate.'[85] In the early stages of the bequests' controversy, Murray blamed MacHale but not O'Connell, and towards the end, Dr Walsh of Halifax largely exonerated O'Connell who, he believed, was under heavy pressure from MacHale and Cantwell.[86]

O'Connell certainly opposed the act; he wrote articles against it during his imprisonment and in answer to Bishop Cantwell, he delivered his very influential legal opinion against it.[87] During the months of July, August, and September, O'Connell had weightier matters on his mind: his imprisonment and successful appeal, his political perplexity, and unsuccessful flirtation with federalism. He claimed that he had 'long hesitated' before going into the bequests affair.[88] His hesitation was due, in part at least, to his anxiety to avoid dissension within his own ranks. Thomas Davis, the leader of the young Repealers associated with the stirring new weekly, the *Nation*, saw the act as a useful measure. He complained bitterly to Smith O'Brien, who was in charge of the Repeal Association during O'Connell's imprisonment, that O'Connell's son, John, had moved a vote of thanks to Dillon Browne without the consent of the Association's committee and did so because Browne opposed the Bequests Bill, which in its final form a majority of the committee approved.[89] Davis, a Protestant like O'Brien, was on the offensive against what he called 'a Browne and MacHale government' or any type of Catholic ascendancy. Smith O'Brien replied in a conciliatory fashion but pointed out that there was much in the new act calculated to awaken well-founded fears

[85] O'Connell to Fitzpatrick, 19 Nov. 1838, Fitzpatrick, *Correspondence*, ii. 160-1.

[86] Heytesbury to Graham, 25 Sept. 1844, Graham Papers; Walsh to Cullen, 10 Mar. 1845, Cullen Papers.

[87] *Pilot*, 26 Aug. 1844.

[88] *Tablet*, 7 Dec. 1844; O'Connell to Fitzpatrick, 12 Oct. 1844, Fitzpatrick, *Correspondence*, ii. 332.

[89] Davis to O'Brien, 20 Aug. 1844, Smith O'Brien Papers, NLI MS 434, no. 1291. For an account of the incident see, D. Gwynn, *O'Connell, Davis and the Colleges Bill* (1948), pp. 7-27. Thomas Davis (1814-45), co-founder of the *Nation*; a leader of the Young Irelanders; a cultural nationalist, he contributed poetry and articles to the *Nation*; William Smith O'Brien (1803-64). Protestant landlord, M. P. Ennis 1835-49, joined the Repeal Association 1843, leader of the Young Irelanders.

among the Catholics, and begged Davis not to lend the approval
of the *Nation* to the measure.[90] Smith O'Brien, however, took
a different line from O'Connell, and in October, O'Connell
had to request him thrice to delay publication of the Association's general report because he was unhappy with the section
on the act and wished to write the paragraph himself for, as
John O'Connell told Smith O'Brien, 'my father fears that as a
layman, you have not perceived the full nature of the case as a
lawyer would, with regard to the "Charitable Bequests Bill"'.[91]
O'Connell himself explained his request for delaying publication on the grounds that he wanted to know first how the
bishops would react:

> The Catholic Bishops meet on the subject of that act on the 12th inst ... I
> would wish their meeting were over before we published. We might easily
> give offence if we were to publish at this particular moment. What we say, or
> what we omit to say, may be taken in bad part. Our not more emphatically
> condemning the bill *may* be attributed to a bad motive, or at least to a desire to
> furnish an argument in its favour.[92]

This letter appears to have crossed with one from Smith O'Brien
expressing his annoyance at the delay. O'Connell still hoped
that O'Brien would wait until he came to Dublin on 20 November to discuss the matter, but he agreed that O'Brien
should omit the whole paragraph on the act.[93] This is what was
done.[94] Although O'Connell disagreed with the point of view of
O'Brien and Davis, he decided (in the interests of unity) to
keep the matter outside the scope of the Repeal Association,
as Davis wanted.[95]

The eventful bishops' meeting created a new situation.
O'Connell was being feted at a Repeal banquet in Limerick,
to which nine of the bishops had sent greetings, many proclaiming their political allegiance to the Liberator and some,
also, their condemnation of the Bequests Act. MacHale, with

---

[90] Davis to O'Brien, [n.d.] Smith O'Brien Papers, NLI MS 434, no. 1293.
[91] John O'Connell to O'Brien, 25 Oct. 1844, ibid., no. 1257.
[92] O'Connell to O'Brien, 9 Nov. 1844, ibid., no. 1273.
[93] John O'Connell to O'Brien, 10 Nov. 1844, ibid., no. 1275.
[94] There is no mention of the Charitable Bequests Act in the 500-page report.
[95] Charles Gavan Duffy, *Young Ireland*, (final revised edition 1896), ii. 166-7;
Gwynn, *O'Connell*, p. 45.

Browne, came straight from the meeting and in the course of his speech declared that:

When the clergy rarely mix in such secular assemblies as this evening, it is to calm not to inflame—to heal not to exasperate—to act as mediators of peace, and even, should agitation run high, to bring with them wherever they go the sacred spirit of God—to move over the troubled deep, and lay the rising elements ... The priesthood of Ireland know no sympathy with sedition ...

At the same time, he condemned 'the more recent and more fatal policy [of the state] in forging Penal fetters to have them fastened on by some of their own deluded members.' Browne echoed his sentiments insisting that 'my duty as a Christian minister and my loyalty as a subject of the crown, are not inconsistent with a desire for the political amelioration of my countrymen'.[96] MacHale, who told Cullen that this was the furthest he had ever travelled in the cause of Repeal, had another motive in coming: to tell O'Connell what had taken place at the bishops' meeting and, as some believed, to ask him 'to commence the crusade' against the 'pro-government' bishops.[97] For O'Connell, the Propaganda rescript came as most unwelcome news. As a politician, he feared that a ban on clerical activity would weaken his movement; as a convinced Catholic, he feared the consequences of a split between priests and people. His close friend, Miley, shed an interesting light on O'Connell's fears in informing Cullen:

So alarmed is he for the consequence to religion in Ireland should any further communications...be sent to rebuke and oppress the efforts of those who alone can sustain the faith and constancy of the oppressed and make head against an unprincipled, crafty and powerful enemy, that he is determined... to send you a letter on the subject for the Holy Father himself ... There is a latent suspicion with multitudes, especially of the imperfectly educated amongst young men of station and amongst the operatives of our towns and cities, that it is solely by accident the church does not happen to be martialled here as it has been too often in other countries on the side of despotism and against the people. Should any declaration, command or counsel corroborative of this suspicion arise out of present combinations, heaven look to us.[98]

---

[96] *Nation*, 23 Nov. 1844.

[97] MacHale to Cullen, 26 Nov. 1844; Cooper to Cullen, 20 Nov. 1844; Cantwell to Cullen, 20 Nov. 1844, Cullen Papers.

[98] Miley to Cullen, 23 Nov. 1844, ibid.

O'Connell's alarm was unfeigned. True to his policy for over a generation, O'Connell had no intention of allowing the government to snatch from his hand the most powerful ally he had nor to allow the state to extend its influence through the collaboration of friendly bishops. He saw in Propaganda's letter, and the willingness of Crolly and Murray to work on a government commission, the shadow of the veto once again. His fear was of a church manipulated and divided by the government, and this consideration (even more than his long-standing obligation to MacHale) made him now decide to enter the campaign against the act and the government's diplomatic activity at Rome and in Dublin. If he succeeded, he would humiliate the government that had so recently humiliated him and check its attempt to divide and rule. Even if he did not completely succeed, he would keep agitation and enthusiasm alive; he might frighten the pro-government bishops back into line and, in addition, make the Roman diplomats more cautious in dealing with Irish affairs.

O'Connell's first move was in keeping with his usual tactics. Great meetings were now held to protest against the act.[99] O'Connell himself set the tone in his speeches at a series of eight meetings from 3 to 19 December in different parts of Dublin. Similar meetings were held in Drogheda, Mullingar, Kells, Tuam, Cork, Longford, Londonderry, Waterford, Limerick, Dungannon, Tullamore, Loughrea, and other parts of the country. An alarmed Heytesbury, viewing the rising tide of opposition, reported that 'having defeated Dr. Mac-Hale, we shall have to fight the battle again with O'Connell', and he begged Graham to gazette the board immediately 'for O'Connell is straining every nerve to defeat our object and to intimidate the Roman Catholic bishops.'[100] He did not exaggerate. O'Connell's meetings aroused popular antagonism to fever pitch. At one Dublin meeting, O'Connell went over the familiar grounds of objection to the act: it brought all bequests into the 'greedy grasp' of the board, it robbed the religious of their property and (as Cullen had argued) it violated church law. The government was a 'No Popery administration'

---

[99] *Catholic Directory,* 1846, pp. 211-12.
[100] Heytesbury to Graham, 3 Dec. 1844, Graham Papers.

and *The Times*, its organ, had raised them to power by denouncing the Irish clergy as 'surpliced villains' and as a 'feloni-
ous, filthy multitude'. Was a Catholic bishop to go to the
Castle and say 'Fair Sir, you spit on me on Tueday last, on
Thursday you called me demon, and in return ... I'll be your
Commissioner?' Was there to be a distinction between 'loyal'
and 'disloyal' bishops? Subtly, he brought the people's mind
back to a previous contest. There had been a similar hesitation
by some bishops on the veto question thirty years before, until
at last 'the people cried out " we will have no Soggart Sassenagh
—we will have no Bishops made by an English Pope"', and
O'Connell, amid roars of approval, made his point clearer:
'People of Ireland, you have the same remedy now.'[101] O'Connell feared that through the collaboration of some bishops, the
government would gain indirect influence over the church,
thus dividing the clergy and undermining their whole-hearted
support for his movement.

The lay Catholics, now taking their cue from O'Connell,
vigorously petitioned the bishops to have nothing to do with the
Bequests Act. Letters poured into the papers, meetings were
held up and down the country protesting against the act.
Munster Catholics petitioned Crolly and Murray to imitate
Slattery's rejection of the law and not to play into the hands of
Peel, the arch-enemy, whose one idea was to bring the church
into his power. The Bequests Act would be followed by academical colleges and finally by payment of the clergy, 'and fare
well then to catholicity in Ireland'.[102] On the day on which
Heytesbury begged Graham to hasten the gazetting of the
board, Blake brought the alarming news of the first results of
this new campaign. The third episcopal commissioner, Kennedy
of Killaloe (whom Heytesbury had praised for being so firm),
'in his terror' at the agitation stirred up against him, was
showing signs of withdrawing. Heytesbury was shaken by the
possibility of this defection, fearing it might be only the first,
'knowing' he added, 'the timid nature of every man in the
Roman Catholic hierarchy, except Dr MacHale'.[103] Graham's

---

[101] *Tablet*, 7 Dec. 1844. 'Soggart Sassenagh' means English priest.

[102] Letter of Munster Catholics, 27 Nov. 1844, Murray Papers.

[103] Heytesbury to Graham, 3 Dec. 1844, Graham Papers. Second letter of same
date.

reaction was more optimistic. The possibility of Kennedy's defection was a serious annoyance, but shame, he thought, would restrain 'the better portion of the Roman Catholics' from succumbing in the face of day to O'Connell: 'We have succeeded in making, what O'Connell terms "a schism" among them, and if we proceed steadily and quietly, I believe that the Game is ours.'[104] Peel was more alarmed and advised the Irish administration to offer to clear up any remaining doubts, if necessary by an explanatory act; but if the archbishops should still show signs of back-tracking, Heytesbury should threaten to reveal all the negotiations and the 1840 memorial. 'I would try conciliation with them to the last ... but I certainly would not allow them basely to submit to the dictations of a mischievous demagogue without exposure'.[105]

The need for employing such 'counter-terror' methods, as Graham described Peel's threat, came closer when Bishop Kennedy, despite the pleas of Eliot and Blake, found the pressure too great in Killaloe. His letter to Crolly shows the force of the pressure which MacHale and O'Connell were able to bring to bear:

Having on my arrival at home, found that a violent storm had been raised against me on account of my acceptance of a place on the Board of Charitable Bequests; after having struggled in vain against it for several days, I found myself at length obliged to give way to it ... I, therefore, hereby resign into your Grace's hands my appointment, wishing with all my heart, that I never accepted it ... It is not, that my opinions on the Bill have been shaken ... but because of the unexpected presence of Dr MacHale at the Limerick Banquet ... and his foul insinuation in his speech on the occasion (and I was expected to attend it) created so violent a feeling against me throughout this and the neighbouring counties as I fear, will not speedily be removed.[106]

Heytesbury's anxious waiting for news was ended when O'Connell triumphantly announced at a public meeting that Kennedy had declined the appointment.[107] As Eliot reported to Graham, 'the screw has been applied in this case with success'.[108] Heytesbury was appalled, and although Blake was on his sick-

[104] Graham to Peel, 5 Dec. 1844, Add. MSS 40450, ff. 354-7.
[105] Peel to Graham, 6 Dec. 1844, ibid., ff. 364-7.
[106] Kennedy to Crolly, 7 Dec. 1844, Murray Papers.
[107] Heytesbury to Graham, 7 Dec. 1844, Graham Papers.
[108] Eliot to Graham, 8 Dec. 1844, Royal Archives, D14/57.

bed, he wrote to him imploring him, if he had any personal influence with Kennedy, to use it now. 'Surely' he pleaded, 'the clamour of individuals interested in preventing the establishment of amicable relations between the Roman Catholic Church and the State, ought not to be allowed to prevail against the true interests of the Church which are involved in the Charitable Bequests Bill?'[109] Blake was in no position to help. On the following day, however, Murray arrived in person at the vice-regal Lodge to see the much perplexed lord lieutenant and brought the answer to his plea. Foreseeing the imminent defection of Kennedy, Murray had moved swiftly and decisively. Supported by Crolly, he asked Denvir, bishop of Down and Connor, to take Kennedy's place. If Denvir refused, the archbishops were determined to call on Haly, although he was still in Rome.[110] Denvir agreed. All he reasonably asked was that the news should not be broken until after the opening of his new church in Belfast, when many of the bishops and clergy would be present at the ceremony.[111] His decision was not forgotten or forgiven. Three years later, Clarendon could still report popular hostility to Denvir for allowing himself to be won over by Crolly to support the hated act.[112]

Heytesbury and Graham readily agreed to have the gazetting so timed that while it should come out as soon as possible, it would arrive in Ireland too late to get to the ears of the clergy assembled in Belfast. Murray had pressed for a further assurance that in the event of the attorney general's opinion on the position of religious orders being incorrect, an amending act would be introduced. Heytesbury, 'most desirous of meeting the fair play of Archbishops Crolly and Murray in a similar spirit', agreed and anxiously asked Graham's approval for this exceptional promise. He need not have worried. Graham told him that the action of the archbishops relieved him 'from a load of anxiety', and that both he and Peel entirely approved of the promises given to Murray 'frankly and at once in return for his adherences to his engagement'. Graham, fearful of further

---

[109] Heytesbury to Blake, 9 Dec. 1844, Graham Papers.
[110] Crolly to Murray, 4 Dec. 1844, Murray Papers.
[111] Heytesbury to Graham, 9 Dec. 1844, Graham Papers.
[112] Clarendon's memorandum of 1 Oct. 1847, Clarendon Papers, letterbook 1, f. 68.

defections, added: 'I wish the next forty-eight hours well over and that the order in Council were secured'.[113] Certainly, the pressure on Murray was building up from many quarters. Slattery appealed to him in the interests of unity and harmony within the church, to withdraw from the commission.[114] Although Murray stood firm, Heytesbury reported that 'the clamour raised by O'Connell and John of Tuam against the Archbishops and their confidential interviews with the Castle, has made them timid and nervous.'[115] Crolly retired to his diocese, while Murray sent a message through Blake asking that some place other than Dublin Castle be found for the board's meetings. Although the existing board met in the Castle, 'Dr Murray fears and not without reason that in going to the Castle he will be exposed to hisses and insults most desirable to be avoided... "Subserviency to the Castle" is the watchword now raised against the Prelates.'[116]

If 'subserviency to the Castle' was one of the cries of the protesters, the other issue now coming to the fore was not less explosive: the position of the regular clergy under the act. The religious or regular clergy were small in number (about 54 in Dublin and 200 in the whole country). To these should be added the religious who were not priests—nuns and brothers whose outstanding work was educational and social. The regulars were influential in Rome and popular in Ireland. No pope, least of all a regular like Gregory himself, would lightly allow their position to be weakened, for they played a necessary role in maintaining the international character of the church and enjoyed age-old privileges. Shortly after the bishops' meeting, Murray came in alarm to Heytesbury to tell him that 'the religious orders ... are ... open-mouthed against the bishops for the decision to which they have come.'[117] They had taken a legal opinion, believed that the act placed them in an infinitely worse position with respect to bequests than previously and were preparing to send a memorial to Rome. The outcry was producing such an effect on the people that Murray urged the

[113] Graham to Heytesbury, 11 Dec. 1844, Graham Papers.
[114] Murray to Slattery, 10 Dec. 1844, Slattery Papers.'
[115] Heytesbury to Graham, 14 Dec. 1844, Graham Papers.
[116] Heytesbury to Graham, 16 Dec. 1844, ibid.
[117] Heytesbury to Graham, 21 Nov. 1844, ibid.

government to instruct Petre 'to do away with any wrong impression the religious orders might endeavour to give' in Rome. Aberdeen wrote immediately to Petre to that effect.[118]

The regulars had sought legal advice from O'Connell, who confirmed their fears. Before the new act was passed, although no religious order could take or enjoy property, nevertheless a single member could do so for the support of the whole order. Clause 15 of the act, O'Connell alleged, made this no longer possible, for it contained 'a distinct legislative declaration or definition and all our courts ... would consider themselves bound to act on that declaration.'[119] The worst feature of all was that the act would bring the Catholic commissioners into direct conflict with the regulars, for they would be obliged by law to sue for charitable property misapplied. In point of law, the property of the regulars was misapplied. Since Catholic bishops would be in a far better position than Protestant commissioners to know who the regulars were, it would be a grievous disadvantage to them if those bishops should become commissioners.[120]

Alarmed, the different orders met in Dublin on 4 December, and passed two resolutions condemning the act as 'a penal enactment against us', which would 'lead to the eventual suppression of the religious orders in Ireland', and appealing to their 'beloved Archbishop' to prevent this penal law from ever being passed into execution.[121] The provincials of the Jesuits, Dominicans, Carmelites, and Augustinians came in a body to Murray to voice their concern. Murray, realizing the gravity of the situation, had moved immediately after he had received O'Connell's opinion. He hurried to the vice-regal lodge, and received full reassurances from Heytesbury who undertook to submit a formal case to the law officers; if they should confirm O'Connell's adverse opinion, the act would be amended. Murray passed on this information to Fr John Spratt, who, no

---

[118] Graham to Aberdeen, 25 Nov. 1844; Aberdeen to Petre, 25 Nov. 1844, FO 43/38.

[119] The wording of the proviso runs: 'Provided always, that nothing herein contained shall be construed to render lawful any Donation, Devise or Bequest to or in favour of any Religious Order ... prohibited by ... the 1829 Emancipation Act... or to or in favour of any Member or Members thereof.'

[120] *Pilot*, 6 Dec. 1844.

[121] *Pilot*, 11 Dec. 1844.

doubt with Murray's approval, had it published in the press.[122] Although Eliot and Graham were taken aback at the publication of what they intended to be a confidential communication, they realized that 'the pressure on him [Murray] was very strong and he thought to diminish it by showing the ground on which he stood.'[123] Murray's letter did not completely reassure Spratt.[124] Later, he and all his community signed another protest against the act.[125]

Protests from the regulars were not confined to Dublin. In Cork, they denounced the act as 'strictly penal and embodying a most wanton and unprovoked aggression upon the civil and religious rights of the regular clergy.'[126] Crolly, from his cathedral town of Drogheda, wrote to Murray of 'a popular ferment occasioned by an outcry of the friars, who persuaded the poor people to believe that their properties and their lives were exposed to a direful persecution, and that I was pledged to co-operate with their enemies.' Crolly met both the Mayor of Drogheda and the regulars, and believed that he had removed their false impressions, but he added, 'the red-hot repealers openly declared that they would be guided by Mr O'Connell, whose opinion they preferred to that of any other person.'[127] Certainly, he had a difficult passage. Richard Bellew reported to Murray that 'the Primate looked worried. Sir Patrick Bellew said he [Crolly] is not as accustomed to the warfare as your grace'. Bellew described the emotional atmosphere at a meeting in Drogheda in terms that were probably typical of such meetings throughout the country:

---

[122] *Pilot,* 6 Dec. 1844; John Spratt (1797-1871), Provincial superior of the Irish Carmelites. He was a well-known social worker in Dublin and founded an orphanage, an asylum for the blind, and a night refuge. He also organized a temperance movement.

[123] Eliot to Graham, 6 Dec. 1844, Graham Papers, Graham to Peel, 8 Dec. 1844, Add. MSS 40450, ff. 374-5.

[124] *Pilot,* 11 Dec. 1844.

[125] *Pilot,* 15 Jan. 1845. The regulars were, in fact, afraid of being abandoned. They were very conscious of the hostility of the diocesan clergy manifested in the eighteenth century and as late as 1815, when they were forced to appeal to Rome for protection. They had been badly dealt with in the Emancipation Act. They now wanted more than verbal assurances. Possibly, their respect for Murray played a part in keeping their protest relatively moderate in Dublin.

[126] *Tablet,* 14 Dec. 1844.

[127] Crolly to Murray, 27 Dec. 1844, Murray Papers.

There was a very numerous meeting in Drogheda ... One of the friars preached to the people and said 'as to this new law, my good people, it is all against us—they can now drag us out by force and shoot us on the side of the ditch'—upon which all the old women set up a most doleful wurrah, wurrah. How would you like to see us murdered! Och, wurrah, wurrah![128]

Crolly may have explained his position well, but the newspapers reported that he promised to petition for the amendment of the act.[129] In Belfast, Denvir told a hostile meeting that he accepted the commission under the condition that the objectionable clauses would be so amended in the next session as to meet the approval of the Catholic hierarchy: if not, 'he for one would resign his office as commissioner'.[130] Some of the regulars had protested to Rome about the act, and the curia was taking no chances on the issue.[131] Lambruschini gracefully accepted Petre's assurances that no new restrictions were intended by the act, but two days later, he asked to have this assurance in writing and Petre was obliged to comply.[132] Still, Murray's point when he asked for Petre's intervention had been achieved. If the regulars made further representations in Rome, Lambruschini would be able to produce this document written on behalf of Her Majesty's government; this was precisely what he did when Fransoni questioned him on how to reply to Mac-Hale's complaints.[133]

Meanwhile, in London, the privy council met on Friday 13 December, the earliest possible moment after the obsequies of Princess Charlotte. Heytesbury had already requested that the gazetting be deferred so as not to become public in Ireland before the following Tuesday; alarmed by O'Connell's campaign, he now implored Graham to gazette the board in London as well as in Dublin. His letter gives an idea of the state of near-panic in the Vice-Regal Lodge:

The outcry against the Act is still so violent and the efforts of O'Connell to defeat it so promising that I cannot but regret the gazetting did not take

[128] R. Bellew to Murray, 29 Dec. 1844, Murray Papers. 'Wurrah' is an Irish invocation of the Virgin Mary.

[129] *Pilot*, 23 Dec. 1844.

[130] *Morning Chronicle,* 28 Dec. 1844 (quoting *Belfast Vindicator*); *Pilot*, 30 Dec. 1844.

[131] Letter from a Jesuit, 25 Nov. 1844, AA.EE.SS., fasc. 21, piece 10, ff. 17-18.

[132] Petre to Aberdeen, 17, 19 Dec. 1844, FO 43/38, PRO.

[133] Lambruschini to Fransoni, 28 Dec. 1844, SC Irlanda, vol. 28 ff. 366-71, Propaganda Fide Archives.

place in London as well as in Dublin. The Queen's warrant cannot reach us, at soonest, 'till tomorrow night, after which some hours must pass, before it can be gazetted and many events may occur in those few hours. Would it be impossible to issue a supplementary Gazette even now? I mean in London. It would be a very awkward circumstance if any other defection should occur before the insertion of the warrant in the Gazette here.[134]

Graham promptly had the gazetting carried out in both cities.[135] When the gazette came out in Dublin on 17 December, the three Catholic bishops were given their full ecclesiastical titles (without, however, mention of territorial title) and accorded precedence over the members of the peerage on the board. This recognition was of constitutional importance and caused much comment. The *Morning Chronicle* remarked that 'This is the first time, since the enactment of the penal laws, that the Roman Catholic prelates have been recognised, by their titles, in an official document emanating from the Queen in Council and published by authority.'[136] Sheil told Greville that it was gallantly done and that the effect would be extraordinary.[137] The government was relieved at the outcome, and Eliot wrote jubilantly and over-optimistically that 'the Roman Catholic party as such has ceased to exist. O'Connell can no longer rely on the support of the Church. He has coaxed and he has menaced the most esteemed prelates of ... the Church and his threats and his cajoleries have proved equally unavailing. Drs Crolly and Murray have withstood both.'[138] Heytesbury felt that they had affected a fundamental change in Irish political life: 'We have erected a barrier, a line of Churchmen, behind which the well-thinking part of the Roman Catholic laity can conscientiously rally and aid us in carrying out those measures of conciliation and peace which her Majesty's government have so deeply at heart.'[139]

In its hurry to gazette the board before O'Connell could wreck it, the government had blundered. It now discovered that the board could not be legally gazetted before the new

[134] Heytesbury to Graham, 16 Dec. 1844, Graham Papers.
[135] Graham to Heytesbury, 18 Dec. 1844, ibid.
[136] *Morning Chronicle,* 20 Dec. 1844.
[137] Graham to Peel, 20 Dec. 1844, Add. MSS 40450, ff. 420-3.
[138] Eliot to Heytesbury, 19 Dec. 1844, ADD. MSS 40479, ff. 211-14.
[139] Heytesbury to Peel, 20 Dec. 1844, Add. MSS 40479, ff. 216-17; Graham to Stanley, 22 Dec. 1844, Graham Papers.

year. The ministers put the best face they could on it, hoping that O'Connell would not advert to the mistake. A fresh Order in Council would have to be made and the board re-gazetted in January.[140] Peel admitted frankly that 'we have this con- solation—that strict obedience of the Law, the postponement of Gazetting until after the first of January might have been a very dangerous delay. If we had not hooked our fish when we did, they might refuse the bait in January.'[141] Eliot confessed that although the gazetting was legally premature, it was so desirable 'to nail the Roman Catholic bishops and to put a stop to the agitation ... that I should not have hesitated even with the knowledge ... There is no saying what might have been the consequence of delay'.[142] These were eloquent tributes to the power of O'Connell's campaign, providing evidence both of the great pressures exerted on the pro-government bishops and of the slender margin by which the ministers gained their victory.

At his final public meeting in Dublin, O'Connell ac- knowledged defeat but reminded his audience that the prelates were only fallible men like himself. The government, he added, could not get a single bishop in Munster to support the measure publicly and only one to do so in Leinster, and he explained the action of the two Ulster bishops on the interesting grounds that the Catholics there 'have not the influence over their pre- lates which ought to be possessed by a Catholic population'. He now revealed that an English agent 'Mr. William Peter' [sic], was in Rome and, aided by the Austrian envoy, was 'negotiating a concordat with England'.[143] This was a shrewd move: nothing was so calculated to arouse Irish Catholics as suspicions of collusion between the English government and Rome behind their backs. With this parting shot, O'Connell went home to Kerry, gone, as his watchful opponents repeated among themselves, to consult with MacHale on the next moves to be taken.[144]

[140] Graham to Heytesbury, 21 Dec. 1844, Graham Papers; Graham to Peel, 21 Dec. 1844, Add. MSS 40450, ff. 426-7.
[141] Peel to Graham, 22 Dec. 1844, Graham Papers.
[142] Eliot to Graham, 24 Dec. 1844, ibid.
[143] Pilot, 20 Dec. 1844.
[144] Heytesbury to Graham, 21 Dec. 1844; Eliot to Graham, 24 Dec. 1844, Graham Papers; Graham to Aberdeen, 23 Dec. 1844, FO 43/38.

Around this relatively minor act of parliament, therefore, a full-scale controversy had raged among Catholics for three months. The timing of the launching of the measure goes some way to explaining the hostility with which it was greeted, for as Cardinal Acton had remarked, to introduce the measure when O'Connell had just been jailed was most inopportune. The efforts of the majority to check the government by dissuading or coercing any bishop from joining the new board had been finally defeated through the co-operation of Murray and Crolly with the Irish administration. Yet the outcome remained long in suspense; the government's willingness to accept a technically illegal gazetting of the board was an indication of the narrow margin of its victory and an indication, too, that deeper issues were involved than the provisions of the Bequests Act. This success made it possible for the government to continue its reform initiatives with some hope of success. Within the Catholic church the controversy deepened and made public a division among the hierarchy over the whole question of co-operation with the government. The meeting of the bishops in November was critical. Crolly's use of Fransoni's letter, instead of achieving unity, had hardened the opposition, impelling O'Connell to intervene and to place the issue of state interference with the church in the foreground of the debate. It remained to be seen if, with O'Connell's defeat and departure from Dublin, Christmas would see an end to the controversy.

5

'THE FRIGHT OF GOBLIN CONCORDATS'
DECEMBER 1844 - JANUARY 1845

The government's jubilant claims of a successful conclusion to the Bequests Act issue with the gazetting of the Board on 17 December have been accepted by most historians. Halévy states that 'his [Peel's] success in December was a victory over the extremists and O'Connell, who could no longer...count upon the support of the clergy'.[1] Apart from the fact that the 'extremists' included the vast majority of the clergy, Halévy's claim that O'Connell had lost the support of the clergy is untenable, and the assertion that the matter ended in December needs re-examining. The controversy, far from ending in December, was to reach a culminating point in the new year. More momentous issues than the collaboration of three bishops with a government commission were to be raised as fundamental questions concerning the relations between church and state and, in particular, the tensions between religious duty and civil rights came to the fore. Fears of collusion between the Vatican and Westminster brought controversy to boiling-point, caused the Roman curia, the English government, and Irish Catholics to declare their positions and regained for O'Connell much of the ground he had lost in December.

Advent began with the two main protagonists among the bishops setting forth their views in pastoral letters. MacHale's letter was a strong restatement of the protesters' case. The act, he maintained, prevented any Catholic, on his death-bed, from bequeathing as much as one acre of land to charity, although he might bequeath all he wished to any profane or profligate purpose. It rendered bequests to religious orders null and void and made the commissioners—including the Catholic members—the legal executioners of the penal laws against them.

---

[1] E. Halévy, *Victorian Years, 1841-1895* (1961), p. 93; see also Parker, *Peel*, iii. 126, 130-3; Gash, *Peel*, p. 424.

The act, he also alleged, transferred to a board dependent on the government the power of deciding, in disputed cases, who was the lawful parish priest or bishop. MacHale's first criticism was a valid one. As regards religious orders, however, it was not clear that the act made their situation in law any worse, and the commissioners were not, as MacHale alleged, constituted their 'legal executioners'. Nor was it the intention of the law to give the board any power of adjudicating who the lawful parish priest or bishop was in disputed cases. MacHale's more fundamental charge was that the state had long tried to establish its control, first by a veto, later by the offers to pay the clergy, and that the Bequests Act was but the latest and most subtle effort in this direction. By this act the government was attempting, with some success, to detach some of the bishops from their brethren and make them dependent on the crown. As a result, the hitherto united hierarchy was becoming 'disjointed, weak and deformed—an object of sorrow to the faithful but of triumphant derision ... to the inveterate foes of Catholic Ireland!'[2] If the expressed intentions of Peel and Graham in introducing the measure and the delight with which they hailed the resulting dissension among the bishops are borne in mind, MacHale's charge, while its interpretation of the main purpose of the act is too narrow, must be seen to contain a measure of truth. Shortly before Christmas, Murray replied indirectly to MacHale and his other critics in a pastoral letter to the Catholics of Dublin. In answer to assertions that Catholic charities were safe enough before the act and that no one sought a change, he quoted in full the 1840 memorial— a shrewd move since it showed that the bishops had then asked for many of the changes now offered in the act. He skilfully praised O'Connell's abortive bill as 'a perfect measure' of which the present act was but a very imperfect substitute. Imperfect though it was, the new act brought substantial benefits to Catholic charities, and his own conscience, that 'stubborn monitor', would not allow him to reject it. The regulars, he claimed, were not adversely affected by the law, nor was there any room given for government interference in the internal affairs of the church. When a question arose as to who the

---

[2] 'To the ... clergy and faithful of the archdiocese of Tuam', *Nation*, 14 Dec. 1844.

parish priest or bishop was, the certificate of the diocesan bishop would be taken as conclusive evidence. Deploring the differences that had grown up 'in his hitherto united flock', Murray ended with a final appeal for unity and charity.[3] Whigs, Tories, and Repealers welcomed the pastoral in different ways.[4] O'Connell himself spoke of its 'exquisite tone and temper', but said nothing as yet about its content.[5] Peel was less enthusiastic than his colleagues in Ireland because he felt that Murray was giving O'Connell an advantage which he might later use.[6]

In Ireland, over Christmas, Murray's pastoral was quickly overshadowed by the far more emotive question of a concordat. For Irish Catholics, an alliance between Rome and the government was a threat which despite their loyalty to the Holy See, they had fought in the veto question and were willing to fight in the future. The immediate origins of the scare are to be found in some letters from Cullen to Cooper and to MacHale concerning Petre's visit to the Irish College in Rome.[7] When the matter was raised in the English newspapers and the advantages and disadvantages of an agreement with the pope to regulate Irish Catholic affairs coolly discussed, the excitement in Ireland grew to an uproar.[8] From then on the Bequests Act and the concordat question were interwoven in what became the most bitter phase of the whole controversy. Violent attacks on the commissioner-bishops became the order of the day. The *Pilot* published a grave editorial on 'The Crisis in the Irish Catholic Church'—a title which for many summed up the situation. An anonymous writer, in the same issue, violently described Murray as 'a man of great self-sufficiency and small intellect, a very unsafe and dangerous person to be entrusted with the most important concerns of the Irish Church ... [who] follows with dogged self-sufficiency his own impressions ... and does not fear to be branded as a bullheaded blockhead.'[9] A threat

---

[3] 'To the ... clergy and faithful of the diocese of Dublin', *Freeman's Journal*, 26 Dec. 1844.

[4] *Morning Chronicle*, 24 Dec. 1844; *The Times*, 24 Dec. 1844.

[5] *Pilot*, 30 Dec. 1844.

[6] Peel to Graham, 24 Dec. 1844, Add. MSS 40450, ff. 438-9.

[7] See pp. 158-9; Cullen to MacHale, undated in O'Reilly, *MacHale*, 1.559; Cullen to Cooper, 5 Dec. 1844, draft, Cullen Papers.

[8] *The Times*, 26 Dec. 1844, 7, 13, 18 Jan. 1845; *Morning Chronicle*, 30, 31 Dec. 1844.

[9] *Pilot,* 30 Dec. 1844.

to Murray's life was reported, and although the protesters treated it as a 'quaint invention' to win sympathy for him and his cause, Graham, who himself did not take it seriously, longed to make it public in order to open the eyes of 'the best portion of the Catholics to the horrid dangers which O'Connell had prepared for them and their religion'.[10] His wish was gratified when the Revd Thomas O'Carroll spoke publicly of the threat in Westland Row Church. According to newspaper reports, the effect was slight—'the attendance at Westland Row Chapel on Sunday was very inconsiderable, the congregation being still dissatisfied with the clergymen officiating there for being favourable to the Charitable Bequests Act'.[11] The Westland Row priests—Dean Walter Meyler, Gregory Lynch, Thomas O'Carroll, and A. Quinn—supported Murray, and Fr James Corr of St. Audeon's alleged that they had lost all the respect of their flock and that one of them had been publicly interrupted in his sermon by the congregation.[12] In the Church of St. Nicholas in Francis Street, the people accused the priests of being 'government men' and 'Peel priests', and told them that 'they must look to Sir Robert Peel in future for support and not to them'.[13] The attendance at Murray's own pro-Cathedral had also 'wondrously diminished', whereas 'all the friaries were crowded to excess'.[14] Corr told Cullen that the people cried out that 'their *archbishop* and many *of their priests* are losing their *faith and betraying them* to the *enemies* of their creed and country.'[15] In Conciliation Hall itself, Murray's name 'was groaned, but O'Connell assailed the parties most violently and soon suppressed it.'[16]

It was not merely in Dublin that signs of revolt appeared. At a meeting in Monaghan, it was alleged of Murray that 'his connection with the Castle as Commissioner of National Education has thwarted his better judgement. What then may we

[10] *Pilot*, 8 Jan.; *Tablet*, 11 Jan. 1845; Graham to Peel, 2 Jan. 1845, Add. MSS 40451, ff. 1-4.

[11] *Tablet*, 11 Jan. 1845.

[12] Corr to Cullen, 17 Jan. 1845, Cullen Papers. Walter Meyler (1784-1864), parish priest of Saint Andrews, Westland Row; vicar-general and dean of the Dublin chapter.

[13] Corr to Kirby, 27 Jan. 1845, Kirby Papers, Irish College Archives, Rome.

[14] *The Times*, 1 Jan. 1845.

[15] Corr to Cullen, 17 Jan. 1845, Cullen Papers.

[16] Edmund Cullen to Cullen, 29 Jan. 1845, Cullen Papers.

expect of a simple old man sitting in council with a great majority of ... implacable enemies of the Catholic religion.'[17] *The Times* reported that Crolly's own two chapels in Drogheda 'have, since the Archbishop's acceptance of office, been literally abandoned by their congregation'.[18] At a meeting of Belfast Catholics, the very mention of Crolly's name was greeted with groans and hisses; he was denounced as a long-standing enemy of O'Connell and accused of leading Denvir astray.[19] The Catholic clergy of Derry sent a memorial to the three bishops who had accepted commissionerships, expressing their astonishment that they had preferred the opinion of Smith and Green, the law officers, to the opinion of 'the most discriminating lawyer of the day, Daniel O'Connell'.[20] Later, in Co. Clare, when Bishop Kennedy tried to vindicate the act, he was greeted with 'audible murmurs', and most of the congregation left the chapel.[21] The *Nation*, the organ of the Young Irelanders, being less involved in the bequests issue and less opposed to the act, took a more moderate view of the concordat question. Remarking shrewdly that the government's policy 'is to divide us', it expressed the belief that 'the joy of the English party and the alarm of the Irish party are equally misplaced'. The Irish were not prisoners whom the pope was about to surrender to the English.[22] In the rest of the nationalist press, however, the concordat question was hotly debated. *The Times*'s correspondent reported that 'the concordat—the concordat with Rome—has been the cry dinned into our ears from one end of the country to the other.'[23]

The second week in January proved even more eventful. When O'Connell returned from Derrynane, he published a letter to Cantwell in which he listed twenty objections to the act and pointed out the fallacies in Murray's interpretation of it. Remarking that Petre was in Rome acting for the government, he then raised another emotive issue: 'I have already asserted ... that ... the Most Rev. Dr Crolly is in possession of a letter

[17] *Tablet*, 11 Jan. 1845.
[18] Ibid.
[19] *Pilot*, 8 Jan. 1845.
[20] Address of the Catholic clergy of Derry, 22 Jan. 1845, Murray Papers.
[21] *Record*, 13 Feb. 1845, citing *Limerick Chronicle*.
[22] *Nation*, 4 Jan. 1845.
[23] *The Times*, 7 Jan. 1845.

from the Propaganda relating to the Repeal agitation in Ireland
... How can we be secure if, under such circumstances, any
minority of our prelates should enter into any arrangements
with the British government ...?' O'Connell expressed the
view that the letter was 'uncanonical' and invited Crolly to
publish it.[24] This unprecedented step was precisely what Crolly
took. Calling O'Connell's bluff he published Fransoni's letter
together with the bishops' resolution, proposed and seconded
by Browne and McNally, accepting it. At the same time,
Crolly avowed complete ignorance of any project of a concordat
and pledged his complete opposition to 'any such insidious
scheme, which would be destructive of the independence ... of
our holy religion'.[25]

The publication, complete with translation, of Fransoni's
letter in the Dublin papers caused a sensation, Eliot seeing in it
'the most remarkable and important event that has taken place
in this eventful time'.[26] Republished in many of the English
papers (and later in the *Annual Register*), it was hailed as a defeat
for the O'Connellite bishops. O'Connell accepted the document as canonical and made no comment on its substance, but
instead he praised the resolution proposed and seconded by
Browne and McNally, 'devoted Irishmen full of zeal for the
restoration of that political state of Ireland ... which ... would
feed the hungry, clothe the naked ...' Adroitly he switched
attention to Petre's activities in Rome: 'He [Petre] has, then a
salary, and is at Rome; doing what? It is not said ... that the
affairs of the English Catholics require any such agent at
Rome. It is plain that his agency can relate only to Ireland.'[27]
Cantwell immediately came to O'Connell's support with an
interpretation of Fransoni's letter which, he asserted, was that
of the majority of the bishops. This interpretation claimed that
it was 'conduct and language ... unbecoming our sacred
characters', not clerical presence at public meetings or dinners,
that was the object of Fransoni's 'wise caution'. Sustainable
though Cantwell's nice distinction was between presence at
meetings and unbecoming language, his interpretation does

[24] *Nation*, 11 Jan. 1845.
[25] *Pilot*, 13 Jan. 1845.
[26] Eliot to Graham, 13 Jan. 1845, Graham Papers.
[27] *Pilot*, 17 Jan. 1845.

not tally with the obvious meaning of the Fransoni letter. Cantwell and those bishops who thought like him could not be classed
as 'a politicarum partium studiis, et saeculi negotiis ... alienos',
as Fransoni would have wished. Cantwell, however, went
further and justified the clergy's political involvement on
grounds similar to those advanced by Crolly in 1839 and later
by Maginn in 1848:[28]

In the present state of Ireland, with her people naked, houseless, and starving
... where the very profession of Catholicity is an apology to justify exclusion
from public offices ... or from private employment ... were the Catholic
religion ... to refuse cooperating *constitutionally* in seeking a redress of such
grievances, a suspicion of their integrity, a want of respect and affection and
total loss of influence would be deplorable but inevitable consequences.[29]

This general principle—the assertion that the church must
involve itself in the struggle to provide decent living conditions
for the people—is a view familiar enough today in regard to
many countries of the third world, where a flourishing 'theology
of liberation' insists that churchmen take an active part in
redressing social injustice: the similarity in reasoning is striking.

A week later, Higgins, availing himself of Fransoni's words
'si ita sint', explained the letter as 'purely hypothetical' and
leaving matters precisely where they were.[30] In view of his own
speeches, his attitude is more difficult to understand. The
Nation took a similar view and, describing the letter as 'very
harmless', wished it farewell.[31] Many of the laity, however, did
not take such a calm view. 'Religion from Rome, politics from
home' became the theme of speeches, articles, and letters as
rumours of a concordat spread and the Fransoni letter was
discussed. 'Ecclesiastical affairs', *The Times* reported, 'suddenly
assumed an interest which bids fair to take the wind even out of

---

[28] See pp. 75-6; cf. Maginn to Crolly, 21 Feb. 1848, Murray Papers; 'A desire to
promote, by *peaceful* and constitutional means the amelioration of the social condition
of our unhappy country made by *misrule* the *most wretched* on *earth*, could not be considered a "political pursuit" ... no clergyman has transgressed the bounds of duty,
which makes it incumbent on every follower of the Redeemer to stand by the
oppressed against their oppressors—for the poor and needy against those who strip
them.' Edward Maginn (1802-49), coadjutor bishop of Derry and apostolic administrator.

[29] *Nation*, 18 Jan. 1845.

[30] *Pilot*, 24 Jan. 1845.

[31] *Nation*, 18 Jan. 1845.

the sails of the Repeal agitation.'[32] 'What!' asked the *Pilot*, in
a biting editorial, 'shall Popes and Bishops reckoning on our
awe of their holiness of place carry on secret negotiations with
our enemies affecting our civil liberties and we shall not know
nor hear anything about it, except by accident?'[33] Repealers
neatly used the allegiance argument by asserting that papal
interference on this matter was contrary to the oath forced on
them in the Emancipation Act. O'Neill Daunt, asserting that
the Catholics of Ireland would treat a Roman rescript denouncing the national movement 'as so much waste paper', emphasized 'the criminal inconsistency of the government in
making men swear that the Pope hath no temporal power in the
Queen's dominions and yet manoeuvring to get his Holiness
to exercise temporal power against Irish freedom ... As much
theology from Rome as you please—but no politics.'[34] Crolly's
own vicar-general presided over a meeting in Dundalk at which
those present solemnly declared their resolve 'as loyal subjects
and Irishmen, to repudiate and resist any and every attempt of
the Pope ... to intermeddle in the political affairs of this kingdom.'[35] The *Cork Examiner* denied most emphatically 'the right
of the Pope to interfere with matters which are merely temporal'.[36] At the meeting on 13 January of the Repeal Association, which had up till then avoided the Bequests controversy,
speaker after speaker denounced any papal interference, and
scornful reference was made to the pope's treatment of the
Poles during their uprising in 1831.[37] No wonder *The Times*
asked in amazement: 'are we in Dublin or in the Strand,—in
the Repeal Association or at Exeter Hall?'[38] The government's
supporters were nonplussed at the able twist which the protesters had given to the allegiance question. 'How ridiculous it
is', one of them wrote,

to hear of men whose trade is sedition and whose importance and whose liveli-
hood are derived from deluding and disturbing the unfortunate people of

---

[32] *The Times*, 15 Jan. 1845.
[33] *Pilot*, 10 Jan. 1845.
[34] *Pilot*, 17 Jan. 1845.
[35] *Nation*, 18 Jan. 1845.
[36] *The Times*, 16 Jan. 1845.
[37] *Nation*, 18 Jan. 1845.
[38] *The Times*, 17 Jan. 1845.

Ireland, protesting against the interference of the Pope in temporal affairs, as an assault on the purity of their sworn allegiance.[39]

As the queen perceptively remarked to Peel earlier in the month: 'the Repealers almost turn Protestant and Englishmen, accusing the government of High Treason for their communion with the Pope and claiming the protection of English statutes against the authority of the Pope.'[40] When Crolly requested McNally to reprimand some 'misguided clerics' in his diocese who had made what he termed 'scandalous political speeches' in Clones, McNally advised against any action lest it be construed into a desire to stifle the expression of public opinion and reminded the primate that 'the great majority of the prelates ... including the humble individual who writes and almost all the clergy and people' were opposed to the Bequests Act.[41] If Crolly wished to act, he would have to act on his own.

Concerned at the turmoil that the scare of a concordat caused, Peel and Graham decided that Crolly should be assured that the report was baseless.[42] When Heytesbury told Murray to make whatever use he wished of his written denial of an impending concordat, Murray promptly published it in the press.[43] Graham, whose tolerance of ambiguity was low and whose disdain for popular pressure was great, saw in Murray's action 'a want of dignity and propriety ... which renders official intercourse with these ... prelates difficult and unsafe.'[44] Understandably, he did not want his assurance misconstrued into a promise that, at a future time, a concordat might not be considered by the government. Heytesbury was quick to point out that: 'Dr Murray saw in the publication of my note a relief from great obloquy ... and a refusal to permit him to make use of it would have given rise to a suspicion that O'Connell was not far wrong in his conjectures, and that we were not acting frankly and fairly by our friends.'[45] The publication of

[39] Lambert to Meyler, 16 Jan. 1845, Murray Papers. Henry Lambert, deputy lord lieutenant for Wexford.
[40] Victoria to Peel, 2 Jan. 1845, Add. MSS 40439, ff. 218-19.
[41] Crolly to McNally, 26 Jan. 1845; McNally to Crolly, 27 Jan. 1845, McNally Papers, Clogher Diocesan Archives.
[42] Graham to Heytesbury, 13 Jan. 1845, Graham Papers.
[43] *Pilot*, 17 Jan. 1845; Heytesbury to Graham, 17 Jan. 1845, Graham Papers.
[44] Graham to Heytesbury, 18 Jan. 1845, ibid.
[45] Heytesbury to Graham, 20 Jan. 1845, ibid.

Heytesbury's assurance only partially relieved Murray's embarrassment. Corr claimed that the assertion was considered by all
to be worthless since the government continually deceived them,
and he added that: 'it is generally believed and publicly asserted
that our metropolitan in his seventy seventh year is cajoled by
them.'[46] The attacks on Murray and Crolly continued un-
abated. The *Pilot* carried a sham advertisement with obvious
allusions to the part of the pope and the bishops in the Norman
invasion of the twelfth century:

> Heytesbury, Brewster and Co., Castle Street, have ... lately added to their
> stock of books the following ... 'Conquest made Easy', or Bulls better than
> bullets, imitated after the Latin of Nicholas Breakespeare ... by Most Rev.
> William Crolly, Archbishop and Commissioner, and the Most Rev. Daniel
> Murray, Archbishop and Commissioner, with notes by the Right Rev. Bishop
> Cornelius Denvir, Commissioner, with a portrait of the Hon. William Petre.[47]

The obvious implication was that, with the connivance of the
pope, the three bishops were prepared to betray Ireland's
liberty.

Events in Ireland were moving fast, and journalists had
rarely had such a succession of sensational church news. Dr
Walsh, bishop of Halifax, a shrewd, well-placed observer who
enjoyed both Murray's and Cullen's confidence and had just
arrived from Rome, described the situation:

> Since I arrived in Dublin important events have followed each other in quick
> succession. O'Connell's long and laboured letter; Dr Cantwell's to the
> Liberator in reply, the Clerical address to Dr Murray; the publication of the
> Rescript of Propaganda to the Primate; his letter to the great O himself; Lord
> Heytesbury to Archbishop Murray on the Concordat: all of which you will
> see in the papers. In fact to use an American phrase we have every morning
> before breakfast a small earthquake and every day people of sober habits lift
> up their hands and cry 'what next?'. I confess my heart bleeds for Dr Murray
> ... the opponents of the Bequests Bill—if ever so sound in principle—have
> carried on the war against it in so furious, so uncharitable and so unnatural a
> manner that the consequent evils ... are in my opinion ten times more disas-
> trous to religion than any mischief this unfortunate bill itself could produce.[48]

The situation for the church was becoming serious. Dr Laurence
Renehan, vice-president of Maynooth, wrote to Cullen of 'the

---

46 Corr to Cullen, 17 Jan. 1845, Cullen Papers.
47 *Pilot*, 29 Jan. 1845.
48 Walsh to Cullen, 18 Jan. 1845, Cullen Papers.

fright of goblin concordats which if not laid in time would soon have ultra-Gallicanised our people, and loosened the foundations of Catholic faith.'[49] Lambruschini had not been lacking in foresight when a year earlier he had expressed fears of precisely this type of reaction.

News of the conflict spread outside Ireland. Montalembert expressed the deepest sorrow of the friends of the Catholic religion at the acceptance of office by the three bishops.[50] In contrast Jules Gondon, the correspondent on English affairs of the influential Catholic daily, *L'Univers,* wrote to Murray supporting him.[51] The paper published articles in favour of Murray, at the instance of Nicholson: Montalembert and Lucas, however, put counter-pressure on the paper, and it published MacHale's pastoral to balance its reporting.[52] *Le Siècle,* the powerful anti-clerical paper, spoke of the pope as abandoning the Irish Catholics for political advantage:

D' après des lettres de Rome, l'Angleterre a enfin obtenu du Pape l'encyclique qu'elle desiroit pour le primat et les évêques Catholiques d'Irlande ... Le Ministère anglais ... a, dit-on, menacé la cour de Rome d'exciter à la révolte les populations de ses Etats ... Ainsi, le Pape auroit préféré l'intérêt temporel à l'intérêt spirituel ...[53]

The French paper which seems to have given the most extensive coverage was *L'Ami de la Religion*; while deploring the controversy, it devoted its front page to the matter on more than one occasion. In mid-January, it admitted that the bequests controversy had been 'augmenté par le bruit ... d'un projet de concordat', but it was at pains to try to dispel the notion: 'Qu'en sa double qualité d'Anglais et de catholique, l'honnête M. Petre ait conçu le désir de voir se rétablir des rapports officiels ... que ... il soit allé jusqu' à communiquer ses idées à des personnages

---

[49] Renehan to Cullen, 6 Mar. 1845, Cullen Papers. Laurence Renehan (1797-1857) president of Maynooth, 1845-57. He wrote a *History of Music* (1855); *Collections on Irish History,* ed. by D. McCarthy (1861-74).

[50] *Pilot,* 8 Jan. 1845.

[51] Gondon to Murray, 15 Jan. 1845, Murray Papers, 1844-5, DDA. Jules Gondon (1812-?73) writer and journalist; interested in Oxford Movement; published *Le Mouvement religieux en Angleterre;* translated many of Newman's works; friend of Dr C. Wordsworth, bishop of Lincoln.

[52] Nicholson to Hamilton, 25 Jan. 1845, Hamilton Papers, DDA.

[53] Cited in *Ami de la Religion,* 9 Jan. 1845.

plus eminens ... il n'y a dans ce désir et dans ces démarches ... rien assurement que de fort naturel ...'[54] The paper's comments were balanced, and it went on to add that to believe, as O'Connell asserted, that Petre had convinced the pope's ministers was to have a false notion of the papal government.

The jibes of *Le Siècle* and the solicitous haste of the *Ami de la Religion* to explain away the concordat rumours threw light on Rome's reaction. Alarmed at the uproar in Ireland, the Holy See became more cautious in its dealings on Irish Catholic affairs. Altieri, the nuncio in Vienna, who had been approached unofficially about an agreement between Rome and the Whigs on measures favourable to the church, was warned off by Lambruschini, and promised him to observe a 'gelosa riservatezza ... circa un si delicato argomento'.[55] Haly, still in Rome, wrote in alarm to Fransoni, enclosing a cutting from *The Times* on the concordat issue.[56] Lambruschini, who not long before had deferred Petre's audience with the pope in order 'to avoid the tattle of the journals', was now visited by two influential English Catholics—Charles Bodenham and his nephew, Charles Weld. Bodenham justified his visit to Lambruschini on the grounds that his brother-in-law, the late Cardinal Weld, hoped that 'he might never live to see the day when the independence of the Irish Catholic Hierarchy would be sacrificed to the manoeuvring intrigues of a Protestant State Policy.' Lambruschini not only denied that there was any basis for the concordat rumour, but asked Bodenham to make it known that the contradiction 'came expressly from himself ("dans mon nom")'. Pressed further by Bodenham as to the activities of Petre, Lambruschini declared solemnly that the agent 'neither had, or could have, anything whatsoever to do with the proposal or arrangement of any ecclesiastical affairs whatsoever.' To make doubly sure, Bodenham and Weld went

---

[54] *Ami de la Religion*, 16 Jan. 1845.

[55] Altieri to Lambruschini, 10 Jan. 1844, Archivio della Nunziatura di Vienna, vol. 280 G., ff. 182-3, no. 2045, Monsignore Altieri; dispacci scritti alla Segretaria di Stato, 1844-Luglio 1845, Archivio Segreto Vaticano. The letter is marked 'riservatissimo' and refers to the private advances of Baron Hummelauer who was for many years 'primo Consigliere' and 'Incaricato di Affari' at the Austrian Embassy in London.

[56] Haly to Fransoni, 23 Jan. 1845, SC Irlanda, vol. 28, ff. 396-400, Propaganda Fide Archives.

to see Brunelli, Acton, and probably Fransoni, and from all they received the same assurance: there was no question of a concordat. Reassured, Weld came to the conclusion that the uproar which the mere rumour of a concordat occasioned was a guarantee against any such effort being made for the immediate future. He summed up the situation thus:

To represent to the Irish Catholics that His Holiness has made an open declaration against repeal, that Propaganda has issued a formal opinion upon a Political question, and that the independence of the Irish Church is about to be sacrificed to the intrigues of the English and Austrian cabinets may be a very effective method of creating panic and dissension in Ireland, but no one can mistake the object of the quarter that adopts this policy.[57]

The 'quarter' referred to was, no doubt, O'Connell and his clerical supporters, whom Weld saw as having invented the whole story.

The pope, too, was concerned to scotch any idea of secret bargains. On 25 January, he saw Cullen and made it clear that there was no question of a concordat. A week later, on 1 February, when Tsar Nicholas's special envoy, Count Struwe, arrived for private negotiations, the pope told him severely that the Holy See did not conduct negotiations in secret on matters of religion; the only correct way was through the Russian ambassador and the normal channels. The controversy in Ireland caused by the rumour of a concordat was referred to:

Gli fu fatto anche riflettere alla cattiva impressione che eccita nei Cattolici sparsi per tutto l'Orbe il timore di essere dalla Santa Sede non protetti, e il solo sospetto di segrete trattative e convensioni tra la Santa Sede e i rispettivi Governi; al qual proposito si accennò il fatto del grande alarme dei Cattolici Irlandesi ed Inglesi per la sola falsa voce di un Concordato che conchiuso si fosse tra la Sante Sede ed il Gabinetto Britannico.[58]

---

[57] Bodenham to O'Reilly, 27 Jan.; Weld to O'Reilly, 28 Jan. 1845, Murray Papers. Both letters are on the same sheet. Charles Thomas Bodenham (1783-1865); married a daughter of Thomas Weld; member of the Catholic Board; supported (with his brother-in-law, Thomas, later cardinal, Weld) Bishop Milner's rejection of concessions on the veto question. Charles Weld; nephew of Bodenham, contributor to *The Rambler*; both Bodenham and Weld were related by marriage to Lord Clifford, then residing in Rome.

[58] Udienza accordata ad instanza del Sig. Conte di Bouteneff e alla di lui presenza al Sig. Struwe 1 Feb. 1845, AA.EE.SS., Carte di Russia e Polonia, vol. viii, parte I, ff. 13-14, cited in R. Lefevre, 'Santa Sede e Russia e i colloqui dello Czar Nicola I nei documenti vaticani (1843-1846)', *Miscellanea Historiae Pontificiae,* xiv (1948), 159-293.

Six weeks later, Gregory came back to this matter in a minute of a reply to Metternich:

Conviene perciò avere in vista qual sinistra impressione sarebbe nei cattolici sparsi per tutto l'Orbe una segreta trattativa di Concordato in cui temerebbero forse abbandonata la loro causa per particolari politici riguardi. E recentissimo il fatto del grande allarme dei Cattolici Inglesi ed Irlandesi per la sola falsa voce di un Concordato che conchiuso si fosse o andasse a concludersi tra la S. Sede et il Gabinetto Britannico.[59]

The pope had no concordat in mind, and was careful not to awaken suspicions in Ireland or elsewhere by secret agreements with governments. Gradually, it became clear that the rumour of a concordat was unfounded. Cullen affirmed that it had been suggested by Petre to give himself importance, while Lucas commented that the government was being rightly blamed for the work of its own agent, whom he described as a 'silly, ill-principled coxcomb'.[60]

While the affair of the concordat was at its height, Murray and MacHale both received communications from the curia. Immediately after the bishops' meeting, the Holy See had received representations from the parties involved. Murray informed Acton that the bishops at their meeting had agreed to follow their own conscience with regard to the act.[61] Crolly assured Fransoni that his rescript was both timely and necessary.[62] MacHale implored both the pope and Fransoni to forbid bishops going on the bequests board, for 'ex quo primum ad fidem Ecclesiae Catholicae Sanctae Romanae gens nostra a Sancta Praecedessore Suo Coelestino adducta est, numquam in majori periculo ista fides versata est'.[63] How to reply to this exaggerated plea was a problem which Fransoni passed on to Lambruschini, who, neatly referring him to the reply given to Petre, Acton's draft reply to Murray and Petre's guarantee on

[59] Minuta autografa di Gregorio XVI sulla possibilità o meno di un concordato con la Russia...ibid., ff. 36-9, cited in Lefevre, 'Santa Sede', pp. 255-7. Lefevre dates this communication for the middle of March 1845. The occasion was the proposed marriage of an Austrian prince and a Russian princess.

[60] Cullen to MacHale, 18 Jan. 1845, O'Reilly, *MacHale*, i. 559; Cullen to Murray, 25 Jan. 1845, Murray Papers; *Tablet*, 8 Feb. 1845.

[61] Murray to Acton, 23 Nov. 1844, AA.EE.SS., Fasc 21, piece 14, ff. 45-7.

[62] Crolly to Fransoni, 25 Nov. 1844, SC Irlanda, vol. 128, ff. 352-3, Propaganda Fide Archives.

[63] MacHale to Pope Gregory, 25 Nov. 1844, AA.EE.SS., Fasc 21, piece 15e, ff. 91-2 (copy).

the regulars, told him he had all the materials to answer MacHale.[64] Replies to both Murray and MacHale were sent at the end of December. Acton's reply to Murray carefully weighed the advantages and disadvantages of the new law and, without committing the Holy See, favoured acceptance of seats on the board.[65] Fransoni's reply to MacHale, dispatched at the same time, was quite different. He remonstrated with him for not awaiting a reply from Rome but instead publicly attacking those bishops who, as Fransoni remarked, acted 'juxta consilium in generali Episcoporum conventu initum unice ex concientiae impulsu rectaque voluntate.' The only way to improve the measure was by acting together:

nonnisi ex mutua sacrorum Praesulum conjunctione, eorumque prudenti, unanimi, pacataque agendi ratione, expectare liceat, ut quae praedicta regii gubernii lex continet Ecclesiae canonibus repugnantia vel religionis catholicae principiis haud consentanea, oblatis opportuna occasione debitaque forma per Episcopos petitionibus, tractu temporis a Gubernio ipso emendentur.[66]

Although this did not prevent MacHale from publishing a further public letter to Peel on 25 January in which he shifted his line of attack to Anthony Blake—'the old Advocate of the veto, and of every measure for fettering the freedom of the Catholic Church'—the Roman replies were a clear indication that the curia was not opposed to the act and a confirmation of Petre's success in that respect.[67] Petre now received orders to keep in contact with Lambruschini and to draw his attention to O'Connell's attacks on concordats, the agitators' defiance of the heads of the Irish church and even local disturbances in Ireland, and to warn the Holy See to be wise in time: 'if the democratic principle prevail over ecclesiastical authority the example is infectious and the effect will not be confined to Ireland'.[68] The Curia was indeed worried by the news from Ireland but its reaction was not quite what Graham had hoped

[64] Lambruschini to Fransoni, 28 Dec. 1844, SC Irlanda, vol. 128, ff. 366-71, Propaganda Fide Archives.

[65] Acton to Murray, 31 Dec. 1844, Murray Papers.

[66] Fransoni to MacHale, 30 Dec. 1844, ibid.

[67] MacHale, *Letters*, pp. 585-92. Murray's friends knew Fransoni's reply within a short time: Nicholson to Hamilton, 20 May 1845, Hamilton Papers, DDA.

[68] Graham to Peel, 23 Dec. 1844, Add. MSS 40450, ff. 434-7; Graham to Aberdeen, 12 Jan. 1845, FO 43/38.

for. Lambruschini had gone out of his way to assure Bodenham
and Weld that Petre had no influence on Irish affairs.[69] He
had, early in January, deferred Petre's request for a papal
audience, and by 10 February the secretary of Propaganda,
Brunelli, told Petre that it would have to be further postponed. 'I mention this to your Lordship', Petre explained to
Aberdeen, 'as one of the many proofs how embarrassed this
Court is by the violence of the Catholic Bishops of Ireland.'[70]
Valid though this comment is, it is also true that Petre's own
position had been weakened by the scare of a concordat.
When, at Graham's request, he pressed for support for the co-
operative bishops, Lambruschini refused:

The Cardinal not infrequently asks me about Mr O'Connell but immediately
I allude to the assistance and support he receives from the clergy, he shrugs
his shoulders, adding perhaps—we have nothing to do with him. If I mention
Dr MacHale, he is sure to turn the conversation on Dr Murray, and in
praise of his wise conduct under many difficulties ... I am sorry to send back
the Messenger without being able to obtain a more open approval of the
bishops who are willing to cooperate ...[71]

A private admonition was, as Lambruschini had indicated a
year earlier, the limit to which the Curia was prepared to go in
advising the Irish clergy to avoid politics. Graham and Heytesbury were disappointed, agreeing that 'it would not do to let
the archbishops know that we had asked, and *asked in vain*, for
some public approval of their conduct, nor that the Cardinal
Secretary for State had studiously avoided all reference to Dr
MacHale.'[72]

The storm of controversy that the issue of a concordat generated laid bare many of the underlying tensions within the Irish
Catholic community and came close to causing a dangerous
and lasting split within it. It showed how clearly Catholics
distinguished between the spiritual allegiance they owed to the
church and their legitimate independence in political matters,
and how far they were prepared to go in defying archbishop,
primate, and pope when they feared that their civil liberties
were involved. It was a warning to the government of the

[69] See p. 204.
[70] Petre to Aberdeen, 14 Jan., 10 Feb. 1845, FO 43/38.
[71] Petre to Aberdeen, 21 Jan. 1845, Add. MSS 43151, ff. 210-11.
[72] Heytesbury to Graham, 13 Feb. 1845, Graham Papers.

doubtful and double-edged value of Vatican support for their Irish policies.

The stand taken by the bishops on the bequests issue remained a subject of debate. After Crolly published Fransoni's rescript, Heytesbury hoped that it would tend to open the eyes of those 'who still build their faith upon Dr MacHale, and to widen the breach ... between the seriously religious Roman Catholics, and those who are merely the adherents of O'Connell.'[73] Jubilantly, a few days later, Heytesbury announced that 'the more respectable of the Parish Priests are taking courage and getting up a dutiful address to their Archbishop Murray.'[74] Fifty-eight Dublin priests (including Dean Meyler and Archdeacon Hamilton) did draw up a memorial expressing their affection for the archbishop, their gratitude for his services to the diocese and their confidence in him.[75] His opponents, however, drew up a memorial condemning the act which was signed by a hundred and forty-eight Dublin priests including one vicar forane, seventeen parish priests, and the community of Carmelite friars in Whitefriar Street.[76] Almost every diocesan priest in the archdiocese had taken sides on the issue, and Murray's opponents in the diocese where he had laboured for half a century outnumbered his supporters by almost three to one.

Even Maynooth College, on the outskirts of the diocese, whose corps of professors formed the intellectual élite of the Irish church, did not remain immune. The college dared not take an open part in the dispute for its every move was watched by hostile eyes, but within its walls controversy raged with the intensity that academic life can produce. Already before the bishops' meeting, Russell had alluded to the excitement that existed, telling Cullen that 'we are all on the *quivive* [*sic*] about the Synod.'[77] Evidence of the private or collective views of the professors, however, is difficult to find but there exist two exceptionally revealing documents which throw light on their reactions. Edmund O'Reilly, Russell's colleague, gave Cullen

---

[73] Heytesbury to Graham, 12 Jan. 1845, Graham Papers.
[74] Heytesbury to Graham, 15 Jan. 1845, Graham Papers.
[75] *Dublin Evening Post*, 14 Jan. 1845; *Nation*, 18 Jan. 1845.
[76] *Tablet*, 8 Feb. 1845.
[77] Russell to Cullen, 9 Nov. 1844, Cullen Papers.

a perceptive appraisal of the situation in the college, going beyond the immediate issues to the roots of the division:

There are notoriously two parties among the bishops, ever since the *Education* contest. Dr MacHale's party whatever be *their cause,* whether good or bad, appear to act in a factious spirit at times. We have here among the professors two representatives of that party, Mr Whitehead[78] ... and Dr O'Hanlon.[79] We had another, Dr McNally now bishop of Clogher. These men did their best to put persons of their side into the situations that became vacant. They machinated at the *concorsi* for professorships. Dr MacHale's party *as operating on this house* is mischievous, and those who wish to promote the interests of this house and... of religion, have considered themselves called on to stand together with Dr Murray (as far as this house is concerned) ... in resisting such a party. I would consider the circumstances of a candidate being put forward by that side as a very good reason why he should not be appointed. I do not look upon them as the friends of *order.* Dr MacHale himself has given occasional signs of being a *turbulent man,* and his party seems to partake more or less of that character. Hence, I think *that party, quatenus party,* an evil and one that is a pity to see encouraged. There are two scopuli to be avoided— passiveness and turbulence. There may be perhaps too much of the former on the one side, too much of the latter on the other side.[80]

The dilemma facing O'Reilly and other Irish ecclesiastics was how to strike a balance between the 'passivity' of Murray and the 'turbulence' of MacHale. Should the attitude of the church to the state be one of willing collaboration and gratitude for favours received, which Cooper denounced as 'the timid and crouching policy of the eighteenth century', or should it be one of eternal and suspicious vigilance which might degenerate into over-sensitivity and intransigence? The past record of the state, particularly of Conservative governments, towards the church justified a wary approach, yet if distrust remained the dominant attitude there was little hope that real co-operation would ever develop. It was a problem that the pre-Famine church had not solved. The controversy surrounding the Bequests Act and the underlying issues involved in it forced many of the staff at Maynooth to take up positions at least on the immediate issue, as the detailed and biting complaint O'Hanlon made to McNally reveals:

---

[78] Robert ffrench Whitehead (1807-79), professor of Mental and Moral Philosophy; later vice-president of Maynooth 1845-72.

[79] John O'Hanlon (1802-71), prefect of the Dunboyne scholars.

[80] O'Reilly to Cullen, 11 Dec. 1844, Cullen Papers.

Your lordship can form no idea of the exertions which this man [Reverend Patrick Murray[81]] and young Crolly[82] in particular are making to sink O'Connell and the other friends of Ireland in the estimation of the students. I never thought I should have to witness such baseness as I have witnessed in this house until the last few months. Murray, Crolly, O'Reilly, Russell and Lee[83] are out and out abettors of the Bequests Act—Renehan, Gaffney,[84] Callan,[85] without formally approving of the act are loud and eloquent in their denunciations to the opposition given to the Primate and Dr Murray. Dixon[86] who was honest in past times takes care almost every day to proclaim his neutrality in the present warfare. Furlong[87] and James[88] I am glad to say, are sincere though not noisy opponents of the bill. I neither heard a word from either Gunn[89] or Farrelly,[90] one way or the other on the subject.

Overwhelmed by the dissensions and piqued by the fact that a majority of his colleagues opposed the uncompromising policy which he saw as the true ideal for the Irish church, the intemperate O'Hanlon called for radical solutions, knowing well that they would never be adopted: 'Instead of granting us additional means of support, I wish to God, the government would suppress the College altogether'.[91] O'Hanlon's list includes almost all the members of the staff, and reveals how deeply the controversy had penetrated the quiet halls of the national seminary. The division among the members of staff reflected the division among the hierarchy and concerned not only the immediate question of the merits of the act but also the underlying issue of the attitude to be adopted to the state and towards O'Connell's national movement. Internal tensions

[81] Patrick Murray (1811-82), professor of theology; author of works on systematic theology. He was not related to the archbishop.

[82] George Crolly (1810-78), professor of theology; author of works on moral theology; nephew of Archbishop Crolly.

[83] Walter Lee, (1811-93), dean; later vicar-general of the arch-diocese of Dublin.

[84] Miles Gaffney (1798-1861), dean; became a Jesuit, 1855.

[85] Nicholas Callan (1799-1864), professor of mathematics and natural philosophy; inventor of the induction coil.

[86] Joseph Dixon (1806-66), professor of sacred scripture; archbishop of Armagh 1852.

[87] Thomas Furlong (1802-75), professor of rhetoric; bishop of Ferns 1857.

[88] James Tully (1800-76), professor of Irish.

[89] John Gunn (1812-93), dean.

[90] Thomas Farrelly (1814-91), assistant bursar.

[91] O'Hanlon to McNally, 3 Feb. 1845, McNally Papers, Clogher Diocesan Archives. O'Hanlon's list does not include the president of the college, Dr Michael Montague (1773-1845), who by 1845 was a complete invalid. Nor does it include Whitehead, whose O'Connellite sympathies were well known to McNally, nor Dr Matthew Kelly (1814-58), professor of Belles Lettres and French, editor of source books on Irish history.

and personal loyalties further aggravated the staff's difficulties. Loyalty to O'Connell was certainly a factor with others besides O'Hanlon; McNally, affirming his unbounded admiration for the great leader, had declared that Ireland owed him a national debt, while another Maynooth cleric, Fr James MacMahon, complained that when O'Connell visited the college in January 1846, although the students and some of the staff received him well, others among whom he named Murray, Crolly, Kelly, Lee, and Russell, 'offered no external mark of respect' to the Liberator.[92]

O'Hanlon believed that Dr Patrick Murray had organized the clerical address of support for Archbishop Murray. Heytesbury now attempted to organize a lay address of support. Despite his earlier claim that 'everything that is respectable in the Roman Catholic body' sided with the archbishop, when the lord lieutenant asked some of those respectable Catholics to draw up an address they shied away with the excuse that it would be 'scantily supported'.[93] While he was finding it impossible to get the lay Catholics to support Murray, other lay Catholics who had protested against the act now took two initiatives. The first was a joint petition to each of the bishops, the second an appeal to Rome. In their petition to the bishops, they asked them to reassemble in synod and to deliver 'a formal, positive, and marked decision upon, not only concordats, pensions, or any kind of vetoistical schemes', but also on the Bequests Act. Seven-eighths of the priests, they claimed, and all the laity had protested against the act. The division 'in our hitherto united body' was the reason they gave for urging the bishops to meet. Over ninety leading citizens of Dublin, including aldermen, town councillors, and barristers signed the petition.[94]

If this address was a remarkable manifestation of disapproval from Murray's own laity, even more remarkable were the replies of the bishops, which shed an interesting light on their

[92] McNally to Fitzpatrick, 17 Nov. 1843; J. J. MacMahon to McNally, 13 Jan. 1846, McNally Papers, Clogher Diocesan Archives. Patrick Vincent Fitzpatrick (1792-1865) was organizer of the O'Connell Tribute. James Joseph MacMahon (1819-84), ordained in Maynooth 1846; later parish priest of Carrickmacross and dean of the Clogher diocesan chapter.

[93] Heytesbury to Graham, 3 Feb. 1845, Graham Papers.

[94] Battersby, *Catholic Directory*, 1846, pp. 408-18.

attitudes. Sixteen of the twenty-seven bishops replied, a high proportion when one excludes the three commissioners themselves and Haly (who was in Rome); all, with the exception of two (possibly three), declared their opposition to the act. Six of the nine bishops in the province of Armagh registered their opposition to it. Higgins termed it 'nefarious' and then went on to express the fervent hope that bishops, priests and people would unite 'to procure a repeal of the detested Union, the fruitful source of all our national miseries'.[95] Blake was willing to wait a few weeks 'in order to test the sincerity of the Premier, who cannot now be ignorant of the opposition which the bill has received'.[96] Cantwell asserted that since the introduction of the act, charitable bequests had 'almost entirely dried up, for during this one month four deeds, conveying property of very considerable amount to religion and charitable institutions within this diocese, have been committed to the flames'.[97] This type of allegation hit hard, for if no bequests were forthcoming then the purpose of the act would be defeated. McNally denounced the act as 'essentially vicious', McGettigan pointed out that he and his priests intended to petition parliament against the act.[98] McLaughlin, who had abstained from voting at the November meeting, declared that the act had no more determined opponent than himself.[99] In the southern province, Slattery reaffirmed the 'unalterable opposition' of his diocese to the act. The only other Munster bishop to reply was Kennedy who still smarted from the injury which MacHale had inflicted on him. His letter is one of the most remarkable of all. The origin of disunity among the hierarchy was not the Bequests Act, he insisted, but lay in an earlier issue:

The education question had, unfortunately, very much disturbed the previously-existing harmony of the Irish Catholic prelates; for it was on that question, sir, and not on the 'Bequests' Bill as has been so often erroneously asserted, that the minority of our body refused, for the first time in my memory, to be guided by the sense of the majority. Who was right on the occasion, the public can now without any difficulty decide.[100]

[95] Ibid., pp. 408-9.
[96] Ibid., pp. 409-10.
[97] Ibid., p. 411.
[98] Ibid., pp. 411-12.
[99] Ibid., pp. 417-18.
[100] Ibid., pp. 408; 415-16.

As it was common knowledge which side Murray and MacHale had then taken, Kennedy's meaning was clear. This was a subtle way to defend the present minority, and to hold up MacHale as the source of discord. Meanwhile, MacHale, in his reply to the petition, asserted that it was only by resigning an office which encroached on the apostolical rights of their brethren that the bishops on the board could restore harmony.[101] Coen contented himself with recording his opposition to the act.[102] Browne went to some pains to denounce both the act and the 'Conservative faction' who introduced it: 'I revere and love the good Archbishop of Dublin ... yet I do even at the risk of incurring his displeasure most respectfully ask, what honest boon or favour can ever be expected from Peel and his minions, the deadliest foes of old Ireland and her religion?' Not above punning, Browne declared that it was 'only *A. Blake* prospect', and 'will not do for Galway or old Ireland'. He went on to give fervent expression to his political faith, a vision of

Ireland for the Irish, united to Great Britain by the golden link of the crown. I care not to whom the reins of government may be entrusted, whether Whig or Tory,...unless we have our own parliament in College-green, an *honest* Bequest Bill, a real emancipation of the religious orders, and freedom for our church ... can never be expected.[103]

Browne's neighbour, French, recording his opposition to the act, claimed that he had attended the synods for the previous thirty-two years and 'invariably protested in common with them [his fellow bishops] against the ''veto'', against any ''state provision'' or any encroachments on the discipline and independence of the Catholic Church...' French, however, forecast that if the government did not expunge all the obnoxious clauses from the act, the three commissioner bishops would resign from the board.[104] McNicholas repudiated with scorn 'an enactment, the direct tendency of which is to extinguish the monastic orders', and intended to resist 'the sacrilegious usurpation of the jurisdiction and canonical rights of the epis-copal orders by any tribunal ... lay or ecclesiastical deriving its

---

[101] Ibid., pp. 415-16.
[102] Ibid., p. 409.
[103] Ibid., p. 416.
[104] Ibid., pp. 413-14.

authority from the secular power.' The act, which had been
pompously announced as an important boon, 'furnished an
illustration of the unfitness of a British Parliament to legislate
for a people of whose religious convictions and most cherished
feelings they are so grossly ignorant.'[105] Feeny believed that the
rights and liberties of Ireland were endangered.[106] The Connaught prelates, almost to a man, had come out more strongly
than before against the act.

Of the four bishops in the province of Dublin, two answered.
Keating merely agreed that there was a very general wish,
not only in Dublin but throughout Ireland, for a meeting of
the prelates.[107] Kinsella courageously pointed out that he did
not see how the Bequests Bill altered the position of the religious
clergy.[108] A week later, he assured his faithful, rather
naïvely, that there was no fundamental dissension among the
bishops:

> There was no difference even about the *MERITS* of the Bequests Bill, for
> all condemned three or four portions of it. The only difference was on a question
> of prudence; some thinking it was best to reject it altogether,... others thinking
> it more prudent to accept it for the sake of the good in it and to try by every
> means to get rid of what was bad; and IF the bad would not be taken away,
> then to have nothing further to do with the Bequests Bill.[109]

In general, the replies showed that the great majority of bishops
was strongly opposed to Murray's policy of co-operating with
the government in implementing the new act. Behind their
criticisms of the act lay a distrust of the Conservative government, while a number of them felt that only a native parliament
could understand Irish needs. Despite the pressure which the
protesters exercised, the minority bishops held a trump card.
Only the primate could call an extraordinary meeting and, as
Crolly had no intention of putting his head on a block, nothing
came of the demand. The propaganda value, however, for the
protesters was immense as bishop after bishop publicly announced his opposition to the provisions of the act.

[105] Ibid., pp. 416-17.
[106] Ibid., pp. 412-13.
[107] Ibid., pp. 410-11.
[108] Ibid., p. 408.
[109] *Pilot,* 3 Feb. 1845.

The Dublin Catholics' second initiative was not as successful. They had planned to send a lay delegation to the pope and
O'Connell proposed his son, John, and Lord Ffrench as delegates.[110] Before the delegation could get under way, however,
alarming news arrrived from the Irish College. When the pope
saw Cullen on 25 January, it appears certain that he rebuked
him for spreading unfounded rumours about a concordat and
for his role in the controversy. A very chastened Cullen wrote
twice in quick succession to Murray, denying the possibility of
a concordat and regretting bitterly the part he had played.[111]
Acknowledging that he had probably helped to circulate the
false report, he humbly told Murray

> ... insipienter locutus sum. God grant that I may do penance for any evil I
> have occasioned. I have come to the firm resolution of *never*, never interfering
> in political reports or discussions. I speak to Your Grace with the greatest
> sincerity and confidence in this matter ... Oh that peace could be restored to
> the Irish Church.[112]

He also wrote to his friends MacHale, Dr Blake and Miley
pleading for moderation. Cullen had been badly shaken. He
fell into a deep depression, could not sleep at night and was so
ill that his friends in Rome and Ireland became alarmed. Miley,
Cantwell, and MacHale warned him he was taking things too
much to heart, and noting his state of 'terror', they came to the
conclusion that there must be strong pressure on him in
Rome.[113]

A remark of Bishop Walsh to Kirby, with its hint of reproach
and warning, sheds a little light on this somewhat veiled in-
cdent: 'Oh, how I grieved for our charming Dr Cullen when I
heard the dear, good man was in such affliction and in such a
state of health; I am quite sure that neither he nor you will ever
again be involved in any trouble of this nature.'[114] Walsh had
reason to be grateful both to Murray and Cullen, and un-

---

[110] Heytesbury to Graham, 21 Jan. 1845, Graham Papers.
[111] Cullen to Murray, 25 Jan. 1845, Murray Papers; Cullen to Murray, 28 Jan.
1845, Cullen Papers, DDA.
[112] Cullen to Murray, 28 Jan. 1845, ibid.
[113] Cullen to Cantwell, 8 Feb. 1845, O'Reilly, *MacHale,* i. 576; Miley to Cullen,
25 Feb. 1845; Cantwell to Cullen, 25 Feb. 1845; MacHale to Cullen, 1 Mar. 1845,
Cullen Papers.
[114] Walsh to Kirby, 15 Mar. 1845, Kirby Papers.

doubtedly would have had ready access when in Dublin to both Murray and Crolly. Cullen had evidently implored him to smooth matters over as best he could with the two archbishops, for Walsh wrote: 'Since I came to Dublin I lost no opportunity of doing what you wished with Dr Murray, and also with Dr Crolly ... if you knew all the two archbishops have suffered you would really pity them and would not be surprised at all they feel. I softened everything as well as I could.' He went on to give good advice to Cullen in a passage that throws light on Cullen's position in Rome:

At all events, my dear friend, there is no use in your *fretting* yourself any longer about the past. I am glad you agree that neutrality is the soundest policy for the Irish College. You must not take *too much blame* to yourself, especially, in Rome. I have represented here that the vague rumours about the Rescript from Rome and the subsequent publication of Cardinal Fransoni's letter, were very instrumental in exciting the people. You can safely affirm the same. Even if you have acted imprudently, there is no use in worrying yourself now on the subject ... If your health not be better when this reaches you, esp. if your natural sleep be not restored I conjure you to take even a short trip from Rome...

The archbishops, he reported, were more angry still at Kirby, going so far as to suggest that he was 'crazed'.[115] Cullen's standing in Rome had been damaged. From Paris, Nicholson reported later in the year, with some glee, that 'there exists no longer "the Pope of Ireland" ... Gregory the XVI now acts for Paddy Land.' Nicholson, delighted at Cullen's fall from favour because he was the support of MacHale and Higgins, nevertheless felt sorry for him since 'his intentions, however mistaken, were always good'.[116] Nicholson later affirmed categorically that Cullen nearly compromised the pope 'by false information on the Bequests Act and for so doing (though it was done unintentionally) was personally reproved by his Holiness.'[117] Although Nicholson was inclined to gossip, the circumstances in which he made this claim and the general evidence indicate its essential accuracy.

Walsh's comments on the reaction of the two archbishops, including their exasperation at Kirby's ill-advised statements,

[115] Walsh to Cullen, 10 Mar. 1845, Cullen Papers.
[116] Nicholson to Hamilton, 15, 23 June 1845, Hamilton Papers.
[117] Nicholson to Murray, 14 Aug. 1846, Murray Papers.

have the authentic ring of a well-informed, judicious observer.
When Walsh went on to recount the reactions within the Repeal
association, he had not the same first-hand information. He
had complained to O'Connell of the disrespectful language
used about the pope and the bishops, but then came to the
conclusion that 'the poor Liberator is very much coerced
himself by Young Ireland and others.' Walsh had heard a
report that MacHale and Cantwell had threatened to resign
from the Repeal movement if O'Connell did not support them,
whereas 'Smith O'Brien and the Protestants were violently
opposed to its [the Bequests issue] being mixed up with the
National Question.'[118] This report of the pressures placed on
O'Connell by the bishops, on the one hand, and by the Young
Irelanders, on the other, is accurate except for one important
point. Although MacHale and Cantwell were prime movers in
the agitation against the act, there is no evidence to indicate
that they threatened to resign from the nationalist movement if
O'Connell did not support them. On the contrary, there is
evidence to show that O'Connell, for good political reasons,
was opposed to the act from the start and actively intervened
when he learned of the unfavourable developments at the
bishops' meeting. It was certain that Cullen was ill, and despite
pleas was quite unable to help the protesters any further. To
Cantwell, who was accused of censuring anyone who supported
the Bequests Act, Cullen appealed for moderation and asked
him 'for God's sake' to oppose 'the intended lay deputation
to Rome'.[119] Cantwell, impressed by Cullen's alarm saw to it
that the idea of the delegation was quietly dropped.[120] With the
failure of the protesters to force the bishops to meet again or to
send a lay delegation to Rome and with the emergence of the
Maynooth question, the fierce controversy died away.

The Charitable Bequests Act and the issues it raised have
not, generally speaking, received the attention from historians
that they deserve. The act was important in its own right
because it provided better financial support for the church's
institutions.[121] The recognition the new commission gave to the

---

[118] Walsh to Cullen, 10 Mar. 1845, Cullen Papers.
[119] Cullen to Cantwell, 8 Feb. 1845, Mac Suibhne, *Cullen*, i. 258.
[120] Cantwell to Cullen, 12 Mar. 1845, Cullen Papers.
[121] See p. 352.

bishops, moreover, according them their full ecclesiastical titles, was a significant step toward the acceptance of the Catholic church within the constitution.[122] On the tactical level, Peel's success in gaining the co-operation of a number of the bishops was of vital importance for his whole programme of reforms, although for months the result remained in doubt, the balance swinging dramatically first in one direction and then in another. The publication of the Roman rescript and the 'fright of goblin concordats' laid bare deep tensions within the Irish Catholic community.

Keenly aware of the many unexpected effects the first instalment of his reform programme produced, Peel detailed them for Gladstone to demonstrate that the government's policy was already attaining its objective:

The consequences of the Bequests Bill, the schism between the Irish agitators and the chief authorities of the Roman Catholic Church, the rescript of the Pope enjoining forbearance from turbulent agitation on the part of the clergy, the declaration of the Papal authorities that they will co-operate with the Civil power in maintaining submission to the law in Ireland, the adherence of the English Roman Catholics to Dr Murray, in preference to O'Connell, are important, many of them unforeseen events.[123]

The controversy and the 'unforeseen events' had overshadowed the act itself whose main purpose had dropped from sight. Peel's satisfaction, however, at the new relationship with Rome was premature, for the curia, alarmed at the uproar over secret agents and concordats, and at the 'Gallican' statements from Ireland, became very cautious in its dealings with the government. The 'rescript of the Pope' from which Peel hoped for so much was lost in the same uproar. To see the 'schism' as a split between the agitators and the chief authorities of the church was naïve, for if two of the archbishops stood out against O'Connell, two others, together with two-thirds of the rest of the hierarchy, supported him. Indeed, there was a certain blindness on the part of Peel, Graham, and Heytesbury in persuading themselves that the small minority of bishops, priests, and laity who supported the government's measure

[122] During the debates over the Ecclesiastical Titles Bill (1851), the recognition accorded to the bishops in the Bequests Act and in the establishment of the bequests board was quoted as a precedent.

[123] Peel to Gladstone, 20 Jan. 1845, Parker, *Peel*, iii. 165-6.

comprised 'the seriously religious Roman Catholics' and in dismissing the great majority as 'merely the adherents of O'Connell'.[124] Although O'Connell had been defeated on the bequests issue, he had retained his clerical support and, during the controversy concerning the concordat, had regained most of the ground he had lost. The real schism was within the ranks of the bishops—a division reflected in the Maynooth staff— which was the most serious of all the consequences of the six months of controversy.

To have won Murray openly to its side against his fellow-bishops was the government's main achievement. Like most pre-Emancipation bishops, Murray, while maintaining a prudent reserve in regard to the state, was willing to co-operate with it. He had seen and often presided over many changes in his church during the thirty-five years since his selection as archbishop—changes which tended to make the church, while still independent, more institutionalized. Emancipation had given it a new status; the Melbourne administration had brought many Catholics into public life, and the national system of education had accustomed Murray himself to working on government boards. His co-operation with the government in 1844 was, therefore, scarcely surprising except in so far as it was with a Tory government. What was suprising was his willingness to co-operate to the point of dividing his church and of supplying information to the government's Roman agent. A clear conviction that the act was beneficial to his church, which Blake subtly strengthened, accounted for this action. Furthermore, the 'factiousness', as he saw it, of the opposition to the national system of education was still fresh in his mind, and in the present controversy the protesters' tactics left him no honourable means of retreat even when it became apparent that the majority of the clergy differed from him. The indecisive Crolly was more timid and appeared more sensitive to the importance of unity but, after the November meeting, he took a firm stand against MacHale and the O'Connellite bishops. MacHale, though he had lost to the government and to Murray and had been rebuked by Rome, sturdily refused to be silenced and was already suspicious of further

[124] See pp. 140, 190.

official measures of reconciliation. His Roman ally, Cullen, suffered more. His influence had been shaken and he appeared intent on avoiding similar dangerous involvement for the future.

The government for its part, had achieved considerable success. It had redressed the blunder of Peel's first appointments: Heytesbury and Eliot had worked as a perfect team in the delicate negotiations with Murray, Crolly, and Blake. Eliot's role as intermediary and his sympathy for reform, combined with Heytesbury's experience and patience, had played no small part in the success of the policy. Graham had co-operated well with them. The Graham of February 1845 was a far cry from the 'no concessions' Graham of June 1843. His increasing knowledge of the complexities of Irish affairs had no doubt helped, but he owed much to his relationship with Peel, who supplied what Graham's mercurial spirit needed—confidence and steadiness. Peel remained the directing mind, ready to give advice and support when needed. While the controversy over the act showed him the strength of the opposition, the split in the monolithic structure of the 'Catholic party' constituted real, if limited, success. The moderate party which he and Heytesbury hoped would spring up was slow in forming, but a start had been made and a further growth could be expected with the granting of generous aid to Maynooth. By February 1845, Peel was able to intimate to Gladstone that some breakthrough on the Irish problem was within the range of possibility. Encouraged with the results of his first attempt to kill Repeal by kindness, he determined to press ahead even if Gladstone or others deserted him. Success in establishing a working relationship with the bishops—who appeared to be the only counterpoise to O'Connell—weighed more with him than cabinet, or even party unity. Indeed, it weighed more with him than the provisions of the Bequests Act itself.

Even as Peel and the Irish clergy were assessing the results of the controversy, one final shock was in store for the government. On the eve of Cullen's disturbing interview with the pope, Heytesbury had an equally disturbing interview in the vice-regal lodge. In cloak and dagger style, Bellew, one of the commissioners, came secretly to him with alarming news concerning Petre. Report had it that Petre was a profligate and a scoffer at all religions—information which, if true, would enable O'Connell to bring further pressure to bear on the commissioner bishops. Bellew warned Heytesbury that he had little idea of the intimidation still being used against the bishops, the final result of which would be that they might break.[125] An alarmed Graham admitted that the accusations against Petre might be true, but implored Heytesbury to keep the bishops firm for otherwise their whole Irish policy would be in ruins. He volunteered to seek out Blake and through him to confirm the bishops in their reliance on the government's intentions. 'No time ought to be lost', he declared, 'in bringing forward an additional grant to Maynooth, for this, after all, is the test of our good-will and will render the position of the archbishops impregnable'.[126] Heytesbury fully concurred with this plan and expressed to Peel his impatience for the opening of Parliament and the development of his Irish policy, adding that 'the Maynooth Bill ... will restore courage to our trembling ... Prelates and to the equally trembling laity.'[127]

When Parliament assembled on 4 February, much of the queen's speech was taken up with those Irish reforms.[128] Graham promised an alteration in the Bequests Act if it should injure the regular clergy—an assurance which pleased Murray who felt that it would rectify his position with those whose objections to the act were conscientious.[129] Then Peel made the following carefully chosen remarks:

I frankly state, ... that it is our intention to propose to Parliament a liberal increase of the vote for ... Maynooth ... I beg to state also, with equal distinctness, that we do not propose to accompany that increased vote by any regulation with respect to the doctrine, discipline, or management of the College which can diminish the grace and favour of the grant. I rejoice in the opportunity at the commencement of the Session, in making frankly this statement....[130]

[125] Heytesbury to Graham, 24 Jan. 1845, Graham Papers (marked 'Secret and Confidential').

[126] Graham to Heytesbury, 26 Jan. 1845, ibid.

[127] Heytesbury to Graham, 28 Jan. 1845, ibid; Heytesbury to Peel, 31 Jan. 1845, Add. MSS 40479, ff. 277-9.

[128] *Hansard,* lxxvii. 3-4, 4 Feb. 1845.

[129] Ibid., 107-10, 4 Feb. 1845; Heytesbury to Graham, 11 Feb. 1845, Graham Papers.

[130] *Hansard,* lxxvii. 82-94, 4 Feb. 1845.

An increased grant to Maynooth, with 'no strings attached', was the government's intention. Peel and his home secretary were keeping their pledge and were about to begin a new and scarcely less controversial phase in their scheme of Irish reforms.

6

THE MAYNOOTH GRANT 1845

'It is not Liberalism but Romanism which Peel is forcing on the nation ... It is not merely Popery; that is unpopular enough in England, especially Irish Popery; but it is Maynooth. It is a name and a thing above all others odious and suspicious to England.' (*The Times*, 17 Apr. 1845)

1. Maynooth College 1796-1845: myths and realities

Assuming that *The Times* here faithfully represents a dominant aspect of English opinion, it is essential to inquire into the reasons behind this remarkable focus on the College of Saint Patrick in Maynooth, Co. Kildare, some fifteen miles from Dublin. When Peel decided in 1844 to treble its annual parliamentary grant, the college which was the principal Roman Catholic seminary in Ireland, was sending out some sixty-five priests a year, so that by 1853 half the parish clergy could claim to be Maynooth-trained.[1] The existing grant, however, had become the subject of hostility outside Parliament and of so much controversy within Parliament that one historian has asserted that 'there is scarcely any one subject that fills a larger space than Maynooth in Hansard's parliamentary debates of the first half of the nineteenth century.'[2] The circumstances in which the college was founded and the growing controversy concerning it now require examination.[3]

[1] L. F. Renehan, 'A Return of the number of Maynooth students ordained during the last twenty years'; *Report of ... Commissioners appointed to inquire into the management of the College of Maynooth, PP 1855*, xxii, 132. Precise figures for ordination to the priesthood were not obtainable, but Renehan explained that the figures for ordination to the sub-diaconate were 'the nearest approximation deducible from the College books to the return contemplated ...'

[2] J. F. Hogan, *Maynooth College and the Laity* (1910), p. 48.

[3] The standard history of Maynooth is J. Healy, *Maynooth College, its centenary history, 1795-1895* (1895), a valuable work in need of revision. See also T. Ó Fiaich, *Má Nuad* (1972); M. R. O'Connell, 'The political background to the Establishment of Maynooth College', *IER*, fifth series, lxxxv (1956), 325-34, 406-15; lxxxvi (1956), 1-16; J. Newman, *Maynooth and Georgian Ireland* (1979). Two recent theses contain valuable new information on Maynooth: P. O'Donoghue, 'The Catholic Church and

As a state-subsidized training college for Catholic priests in a staunchly Protestant state, Maynooth's position was unusual. What is even more remarkable is that adequate provision was not made for state control in 1795 when the college was established with an annual grant of £8,000. By 1801 John Fitzgibbon, the Irish lord chancellor and a determined opponent of the Catholics, was already noting bitterly that 'we have most giddily made this establishment, and have never looked to the necessity of making regulations to guard it from abuse.'[4] For acting so 'giddily', the state was to pay a heavy price throughout the nineteenth century, and Parliament was to be convulsed almost yearly by the Maynooth grant until the great upheaval of 1845. The question arises as to why the government in 1795 bequeathed such a thorny problem to its successors. The explanation is to be sought in the complex political situation at the end of the eighteenth century. By 1793 England was at war with France and concessions to the Catholics were considered desirable. By that same year the Catholic church in Ireland was facing its own crisis brought about, too, by the revolution in France. During the penal years, it had successfully built up and maintained its structure of bishops and priests by training its candidates for ordination in Irish colleges on the continent. At the outbreak of the revolution, 478 students were being trained in these colleges: 348 in France, the remaining 130 in Rome, Spain, Portugal, and the Netherlands. The revolutionaries, however, closed the colleges; and when in 1793 they took over the Collège des Lombards in Paris, the principal training centre for Irish priests, the bishops were forced to consider the possibility of training the priests in Ireland.

It was not that the bishops wanted education in Ireland for the clergy. Their spokesman, Dr John Troy, archbishop of Dublin, avowed that 'nothing but absolute necessity can

---

Ireland in an age of Revolution and Rebellion, 1782-1803', (NUI, PH.D. thesis, 1975); and K. Wöste, 'Englands Staats-und-Kirchenpolitik in Irland 1795-1869, dargestellt an der Entwicklung des irischen Nationalseminars Maynooth College' (inaugural-Dissertation zur Erlangung des Doktorwürde der Rheinischen Friedrich-Wilhelms-Universität zu Bonn, 1976).

[4] Memorandum of the Earl of Clare upon the original Institution of Maynooth, 28 Dec. 1801, C. Ross ed., *Correspondence of Charles, first Marquis Cornwallis* ... (1859), iii. 373.

reconcile me to it, as I think it almost impossible to render it as useful as we wish.'[5] His fears were well founded, for influential parties in Ireland were not content to leave the priests' training to the bishops. Fitzgibbon had attached an amendment to the Relief Act of 1793 providing that any future college 'shall be a member of the university of Dublin and shall not be founded exclusively for the education of papists'.[6] Nevertheless, the closure of the continental colleges created that 'absolute necessity' of which Troy spoke, for the provision of priests for an ever-increasing population was the bishops' first priority. Encouraged by Rome, the bishops met in December 1793 to review the situation and investigate the feasibility of establishing seminaries in Ireland that would meet their needs. In January 1794, Troy presented a memorial to the lord lieutenant, Lord Westmorland, recounting the difficulties created by the closure of their continental colleges, expressing reluctance to expose students 'to the contagion of sedition and infidelity' of France and soliciting the royal licence for the endowment of seminaries for training priests. The memorial ruled out the University of Dublin as unsuitable, pleading the special character of priestly training, and requested instead that the seminaries be 'under Ecclesiastical Superiors of their [the students'] own Communion'. Although a grant was not directly sought, in expressing the hope that the moral instruction of the people 'may appear to his Majesty's Ministers a subject not unworthy of his Royal Consideration and Bounty', it is clear that the bishops expected endowment.[7] A year passed before the government replied rejecting this petition as incompatible with the act of 1793.[8] Within a few days, however, Lord Fitzwilliam became lord lieutenant, and his ambitious programme of Catholic reforms included the provision of a grant for the education of priests. Although Fitzwilliam was dramatically recalled and his reform programme scrapped, Portland, the home secretary,

---

[5] O'Donoghue, 'Catholic Church', p. 247.

[6] 35 Geo. III. c. 21, section vii (Ir); *A full and accurate report of the Debates in the Parliament of Ireland in the session 1793; on the bill for the Relief of His Majesty's Catholic subjects ...* (1793), pp. 388-9.

[7] Troy to Westmorland, 14 Jan. 1794. Maynooth College Archives.

[8] S. Hamilton to Troy, 2 Jan. 1795, Troy Papers, DDA, cited in O'Connell 'Political background', *IER*, lxxxv. 332-3.

reassured Dr Thomas Hussey, whom he had sent to Ireland to assist in planning the projected seminary, that it would be proceeded with; and he instructed the new lord lieutenant, Lord Camden, and the chief secretary, Thomas Pelham, to press ahead with the plan.[9] Pelham, Troy, and Hussey speedily worked out an agreement and on 23 April 1795, a bare three weeks after the arrival of Camden, the bill was introduced into the Irish House of Commons and passed without difficulty.[10] The only discordant note sounded was a petition by Catholic laymen criticizing the concentration of authority in the hands of the trustees of the new college and the exclusion of Protestants.[11] The trustees acquired a property at Maynooth in Co. Kildare and courses began there in October. On 20 April 1796, Camden, accompanied by Fitzgibbon, the chief justices, and Catholic prelates, ceremoniously laid the foundation stone for new buildings. Church and state had combined to launch the Royal College of St. Patrick at Maynooth.

The failure of the state to establish complete control over the college is largely attributable to the determined stand taken by the bishops. Already at their meeting in December 1793 they left the Congregation of Propaganda in no doubt as to their feelings:

ab omnibus in eam sententiam concordibus suffragio itum est, nihil commercii, nihil eos commune habituros cum Universitate hac Dubliniensi Protestantium, in Cleri nostri institutioni, vel in Seminariorum nostrorum erectione aut administratione; etsi contrarium statutum sit in nupero quodam decreto, seu Acto Parlamentario. Moriendum potius in simplicitate nostra omnes Praesules censuere.[12]

Again, in February 1795, their negotiators, reporting back to a meeting of the bishops, put the following query to them: 'Can

[9] O'Connell, 'Political background'; R. B. McDowell, 'The Fitzwilliam episode', *IHS*, xv (1966), 115-30. Thomas Hussey (1745-1803), chaplain of the Spanish Embassy in London; first president of Maynooth College 1795-8; bishop of Waterford, 1797-1803.

[10] 35 Geo. III. c. 21 (Ir). The act was entitled 'An act for the better education of persons professing the Popish, or Roman Catholic religion' and did not specify that the college was to be reserved exclusively for the training of priests, but the circumstances surrounding its establishment indicate that such was its primary purpose; see Hogan, *Maynooth College and the Laity*, pp. 7-47; O'Connell, 'Political background', *IER*, lxxxvi. 6; Newman, *Maynooth*, pp. 13-20.

[11] *Journal of the House of Commons ... of Ireland from 22 Jan. 1795 to 5 June 1795* (1795) pp. 111-12, 29 Apr. 1795.

[12] Letter of the four archbishops and five bishops to the cardinal prefect of Propaganda, 5 Dec. 1793, Moran, *Spicilegium,* iii. 458.

the Acting Prelates ... agree to the appointment of President or Professors in the intended Colleges by Government, Parliament or any lay authority; and if not, what degree of interference on the part of any of these is admissible?' The answer was 'Negatively; no interference is admissible.'[13] The hard line taken by the bishops on this issue is all the more surprising in view of the more flexible attitude adopted by the same meeting on the possibility of royal nomination of bishops. Of great importance and support was the advice of their powerful ally, Edmund Burke, who, urging them to reject 'government interference', warned them not to be deceived by the 'fine specious, general name of *government*'. In effect they would hand over the training of their priests to men like Fitzgibbon and Duigenan, avowed enemies of their church, as soon as they accepted 'government interference.'[14] Still, the fact that this question was put to the bishops is indication enough that the government hoped for some control. The Fitzwilliam debacle changed matters. Portland was anxious to conciliate the bishops, and Camden found the Irish Protestants desirous that the Catholics should enjoy every advantage which 'may not endanger the established Constitution'.[15] As Tighe, the MP for Wicklow remarked, Maynooth was a sop for the abandonment of Emancipation.[16] Furthermore, there was now no comprehensive government plan to deal with the Catholic question in the context of which the relations of the Catholic church and the Protestant state could be fully worked out.[17] Portland, nevertheless, proceeded cautiously, submitting the draft legislation to the scrutiny of the archbishop of Canterbury, 'because' as he told Camden, 'upon a subject of this kind there can not be too much consideration.'[18] Fitzgibbon successfully opposed Hussey's plan for vesting the college in the Catholic bishops, persuading Camden that such

[13] Ibid., iii. 474-5.

[14] Burke to Hussey, 17 Mar. 1795, *Correspondence*, viii. 199-205. Patrick Duigenan (1735-1826); advocate-general 1785; MP for Armagh; a resolute opponent of concessions to Catholics.

[15] Camden to Portland, 6 Apr. 1795, Secret ministerial letters from ... Camden ... to ... Portland ... 1795-7. Letterbook, p. 3. Trinity College, Dublin, MSS 1762, Pelham Papers.

[16] *Freeman's Journal*, 2 May 1795.

[17] O'Connell, 'Political background', *IER*, lxxxvi. 8-16.

[18] Portland to Camden, 20 Apr. 1795, Secret ministerial letters from Camden to Portland, p. 286.

an arrangement might encourage the idea of an establishment for the Catholic church.[19] As a result of his action, the act of 1795 appointed the lord chancellor, the two chief justices, and the chief baron of the exchequer (all positions reserved by law for Protestants) *ex-officio* members of the Board of Trustees. Eleven other trustees, however, were Catholic ecclesiastics (all bishops except Hussey, the first president) and the remaining six were Catholic laymen. The trustees were empowered to appoint a president and professors, to draw up bye-laws and the property of the college was vested in them. They also had the important role of college visitors. The Protestant members attended only two meetings. In 1800 Fitzgibbon attempted to increase governmental control in an amending act which set up a body of eight visitors. Two of those were the Catholic archbishops of Armagh and Dublin, a third was the Catholic Earl of Fingall but the five remaining were Protestant. These were the four *ex-officio* members of the Board of Trustees who now ceased to be part of that body, and the chancellor of the Irish exchequer.[20] The lord lieutenant had the power to veto the byelaws, rules, regulations, and statutes of the college. Finally, the trustees had to account annually for the parliamentary grant.

From the point of view of the bishops, whose first aim was to prevent external interference with the training of students for the priesthood, there were possible flaws in this arrangement. The governing body of the seminary—the trustees—included laymen; five of the eight original visitors were Protestant and the lord lieutenant possessed a wide-ranging veto. Impressive though these restrictions seemed, they were more apparent than real. Section 3 of the Act severely limited the powers of the Protestant visitors, laying down that their authority 'shall not extend to, or in any manner affect the exercise of the Roman Catholic religion, or the religious doctrine or discipline thereof within the College...' Sections 4 and 9 confirmed this power in the hands of the Catholic bishops. The triennial visits proved to be a mere matter of form.[21] Similarly, the lord lieutenant's veto

[19] Camden to Portland, 14 Apr. 1795. ibid., pp. 12-14.

[20] 40 Geo. III, c. 85 (Ir). When the office of chancellor of the Irish exchequer ceased in 1813, the number of Protestants dropped to four.

[21] *Report of the Parliamentary Committee of the Loyal National Repeal Association* (1845), ii. 312.

applied only to regulations not affecting the exercise of the
Catholic religion and its religious discipline within the college.
Since there is little in a Catholic seminary that cannot fit into
that category, the veto was practically worthless. On the Board
of Trustees, the bishops were in a commanding position, and a
report of the Repeal Association in 1844 commented that 'the
lay trustees appear to be in reality rather honorary and nominal
than efficient trustees.' Despite the inconvenience of a triennial
visit and the annoyance of annual questions in Parliament, the
bishops possessed all the control they could reasonably expect
over the running of the college. Their position was enhanced
when, in 1817, the lay college, which was attached to the
seminary, was closed down.[22] Thenceforth, Maynooth was run
by the Irish church exclusively to train its clergy. Fitzgibbon's
misgivings were well-founded. Although subsidized by the
state to the tune of £8,000 a year, Maynooth was free of its
control.

The first major criticism of Maynooth came in 1798 when it
was alleged that some of the students were involved in the
rebellion.[23] From then on the college came in for bitter, if
sporadic, attacks from those who opposed state support for a
Catholic seminary, disliked the type of priest it produced and
cast doubts on its doctrine.[24] In 1826 a thorough inquiry into
the college amassed detailed information concerning the courses
followed, the lecturers, the students, and the general regime,
but it could come to no conclusion for the commissioners disagreed in their findings.[25] Anthony Blake, who had been one of
the commissioners, told the lord lieutenant in 1844 that three of
the five commissioners favoured a more liberal endowment for
the college under new regulations while the other two would
have liked to suppress it.[26] In the agitation that led to Eman-

---

[22] A lay college was set up in 1800 and continued in existence until 1817.

[23] Journal of the Trustees of Maynooth College, pp. 14-15, 11 May 1798, Maynooth
College Archives.

[24] *Hansard* 1, xxxvi. 325, 9 May 1817, John Leslie Foster; *State of Ireland; Report and
Minutes of Evidence, PP 1825,* viii. 807, 7 June 1825, William Magee, archbishop of
Dublin.

[25] *Eighth report of the Commissioners of Irish Education: Roman Catholic College of Maynooth,
PP 1826-7,* xiii. 537-998.

[26] Heytesbury to Graham, 16, 20 Oct. 1844; Eliot to Graham, 16 Oct. 1844; Graham
to Heytesbury, 20, 24 Oct. 1844, Graham Papers. For Blake see pp. 136-9.

cipation, 'Maynooth began to be felt', as Thomas Wyse, O'Connell's able lieutenant, remarked; and the spectacle of priests leading tenants to the polls to vote against their landlords increased hostility to the college.[27] The efforts, too, of zealous missionaries of the New Reformation, reporting back to sympathetic English audiences who provided their main financial support, brought Irish religious affairs, including Maynooth College, before a wider audience. It was at Exeter Hall and among the Evangelicals that this Irish mission received most support. Within the Evangelicals a militant wing had developed, 'the product of a new apocalyptical evangelicalism which emerged in England during the 1820s'.[28] These were the 'Recordites' who took their name from *The Record,* a dynamic thrice-weekly evangelical paper. Through the opposition of the Recordites in Parliament, the annual debates on the Maynooth grant became more acrimonious during the 1830s.[29]

There were other factors bringing Irish religious controversy to the forefront of English politics. The Established church felt threatened. Many churchmen were still upset by the 'betrayal' of 1829. The Reform Act of 1832 embittered feelings and it appeared likely that the reformed Parliament would interfere with the church. Concerned with the situation in Ireland where the Tithe war had broken out, the Whig government brought in a Church Temporalities (Ireland) bill in 1833 which suppressed ten Irish bishoprics. It was the appropriation clause of the bill, however, that roused most feeling for it provided that the government could use for whatever purposes it thought' proper the surplus revenues of the suppressed bishoprics. In 1835, with the return to power of the Whigs allied to O'Connell's party, the Anglican primate of Ireland, Lord John Beresford, aware of a renewed threat of appropriation, sent the Rev Mortimer O'Sullivan and the Rev R. J. M'Ghee to England to rally support for the Irish church.[30] The Recordites; particularly

---

[27] T. Wyse, *Historical Sketch of the late Catholic Association of Ireland* (1829), i. 203. For Wyse see p. 291.

[28] I. C. Bradley, 'The Politics of Godliness: Evangelicals in Parliament, 1784-1832' (Oxford Univ., D. Phil. thesis, 1974), p. 253.

[29] *Hansard,* iv. 268, 23 June 1831; v. 16-28, 19 July 1831; xii. 306-9, 11 Apr; xiv. 214-15, 10 July, 1832; xxii. 976-9, 18 Apr. 1834; xxviii. 529, 4 June 1835; xxviii. 896-8, 19 June 1835.

[30] I. S. Rennie, 'Evangelicalism and English public life, 1823-50' (Toronto Univ., Ph. D. Thesis, 1962), pp. 236-9.

Captain James Gordon, MP for Dundalk, gave them a warm
welcome. A well-advertised meeting at Exeter Hall on 20 June
1835 promised the sensational revelation of documents which
would prove conclusively the intolerant and persecuting nature
of Irish Catholicism. Gladstone, Ashley, and over a score of
other MPs were among the distinguished audience at this
meeting where M'Ghee produced as his evidence the moral
theology textbook of Pierre Dens.[31] *Dens*, he claimed, as he
read extracts from it, sanctioned false oaths by Catholics,
intolerance, and the odious practices of the confessional and yet
was a textbook for Maynooth, specially reprinted on Dr
Murray's orders. At the close of the meeting, Gordon announced the establishment of a Protestant Association, which,
with similar associations throughout the country, was destined
to play a significant part in stirring up anti-Catholic feeling.[32]
The meeting impressed Gladstone and was the proto-type of a
series of meetings which denounced the evil influence of Dens
in Maynooth and the alleged perjuries of Murray, whom some
ultra-Protestants re-christened 'Dr Dens Murray'.[33] Dr
Phillpotts, bishop of Exeter, raised the question in the House of
Lords:

Is not *Dens' Theology* one of the reference books of Maynooth College ...?
Is not that book left in the public library for the perusal of all the students ...?
Dens' opinions are as much respected in Maynooth as Blackstone's Com-
mentaries in the Protestant universities of England.[34]

[31] P. Dens, *Theologia moralis et dogmatica...* 8 vols. (Dublin 1832); Pierre Dens (1690-
1775), a Belgian theologian who wrote mainly on the sacrament of penance and the
confessional. His most important work was the *Theologia ad usum seminariorum et sacrae
theologiae alumnorum* (Louvain, 1777) which, published posthumously, was not
completely his own composition. Its pedagogical method of question and answer made
it popular. This was the work which Coyne, the Catholic publisher, re-edited in
Dublin in 1832, with a fulsome dedication to Murray. Coyne's edition contains many
additional Roman documents.
[32] M. O'Sullivan and R. J. M'Ghee, *Romanism as it rules in Ireland* (1840) i. 1-74.
Newman's witty sketch of a Muscovite orator denouncing to a shocked audience in
Moscow the 'blasphemous' doctrines contained in Blackstone's *Commentaries* ('the king
can do no wrong' etc.) was deliberately modelled on M'Ghee's dramatic disclosure of
the 'evil doctrines' contained in *Dens*; J. H. Newman, *Lectures on the present position of
Catholics in England ... 1851* (1893 ed.), pp. 25-41.
[33] W. E. Gladstone, *Diaries*, ed. M. R. D. Foot and H. C. G. Matthew (1968),
ii. 176, 20 June 1835; O'Sullivan and M'Ghee, *Romanism*, vols. i and ii give full
accounts of those meetings. Sugden complained of an article in the *Standard* calling the
archbishop 'Dr Dens Murray'; Sugden to Graham, 25 May 1843, Graham Papers.
[34] *Hansard*, xxix. 608, 16 July 1835.

No less than thirty columns of *Hansard* were filled with the
debate on the theology and influence in Ireland of this obscure
Belgian theologian. *Dens* was so often cited in speeches and in
the press that one of the Maynooth professors, questioned
about him during the 1853 inquiry, finally exclaimed in exasperation that 'the name and authority of Dens have been for
the last twenty years, so incessantly and pertinaciously obtruded
upon us - as if he were a Pope addressing the whole church *ex
cathedra* or a second Council of Trent.'[35] Pamphlets criticizing
Maynooth began to multiply in the 1830s.[36] Not untypical of
their content was the assertion of the Rev Edward Bickersteth,
a prominent Evangelical, that the Maynooth grant 'is paying
money to undermine the Throne as much as if it had been
spent in buying the barrels of gunpowder which were used by
Guy Fawkes.'[37] The press, too, led by *The Times,* whose influence was in the ascendant, published numerous hostile
articles in which the Irish problem was seen as a complex of
O'Connell, a slavish peasantry, popish priests, Maynooth,
Dens, and Repeal.[38] Blackwood's Magazine, Fraser's Magazine, and other influential journals took up the same themes.
The religious literature current in most homes had always been
anti-Catholic, from the commentaries on the Bible and the
Homilies down to the religious tracts of Hannah More. Now,
in the second half of the 1830s, Foxe's *Book of Martyrs,* the best-
known anti-Catholic text, was frequently republished.[39] These

[35] *Maynooth Commission: Report of Her Majesty's Commissioners PP 1854-5,* xxii. 368.
When Thomas Raikes, the diarist, visited the library in Maynooth in 1846, he commented that 'one of the prominent books was P. Dens' Theology, which is the ground-
work of their [Maynooth's] statutes, though denied by Dr Murray ...', Journal,
4 Jan. 1846, *A portion of the journal kept by Thomas Raikes ...* (1857), iv. 323.

[36] Books and pamphlets on Maynooth included: E. F. O'Beirne, *An impartial view
of ... Maynooth: Containing an account of the system of tyranny—mental, moral and physical—
pursued therein* (1836);—*Maynooth in 1834* (1835); A. Irwin, *Roman Catholic morality, as
inculcated in the theological class-books in Maynooth College.* (1836); J. C. Colquhoun, *Speech
at Exeter Hall on the Maynooth Grant* (1836); *The case of Maynooth considered ...* (1836); *Popish
College of Maynooth* (1836), R. J. M'Ghee, *Popery in Maynooth* (1839); *Maynooth College;
its teaching ... from its own class-books,* 2 vols. (1841); J. Lord, *Maynooth College* (1841).

[37] *Endowment of Popery* (London, n.d.); Edward Bickersteth (1786-1850).

[38] G. A. Cahill, 'Irish Catholicism and English Toryism', *Review of Politics,* xix
(1957), 62-76.

[39] The catalogue of the British Museum lists editions of the *Book of Martyrs* for
1837, 1838, 1839, 1841, 1843-9, 1848; extracts from the work were published in 1835,
1837, 1846, 1851.

editions, complete with woodcuts depicting burnings of heretics, showed a 'progressive corruption and vulgarization of the original for the propagation of an increasingly narrow evangelical Protestant piety ... The book opened now with the stories of the sufferings inflicted on Protestants in the days of ''Bloody Mary''.[40] Pamphlets, articles, speeches, and the increasing number of questions raised in Parliament are an index of rising hostility to Catholicism and of the focus on Maynooth.

The undercurrent of 'No Popery' which, as Professor Chadwick noted, bubbled to the surface from 1835 onwards had deep roots in English life.[41] Greville, who pleaded strongly for an increase in the grant to Maynooth, noted at the same time the difficulties involved in granting any concessions to Catholics 'for the good people of England have, for the most part, sucked in with their mothers' milk a dislike to the [Roman] Catholic religion.'[42] The high-minded, if less tolerant Lord Ashley, noted in his diary, in reference to the opposition to the increased grant, 'the deep solemn, Protestant feeling in the hearts of the British people'.[43] Newman, who had the advantage of seeing both sides, delivered a series of lectures on this 'anti-Catholic tradition' which he described as 'so multitudinous, so elementary' that a Catholic had no chance against it.[44] Apart from the influence of the Evangelicals there were other influences at work from 1835 onwards to stir up this deep-rooted antagonism to Catholicism. For some it was O'Connell's political influence and activities that roused their hostility to Catholicism. A devoted churchman like Newman avowed that he harboured 'an unspeakable aversion' to O'Connell's policy because he appeared to associate himself 'with men of all religions and no religion against the Anglican Church, and advanced Catholicism by violence and intrigue.'[45] Other Anglicans were disillusioned with the effects of Emancipation: William Whewell, master of Trinity College, Cambridge, told

---

[40] W. Haller, *Foxe's Book of Martyrs and the Elect Nation* (1963), p. 252.

[41] O. Chadwick, *The Victorian Church* (1966), i. 166.

[42] Greville, *Past and Present Policy,* p. vii.

[43] Diary, 7 Apr. 1845, E. Hodder, *The Life and Work of the seventh earl of Shaftesbury* (1880-2), ii. 101.

[44] Newman, *Present condition of Catholics,* pp. 24-41.

[45] J. H. Newman, *Apologia Pro Vita Sua,* ed. M. J. Svaglic (1967), p. 117.

Henry Goulburn, Peel's chancellor of the exchequer, that 'the results of the Relief Bill had made people feel how little liberal concession could allay Roman Catholic hostility and that he felt satisfied that any attempt to repeat such an experiment in the case of Maynooth would cause universal excitement in the Protestant mind.'[46] A further, and very powerful, contributory factor was the growing alarm aroused by certain tendencies manifested within the Oxford movement which had begun as a protest against state interference with the church, especially in Ireland, but was now accused of 'creeping Romanism'. In 1838 Newman and John Keble had edited the first volumes of Hurrell Froude's *Remains*; and its contemptuous remarks on the Reformation, the leading Reformers and 'odious Protestantism' had scandalized many churchmen and provoked reactions against the movement. When on 27 February 1841 Newman published *Tract XC* with a view to showing that the thirty-nine Articles were not inconsistent with Catholic faith, alarm became widespread that the church of Rome and her doctrines were gaining a foothold within the citadel of the Anglican church. When a few days later the usual objections against the annual grant to Maynooth were raised in Parliament, O'Connell and his friends retaliated by referring to the Oxford clergymen who were, he alleged, 'acting contrary to their oaths in teaching Popery while they were paid by the Protestant Church'.[47] As alarm at the Rome-ward trend increased with the secession of some Tractarians, anti-Catholicism grew.[48] Referring to the prevalent mood of 'No Popery', the *Morning Chronicle* alleged that were it not for 'the Puseyite extravagance it would soon have become as purely historical as the "no-Excise" cry which frightened Sir Robert Walpole.'[49] In an age of Romanticism, Catholicism could be tolerated, even cherished, as an interesting medieval survival—as Scott depicted it in his writings. Now, however, it seemed to pose a real threat and from two quarters:

[46] Goulburn to Peel, 6 Jan. 1845, Add. MSS 40445, ff. 5-7; see N. Gash, *Reaction and Reconstruction in English Politics 1832-52* (1965), p. 95. Gash gives examples of similar sentiments, op. cit. pp. 93-5. Greville admitted that others shared the dis-illusionment attributed to Whewell but he argued that it was not justified; *Past and Present Policy*, p. 169.

[47] *Hansard,* lvi. 1239-54, 2 Mar. 1841.

[48] Chadwick, *Victorian Church,* i. 166-89.

[49] *Morning Chronicle,* 26 Mar. 1845.

one from the Maynooth-dominated masses of Ireland, many of whom were pouring into English cities, and another, more insidious, from the very heart of Protestantism and from those sworn to defend it. When the *Record* announced in 1845 that what the country had to dread was 'POPERY; popery within and popery without the church', it was using the same language that Lord John Russell was to use in the Durham Letter when, linking Tractarianism and Papal Aggression, he denounced 'the danger within the gates' as the greater of the two.[50]

Since Maynooth College was a focal point of criticism, the question arises as to the justification for the charges made against it. It should be noted that not all the diocesan priesthood were educated at the college; in 1826, besides the 391 students in Maynooth, about 120 were being educated in other colleges in Ireland and a further 140 in colleges on the continent.[51] On the question of the training imparted, neither the 1826 commission nor a more thorough one in 1853 found anything seriously amiss.[52] Maynooth did not teach that the pope had power to depose the monarch, nor that it was lawful to break oaths with heretics. The authorities, realizing only too well the vulnerability of the college, were at pains to prove their loyalty, and the questions raised in Parliament and in the press by suspicious Protesants kept them alert and careful. The severe judgment passed on *Dens* and Maynooth's other textbooks was unwarranted. *Dens* was only one of many manuals competing in the theological market in Catholic seminaries throughout the world, and professors of theology tended to select only those sections which appealed to them. Undoubtedly, many passages in these books could be interpreted in a way that would seem to encourage casuistry, papal power to dissolve oaths and prurience in confessional interrogation. The extracts, however, were forced out of their highly specialized context. Murray protested that, 'until the Church of England shall have reformed its Book of Homilies, and the Church of Scotland its Confession, no one of either communion has a right to utter one word against the

---

[50] *The Record,* 6 Feb. 1845; Lord John Russell to the Bishop of Durham, 4 Nov. 1850, Spencer Walpole, *Life of Lord John Russell* (1891), ii. 120.

[51] *Eighth Report, Maynooth, PP 1826-7,* xiii. 8-9.

[52] *Report of H. M. Commissioners appointed to inquire into the management and government of the College of Maynooth, PP 1854-5,* xxii.

publication or reading of *Dens*.'[53] Dr Thirlwall, bishop of St. David's, came to a similar conclusion, affirming in 1845 that the passages were selective and that 'there was no difference between the teaching of these books and of the most approved treatises by any Protestant ethical writer.'[54] The charge concerning the manner of interrogating in matters of chastity in the confessional was specially investigated by the 1853 commission and was found to be without foundation.[55] The confessional practices which M'Ghee discovered in *Dens' Theology* could have been found in contemporary manuals of moral theology. The moral theologians over-emphasized the categorization of sins according to genus and species, and specified minutely the type of question a confessor was obliged to ask in assessing the measure of guilt. This over-specification applied to sins against justice as much as to sins against chastity but, in the nature of things, specification of questions on sins against chastity gave the impression of prurience. Undoubtedly, the treatment of this subject by the manuals was to blame; moral theologians, like writers of medical manuals, felt they had to treat of all pathological cases as well as the more ordinary ones, and such cases took up an unwarrantedly large space. The insertion of a minute list of questions which so shocked O'Sullivan when he found it in *Dens* goes back to the early middle ages. Protestant difficulties about the confessional stemmed not from proven facts, but from an outlook that regarded with suspicion a practice foreign to its own tradition and which appeared as unwarrantable interference with the rights of the head of the family.

As Catholic seminaries everywhere used standard theology textbooks in Latin, the teaching in Maynooth would not have differed much from Catholic teaching on the continent. Indeed, a comparison with foreign seminaries, undertaken by the Commission of 1853, and an examination of the textbooks in use showed that the academic course in the college was extensive.[56] The standardized textbook and the lack of breadth in the tight structure of seminary curricula, however, reflected

---

[53] Murray, *A pastoral address to the Catholic clergy of the diocese of Dublin* (1836), p. 151.
[54] *Hansard*, xxxi. 87-8, 4 June 1845.
[55] *Report on Maynooth, PP 1854-5*, xxii. 64-5; 727-73.
[56] *Ibid.*, pp. 21-2, 237-349.

the indifferent quality of contemporary Catholic theology. The system was, on the whole, a somewhat restricted one. Apart from texts in theology, the Commission of 1826 found the rooms of the senior students furnished 'with a very considerable collection of books in different classes of literature'.[57] Nevertheless, entrance standards left room for improvement, and as late as 1854 the Commission of Inquiry after hearing the evidence of Dr Dixon, archbishop of Armagh, Lord Ffrench, and Anthony Strong Hussey, all visitors of the college, came to the conclusion that there was a great defect in the entrance examination in regard to the English language. The poor state of preparatory schools was seen as the root of the problem.[58] The complaint that the general training, with its rigid discipline, seclusion from ordinary life, and apparent invasion of students' private lives was too narrow, had a certain validity. It was quite foreign to the mode of training for the Anglican ministry with which its critics compared it. It is doubtful, too, if the seclusion practised was the most apt way of preparing young priests for their later ministry. This mode of training, however, was common throughout the Catholic world and was not peculiar to Maynooth. The Council of Trent, in a successful attempt to weed out unsuitable candidates, established seminaries in each diocese where the students—over a period of six or seven years—were given a uniform and thorough course in Catholic theology, received continuous guidance in spiritual matters and were subjected to close supervision and exacting discipline. At the end of this period, the seminary authorities decided whether or not the candidate was suitable for ordination. The result was generally a pious, well-instructed, obedient priest devoted to the Catholic church, but the exaggeratedly clerical education did make for a certain narrowness.

Another recurring criticism levelled at Maynooth, which was first voiced by Fitzgibbon as early as 1799, was that the free education at the college would mean that the priests would be taken from 'the dregs of the people'.[59] In 1808 Parliament

---

[57] *Eighth Report, Maynooth, PP 1826-7*, xiii. 548.

[58] *Report on Maynooth, PP 1854-5*, xxii. 282-6; 47.

[59] Cornwallis to Portland, 18 Apr. 1799, *Correspondence of Charles, first Marquis of Cornwallis*, C. Ross ed. (1839) iii. 91.

required the college to furnish a list of the occupations of the students' fathers. The list showed that out of 205 fathers, 148 were 'farmers'—a term that could include rich and poor farmers alike—and 11 others were 'graziers', who would represent a wealthier class than the ordinary farmer. Three-quarters of the students, then, were sons of the soil, but it is not possible to indicate with precision their family circumstances. The remaining 46 included 10 grocers, 7 merchants, 2 innkeepers, 2 flour factors, a ship's captain, a land surveyor, a land agent, a clerk of coal mines, a tax-collector, and one or two representatives of a dozen other trades.[60] The information for the non-agricultural group is more revealing for it shows that some of these students were drawn from the professional and mercantile classes and the others were sons of tradesmen. These returns would indicate that the students did not come from the lower echelons of society. The information, however, is too vague and incomplete—some of the dioceses made no returns—to enable more than tentative conclusions to be drawn from it. Although these and other papers on Maynooth were again laid before the House of Commons in 1817, the criticisms of the social origins of the Maynooth students did not abate; and in the early 1820s, the president of the college, Dr Bartholomew Crotty, complained to the lord lieutenant, Lord Wellesley, of the slur cast on the college by allegations in a newspaper that 'the Roman Catholic clergy of Ireland was composed of men taken from the plough, and trained up in the College of Maynooth in the principles of *treason and sedition.*'[61] Maxwell Blacker, KC, told a Select Committee investigating the State of Ireland in 1824 that the Maynooth clergy were taken 'from the very humblest class of men, whose brothers were carpenters and shoemakers, and overseers and under stewards'.[62] Similarly, Major George Warburton stated that they were of a lower class of individual than the former clergy.[63] O'Connell's evidence before the Committee was ambiguous. Intent on praising the Maynooth clergy, he remarked that 'being most of them the

---

[60] *Papers presented to the House of Commons relating to Maynooth College, PP 1808*, ix. 371-99.

[61] *Eighth Report, Maynooth, PP 1826-7*, xiii. 639-40.

[62] *Minutes of Evidence, Select Committee on Disturbances in Ireland, PP 1825*, vii. 63.

[63] Ibid., p. 162.

sons of very low persons, they have astonished me not only by their manners, but by the classical facility and elegance of their style in writing.' He was immediately asked from what class the former clergy were taken, and replied that they were taken from nearly the same class, perhaps a little superior. He went on to make the point, not entirely convincingly in the light of his earlier remarks, that several sons of the gentry, including his nephew and another near relation, were educated at Maynooth.[64]

Maria Edgeworth complained that the priests educated there were 'so vulgar that no gentleman can, let him wish it ever so much, keep company with them.'[65] Inglis, Lord Alvanley, and the Halls contrasted the benevolent, courteous, foreign-educated priest with his polished demeanour and knowledge of the world to the vulgar-minded or stiff and conceited product they saw emerging from Maynooth.[66] The most violent accusation on this score came from Eugene O'Beirne, who had been expelled from Maynooth but had conformed to the Established church. To secure training in the continental colleges, he asserted, it was necessary to muster about £100. For Maynooth, however, 'the rudest ploughboy, if he have but managed to obtain the interest of his parish priest, is infallibly certain of having the way smoothed for him ... No one acquainted with Ireland can deny, that the vast majority of Maynooth students, for twenty years past, have been composed from the lowest grades of society!' An Irish priest, he affirmed, was almost invariably the son of some petty farmer, labourer or artisan.[67] In 1844, when Peel was contemplating improving Maynooth, De Grey, in an effort to dissuade him, made a similar criticism: 'They are born in poverty and want, they do not feel the misery of dirt and poor fare during their period of education ... An institution on a better footing in England ... would never run

---

[64] *Minutes of Evidence, Select Committee, Lords, on State of Ireland, PP 1825*, ix. 155.

[65] Maria Edgeworth to Honora Edgeworth, 12 Aug. 1831, Edgeworth Papers, cited in Hurst, *Maria Edgeworth*, p. 66.

[66] H. D. Inglis, *Ireland in 1834: a journey through Ireland during the spring, summer and autumn of 1834* (3rd ed. 1835), ii. 338-42; Alvanley, *State of Ireland*, pp. 18-23; Mr and Mrs S. C. Hall, *Ireland: its scenery and character* (1841-3), ii. 278-83.

[67] E. F. O'Beirne, *A succinct and accurate account of the system of discipline, education and theology adopted and pursued in the Popish College of Maynooth* (1840), pp. 2-4.

the risk of being swamped with the sons of day labourers (an old woman at my gate earning a few shillings a week has her son a Maynooth priest).'[68]

The Maynooth priest, however, had his defenders. In 1817 a Maynooth student claimed that he scarcely knew one respectable Catholic family which had not some relative in the church, adding that 'considering the exertions that have been made to confine the acquisition of rank and property, to the members of the established church, it is by no means singular that the mission of Ireland should be generally supplied from the middle classes of society'.[69] The point was sound, for with the decimation of the Catholic aristocracy it was not to be expected that a majority of priests should be from the upper classes. Nevertheless, as Daniel Madden, the Young Irelander, correctly noted, the remaining Irish aristocracy, in contrast to the Catholic aristocracies on the continent, gave few of its sons to the church.[70] The question of the students' origins was discussed during the Commission of 1826. Crotty, the president of Maynooth, Michael Montague, vice president, and Crolly, then bishop of Down and Connor, defended the type of student, Crotty maintaining that they were 'generally the sons of farmers, who must be comfortable in order to meet the expenses ...; of tradesmen, shopkeepers; and not a very small proportion of them are the children of opulent merchants and rich farmers and graziers.' Although he accepted that some few might come from a lower class, he maintained that the students in general came 'from what in Ireland is considered the middling class'. He backed up his case by adducing figures to prove that the cost of education in Maynooth was as high as the cost of educating a student on the continent.[71] In 1844 the well-informed Anthony Blake, in a secret memorandum which the cabinet adopted as the basis for its Maynooth bill, affirmed that

those who are acquainted with the present Roman Catholic clergy, and who speak of them from actual intercourse, not mere rumour, know that they

[68] De Grey to Graham, 27 Feb. 1844, Graham Papers.
[69] *Calumny refuted, or remarks on a pamphlet of the Rev. William Phelan, F.T.C.D., entitled 'The Bible, not the Bible Society'*; by a student of the R.C. College of Maynooth (1817), p. 34.
[70] Madden, *Ireland*, ii. 258-9.
[71] *Eighth Report*, pp. 594, 632-3, 909.

come, for the most part, not from the lower orders, but from the middle class. They do not, however, come from the wealthier sections of it; they come ... from struggling families that could not pretend to send them to any college, unless to one that would receive them free.[72]

John Harold, curate at Kingstown, who had entered Maynooth in 1838, told the 1853 Commission that he thought the students were 'the sons of persons in business and trade in the cities and provincial towns and the sons of comfortable, middle and humble farmers in the country.'[73]

On the difference between the old-style priest trained in France or Spain and the home-educated priest, Maynooth's defenders had interesting comments. O'Connell, who had studied at St. Omer and Douai and who, furthermore, was well placed to understand the political attitudes of both old and new clergy, told the 1826 Commission that 'the priests who were educated in France ... were very strong anti-Jacobins ... there ... [was] among them a great deal of ... ultra royalism; but with the priests educated at Maynooth, the anti-Jacobin feeling is gone by, and they are more identified with the people.'[74] Bishop Doyle, who favoured the broadening influences of travel, was convinced from his own training at the university of Coimbra that, although the education in Irish colleges was as good as could be had in continental colleges, the universities abroad provided better education for they had men of more extensive learning to teach and genius was better cultivated.[75] MacHale's tart comment on the controversy was that 'when Maynooth did not exist, the continental clergy were sure to return to their country with foreign disaffection; and now, when that venerable body is gradually retiring from the scene, they are panegyrised by their enemies, as if they thought they could injure Maynooth by contrast.'[76] MacHale's criticism is a fair comment on a normal nostalgia for the past but he did not make sufficient allowance for the growing apprehension felt by

---

[72] Blake's memorandum on Maynooth College, 4 Nov. 1844, Derby Papers, Box 37/1.

[73] Report on Maynooth, *PP 1854-5*, xxii. 408.

[74] *State of Ireland: Report and Minutes of Evidence, PP 1825*, viii. 120, 4 March. 1825.

[75] *Minutes of Evidence on the State of Ireland, PP 1825*, ix, 243, 21 Mar. 1825.

[76] MacHale to the editor of the *Morning Chronicle*, 5 Sept. 1831, J. MacHale, *Letters* (1847), p. 220.

Protestants at the increased political involvement of the Irish Catholic clergy.

Evidence of the students' own attitude to the criticisms of their social origins is not readily available. Some insight may, however, be gained from an incident in the college which began as a trivial row between a student and a college servant but grew into a serious confrontation between the students and the college authorities. According to the students' account the affair began when the servant spoke to the student 'in a stile which from the contrasted condition of the student and the servant roused his [the student's] feelings.' The matter became serious when the servant appealed to the professorial staff:

The servant was redressed by R. M. Delahogue in the presence of the other professors with language to the following import: the students of this College from the continual and habitual tenor of their conduct may with truth be called a *community* of peasants. What were his reasons? They never observed the ceremony of saluting him by taking off their hats; secondly, they sometimes had the rudeness to sit at the parlour fire during the absence of the professors.

Stung by Delahogue's contemptuous remarks, the whole student body revolted. Having appealed in vain first to the dean and then to the president, they solemnly put their case to the trustees in a memorandum that laid bare the very heart of their grievance:

The respectability of this College *especially* of the students has often been assailed in public by the enemies of their faith; they have read and repeated the calumnies with indignation which the silence of individual feelings could allow [*sic*]. They have seen a Duigenan attempt to draw on [them] the contempt of the empire by the appelation of paupers. But when they beheld their professor not merely countenance but confirm this calumny by a term still more contemptuous the feelings of their resentment were mingled with sorrow. This sorrow operated powerfully and generally.[77]

The trustees, deeply concerned at 'the spirit of insubordination ... which has of late pervaded almost the whole of the Students', took a firm stand. They expelled five ring-leaders and ordered the president to punish the whole body.[78] Although the affair

[77] Memorial of the students..to the Trustees, 3 Jan. 1803, file marked 'Maynooth College 1795-1849', DDA.
[78] Journal of the Board of Trustees, 28 Feb. 1803, pp. 33-4, Maynooth College Archives.

ended there, the unanimous rejection of the term 'peasant' is remarkable. While to Delahogue, a Sorbonne professor of the *ancien régime*, they may indeed have appeared to deserve to be called peasants, to them it was an insult more injurious and unacceptable than to be called paupers. Their outraged reaction shows how far they were from regarding themselves as 'the dregs of the people'. It is an indication too, of complex stratifications within Irish 'peasant society' whose existence outside observers often did not even suspect. The evidence given by the students to the 1826 Commission was more telling than that of the staff because it was more specific. Questioned about their parents' position in life one replied that they held land in the barony of Firth,[79] another that his father was a general shop-keeper in Kilcock who also held over two hundred acres,[80] a third that his father was engaged in the 'surveying and engineering department'.[81] Yet another said that his mother held between two hundred and fifty and three hundred acres under the Marquess of Ely, in the barony of Shelbourne,[82] another that his father was a farmer, without adding any qualifications.[83] Another replied that his father was a 'woollen draper and an army contractor for mens' necessaries on a large scale'.[84] One volunteered the comment that his parents, like the majority of parents of other students, belonged to that state of life 'which we call the middle class of society'.[85]

Most of the many visitors to Ireland during this period commented on the priests and although some of them contrasted the Maynooth priest and the foreign-educated priest, in general the opinions they expressed lent little support for the idea that the priests were recruited from the lowest class of society. Baptist Noel accepted Crotty's contention that the expense of a Maynooth education excluded students from the lowest classes.[86] The novelist Thackeray, who was severely critical of the college, came away with the impression that the students

---

[79] *Eighth Report*, p. 948.
[80] Ibid., p. 959.
[81] Ibid., p. 960.
[82] Ibid., p. 964.
[83] Ibid., p. 966.
[84] Ibid., p. 971.
[85] Ibid., p. 969.
[86] Noel, *Tour*, p. 339.

were the sons of tradesmen and farmers.[87] James Johnson, a
noted physician, reported that 'the students were by no means
a vulgar-looking class ... They were stout-built farmers' sons
apparently.'[88] The author, James Grant, specifically rebutted
the charge that the students were from the dregs of the peasantry:
'A majority of them consist of the sons of small farmers, not it
is true, abounding in wealth, but persons of good character and
of respectable standing in the rural society of Ireland ... Not
a few of them are the sons of persons in the better class of
society.'[89] Those two fair-minded and observant aristocrats—
Tocqueville and Beaumont—who mingled with priests in
many parts of Ireland, were not struck either by the lowly social
origin of the clergy or by coarseness in their manners. Instead,
Tocqueville received a favourable impression when he dined
with them in Carlow: 'An archbishop was there, four bishops
and several priests. All these gentlemen carried themselves
very well. The meal was decently but unostentatiously served.
The dinner was good but not elaborate. These ecclesiastics
drank very little. They all appeared to be gentlemen.'[90]

When we turn to the literature of the period, we find, as
a literary critic has aptly put it, that many 'Protestant novelists
... were fond of elderly, unworldly priests, who deplored the
intrusion of their Church into politics'.[91] The Revd George
Brittaine, the Anglican rector of Kilcormac, Co. Wexford, in
his novel *Irish Priests and English Landlords*, shows the older
priest, Mr Moloney, blaming the loss of members of his flock
on the 'blustering', the 'trampling and reviling' of the young
priests issuing from Maynooth.[92] Carleton, who originally
intended to study for the priesthood at Maynooth, satirizes the
peasants' veneration for the Maynooth student.[93] Trollope,
a keen and sympathetic observer of the Irish scene, sharply
contrasts the two types of priests. Fr McGrath, the parish
priest, trained at St. Omer and Paris, is a cultivated gentleman:

[87] W. M. Thackeray, *Irish Sketch Book* (1843), p. 238.
[88] J. Johnson, *A tour in Ireland with meditations and reflexions* (1844), ii. 256.
[89] J. Grant, *Impressions of Ireland and the Irish* (1844), i. 172-3.
[90] Tocqueville, *Journeys*, p. 130.
[91] T. Flanagan, *The Irish Novelists, 1800-1850* (1959), p. 239.
[92] G. Brittaine, *Irish Priests and English Landlords* (1830), pp. 18-19.
[93] Carleton, 'Denis O'Shaughnessy'.

'he had ... seen more of French manners and society than usually falls to the lot of Irish theological students ... He was, also, which is equally unusual, a man of good family and ... was more fitted, than is generally the case with those of his order, to mix in society.' Unlike him in every way, except in his zeal for the church, was his Maynooth-trained curate, Fr Cullen:

... the son of a little farmer in the neighbourhood, [he] was perfectly illiterate—but chiefly showed his dissimilarity to the parish priest by his dirt and untidiness. He was a violent politician ... Father Cullen's redeeming point was his earnestness,—his reality; he had no humbug about him ... his heart and mind were full of the Roman Catholic Church and of his country's wrongs; he could neither think nor speak of aught beside.[94]

Lever also contrasts the two types, although his characterization lacks Trollope's depth. Fr Malachi Brennan, the parish priest, was 'the beau ideal of his caste ... the general expression, a mixture of unbounded good-humour and inexhaustible drollery'. The curate, Mr Donovan, was the 'very antipodes to the *bonhomie* of Fr Malachi:

he was a tall, spare, ungainly looking man ... with a pale, ascetic countenance the only readable expression of which vibrated between low suspicion and intense vulgarity ... Fr Malachi was an older coinage, whereas Mister Donovan was the shining metal, fresh stamped from the mint of Maynooth.[95]

Neither the Banims nor Humphrey O'Sullivan, who were Catholic, draw any distinction between the old-style and new-style priest. Interesting though the literary evidence is, however, it is often too polemical to convey an accurate picture.

In the absence of a proper sociological study of the Maynooth priests, it is difficult to come to more than tentative conclusions. The products of Maynooth were not, it appears, of lower social origin than the eighteenth-century priests. One suspects, with MacHale, that the alleged difference between pre-Revolutionary and post-Revolutionary priest was due in part to a nostalgia for the past. What difference there was came from the broaden-

---

[94] Trollope, *MacDermots*, i. 65-73.

[95] Lever, *Harry Lorrequer*, pp. 41-2. In real life, Fr Malachi was Fr Malachy Duggan and bore not the 'impress of Douay or St Omers' but of Maynooth where he trained from 1808-12; P. J. Hamell, *Maynooth Students and Ordinations, 1795-1895; Index, Part II* (1973), p. 11.

ing effect of foreign training, the long separation from Ireland and, above all, from the gap between the generations trained under the *ancien régime* and those trained in the new century. To this must be added the new feeling of confidence that O'Connell's successful campaign for Emancipation had engendered.

At the root of the difference of opinion about the social origins of Maynooth priests lay a misconception as to the meaning of the term 'the lowest classes'. The distinction between farmers on the one hand, and cottiers and labourers on the other, was fully as real as that between the peasants generally and the landed gentry and aristocracy. Within the farming class again, there were important distinctions between what John Harold called the 'comfortable', 'middle', and 'humble' farmers. In general it appears that most students came from the 'middle' farming class, others from 'comfortable' and 'humble' farming families, while some were merchants' and tradesmens' sons. The cost of an education at Maynooth placed it beyond the reach of the poor. Apart from that a candidate had to be accepted by his bishop and his parish priest. Although wealth and social standing were not nominally criteria, 'good stock' and a certain degree of education were regarded as necessary. Given the church's insistence on these qualities and the sharp social distinctions within the Irish community, it was only in exceptional cases that the badly educated children of the very poor could aspire to the ministry. The Maynooth clergy were mainly farmers' sons; they were not from the lowest echelons of society.[96] Their higher social standing made them more formidable political opponents of the established order than if they had been drawn, as De Grey and others supposed, from the sons of labourers. Criticisms of the lowly origin of the Maynooth priest came largely from political opponents and from those accustomed to an Anglican clergy drawn from the gentry and the middle class.[97] The debate could be seen as

[96] The criticisms of the social origins of the Irish Catholic clergy were more applicable to the Anglican clergy of Wales and Cumberland, if one is to judge by W. J. Conybeare, 'The Church in the mountains', *Essays Ecclesiastical and Social* (1855), pp. 1-56.

[97] In 1841 Oxford and Cambridge provided 86 per cent of the candidates for holy orders; the universities of Dublin and Durham 7 per cent between them; M. Crowther, *Church embattled: religious controversy in mid-Victorian England* (1970), p. 221.

reflecting English views of the social role of a clergyman in England, the shock at observing the influence of the Irish priests and attempts, in social terms, to explain it. It is remarkable, too, that no mention was made—even by Maynooth's defenders—of the church of Rome's claim that all its clerical ranks, including the papacy itself, were open to the poorest of its faithful—a claim closely linked with its theology of the priesthood as a 'divine call' or vocation.

For fifty years, Maynooth College had enjoyed an independence that the hierarchy deemed essential but which aroused growing fear and suspicion as the priests it trained began to make their influence felt throughout Ireland. The allegations concerning the type of priest recruited and trained in Maynooth rested on misconceptions of Irish society, particularly of peasant society. On the other hand, the strictness of the discipline and the isolation of the students during their training lent weight to the criticism that the seminary system practised there provided too narrow a preparation for their future ministry and place in society. The criticisms levelled against Maynooth's doctrines were not well founded and were based, for the most part, on misunderstandings resulting from different traditions. The claim that the college trained students in 'principles of treason and sedition' was no more than wild exaggeration; indeed the Maynooth staff appear to have been the only body of clergy of which a majority supported the moderate line taken by Murray. Much of the antagonism manifested against Maynooth arose from a latent anti-Catholicism which many factors, religious and political, combined to bring to the surface from the 1830s until beyond our period. By 1845 the unfavourable notice which Maynooth had been receiving had made it, for many, 'a name and a thing above all others odious and suspicious'. The government by now had ample evidence that the clergy in general and the younger Maynooth-trained priests in particular were actively involved in O'Connellite politics. To wean them away from such involvement Peel would be forced to consider increasing substantially the grant to Maynooth, even though he realized that the controversy that had grown up about that institution had made it a minefield of difficulties and dangers for all parties, and particularly for his government.

2. Maynooth's finances and ministerial deliberations

If the social standing of the student that Maynooth College recruited and the type of priest it produced was a cause of serious concern for politicians and churchmen, the college's inability to train a sufficient number of pastors for the Irish mission was the main worry of the Catholic bishops. The college had served the Irish church well but the sixty or more priests it produced annually, even when supplemented by the other Irish and continental seminaries, were wholly insufficient to meet the needs of the rapidly increasing population.[98] Before the French Revolution there were 478 students in training on the continent. By 1826 the population had grown by two-thirds, but the number of students had risen by only 36 per cent to 651, of whom 391 were in Maynooth, 120 in other colleges in Ireland and 140 on the continent.[99] Although by 1843 the number in training in Maynooth had risen by a further 11 per cent to reach 433, the growth in population had matched this increase if not outstripped it. By then, too, the colleges in Spain and Portugal were no longer functioning.[100]

The expansion and improvement of Maynooth, now the main source of priests for the Irish church, were limited by its meagre resources. The total income of the college from all sources in the 1840s amounted to approximately £15,000, two-thirds of which came from the annual parliamentary grant which had scarcely changed since its inception. The grant, originally £8,000 in 1795, had risen to £8,928 sterling (£9,673 Irish currency) by 1813, at which figure it had remained unchanged. Yet the number of students had increased from 40 in 1795 and 250 in 1809 to reach 437 in 1840, as the bishops crowded recruits into its mean, unhealthy buildings in an intensive effort to provide pastors for the ever-increasing flock. Accommodation had become grossly inadequate. From time to time, the government made special grants for building purposes but the Commission of 1826 was told that two, three, or

[98] The average number of students who left the college in holy orders in the years 1841, 1842, and 1843 was sixty-six. *Returns relating to the College of Maynooth, PP 1845,* xxviii. 334.

[99] *Eighth Report, Maynooth, PP 1826-7,* xiii. 8-9.

[100] Memorial of the Trustees...to Lord Heytesbury..., [n.d. Nov. 1844], cited in full in Healy, *Maynooth,* pp. 408-10.

four students (sometimes as many as six) were forced to share a room. From 1836 on, not a penny was spent on new buildings, and only a paltry amount (£189 18s. 10d. in 1843) on repairs.[101] Noel described the college as a 'mean, rough-cast and white-washed range of buildings' and, in 1843, Thackeray, complaining of its dilapidation, alleged that 'an Irish union-house is a palace to it'.[102] The visitation in 1846 revealed that there were only 346 rooms for 512 students and that five rooms contained six students each.[103] A year later, and after the increase in the grant, Clarendon was to describe the wretched condition of the rooms:

> I saw the rooms of which we heard so much in England. They have three or four beds in them and are wretched comfortless and ill ventilated, such as no one in England would ask a servant to sleep in for a night, ... The single bedded rooms are not much larger or better than those at Pentonville Prison.[104]

Appeals for an increase in the grant had been made from time to time. In 1823, the president, Dr Crotty, had set out the college's financial difficulties to Eneas MacDonnell, asking him to use his good offices to procure an increase in the grant.[105] O'Connell complained to the Committee reporting on the State of Ireland in 1825 that 'there is ... a miserable penury in the way that Maynooth college is treated', and Lord Cloncurry in 1835 had appealed to Melbourne for an increase in the grant.[106]

In the later 1830s, the problem reached critical proportions, for the college fell into debt and seemed unable to get out of it. Determined to increase the number of priests, the trustees in 1834 lowered the entrance age from eighteen to seventeen and at two separate meetings granted each diocese an extra free

---

[101] Healy, *Maynooth*, p. 740; Larkin, 'Economic Growth', pp. 859-60.

[102] Noel, *Notes*, p. 353; Thackeray, *Sketchbook*, p. 337.

[103] *Report of a Visitation held at the College of Maynooth, on the 20th day of April, 1846, PP 1846*, xlii, 211.

[104] Clarendon to Russell, 31 July 1847, Clarendon Papers, Letterbook 1, f. 12.

[105] Crotty to MacDonnell, 3 Mar. 1824, *IER*, xlvii (1936), 644-6. MacDonnell was London agent for the Irish Catholics in the 1820s.

[106] *Report from Select Committee on the State of Ireland, PP 1825*, vii. 128, 4 Mar. 1825; Holland to Cloncurry, 29 Apr. 1835; Melbourne to Cloncurry, 4 June 1835, Cloncurry, *Life and Times*, pp. 345-6.

place.[107] The following year in addition to those fifty-four new places, the trustees established a further forty-five new places.[108] Both of these expansions, however, were to last as long as the funds of the college would permit and, unfortunately, that was not to be for very long. By 1838, the college was forced to borrow £1,000 'for the purpose of relieving the present embarrassed state of the College', and the trustees sent the four archbishops and Lord Fingall, Sir Patrick Bellew, Lord Ffrench, and Anthony Hussey to plead with the lord lieutenant for an increase in the grant.[109] As nothing came of this petition, the trustees suppressed forty-one of the forty-five free places established four years earlier.[110] Since a debt of £2,500 remained on 31 March 1840, the trustees suppressed another twenty-seven free places, and Murray suggested that they consider the advisability of applying to Parliament for an increase in the grant.[111] The year 1841 proved to be a decisive one. The cut-backs they had made in 1840 had not taken them out of their difficulties, and they met four times in 1841 in an effort to make Maynooth solvent. In April, after seeing the balance sheet, they were forced to negotiate a loan of £1,500.[112] In June, they told the president to send the students home for the vacation and to limit the number of senior students 'until the debts on the College shall be entirely discharged'.[113] When they met again in August, however, the debt stood at £4,600 and they decided to suppress a further thirty-one free places.[114] Clearly, a new initiative had to be taken, and in November they decided in desperation to appeal to the newly formed Conservative government for help.[115] At the bishops' meeting, the proposer and seconder of the motion to seek aid from the government were respectively Dr MacHale and Dr Higgins, the two most outspokenly nationalist prelates on the bench.[116]

[107] Meeting of the Trustees, 26 June, 18 Sept., 1834. Journal of Trustees, pp. 186-7, 193, Maynooth College Archives.
[108] Ibid., 25 June 1835, pp. 200-1.
[109] Ibid., 28 June 1838, p. 225.
[110] Ibid., 26 June 1839, p. 234.
[111] Ibid., 29 June 1840, pp. 236-7.
[112] Ibid., 15 Apr. 1841, p. 239.
[113] Ibid., 24 June 1841, p. 240.
[114] Ibid., 27 Aug. 1841, p. 242.
[115] Ibid., 10 Nov. 1841, pp. 245-6.
[116] Meeting of the Irish Bishops, 9 Nov. 1841, DDA.

Table 3

Revenue and Expenditure of Maynooth College, 1826-1845

Columns A, B, and C give the amounts received respectively from pensions and fees of admission, expenditure on provisions and the amount of the annual saving or loss; columns F and G give the total Charge (revenue) and Discharge (expenditure). The sources are MSS in Maynooth College Archives. Column D gives the total number of students for every year between 1826 and 1845 for which figures are available.[a] Column E lists the prices of a composite unit of consumables in southern England, taken from E. Phelps Brown and S. V. Hopkins, 'Seven centuries of the prices of consumables, compared with builders' wage rates', in P. H. Ramsey ed., *The Price Revolution in Sixteenth-Century England* (1971), pp. 18-41.

Year	A Pensions and Fees £	B Provisions £	C Saving/ Loss £	D Total Number of Students	E Price of Unit of Consumables	F Total Charge[b] £	G Total Discharge £
1826	2,862	6,989	1,829	391	1322	15,702	14,282
1827	2,191	6,606	1,236		1237	15,693	12,863
1828	2,659	6,730	443	388	1201	14,510	11,445
1829	2,636	6,691	1,549		1189	16,779	12,288
1830	2,541	6,415	273	377	1146	17,983	13,433
1831	2,514	6,354	2,263	380	1260	18,576	17,688[c]
1832	2,669	6,945	1,972	388	1167	14,672	11,804
1833[d]	2,271	7,432	4,898		1896	20,659	19,284[e]
1834[d]	2,817	6,841	157		1011	13,212	12,363
1835	2,759	7,635	1,430		1028	15,324	14,621

Year						
1836	2,125	7,442	849		1141	14,504	14,342
1837	2,111	9,256	795 (loss)		1169	16,258	15,008
1838	2,044	9,016	975 (loss)		1177	14,878	14,827
1839	1,960	8,899	600 (loss)	425	1263	13,586	14,387
1840[f]	2,321	10,339	1,600 (loss)	437	1286	14,215	15,756
1841[f]	2,016	10,029		427	1256	15,116	15,001
1842	2,995	8,075		425	1161	16,486	16,093
1843	3,278	7,270		433	1030	15,109	13,898
1844	3,194	7,516		438	1029	15,755	13,587
1845	3,011	7,984		522	1079	16,809	13,436

[a] The figures for 1828, 1830, 1831, and 1832 are based on incomplete manuscripts in a file entitled 'Maynooth College, 1796-1849' in the Dublin Diocesan Archives. The figure for 1839 is based on the names of students given in a bound ledger of 'The Account of the R.C. College from 6th Jan. 1829', in the bursar's office, Maynooth College. The other figures are contained in various Parliamentary Papers. A careful search has failed to establish the total number of students in the college for the other years between 1833 and 1838. Noel, in his *Tour*, p. 338, gives the figure of 450 for 1836.

[b] This amount includes the annual grant of £8,928 for all the years from 1826 to 1845.

[c] £5,842 was expended on buildings in 1831.

[d] Up to 1832 inclusive, the financial year ran from January to January; from 1833 it ran from March to March. The transition may explain the unusually high figure for both the charge and discharge in 1833 and the unusually low figures for 1834. The grant for 1833 was £11,160, and for 1834 £6,696. Taken together they give the average for each year as £8,928, the normal amount of the grant.

[e] £6,574 was expended on buildings in 1833. There was no special grant for either these buildings or those of 1831.

[f] Loans of £1,500 and £2,069 balanced the budgets of 1840 and 1841.

The bishops' memorial to the government explained that despite economies, the college still carried a debt of £4,600. While claiming that double the number of priests was needed to cope with the growing population, they explained that 'the increasing distress in the country during the latter years, has so affected the condition of the middle classes of Society, from which candidates for the Roman Catholic priesthood are usually presented, that there has been a very considerable reduction in the numbers who pay for their support and a far greater reduction is to be apprehended.'[117]

The reason given by the bishops for the financial embarrassment of the college needs scrutiny and correction. An examination of the financial statements shows that the income received from pensions (fees) decreased sharply in 1836 and continued to decrease more slowly over the next three years. In this sense, the bishops' statement is correct. Yet the decrease from this source between 1835 and 1839 was only £800 and, in 1840, which proved the critical year for the college, this loss had been halved. The main cause of the deficit after 1836 was not a dramatic decrease in income but a dramatic rise in expenditure, as revealed in Table 3. The year 1840 was clearly a crucial year, for although the receipts from pensions and fees rose slightly, the cost of provisions, which had been £7,442 in 1836, rose to £10,339 in 1840—an increase of almost 40 per cent. Since the total income was £15,000, this increase was seriously inflationary and upset Maynooth's precarious financial balance. As the figures in Table 4 indicate, the main increase was in the amount spent on meat and bread. From 1841 to 1844 the amount spent on those two commodities fell as dramatically as it had risen over the previous five years.

One reason for the increase in expenditure on provisions was that the number of students increased from 388 in 1832 to 437 in 1840. Annual entrances to the college were at their highest in 1833 and 1834, when they reached 102 and 104 respectively, compared to an average of 77 for the period from

---

[117] Memorial of the archbishops and bishops of the Roman Catholic Church in Ireland to Lord De Grey, Add. MSS 40612, ff. 171-2; n.d. but clearly between 10 and 13 Nov. 1841; see Journal of Trustees, pp. 245-6.

Table 4

Expenditure on provisions of Maynooth College 1836-1845[a]
(in £)

	1836	1837	1838	1839	1840	1841	1842	1843	1844	1845
Meat	3,983	4,638	4,629	4,226	4,888	4,703	3,818	3,774	3,585	3,774
Fish	116	121	84	114	68	141	96	52	77	91
Bread (and flour in 1838)	758	1,434	1,280	1,614	2,072	2,030	1,431	1,128	1,139	1,195
Potatoes	135	328	321	220	340	374	373	192	245	337
Butter	438	510	542	483	506	578	487	354	400	455
Milk	597	666	678	598	646	713	655	702	673	676
Beer	794	771	714	798	968	557	380	409	631	645
Wine	65	71	61	73	79	71	61	69	64	102
Groceries	220	317	308	337	325	436	377	304	325	343
Eggs	158	176	164	205	192	212	171	130	135	146
Fowl	49	62	65	72	75	67	54	40	54	63
Oatmeal, fruit, salt	130	162	170	161	180	148	171	115	188	155
Total:	7,442	9,256	9,016	8,899	10,339	10,029	8,075	7,270	7,516	7,984

[a] The source for this table is an unmarked, handwritten bound volume in the bursar's office, Maynooth College, containing the accounts of the trustees of the college.

1830-44,[118] and remained high at an average of 89 in the period from 1835-41. Total numbers may well have reached 450 in 1836. Still, the increased number of students does not fully explain the expenditure. Increased food prices also played an important part: Dublin market prices for corn, butter, and meat showed a remarkable and steep increase for the period 1836-40.[119] There is reason to suspect that the bursar, Dr John Fennelly, who took up office in 1834, was also at fault.[120] The trustees never officially attached blame to him but when he resigned in 1841 to go on missionary work in India, they accepted his resignation without any mark of regret. Maynooth's official historian notes 'that no donation of a quarter's salary was made to him'.[121] The warmth with which the trustees on more than one occasion praised his successor, Renehan, 'for his zealous and efficient and successful discharge of the duties of Bursar', contrasts strikingly with their silence as regards Fennelly.[122] The president, Montague, complained to Crolly of Fennelly's 'gross neglect' which 'will much increase our enormous debt'.[123] When Renehan reluctantly undertook the task of attempting to make the college solvent, on his appointment in June 1841, the outlay on povisions dropped from £10,029 in 1841 to £7,516 in 1844, which represented a return to the levels of 1835 and 1836. The fact that a variation of £3,000 could plunge Maynooth into crisis emphasizes the

[118] *Maynooth College Calendar for the year 1872-3* (1873), pp. 117-69. This calendar gives the matriculation register for the period 1821-45. A bound manuscript in the Maynooth College Archives contains lists of students promoted to holy orders within the college for the years from 1798 to 1845. It does not list those who were ordained outside the college.

[119] *Dublin market prices: Pence per cwt*

	Wheat	Oats	Barley	Butter	Bacon	Beef	Mutton
1831-5	126	76	86	879	465	509	584
1836-40	165	93	102	1,118	576	599	666

R. D. Crotty, *Irish agricultural production: its volume and structure* (1966), p. 35. An increase of 1*d.* per lb in the price of meat cost an extra £800 a year according to the calculations of Thomas Farrelly, the college bursar, in 1867 when the number of students was over 500; Bursar's financial statement for the year ending 31 March, 1867, Maynooth College Archives.

[120] Journal of the Trustees, 15 Apr. 1841, pp. 238-9. John Fennelly (1806-68), bursar 1834-41; bishop *in partibus* and vicar apostolic of Madras 1842-68.

[121] Healy, *Maynooth*, pp. 349-50.

[122] Journal of the Trustees, 10 Nov. 1842, p. 248; 24 June 1843, p. 251.

[123] Montague to Crolly, 7 May 1841, Cullen Papers, 1850-60, DDA.

precarious nature of its finances and the reasonableness of the bishops' plea for an increase in the grant. The bishops were unable to provide the money themselves as their recourse to raising loans in the years 1838 and 1841 showed. Although the rapid growth in the Catholic population and the consequent rise in amount of stole fees for baptisms, marriages, and deaths had benefited individual priests, the bishops had no extra capital available to provide training facilities for the increased number of priests needed.[124] The bishops' first concern was for their own local diocesan needs, and as for Maynooth College they hoped it would be able to manage on its own scanty resources even though the numbers in training had increased by 16 per cent in the decade from 1830 to 1840. Indeed, they acted as if the financing of the college was principally the state's affair; and since successive governments had been maintaining Maynooth for half a century, they had the weight of tradition on their side. It remained to be seen how the new conservative government would react.

A delighted Eliot saw in the bishops' request an opportunity 'of securing to the Government an effectual control over the management of Maynooth College'. He was convinced that the advantages to be gained by establishing a proper system of visitation would be cheaply bought by the outlay of a few thousand pounds. Since Parliament had engaged itself to educate the priests, Eliot argued that it was bound to ensure that the education was good and that sufficient priests were provided. The existing system provided only half the necessary number of priests and educated them so badly that raw and ignorant youths, after a residence of only a year and a half or two years in the college, were sent out to instruct the peasantry. The improvement of the priest was the best means of improving the peasant.[125] Although Eliot was correct in stressing the insufficiency of priests, he was wrong in claiming that the students were sent out after so short a time: courses lasted a minimum of four years and were normally six. In any case he was alone in his enthusiasm. Graham took the line in 1841 that the Maynooth question 'must ... be decided with reference

[124] Larkin, 'Economic Growth', pp. 858-62.
[125] Eliot to Graham, 12, 18 Nov. 1841, Graham Papers.

to the Protestant mind and Protestant policy in Ireland, not
forgetting the Presbyterians of the North, who are the firm
friends of Britain'.[126] After Peel and Graham discussed the
matter, De Grey was instructed to inform Murray that the
government could not promise an increase, for any such proposal must be the result of 'deliberation and inquiry'—meaning
no more in this respect than some inquiries which Graham had
told Eliot to make of the primate, Foster, Jackson, and others.[127]
Murray, interpreting it to mean inquiry into the running of the
college, welcomed it.[128] Eliot, whom De Grey suspected of
being influenced by Blake, took up this idea of formal inquiry
in September 1842, and bypassing the unsympathetic lord
lieutenant, pressed the idea on Peel.[129] Stanley, whose views on
Irish education naturally carried weight and who was influenced
by his ministerial dealings with Catholic hierarchies in the
colonies, saw merit in any inquiry which 'might render familiar
ideas which at present would not even be permitted to be discussed.'[130] Peel was cautious, however, fearing that 'the
MacHales, on the one hand, and the M'Ghees, on the other,
might seek to convert the unfortunate commissioners into
judges of an interminable ... controversy.'[131] He put Eliot's
views to the cabinet and told him of the decision: 'An increased
grant to Maynooth or an enquiry as a foundation of an increased grant would, in our opinion, rouse into action feelings
and passions which are now slumbering, and which if their
slumber be not disturbed may peacefully die away.' Peel
pointed out that the Whigs had earlier refrained from increasing
the grant probably 'from prudential considerations having
reference to the inflammable state of the public mind on a
question of this nature'.[132] The Intrusion controversy in the

[126] Graham to Eliot, 14 Nov. 1841; Graham to De Grey, 27 Nov. 1841, ibid.

[127] Graham to De Grey, 27 Nov. 1841, Graham Papers, De Grey to Murray,
30 Nov. 1841, Maynooth College folder 1796-1849, DDA.

[128] Murray to De Grey, 2 Dec. 1841, Murray Papers, Maynooth College folder
1796-1849, DDA.

[129] Eliot to Peel, 23 Sept. 1842, Add. MSS 40480, ff. 118-19; De Grey's suspicions
were well founded; Eliot frequently consulted Blake e.g. Eliot to Blake, 30 June
1843, Blake Papers.

[130] Stanley to Peel, 21 Oct. 1842, Derby Papers, Letter-book 1841-5, pp. 52-4; this
letter is wrongly dated in Parker, *Peel*, iii. 66-7 and Gash, *Peel*, p. 414.

[131] Peel to Eliot, 27 Sept. 1842, Add. MSS 40480, ff. 120-3.

[132] Peel to Eliot, 13 Nov. 1842, ibid., ff. 145-8.

Church of Scotland was just then at its height, embroiling the government in a matter where religious feelings ran very high indeed.

While the government was not prepared in November 1842 to attend to this appeal of the bishops, it was forced to take the initiative within less than a year. The events of the 'Repeal Year' had overtaken its immobile policy. Eliot's proposals of Janaury 1844 contained recommendations for the improvement of Maynooth College and were to provide the basis of the plan which Peel circulated to his cabinet in his memoranda in February.[133] In the third memorandum, written shortly after the nine-day debate in the Commons, Peel's determination to take action on the Maynooth question became manifest. Appealing to the general, moral and political outlook of his cabinet he stressed the evil of the existing system: '...we incur a great responsibility, not parliamentary but moral; by leaving the vote as it is, by sending out annually fifty spiritual fire-brands, prepared for mischief by ourselves to convulse the country ...the wit of man could not devise a more effectual method for converting them into sour malignants ...' Following Eliot's suggestion, he proposed that a commission be set up 'in a friendly spirit—not to Maynooth—but to carrying out the principle which was recognized by the original establishment of Maynooth.' It would investigate the possibility of the com-bined education of clerics and laity, the extension of Trinity College and, if nothing else proved practicable, those improve-ments which could be introduced into the Maynooth system.[134]

There was opposition to Peel's plan. De Grey complained that an increased grant would only 'perpetuate the poison now infused throughout the land' and that no improvement in the college would be beneficial as long as it was impossible to provide for the priests when they left it.[135] More serious for Peel was the opposition, from within the cabinet, of Gladstone, whose difficulties on the subject reflected those of many of his contemporaries. In the 1830s, he had viewed with alarm the growing split between church and state, and in 1838 he vigorously

[133] See pp. 112-19.
[134] Peel, memorandum, [28] Feb. 1844, Add. MSS 40540, ff. 40-55.
[135] De Grey to Graham, 27 Feb. 1844, Graham Papers.

asserted in *The State in its relations with the Church* the duty of the state to uphold the church.[136] Looking to the Tory party as a means for regenerating society, he hailed its victory in 1841 as a victory for the Anglican church. Abstract ideals and practical policies do not often mix, however, and from his severely practical job in the Board of Trade and his collaboration with politicians such as Peel, Graham, Aberdeen, and Stanley, it dawned on him that his views on the relationship of church and state were no longer practical. Although in his book he had denounced the Maynooth Grant as wholly vicious in principle, he now found himself voting silently for it, to the indignation of some ultra-Tories.[137] An increased grant was a different matter however, and he determined to oppose it.

During the year 1844 an ideological battle was fought out between Gladstone and the rest of the cabinet, a battle which sheds an interesting light not merely on Gladstone's views, which are well known, but on those of the other ministers. Peel explained to Gladstone the necessity for some reforms in view of

the anomaly of the [Established] Church—of its revenues nearer £700,000 than £500,000 ... of the impossibility of governing Ireland without breaking up the Roman Catholic combination for Repeal, of maintaining the law, of looking foreign powers in the face—of the effect that a secession from the Government on religious grounds would produce in raising a clamour...of his belief that the breaking up of the Government would be followed by the accession of a very democratic Ministry,—but that nevertheless it would be a question for consideration whether in the event of a secession from it on this question such a dissolution ought not to take place.[138]

Wharncliffe and Lyndhurst feared that Gladstone's resignation would create an extreme high church party.[139] Stanley believed that it was impossible to govern Ireland without concessions and went so far as to say that 'he could see nothing ahead if there were a break up on this question but a civil war.'[140] Gladstone, for his part, questioned the effectiveness for concili-

---

[136] W. E. Gladstone, *The State in its relations with the Church* (1838), p. 252.

[137] *Hansard,* lv. 387, 20 July 1842.

[138] Gladstone's memorandum, 2 Mar. 1844, Add. MSS 44777, ff. 131-6, Gladstone, *Prime Ministers' Papers,* ii. 238.

[139] Ibid., p. 240.

[140] Gladstone's memorandum, 7 Mar. 1844, Add. MSS 44777, ff. 139-48, ibid. ii. 244-9.

ation of an increased grant, suggested that any settlement of the Catholic question should be prefaced by the restoration of relations with Rome and insisted that in view of his published opinions, he was in honour bound to resign from a government which introduced such a measure.[141] It should be emphasized that in the course of the year 1844 he opposed the increased grant mainly on the grounds of principle.[142] But by the end of the year, the sole ground on which he based his opposition was that of personal and public consistency: he thought that the public thought that he still held the views expressed in his abstruse publication, since he had not publicly recanted them.[143] Peel, although a good churchman, did not share Gladstone's passionate absorption with the church or his religious enthusiasm, and he had no intention of being deflected from his course of essential Irish reforms by the pleas of his able but junior minister. Consequently, when Thomas Wyse, M.P. for Waterford, raised the question of universities for Ireland on 19 July, the prime minister, in a speech which caused some stir, promised that the government would consider not merely the university question but also Maynooth.[144]

Before the November cabinets—which were devoted to these two questions—took place, Graham circulated several useful documents to the ministers.[145] Stanley's original idea had been that the priests and laity should receive their education together but Graham decided to present the two matters separately. The important part that Blake had in the formulation of the Maynooth bill has not been recognized. Through Heytesbury, he submitted a comprehensive paper on Maynooth (based on an earlier one prepared for Wellesley) for the cabinet meeting of 25 November. This paper, together with later modifications suggested by Blake or transmitted by him from the bishops, formed the basis of the government bill. Before making his recommendations, Blake cleared up two preliminary points. The first was on the question of a combined

---

[141] Ibid.

[142] Gladstone's memoranda, 11, 29 Feb. 1844, Add. MSS 44777, ff. 119-26, 129-30, ibid., ii. 230-2, 237.

[143] Gladstone's memorandum, 14 Jan. 1845, Add. MSS 44777, ff. 212-15, ibid. ii. 272.

[144] *Hansard,* lxxvi, 1129-33.

[145] Graham's memorandum to cabinet, 16 Nov. 1844, Derby Papers, Box 37/1.

education for clergy and laity. He strongly opposed such a system, quoting Edmund Burke to this effect:

... if a Roman Catholic clergyman, intended for celibacy and the functions of confession, is not strictly bred in a seminary where these things are respected, inculcated and enforced as sacred and not made the subject of derision and obloquy, he will be ill-fitted for the former, and the latter will be indeed in his hands a terrible instrument.[146]

The second point which Blake was anxious to scotch was the notion that the Maynooth priest was of a lower social origin than his eighteenth-century predecessor. Here again his authority was Burke, who affirmed that the pre-Revolution clergy came from 'the lower orders of the people'.[147] Blake then proceeded to give his positive suggestions. The trustees should be incorporated so that they could acquire land, and they should be empowered to grant degrees. Salaries, exhibitions, and free-place allowances should be doubled; fifteen new fellowships should be founded. A novel feature of Blake's plan was the proposal to set up a separate seminary near the college for the four junior classes, with one hundred and fifty free places. As to the question of visitors, which Graham regarded as all-important, Blake recommended that the four judges who were visitors in name only should be replaced by more qualified persons who could act as links between the government and the college. Blake set the new figure for the grant at £25,000— treble the existing grant and far higher than the extra £2,000 or £3,000 a year which Eliot had suggested in January.[148]

Both Heytesbury and Graham in their covering memoranda warmly supported Blake's proposals. Graham, warning against any hasty 'liberalizing' of clerical education, argued that

the celibacy of the priests may be an evil; confession may lead to gross abuses; but the vow of celibacy must be taken by every Roman Catholic priest and confession remains a sacrament of the Church of Rome. Millions in Ireland adhere to this creed and priests must be provided for the decent performance of their sacred ordinances.

An increase in the grant, Graham argued, would constitute no

---

[146] Edmund Burke, 'Letter to a peer of Ireland, on the penal laws against Irish catholics, 21 Feb. 1782', *The Works of ... Edmund Burke* (1887), iii. 290.
[147] Ibid., p. 287.
[148] Blake's memorandum on Maynooth, 4 Nov. 1844, Derby Papers, 37/1.

violation of principle, and the real fault with Maynooth was the failure of the state to fulfil its own original, more generous designs. To the popular objection that the college thus favoured by the state was 'the hot-bed of sedition', he replied that 'gratitude is now expected for favours doled out with a sparing hand', whereas the policy he was recommending proceeded on the assumption that 'kinder and more generous treatment will create a better and more loyal feeling'.[149]

While the home secretary had been busy collecting material for the cabinet meetings, the Maynooth trustees, inspired by Peel's promise during the debate on Wyse's motion, decided to approach the government again for help. The college's finances had improved, thanks mainly to the work of a thrifty bursar, but the budget was still meagre. Their memorial pointed out that the college had to practise rigid economy, pay low wages, and, during the vacation, send the students home and dismiss the servants. Some students were withdrawn before their course was completed. The buildings were inadequate and in bad repair. Fewer students were able to pay for their keep. Yet more, not less, priests were needed for the growing population, and with the closure of the Spanish and Portugese colleges, which had provided a certain number of priests annually, the demands on Maynooth had increased.[150]

When Heytesbury, in the course of his meeting with the four archbishops, raised the question of visitation, MacHale protested vehemently against any change.[151] Heytesbury, however, believed that the other three archbishops were not so adamantly opposed, and the cabinet saw this as an encouraging sign for the reforms they had in mind, Stanley even hoping that Gladstone might be won over.[152] By 25 November, the cabinet knew the contents of the memorial and was disappointed to note that the bishops sought an increase of the grant upon the same terms as for the existing grant, 'thus striking', as Gladstone remarked, 'at the root of the proposal to modify the visitorial

---

[149] Graham's memorandum, 16 Nov. 1844, ibid.

[150] Memorial of the Trustees of the Roman Catholic College at Maynooth to His Excellency Lord Heytesbury, Nov. 1844; Healy, *Maynooth*, pp. 408-10.

[151] See p. 176.

[152] Stanley to Buccleuch, 23 Nov. 1844, Derby Papers; Peel to Prince Albert, 22 Nov. 1844, Add. MSS 40439, ff. 157-8; Graham to Heytesbury, 22 Nov. 1844, Graham Papers.

power to which Sir J. Graham clings very much.'[153] A final decision was postponed while Graham tried to ascertain if the bishops would consent to a change in the visitorial system. Seizing hopefully, too, on Blake's claim that Maynooth's divinity course corresponded with that of the Sorbonne, Graham asked Heytesbury for more information:

we wish to know from you what is your own impression as to the precise nature in the composition of the Board of visitors to which Archbishop Crolly, Archbishop Murray and Mr Blake would consent. This is a very important question with regard to public impression in this country ... Now, if by effective visitation on the part of responsible persons nominated by the Crown, some of whom were Protestants, it would be ascertained that the Sorbonne system is strictly followed and that all the slanderous imputations as to the immoral effect and tendency of the teaching at Maynooth are false, a strong additional argument would be supplied in defence of the increased grant, and much of the prejudice against it in this country would be removed.[154]

Graham even considered changing Maynooth's location, musing that 'a change of place would operate almost as much on public opinion as a change of system'.[155] His attitude shows some of the difficulties the government knew that it would face from popular prejudice and indicates their efforts to forestall them. The replies from Dublin were less than satisfactory. All Heytesbury could tell him about visitorial powers was that although Blake and Murray had appeared to be flexible on the matter, the bishops' memorial asked for an increased grant upon the old terms. Again the similarity between the Sorbonne and Maynooth courses turned out to be based on no more than Blake's assurance to Heytesbury, and although Blake now produced some of Maynooth's textbooks, this was scarcely the type of proof that would influence public opinion in the manner intended by Graham.[156]

Aware that Maynooth constituted the thorniest problem in the programme of reform, the cabinet decided to complete the bequests question and to initiate the colleges project, before

---

[153] Gladstone's memorandum, 25 Nov. 1844, Add. MSS 44777, ff. 206-9, *Prime Ministers' Papers*, ii. 270.

[154] Graham to Heytesbury, 25 Nov. 1844, Graham Papers.

[155] Graham to Eliot, 27 Nov. 1844, Graham Papers.

[156] Heytesbury to Graham, 27 Nov. 1844; Eliot to Graham, 27 Nov. 1844, Graham Papers.

devoting full attention to Maynooth. Nevertheless, Peel and Graham in London, Heytesbury and Eliot in Dublin realized that the problem had to be faced soon. Graham saw it as 'the key which will open to the Queen's government influence over the Roman Catholic priesthood.' Pointing out that the cabinet had 'the facts and arguments', he pressed for an early decision, adding that: 'There is hardly any concession which we could make to the Roman Catholic hierarchy with respect to this seminary but would not be safer to the state and more creditable to the government than to have it in its present condition.'[157] Peel, too, while still hoping for concessions as to visitation and public examinations in order to diminish 'Protestant jealousy', reiterated his view that an increased grant without conditions would be preferable to the existing situation.[158] From Ireland Heytesbury urged the necessity for dealing generously and rapidly with Maynooth.[159] The bequests controversy, however, complicated matters, for Murray and Crolly, harassed by MacHale and O'Connell and accused of subserviency to the government, were unwilling to come into contact with Eliot or Heytesbury. Blake remained the indispensable middleman. On 22 December, in the course of an important interview with Heytesbury, Blake restated more specifically his solution to the problem of visitation: to retain the three Catholic visitors but to replace the four judges with Protestant visitors 'of a different description', mixing a Catholic or two with them. Public examinations in the presence of the visitors would not, he thought, raise any difficulty. He agreed that the exhibitions should be granted for a period extending beyond the college course, but prudently advised Heytesbury to induce the trustees themselves to make such a proposition.[160] Graham was very satisfied with these proposals. 'I know not that we can with propriety ask or desire more', he told Peel.[161] To benefit to the utmost from Blake's advice, he told Heytesbury to prepare a bill before Blake left Dublin which, he enthusiastically expected, would re-enact the whole settlement 'on the new basis such as

157 Graham to Peel, 15 Dec. 1844, Add. MSS 40450, ff. 396-7.
158 Peel to Graham, 16 Dec. 1844, ibid., ff. 406-7.
159 Heytesbury to Graham, 12 Dec. 1844, Graham Papers.
160 Heytesbury to Graham, 22 Dec. 1844, ibid.
161 Graham to Peel, 24 Dec. 1844, Add. MSS 40450, ff. 440-1.

you and Mr Blake may jointly approve'. A major difficulty of the negotiations was that although Blake could supply information and give his opinion, 'what he says binds nobody', as Heytesbury reminded Graham. Nevertheless, the lord lieutenant insisted, they must press on:

we are certainly arrived at a crisis. Although nothing has been specifically promised, the speech of Sir Robert Peel, the discussions in the newspapers, and all that has been passing here have excited hopes and expectations amongst the Catholics which if now disappointed, will make all the advances we have already made of no avail and our future relations with our Catholic subjects in this country more complicated and perhaps more embittered than ever.[162]

Graham, warned by Heytesbury, abandoned his idea of re-enacting the whole settlement of Maynooth, but asked Heytesbury to prepare a bill excluding incorporation for the college.[163]

When, however, in early January the Irish attorney general, under the close supervision of Heytesbury, produced a draft based on Blake's suggestions, it included incorporation. It also provided that there was to be no interference with Maynooth's teaching or discipline. The grant was to be trebled and a sum allotted for building and repairs. Instead of a junior seminary, free places were to be provided for two hundred and fifty juniors, a scheme which, according to Blake, the bishops preferred and which represented an increase of a hundred in the total number Blake had first suggested. Since the bishops did not want exhibitions (except for the Dunboyne students) or fellowships, both ideas were abandoned. The Dunboyne students were the more distinguished students who remained on in the college for three years of more advanced studies. At the bishops' suggestion, too, the upkeep of the college was to be the responsibility of the Board of Works. The system whereby the trustees elected three Catholic visitors was left unchanged, but in place of the five judges, the crown could now nominate any five persons as visitors. Visitations were to take place annually rather than triennially. By another reform, the government hoped to increase its influence over the seminarians. The existing grant was a gross sum towards defraying the costs of

---

[162] Heytesbury to Graham, 28, 29, Dec. 1844, Graham Papers.
[163] Graham to Heytesbury, 30 Dec. 1844, ibid.

the college, but it was now proposed that the individual professors and seminarians would each receive a certain sum, subject only to stipulated deductions for their expenses. This was a new principle. Blake had suggested some such measure, and the attorney general and, presumably Heytesbury, had worked out the details. The monies for Maynooth were to come from the consolidated fund; the government had no intention of appropriating church funds for the purpose and Graham was anxious to remove this annual bone of contention from Parliament.[164] Throughout the negotiations, Blake was Heytesbury's informant on 'the bishops' views', although with what authority it is impossible to ascertain. More than likely, Blake was retailing the views of Murray, combined with his own personal ones.

Graham's reactions to the Maynooth draft bill were favourable. 'This Child of Terror', as he called it, was not as terrifying as he had feared. He made two suggestions. With a view to attaching the seminarians more firmly to their pensions from the state, he wanted the college authorities to forgo their power to expel students and so terminate their grants, but Heytesbury warned him that the authorities would never consent to this. Graham also opposed entrusting the upkeep of the college to the Board of Works, for he feared that it might cause critics to complain that this was according the college a 'national' character. When both Eliot and Heytesbury urged that it was necessary from a practical point of view and would keep Maynooth more dependent on the state, he did not press the matter further. Graham was now satisfied and decided to introduce the measure for early decision in cabinet.[165]

Before the cabinet met, Peel made his last effort to retain Gladstone, pointing out to him the benefits that had flowed from the government's Irish reform policy both as regards relations with Ireland and with Rome.[166] Gladstone, however, was determined to go, but promised to make it clear that he left on a question of personal honour connected with Maynooth,

[164] Draft of Maynooth Bill, circulated by Graham 14 Jan. 1845, Derby Papers Box 37/1.

[165] Graham to Heytesbury, 13 Jan. 1845; Heytesbury to Graham, 15 Jan. 1845; Eliot to Graham, 16 Jan. 1845, Graham Papers.

[166] Peel to Gladstone, 20 Jan. 1845, Parker, *Peel*, iii, 165-6; see p. 219.

and that he would not countenance a no-Popery campaign. On 21 January, Eliot succeeded his father as Earl of St. Germans and retired from the chief secretaryship, thus snapping a most useful line of communication with the bishops. Graham's comment on both these losses is picturesque:

on Friday evening we found ourselves not only without a secretary for Ireland, but also without a president of the Board of Trade. Gladstone's secession on Religious Grounds exposes our Maynooth measures to danger, and of course, brings into peril the existence of the government. It is true that Gladstone's scruples are placed by him not so much on the ground of political misgivings or religious qualms, as of written pledges ... but still the general impression would be that he is a martyr to the Protestant cause ... and it is impossible to foresee how strong may be the excitement ... We are, however, steady to our purpose ... It is necessary to repair the breach in our line ... and restore our wasted strength on the eve of the day of battle and almost in presence of the enemy ...[167]

Graham's forebodings were well grounded, yet neither he nor Peel intended to be deflected from their course. On the same day, the cabinet approved the Maynooth draft bill with some minor changes which Graham immediately communicated to Blake. Blake approved of them and added some of his own. Graham was now optimistic: 'my conversation with Mr Blake has convinced me that the Roman Catholics will accept this additional grant on these terms if not with gratitude, at least with avidity; and no one can foretell the consequences, which may flow from the healing effects of such a measure'.[168]

This analysis of the negotiations on Maynooth brings out further the important part played by Anthony Blake, for the bill was mainly his, and virtually all his points were accepted, including that of incorporation, although Graham resisted this almost to the end. The only changes made were those which Blake represented as requested by the bishops. Despite much talk about establishing effective visitation, the bill made no serious attempt to gain control over the college, its main thrust being towards its adequate endowment. The amount of the grant suggested by Blake and accepted by the government was far more generous than that envisaged by either the bishops in their 1841 appeal or by Eliot in 1843. In framing the bill, the

[167] Graham to Heytesbury, 26 Jan. 1845, Graham Papers.
[168] Ibid.

government avoided the mistake of non-consultation which had jeopardized the success of the Bequests Act. This had been possible because negotiations concerning that act had opened, as Graham had hoped, a line of communication with an influential section of the Catholics—a link further strengthened by Heytesbury's appointment as lord lieutenant. Peel had prudently avoided an investigation into the college, but it remained to be seen whether he had thus, as he hoped, prevented the recriminations which Maynooth had excited over the previous decades being voiced again. Although much parliamentary and even some popular opinion was favourable towards concessions to Ireland, Peel's underestimate of the difficulties raised by Gladstone over Maynooth was itself a bad omen for the future. Nevertheless, by January 1845, he could no longer avoid proceeding with this fateful measure. An inner dynamism in his reform programme made it impossible to draw back, for as Heytesbury, expressing his fervent desire that they had 'turned the corner of Maynooth', wrote: 'the expectations of the Catholics have been greatly raised and any disappointment there would react upon all your conciliatory projects.'[169] At the end of January, it was apparently still intended that the colleges bill should precede the Maynooth bill, but, as we have seen, events in Ireland forced the pace. As a result of Bellew's visit to Heytesbury warning him of the heavy pressure on Murray and Crolly, the government decided to press ahead immediately with the Maynooth bill; and on the first day of Parliament Peel announced that the grant would be liberally increased.[170] The focus on Maynooth shifted dramatically from cabinet discussion and secret negotiations to the full glare of hostile publicity.

3. The Passing of the Act of 1845

Peel's first forthright announcement of an unconditional grant to Maynooth caused no immediate general stir—to judge from the lack of comment in *The Times* and *Morning Chronicle*—except among Exeter Hall Protestants. Despite (perhaps because of) his explanatory speech, Gladstone's resignation mystified

---

[169] Heytesbury to Peel, 28 Dec. 1844, Add. MSS 40479, ff. 242-3.
[170] See p. 221.

people, and his leap out of the ministry to follow his book was likened to the footman who jumped off the express to go after his hat.[171] Churchmen were intent on the Tractarian crisis as the meeting of Oxford University Convocation, which was to consider Ward's *Ideal of a Christian Church* and Newman's *Tract XC*, approached. Parliament was preoccupied with income tax, sugar duties, and other financial matters, the dispute with the U.S.A. on Oregon, and with resuming the amusing sport of baiting Graham on post-office espionage. As Graham remarked, 'Ireland is for the moment forgotten and we should not do justice to our measure if we did not wait for a lull before we launch our boat on this troubled sea.'[172]

The first protests came from the ultra-Protestant press. *The Record*, in its first number after Peel's speech, called for 'RESISTANCE' to the threat of popery.[173] Subsequent articles denied the existence of any 'national compact' to maintain the grant, denounced Maynooth's teaching on oaths, theft, the oath of allegiance, and the confessional, and asserted the folly of attempting to wean the priests from Rome. It urged Protestants to petition ceaselessly and to lobby members of Parliament, especially those with marginal seats, such as the City of London, Brighton, and Bath.[174] On 6 February, the Protestant operatives in Dublin deplored 'that idolatry was to be taught at a large increase of expense to the public purse'.[175] Dudley Perceval was early on the scene too, with a letter of protest to the *Morning Chronicle*.[176] At Exeter Hall, the Protestant Association set up a standing committee on 25 February to organize opposition.[177] Hostility to the grant was at this stage mainly Anglican in inspiration. The vastly improved subsidy and the permanent nature given to the grant seemed to imply

---

[171] *Record*, 10 Feb. 1845.
[172] Graham to Heytesbury, 19 Feb. 1845, Graham Papers.
[173] *Record*, 6 Feb. 1845.
[174] Ibid., 10, 13, 17, 20, 27 Feb. 1845.
[175] *Record*, 13 Feb. 1845.
[176] *Morning Chronicle*, 8 Feb. 1845.
[177] A. S. Thelwall, *Proceedings of the anti-Maynooth conference of 1845, with an historical introduction and an appendix* (1845), p. vi. Thelwall published this volume at the request of the Central Anti-Maynooth Committee of which he was a member. The introduction contains a first-hand account of the history of Protestant opposition to the bill from February to June, 1845.

concurrent endowment and the beginning of the end of the special relationship between the state and the Established church. As Archdeacon Samuel Wilberforce, who regarded the measure as necessary, noted, church and state were 'at the fag end of an old alliance'.[178]

It remained to be seen whether the Protestant Dissenters would bury their distaste for the Establishment and, united by a common Reformation heritage, make common cause with Anglicans against the endowment of Catholicism. Some indeed, chiefly the Methodists, had little difficulty in doing so, for they felt they were now fighting the second battle of the Reformation.[179] The Catholics had been able to rely on the support of other Dissenters in their demands for civil rights. On 26 March, however, the Baptist Union declared their absolute objection 'to the application of the resources of the State to ecclesiastical purposes', and the Congregationalists and Presbyterians soon followed suit.[180] Their attitude was a logical consequence of the turn which many nonconformists had taken, when, under the leadership of Edward Miall, they made 'voluntaryism' their guiding principle and founded the British Anti-State Church Association in April 1844. The Dissenters were so vehement in denouncing the grant that Peel wrote off the agitation as 'mainly the opposition of *Dissent* in England,— 'partly fanatical, partly religious'—a view not borne out by the facts.[181] There were 39 Anglicans on the anti-Maynooth Committee in addition to 19 Congregationalists, 9 Wesleyans, and 4 Presbyterians.[182] This central Committee had set up at the London Coffee House, Ludgate Street, and from there it urged all Protestants to organize public meetings to stir up 'Protestant feeling and principle'.[183] It circulated a form of petition to parliament which only needed signing and forwarding. The

---

[178] Wilberforce to Anderson, 26 Apr. 1845, A. R. Ashwell and R. G. Wilberforce, *Life of Samuel Wilberforce* (1880), i. 265. Samuel Wilberforce (1805-73) dean of Westminster, May 1845; bishop of Oxford; Oct. 1845; trs. Winchester 1869.

[179] R. G. Cowherd, *The politics of English Dissent* (1956), p. 160 citing *Congregational Magazine*, 2nd series, ix (1845), 321.

[180] *The Times*, 1 Apr. 1845; *Record*, 12 Apr. 1845.

[181] Peel to Croker, 22 Apr. 1845, *The correspondence and diaries of ... John Wilson Croker ...* (1884), iii. 32.

[182] Machin, 'Maynooth Grant', p. 69.

[183] Thelwall, *Proceedings*, p. xvii.

strength of the movement was to give the government an un-
pleasant shock when the bill received its first reading on 3 April.
The scene in the House of Commons on that day was certainly
an extraordinary one. No sooner had the measure been introduced than 'a vast number of Members, especially on the ministerial side of the House, instantly started up, rustling with
parchments and occasioned considerable laughter in the
House.'[184] Although surprised at the number of petitions, Peel
introduced the bill in a speech in which he presented the Commons with his characteristic choice of three options. The grant
could be abolished, it could be left unchanged, or a more liberal
provision could be made. The first course would involve repudiating the policy inaugurated by Pitt and upheld by both
the Irish and Imperial parliaments. The second was also
wrong, for any arrangement was better than leaving Maynooth
in its present miserable plight. The third course was the only
one which the government proposed in order to improve the
college and to elevate the tone of education there. Despite his
well-reasoned case, no less than one hundred and fourteen
members, mainly of his own party, divided against him.[185]
Heytesbury and Graham agreed that the division 'was not such
a one as we could have wished'.[186]

Encouraged by this excellent showing, the opponents of the
grant renewed their efforts. Seizing on Russell's reference to
the necessity of endowing the Catholic clergy, they summed up
the issue in one question: 'Protestants of England, are you
prepared to pay for a Popish Establishment?'[187] They tried to
have the second reading postponed to allow time to organize
petitions. Peel curtly refused to listen to a deputation led by
Sir Culling Eardley Smith. He told the delegates that he would
have had more regard for the petitions but that he knew that
they were merely the echoes of a committee in London. Lord
John Russell likewise declined to help them.[188] Denied any

---

[184] *Record,* 7 Apr. 1845.

[185] *Hansard,* lxxix. 18-111, 3 Apr. 1845.

[186] Heytesbury to Graham, 6 Apr. 1845, Graham Papers.

[187] Thelwall, *Proceedings,* pp. xxii-xxiii.

[188] Ibid., pp. xxxii - xxxiii. Sir Culling Eardley Smith (1805-63); philanthropist; 3rd
bart. 1829; MP for Pontefract 1830; founded Evangelical Alliance 1846. He was one
of the most active members of the anti-Maynooth committee of which he was chairman.

extension of time, the committee went into action with amazing energy. From the London Coffee House, it dispatched circulars, appeals, and petitions throughout the country. There was a splendid response to this well-organized campaign. In the week's interval between the first and second reading, aggrieved Protestants held meetings up and down the country, lobbied members of parliament and drew up petitions. At the second reading of the Bill on 11 April, 2,400 petitions were presented, one of them bearing as many as 19,000 signatures. High Churchmen and Evangelicals, Methodists and Dissenters of the three denominations agreed to bury their differences, in what the Earl of Roden called a 'holy union' to defeat the bill. Gladstone admitted that 'the general and prevailing sentiment of the great majority of the people of England and of Scotland' was opposed to the Bill.[189] Alarmed at the fury of opposition, Heytesbury kept up pressure from Ireland, telling Graham that the whole future of their Irish policy was now at stake; if the bill were rejected, 'every bad passion will be roused —the Roman Catholics will unite again as one body, the force and power of the Agitators will be enormously increased.'[190] Peel and Graham communicated to the queen Heytesbury's anxieties and favourable comments from Murray, O'Connell, Blake, and John Corballis, Catholic commissioner on the Board of National Education. The queen wholeheartedly backed Peel's measure, regarding it as 'great and good', and complained to her uncle, King Leopold, of the narrow-minded opposition: 'I blush for Protestantism', she told him.[191]

Despite the opinion of the country, the decision lay in the Houses of Parliament. On the first night of the second reading, Gladstone made a speech supporting the bill that annoyed both the opponents and the government. *The Record* accused him of outdoing 'all his other inconsistencies', on the grounds that he demolished the case for the grant and then pleaded for it on the grounds that it would be 'a great boon' to the Irish Catholics.[192]

[189] *Hansard,* lxxix. 520-54, 11 Apr. 1845.

[190] Heytesbury to Graham, 11, 12, 14 Apr. 1845, Graham Papers.

[191] Peel to the queen, 9 Apr; the queen to Peel, 15 Apr. 1845, Parker, *Peel,* iii. 173-6; the queen to the king of the Belgians, 15, 23 Apr. 1845, *The letters of Queen Victoria: a selection from her majesty's correspondence between the years 1837 and 1861,* ed. A. C. Benson and Viscount Esher (1908), ii. 36-7.

[192] *Record,* 14 Apr. 1845.

Plumtre asked what was the use of 'these great principles, pedantically argued in interminable books, if the first pinch led to their abandonment.'[193] In the House of Commons, George Smythe commented humorously, but accurately, that Gladstone had voted against the grant, then in favour of it, had then left the government because of his opposition to it, now voted for it and might possibly change again.[194] Contradictory though his conduct appeared, Gladstone's action marked the end of a period of great change in his life. 'I had [after Maynooth] no great or serious mental change to make', he related in his autobiography.[195] It was clear to him that the ideal relationship between the state and the church, so clearly delineated in his book, was no longer feasible.

Disraeli used the occasion to make a savage and effective attack on Peel, alleging that he was 'a Minister who habitually brings forward as his own measures those very schemes and proposals to which, in opposition, he always avowed himself a bitter and determined opponent'. Denouncing Peel's inconsistency, he described him as 'a great Parliamentary middleman ... who bamboozles one party and plunders the other ...'[196] Macaulay made the most stirring speech of the debate, drawing a striking contrast between the poverty of Maynooth and the splendour of Cambridge, his own university. Although he supported the measure, he took fierce revenge for Peel's opposition tactics during the Whigs' administrations. Because his is an important indictment of Peel's past and present conduct, it merits quoting at length:

You offer to the eager, honest, hotheaded Protestant a Bill [? Registration Bills (1840-1)] to take privileges away from the Roman Catholics of Ireland if he will only assist you to power ... then, when you are in power, you turn round on him and give him a Bill for the religious endowment of the Roman Catholic College in Ireland ... Is it possible that the people out of doors should not feel indignation at seeing that the very parties who, when we were in office, voted against the Maynooth grant, are now being whipped into the House in order to vote for an increased Maynooth grant?...Can you wonder that all those fierce spirits, whom you have taught to harass us, now turn round and begin to worry you. The Orangeman raises his howl and Exeter-

193 *Morning Chronicle*, 18 Apr. 1845.
194 *Hansard*, lxxix. 833-40, 15 Apr. 1845.
195 Gladstone, *Prime Ministers' Papers*, i. 51.
196 *Hansard*, lxxix. 555-69, 11 Apr. 1845.

hall sets up its bray. Mr M'Neile is horror-stricken to think that a still larger
grant is intended for 'the priests of Baal' at the table of 'Jezebel' and your
Protestant operatives of Dublin call for the impeachment of the Minister in
exceedingly bad English...Did you think, when Session after Session you went
on attacking those whom you knew to be in the right and flattering the prejudices of those whom you knew to be in the wrong, that the day of reckoning
would never come? That day has come; and now, on that day, you are doing
penance for the disingenuousness of years.[197]

Macaulay recalled eight years later 'how white poor Peel looked
while I was speaking'.[198] Macaulay's onslaught was the bitter
and partisan attack of a politician out of office, yet it shows how
Peel's Irish reform policy suffered from his past record. It was
not just to say of Peel, as Macaulay did, that he called up the
devils of religious animosity, but he had used prejudices against
the Irish Catholics for opposition purposes.[199] It was true that a
resurgent Anglicanism had contributed significantly to raise
Peel to power, but that was not by any means a complete
explanation of his success in 1841. Macaulay's analysis of the
'natural consequences' is accurate enough; the ultra-Protestants
now felt that he had betrayed them and for the second time.
Yet Macaulay gave no credit to the courage Peel showed in
publicly making such a change. Eager to score a party point
and to display his own forensic power, he could not rise to the
generosity of his own chief, Russell, who, by his constant
championship of Irish causes, had more cause than Macaulay
to feel piqued by Peel's stealing of his clothes.[200]

The record of the government became a major theme of the
debates, and attacks on Peel's alleged inconsistency became so
regular a feature that the *Morning Chronicle* smugly commented:
'Dante represents the head of the archtraitor, as consigned to
the eternal gnawing of his victim; but here the one head is in
the jaw of the multitude, who leap up by dozens to shed their
venom, and gratify their revenge.'[201] The unpopular Graham,

[197] Ibid., 646-58, 14 Apr. 1845.
[198] G. O. Trevelyan, *The life and letters of Lord Macaulay* (1893), pp. 453-4.
[199] Peel was accused of attacking 'the encroachments of the Church of Rome' in
1838; *The Times,* 21 Apr. 1845. He repudiated it and said, 'I never raised a no Popery
cry', *Hansard,* lxxix. 1422-3, 28 Apr. 1845.
[200] Russell later associated himself with Macaulay's charges, though in a muted
fashion, *Hansard,* lxxix. 1229-30, 23 Apr. 1845.
[201] *Morning Chronicle,* 16 Apr. 1845, see also *The Times,* 19 Apr. 1845.

too, suffered with his chief and, when he now urged conciliation
for Ireland, his own uncompromising words of June 1843 were
flung in his teeth. He rose to the occasion and, in a most remarkable admission for so haughty a man, declared simply: 'I am
sorry for the use of that phrase; it has given offence in Ireland;
I deeply regret it.' Then, to cheers from both sides of the
House, he went on: 'I can only say, ...from the bottom of my
heart, that my actions... have been better than my words.' He
added the significant comment that the days of 'Protestant
Ascendancy' were passed and that he would not be responsible
for any attempt to govern Ireland on these principles.[202] It is
remarkable how both he and Peel were prepared to subordinate
a defence of their consistency to the central aim of getting the
measure through. Peel was willing to allow the credit for conciliatory measures to go to his political opponents provided that
the bill should pass: '... you may think, and perhaps not unjustly, that ... this measure should have proceeded from the
constant ... friends of the ... Catholics. You may think it right,
that those who have proposed [it] should forfeit your patronage
... punish the men; but do not disregard the consequences of
rejecting this measure as it has been introduced.'[203] The
Maynooth debate brought out many divisions. It divided Young
England for, although Disraeli opposed it, Smythe and Lord
John Manners supported it, the former deprecating any attempt
to make the Irish clergyman 'something more of a chaplain and
something less of a priest', the latter defending the type of priest
which Maynooth had produced on £9,000 a year.[204] Ashley
opposed the increased grant in a speech, which he noted, in his
diary not without self-satisfaction, as being good and impartial
and well received by the Catholics.[205] The leaders of the Anti-
Corn Law League were split: Cobden praised the grant as an
educational measure, while Bright appealed to Catholics to
resist this 'hush money' whose aim, he remarked perceptively,
was intended to make their clergy 'as tame as the clergy of
Suffolk and Dorsetshire'.[206] Thomas Duncombe, speaking for

[202] *Hansard*, lxxix. 914-29, 17 Apr. 1845.

[203] Ibid., 1025, 18 Apr. 1845.

[204] Ibid., 823-31, 833-40, 16 Apr. 1845.

[205] Ibid., 774-81, 16 Apr. 1845; Diary, 18 Apr. 1845, cited in E. Hodder, *Life and work of Lord Shaftesbury* (1880-2), ii. 102.

[206] *Hansard,* lxxix. 963-8, 18 Apr. 818-23, 16 Apr. 1845.

the voluntaryists among the Dissenters while expressing sympathy for the Catholics, opposed endowment of any religion.[207] John Colquhoun, Col. William Verner, Col. Charles Sibthorp, William Ferrand, and Inglis took their stand on Anglican principle.[208] The two members for Dublin, Edward Grogan and William Gregory, opposed the grant, as did the two members for Dublin University, Frederick Shaw and James Hamilton.[209] The members for Oxford and Cambridge were divided: Sir Robert Inglis and Charles Law opposed it whereas Thomas Bucknall Estcourt and Henry Goulburn supported it.[210]

Outside the House of Commons, the duke of Newcastle, bitterly disappointed by Gladstone's 'betrayal', called on all members of the 'almost persecuted' Church of England to resist this sinful endowment of a rebellious Popish seminary and to 'Petition, Petition, Petition'—a plea that became the banner-heading of one of the Anti-Maynooth committee's advertisements.[211] Petitions showered 'thick as a snow-storm, on the Table of the House'.[212] *The Times* had at first shown no great opposition to the new measure but from the beginning of April it came out strongly against it: 'It is not Liberalism but Romanism which Peel is forcing on the nation... It is not merely Popery; that is unpopular enough in England, especially Irish Popery; but it is Maynooth. It is a name and a thing above all others odious and suspicious to England.'[213] Most of the press took the same line as *The Times*. Punch published an amusing verse that was not without an element of truth:

> How wonderful is Peel
> He changes with the time...
> He gives whate'er they want
> To those who ask with zeal
> He yields the Maynooth Grant
> To the clamour for Repeal.[214]

[207] Ibid., 999-1004, 18 Apr. 1845.
[208] Ibid., 501-12, 11 Apr.; 700-5, 15 Apr.; 968-80, 18 Apr.; 1016-24, 18 Apr. 1845.
[209] Ibid., 512-20, 11 Apr., 642-5, 14 Apr., 658-66, 14 Apr., 762-8, 16 Apr. 1845.
[210] Gash, *Peel*, p. 474.
[211] *Morning Chronicle*, 16 Apr. 1845; Thelwall, *Proceedings*, lii-liii.
[212] Macaulay, 14 Apr. 1845, *Hansard*, lxxix. 657.
[213] *The Times*, 17 Apr. 1845; see also 16, 18, 19 Apr. 1845.
[214] *Punch*, viii. 191.

The *Morning Chronicle*, although pleased at the split in the Tory party, supported the measure and appealed to those dissenters who opposed the grant on voluntaryist grounds to take Irish conditions into account: 'The Irish Catholics are very well disposed to the voluntary principle, but if they find its English advocates employ it to defeat a Maynooth grant, while they are unable to disturb the rich establishment of the Protestant minority, they will hardly give those advocates credit for ... love of equal justice.'[215]

Abroad, the debate was followed with great interest, especially by Catholics.[216] *L'Ami de la Religion*, which devoted considerable space to it in all its issues, remarked that: 'la gravité de cette question et la sollenité de la discussion qu'elle provoque fixent, en ce moment, toute l'attention et l'intérêt religieux du monde catholique.' Its own judgement on the matter was 'Gloire à Sir Robert Peel!'[217] On 17 April, *The Times* published a comprehensive review of the question from the *Journal des Débats*, which saw the measure as a revolution in England's religious policy and as the first step leading to 'the general and regular maintenance of the Catholic clergy by the State'.[218] This comment from the *Journal des Débats* touched on one of the most sensitive issues raised during the debate.[219] Many Protestants, in and outside Parliament, feared that the increased grant was indeed such a first step. In reply to Inglis, Peel made it quite clear that that was not intended, but he did not dispel the fears of the opponents of the grant since he significantly refused to hamper any future government by a statement that the difficulties in the way of such an endowment of the Catholic church were altogether insuperable.[220]

The measure was not in real danger, for Peel could count on the massive support of the Whigs and Liberals. Russell, whatever his private feelings at having to rescue Peel, was determined to forgo party advantage and supported the bill as 'calculated, in some degree, to heal the still bleeding wounds of Ireland', although he realized that he would thereby alienate

---

[215] *Morning Chronicle*, 16 Apr. 1845.   [216] *The Times,* 21 Apr. 1845.
[217] *Ami de la Religion*, 19, 24 Apr. 1845. The first seven pages of this latter issue were devoted to the Maynooth debate.   [219] Ibid., 18, 19 Apr. 1845.
[218] *The Times,* 17 Apr. 1845.
[220] *Hansard*, lxxix. 1035-6, 18 Apr. 1845.

some of his own constituents in the City of London.[221] Ashley correctly assessed the situation when he remarked with chagrin that Peel 'lives, therefore, moves and has his being through John Russell.'[222] Peel concluded the debate with a moving appeal to members to let their indignation fall not upon the measure but upon those who prepared it. Then, justifying the course he had pursued, he recalled the situation at the height of the Repeal campaign:

There was a universal feeling at that time that you ought not merely to rely on applications of force ... that it was the duty of the Government to take into consideration the condition of Ireland ... you must break up ... that formidable confederacy which exists in that country against ... the British connexion. I do not believe you can break it up by force ... You can do much to break it up by acting in a spirit of kindness, forbearance and generosity.

In a remarkable conclusion he declared that on the day that he had announced the government's intention of maintaining England's rights in Oregon, he had recollected, with satisfaction and consolation, that the day before he had sent a message of peace to Ireland.[223] This admission 'called forth much anim-adversion'.[224] 'Everybody said', Greville noted in his diary, 'it was a recognition of the truth of what O'Connell had said in his clever and ingenious speech at Dublin.'[225] 'Mr O'Connell and Mr Polk [the President of the United States] have between them made you very uneasy', complained Macaulay and he could not now deny that 'the place where an Irish gentleman may best serve his country is Conciliation Hall.'[226] The general reasons, however, which Peel assigned for his policy have an entirely genuine ring about them, for they correspond to those he put to his cabinet in his memoranda of February 1844 and to his briefing of Heytesbury when the latter took up office in Ireland. Peel's chief concern was not to reform or control May-nooth but to break up 'that formidable conspiracy' against the government—a task that he saw as necessary both for domestic

[221] *Hansard,* lxxix. 1004-16, 18 Apr. 1845.
[222] Diary, 18 Apr. 1845, Hodder, *Shaftesbury,* ii. 103.
[223] *Hansard,* lxxix. 1027-42, 18 Apr. 1845.
[224] Thelwall, *Proceedings,* p. lxii.
[225] Greville, *Journal,* v. 215; 22 Apr. 1845. For O'Connell's speech in Conciliation Hall see p. 287.
[226] *Hansard,* lxxix. 1195, 23 Apr. 1845. .

and foreign reasons. In short, his policy was to kill Repeal by kindness.

The measure passed its second reading by an almost two to one majority. Of the Conservatives, 161 voted for it and 148 voted against.[227] The large majority was accounted for by the Whigs and Liberals, 164 of them supporting the measure as against a mere 30 who opposed it. Three quarters of the Irish conservative members who took part in the division—27 out of 37—voted against the bill. The only danger that Peel faced was on Ward's motion that the provision for the grant be taken from the resources of the Established church in Ireland. It appeared possible that some of the ultra-Protestant Conservatives might ally with the Liberals to defeat the government on this issue, but Peel did not lose his nerve.[228] Ward suspected what was afoot and, warned by Russell, postponed his motion, stating, as Peel told the queen, 'that he would not be a party to a factious combination'.[229] When it finally came up in committee, it was easily defeated.[230] In the House of Lords, the same arguments were gone over again, Lord Roden leading the opposition. Six of the bishops, including Whately of Dublin, supported the bill and seventeen (including the archbishops of Canterbury and York and the bishop of Cashel) opposed it. De Grey and Eliot (now St. Germans), so long and so bitterly divided on it, were now united in voting for it. Supported by most of the Liberal peers, the government had a comfortable majority of 157 on the second reading, the voting being 226 to 69.[231] Despite the Anti-Maynooth Committee's last minute appeal to the queen, the royal assent was given on 30 June. From May on, the opposition to the bill was split because the Ultra-Voluntaryists, protesting against the 'no-popery' stand of the Anti-Maynooth Committee, set up their own meetings at Crosby Hall. Unity was never restored among the Protestant opponents of Maynooth. Many churchmen, frightened by the Ultra-Voluntaryists, began to see in concurrent endowment a

---

[227] Ibid., lxxix. 1042, 19 Apr. 1845; Thelwall, *Proceedings*, p. lxiv. Gash gives the figures as 159 to 147, *Peel*, p. 477.

[228] Peel to Victoria, 9 Apr. 1845, RA D14/101.

[229] Peel to Victoria, 17 Apr. 1845, RA A17/71.

[230] Gash, *Peel*, pp. 474-5.

[231] *Hansard,* lxxxi. 118, 2 June 1845.

safeguard for their own church. The attitude of these Ultra-Voluntaryists prevented united action and helped the government to discount the opposition; it also marked an important stage in the growing influence of that section of the dissenters.[232]

The debate on the Maynooth grant was interesting both because of the issues it raised and those it omitted. The fundamental issue raised by the opponents was the relationship of the state to the Established church, to the Catholic church and to churches in general. The supporters of the measure tended increasingly to base their case on the political argument that the increased grant was a necessary concession to Irish Catholics. Predictably, Maynooth's record (including the type of priest it produced) was attacked and defended without any conclusive result. The government's record was introduced and developed as a major theme. This, too, was understandable, although less relevant to the debate. On the other hand, there was no scrutiny of the provisions of the act, even of those important details which had cost Graham, Peel, and Heytesbury much anxiety, such as the system of visitation or the question of incorporation of the trustees. Details, carefully worked out in order to soften opposition, were ignored, and attention was focussed on the broader issues. The key issue was not effective control of Maynooth, but the constitutional and political validity of endowing Catholicism and conciliating the Irish Catholics. As Gladstone now realized, the relation of the state to the church was changing, for statesmen were forced to think in terms of practical government rather than of the ideals of church and state, whatever might still be the view of the rank and file of the Tory party. The Maynooth bill had proved a watershed.

Peel's party had split down the centre. On the third reading, it had divided 148 to 149 against. The Maynooth controversy has been seen as a rehearsal for the great political crisis of 1846. Indeed the Maynooth Grant may have inflicted the deeper wound on the Conservative party for, if the repeal of the corn laws hit its pocket, the grant to the Catholic seminary for priests struck at a fundamental principle upon which the party had been painfully reconstructed after the debacle of 1829 and

[232] Norman, *Anti-Catholicism*, pp. 39-41.

1832. In the election of 1847 Francis Bonham, the party election agent, reported to Peel that 'Maynooth has certainly destroyed several of our friends; Free Trade hardly any.'[233] His assessment was confirmed by Thomas Wood, the unsuccessful Peelite candidate in Middlesex, who told Peel that the principal reason for the withdrawal of support was 'an apprehension of the endowment for the Catholic priesthood in Ireland and my vote on Maynooth. I do not believe that the Corn Laws ... had much effect in keeping our friends away from the Polls.'[234] It would be a mistake, however, to see the crisis in isolation. Peel was right when he observed to Croker that: 'Tariff, drought, 46s a quarter for wheat, quicken the religious apprehensions of some; disappointed ambition and the rejection of applications for office, of others.'[235] Undoubtedly religious apprehensions were quickened by developments within the Oxford Movement for many were 'alarmed at the doctrines not of Maynooth but of Oxford ... who dread the *Tracts for the Times* as much as ... the Secunda Secundae of Aquinas.'[236] Nevertheless, the cabinet's actions on the Factory Bill and on sugar in 1844 and more recently the 1845 budget had produced increasing discontent in the rank and file of the Tory party. Graham's unpopularity helped to make the position of the government more precarious with its own party, and dissatisfaction reached its climax on the Maynooth Bill. Peel himself was stiff, pompous, and far from conciliatory to those of his followers who saw issues less clearly than he did. The country gentlemen no longer felt that he was as indispensable as he had been when the radical danger was greater, and, deeply offended by both religious and commercial issues, they staged a protest that was to be a full rehearsal of the corn law crisis. Both Peel and Graham bitterly resented the lack of appreciation for their achievements since 1841 and appeared to have lost some of the will to survive. In January, Peel had told Gladstone that he felt that the Maynooth issue would be 'fatal to the Government'.[237] In April, he told Croker that he was

[233] Bonham to Peel, 2 Aug. 1847, Add MSS 40599, f. 122, cited in Gash, *Peel*, p. 625.

[234] Wood to Peel, 25 Aug. 1847, Add. MSS 40599, ff. 226-7, cited in Machin, 'Maynooth Grant' p. 83.

[235] Peel to Croker, 22 Apr. 1845, Parker, *Peel*, iii. 176.

[236] *Hansard*, lxxxi. 79, 4 June 1845, Lord Monteagle.

[237] Gladstone's memorandum, 14 Jan. 1845, Add. MSS 44777, ff. 212-15, Gladstone, *Prime Ministers' Papers*, ii. 272.

resolved on carrying the bill and was 'very careless as to the consequences which may follow its passing, so far as they concern me and my position.'[238] Not surprisingly after such an exhausting session he felt 'a sense of *fatigue* upon the brain'.[239] An even more despondent Graham told St. Germans that the Maynooth question 'would prove fatal to the Administration' and repeated the same gloomy sentiments to Heytesbury, Hardinge, and Croker.[240] To the latter he expressed what amounted almost to a death-wish, fatalistically declaring that 'the country gentlemen cannot be more ready to give us the death-blow than we are prepared to receive it.'[241] It was against this background of seething party discontent and Peel's and Graham's feelings of frustration that the Maynooth Bill became law. Why they persisted in forcing through this measure even when they felt that they were riding to political doom is puzzling and can only be explained on the grounds that Peel believed that the Maynooth Grant was of crucial importance in his efforts to reconcile Ireland—a conviction that had been growing since the crisis of the Year of Repeal. By January 1845, too, he had so deeply committed himself to Irish reforms that it would have been fatal to turn back for, as Heytesbury reported, to disappoint the expectations that had been raised, particularly among his episcopal allies, would have ruined the whole policy of reconcilation.

The controversy over the Maynooth Grant is normally evaluated in terms of the effects it produced in England where it split the Conservative party, contributed to the growth of voluntaryism among the Dissenters, and manifested a deep-seated antagonism to Catholicism both in its Roman and Tractarian guise. The effects of the grant in Ireland, whether on Maynooth College itself or on Peel's attempted reconcilation of the Irish Catholics, have been largely ignored. The stormy controversy that raged in England found little echo in Ireland. Heytesbury was able to report that: 'People here cannot get over their astonishment at the flame which has been raised in England ...

[238] Peel to Croker, 22 Apr. 1845, *Croker correspondence,* iii. 32.
[239] Gladstone's memorandum, 14 Aug. 1845, Add. MSS 44777, ff. 229-32, Gladstone, *Prime Ministers' Papers,* ii. 279.
[240] Graham to St. Germans, 19 Apr. 1845, Port Eliot Archives; Gash, *Peel,* 477-8.
[241] Graham to Croker, 22 Mar. 1845, *Croker correspondence,* iii. 31.

Even those who are opposed to the Catholics cannot understand this excess of indignation'. His comments were re-echoed
by Lord Clare and others.[242]

The leaders of Irish presbyterianism supported the grant.
Henry Cooke, although opposed to the principle of aiding the
dissemination of popery, believed that 'if the thing is to be done
it is not only *as well* to do it generously but it is better', and
with characteristic independence declared that he would 'not
be goaded by all the taunts of the English dissenters to join in
the outcry against it.'[243] His rival, the Unitarian Henry
Montgomery, sending on a petition from the Remonstrant
Synod in favour of the bill, declared that: 'we are shocked at
the possibility of being identified for a moment with those
degenerate Presbyterians who receive nearly £40,000 every
year from the public purse for their own half million of adherents and would withold the mere trifle of £26,000 from *seven*
millions of Catholics!'[224] Montgomery, a long-standing advocate
of Catholic liberties, was right in asserting that some Presbyterians opposed the increased grant, but the main opposition
would seem to have come from the Established church and
from the Wesleyans if one is to judge from the membership of
the Anti-Maynooth Committee for Ireland.[245] Some protest
meetings were held in Belfast, and Culling Eardley Smith
organized a conference and meeting in Dublin for 4 and 5 June.
The scene in the Round Room of Dublin's Rotunda on 5 June
was a colourful one. Dignitaries of the Established church
thronged the platform mingling with Presbyterians, Moravians,
Wesleyans, Independents, Primitive Wesleyans, and Cov-
enanters in a remarkable display of solidarity. 'Bands of Orangemen ranged round the room ... with orange sashes over their
shoulders, broad orange ribbons tied on sticks and held up in
different parts of the room.' Resolutions were passed condemning the 'virtual apostasy' of the government and insisting

[242] Heytesbury to Peel, 24 Apr. 1845, Add. MSS 40479, ff. 333-4, Clare to Peel,
20 Apr. 1845, cited McDowell, *Public Opinion*, p. 222; Heytesbury to Graham, 8 Apr.
1845, Graham Papers.

[243] Cooke to —— 24 Feb. 1845 (enclosed with Peel's letter to Prince Albert
12 Apr. 1845), RA D.14/109.

[244] Montgomery to J. E. Tennant, 8 Apr. 1845 (enclosed with letter of Peel to
Prince Albert, 12 Apr. 1845) RA D14/109.

[245] Thelwall, *Proceedings*, pp. cxxxvi-cxxxvii.

that 'no assistance ought to be given out of the national resources to train a body of men for propagating and extending
doctrines and practices, inconsistent with the Word of God
and idolatrous and superstitious.'[246] Despite such a show of
unity there was no effective sequel to this meeting which, in
any case, had not been called until after the bill had passed its
second reading in both Houses.

Protestant anti-Maynooth meetings in Ireland were predict-
able enough; more important to the government was the reaction of the Catholics for it was to conciliate them that Peel
had brought in this highly controversial and divisive measure
and stuck to it during a gruelling session. The sensitive and
suspicious state of Catholic opinion, of which the bequests
issue and, especially, the concordat question were both symp-
toms and causes, meant that concessions from the Conservative
government would be regarded with suspicion. In Maynooth
College, O'Hanlon was not alone in viewing the government's
proposals with extreme caution although none of his colleagues
appear to have gone so far as to wish for the complete suppression of the college as, in a bitter moment, he did.[247] O'Reilly
portrayed well the critical atmosphere in which the government's proposals would probably be received:

they [the ministers] may propose conditions, which will either be objectionable in themselves or will *appear so* to our, perhaps over-sensitive, bishops and
still more to their political partisans. Some of us in the college have said in
joke that if the government required *an additional candle* to be put on the parlour
table after dinner, the innovation would be denounced as unsufferable. I fear
such would in matters of not much more importance be the case.[248]

When the text of the bill became public, Renehan, Maynooth's
bursar and soon to be its president, explained to Cullen his own
attitude of prudent reserve: 'As *yet* we have no reason to dread
any inconvenient interference with our government or internal
arrangements of education or discipline. But *timeo Danaos* etc.'
With the memory of the bequests controversy fresh in his
mind, he avowed that he would rather not receive the badly
needed increase 'than that any bishops in the newspapers

[246] Ibid., pp. cxxv-cxxxvii.
[247] See p. 211.
[248] O'Reilly to Cullen, 21 Jan. 1845, Cullen Papers.

disagree about the terms or that the people's respect for the clergy should again be endangered.'[249] As the bill progressed through Parliament, however, the nationalist newspapers showed themselves very favourable to the measure and to the government's stand. A delighted Heytesbury assured Graham that 'the feeling of satisfaction it excited amongst all classes of the Roman Catholic population exceeded my most sanguine expectations.'[250] Dean Meyler, one of Murray's strongest supporters, described the measure as 'munificent in its substance and noble in its Manner' and declared that Peel would soon be the most popular man in Ireland.[251] From Maynooth, Russell wrote to Henry Bagshawe, the editor of the *Dublin Review*: 'By the way, is not Sir Robert Peel a noble fellow? His bill for us is a magnificent one.'[252] Of more direct use to Peel was a joint letter signed by the entire Maynooth staff which he read in the House of Commons to prove, against assertions to the contrary, that the priests of the college welcomed and were grateful for the measure:

The undersigned beg leave most respectfully to express our deep sense of gratitude for the very liberal provisions which you, as head of the Government, have proposed for the education of the Roman Catholic clergy, and still more for the kind and gracious manner in which you have recommended the measure to the friendly consideration of the House.[253]

Whatever distrust O'Hanlon, O'Reilly, or Renehan may have previously entertained had been dissipated by the generous terms of the bill and the warmth with which the government pressed it forward. Even MacHale publicly praised the bill, while Murray called at the Castle to express his gratitude.[254] Collectively, too, the bishops expressed their thanks to the government, and when Heytesbury later visited the college, the authorities showed their appreciation.[255] There were a few dis-

---

[249] Renehan to Cullen, 6 Mar. 1845, ibid.

[250] Heytesbury to Graham, 11 Apr. 1845.

[251] Meyler to McDonnell, 8 Apr. 1845, RA D14/110.

[252] Russell to H. R. Bagshawe, 6 Apr. 1845, Westminster Diocesan Archives.

[253] *Hansard*, lxxix. 1034, 18 Apr. 1845. The president, Montague, did not sign the letter; he was too ill to take any part in the college's affairs.

[254] *Pilot*, 30 Apr. 1845; Heytesbury to Graham, 23 Apr. 1845, Graham Papers.

[255] Meeting of 23 May 1845, Meetings of the Irish Bishops, DDA; Heytesbury to Graham, 30 July 1845, Graham Papers.

senting voices among the Catholics. Some of Cullen's friends feared that the grant would produce a 'softer' type of priest, who, having become accustomed to government support, would accept a pension from the state.[256] Lucas described the increased grant as 'hush money' and alleged that 'Exeter Hall is to be bullied; the Conciliation Hall is to be cajoled.' Lucas was unrepresentative, however, for, as he complained, 'all our friends are ... running wild with gratitude to Sir Robert Peel'.[257]

Irish Catholic opinion on the bill was partly the result of O'Connell's attitude which deserves more attention than it has received. The Repeal Association had set up a committee to study the bill and O'Connell, in presenting the report, stated his considered opinion that 'the bill appears to be framed in a just and conciliatory spirit.'[258] In a speech at Conciliation Hall, while alleging of Peel that he had at one time had 'almost every young man in the north of Ireland sworn in as an Orangeman', O'Connell avowed that 'nothing was ever more fair, manly and excellent in all its details, than his plan respecting Maynooth'. He himself took what credit he could, and in witty phrases that rankled in the minds of opponents, he intoned a litany of praise to his own movement: 'Agitation, I thank you, Conciliation Hall, I am obliged to you, Repeal Association, Maynooth ought to pray for you.'[259] As the debate developed, it was not merely the terms of the measure but the courage of the ministers that impressed O'Connell. Privately and publicly, he highly commended Graham, forgiving him everything, 'trial, persecution, sentence and all'; and, with customary exuberance, declared that the Irish people would place Graham 'upon a pedestal, the basis of which shall be "Justice to Ireland".'[260] O'Connell, for the first time, was showing confidence in the Conservative administration.[261] To his cousin Pierce Mahony—who promptly passed on the word to Graham—

[256] J. O'Ferrall to Kirby, 4 June 1845, Kirby Papers; J. Maher to Cullen, 9 June 1845, Cullen Papers; Cullen to Kirby, 3 Aug. 1845, Kirby Papers.

[257] *Tablet*, 19 Apr. 1845.

[258] *Report of the Parliamentary Committee of the Loyal National Repeal Association*, ii. 311-15.

[259] *Nation*, 12 Apr. 1845.

[260] Ibid., 26 Apr. 1845.

[261] W. E. H. Lecky is unfair to O'Connell in claiming that he supported the bill in the most grudging manner; see his *Leaders of Public Opinion in Ireland*, vol. ii. *Daniel O'Connell* (1912), p. 280.

O'Connell wrote that 'the Ministry appear to be really sincere in their determination to do something for Ireland', adding significantly that 'they have raised hopes infinitely beyond the Maynooth grant'.[262] In the eyes of many Irish Catholics, Maynooth was an important symbol, and the government's generous treatment of it a pledge for the future. In answer to Mahony, who was anxious for a *rapprochement* with the government, O'Connell now drew up a policy statement which compares in importance to his letter to Buller two years earlier. Surely, he wrote, the ministers after their speeches upon the Maynooth question ought to bring in political reforms, such as a proper Municipal Corporations Bill. The desperate situation of the peasant was quite alarming and he feared a 'servile war', a 'French Jacoterie' [*sic*] unless something were done for him: 'The peasant must be relieved or, depend upon it, he will go mad.' The evidence being published by the Devon Commission showed the terrible condition of the poorer peasants and gave urgency to O'Connell's plea for substantial reforms. He believed that the government, by its recent actions, had created the right atmosphere, for 'the *manner* of the Maynooth grant has put the people into good humour.' As he perceptively remarked, however, some more 'substantially good measures' were urgently needed. Again, O'Connell reiterated his faith in the government: 'you see', he concluded, 'I do think the Ministry sincere.'[263]

Whatever the consequences within the Conservative party, Peel and Graham had succeeded in Ireland far more than they may have imagined. Certainly, a few thousand pounds to Maynooth was no more than one of those 'skin-deep remedies' mentioned by O'Connell. Yet the manner of its passing, the language used by Peel and Graham during the debate and the way in which they had stood up to popular anti-Catholic pressures, had made a deep impression on the clergy, on Irish Catholics in general, and even on O'Connell. Following on the real, if limited, achievement of the Bequests Act, the favourable reception of the Maynooth Grant had strengthened the possibility that Peel's programme of concessions might achieve its

---

[262] O'Connell to Mahony, 19 Apr. 1845, Parker, *Graham,* ii. 9; *Nation,* 26 Apr. 1845.
[263] O'Connell to Mahony, 25 Apr. 1845, Rathcon Papers.

aim of conciliating a large section of the Irish Catholic community.

The first Maynooth Act of 1795 sprang from the converging desires, though prompted by different motives, of the Catholic bishops and the English government. The major revision of that act in 1845 derived from a similar accord. The bishops needed a college capable of providing more and better-educated priests to cater for an increasing population. The government also wanted better-educated priests in the hope that they would prove more attached to the British connection. In the short term, too, it hoped that the munificence of this unconditional grant would conciliate some of the clergy and wean them away from the Repeal movement. The 1795 act was a sop to the Catholics after the dismissal of Fitzwilliam, the 1845 act a sop after the arrest of O'Connell. By 1845, however, a deep-rooted and widespread anti-Catholicism, focussing particularly on Maynooth College—a movement virtually non-existent fifty years earlier—had sprung up. Peel had courageously withstood this public hostility because he felt that

... it is absolutely necessary to prove to the Roman Catholics of Ireland that the manifestation of that [anti-Catholic] feeling should not induce public men to swerve from the course which ... appears to have produced a lively feeling among those in whose favour it is to be given.[264]

There was much truth in his claim. The question now was whether this second and highly successful instalment of his policy of killing Repeal by kindness would lead to a more lasting reconciliation. Hard on the Maynooth bill came the government's third, and as it proved, final reform measure. On 9 May, Graham introduced the Academic Colleges Bill and the controversy that ensued upset once again the unstable balance that existed in Ireland.

[264] *Hansard,* lxxix. 1425, 28 Apr. 1845.

7

THE 'GODLESS COLLEGES' 1845 - 1846

Education, not emancipation, may well have been the major achievement of the Catholic church in Ireland during the nineteenth century. Certainly, it had struggled for long to obtain a satisfactory elementary education for the poor and had been rewarded with the more or less satisfactory system of national education in 1832. Later in the second half of the century it was to build up its own comprehensive system of secondary education. Tertiary education did not figure high on its priorities until the middle of the century, and even then it could be argued that its quickening interest in a Catholic university was a reaction to Peel's efforts to impose his own solution.[1] When the question of university education for Catholics and Nonconformists had first been raised at the end of the eighteenth century, a number of solutions had been envisaged. Trinity College, Dublin—the sole existing university—might be opened by the abolition of religious tests. A second possibility was to create a new college within the University of Dublin. A third solution was to create new university institutions.[2] These three possibilites were to recur constantly in every attempt to solve the university problem. In 1794, Catholics and, by implication, Nonconformists were permitted to enter Trinity College, a useful though limited concession: they were still ineligible for scholarships and fellowships. Trinity, for economic and geographical reasons, was not easily accessible to students from the south, west, and north of the country. In any case, since only thirty Catholics entered each year as against three hundred and fifty Protestants, the question of higher education for

[1] Two important studies on this question are F. McGrath, *Newman's University, idea and reality* (1951); and T. W. Moody and J. C. Beckett, *Queen's, Belfast, 1845-1949: the history of a university* (1959).

[2] T. W. Moody, 'The Irish University question of the nineteenth century', *History*, xlii (1958), 90-109. Trinity College was founded as a constituent college of the University of Dublin but remained its only college.

Catholics remained effectively unsolved.[3] Further, it was alleged that pressure was brought to bear on Catholics in Trinity to conform to the Established church, and the fact that a number did conform temporarily or permanently, generated suspicion and hositility among Catholic clergy as different in outlook as Cullen and Murray.[4]

The first to broach the possibility of academical colleges was Denis Bullen, professor at the Royal Cork Institute, who, in 1829, wrote a pamphlet advocating a system of 'secular Collegiate education'.[5] He joined forces with Thomas Wyse, a leading member of the Catholic Association and a tireless campaigner for educational reform.[6] The prescient Dr Doyle, in a letter to Slattery, suggested that Wyse should try 'to turn the attention of the government to the establishment of four provincial academies, in which the sciences would be taught'.[7] Wyse, whom Peel justifiably singled out in the 1845 debate as 'the consistent promoter of education in all its gradations', pressed for comprehensive educational reforms for over a decade before the act of 1845. He was the principal speaker at a meeting in Cork, in 1838, when a committee was set up to obtain a lay college for Munster.[8] In 1835 he was chairman of a Select Committee on Foundation Schools and Education in Ireland, and in 1841 he summarized its recommendations in an important letter to Lord Morpeth, the chief secretary.[9] The letter was later printed by order of the House of Commons but no action was taken.

---

[3] McGrath, *Newman's University*, p. 5.

[4] An unsigned list in the Dublin Diocesan Archives, drawn up at about this time, names 74 students who, during the period 1801 to 1831, abandoned the Catholic faith while studying at Trinity College.

[5] *Report of her Majesty's commissioners appointed to inquire into the progress and conditions of the Queen's Colleges at Belfast, Cork and Galway, PP 1857-8,* xxi. 221-3. Bullen was later professor of surgery at the Queen's College, Cork.

[6] Thomas Wyse (1791-1862), a Waterford landowner; MP for Tipperary, 1830; MP for Waterford city 1835-47; member of the Melbourne administration, 1839-41.

[7] Slattery to Wyse, 28 Nov. 1830, cited in W. M. Wyse, *Notes on education reform in Ireland ... compiled from ... the unpublished memoirs of ... Sir Thomas Wyse* (1901), p. 14.

[8] *Pilot*, 16, 19 Nov. 1838.

[9] *Report from the Select Committee on Foundation Schools and Education in Ireland, PP 1837-8,* vii. 345-436; *Copy of a letter to the Right Honourable Lord Viscount Morpeth from Thomas Wyse, Esq... relative to the Establishment and Support of Provincial Colleges in Ireland, PP 1843* li. 339-46.

Higher education did not figure in the programme of reforms which O'Connell put to Buller in January 1844, nor in Eliot's proposals of the same month. It was Peel who, half-way through the debate in February 1844, put forward the suggestion to his colleagues for consideration: 'Are there any measures other than those which we have in contemplation which we can ... adopt?...Can we do anything or hold out any hope with regard to the extension of Trinity College?...Can we establish ... Provincial academies...perfectly open to the Roman Catholic youth ...?'[10] Stanley, keenly interested in education, came out strongly in favour of educational reform in a comment that influenced the cabinet's discussions:

From a few words which I have had with Gladstone, I think he might be brought to assent ... to ... a remodelling of Maynooth and its establishment as one of three or more Provincial Colleges ... the promotion of Catholic Ecclesiastical (combined with civil) education should be the point at which we should endeavour to meet the wishes of the Roman Catholics.[11]

His proposal held attractions for Peel, for apart from the intrinsic importance of an educational reform, it suggested a way of reconciling Gladstone and those who thought like him to a Maynooth measure. Peel, in his third memorandum, suggested that the commission set up to investigate Maynooth should examine: 'whether combined academical Education for Clergy and Laity be possible; whether the establishment of Trinity College can be extended.'[12] Gladstone, however, despite Stanley's 'few words' with him raised objections to the whole principle of promoting Catholic education.[13] Outside pressure helped to advance matters; Wyse had put down a motion on academical education and Peel used this as a means of forcing Gladstone to rethink his position, while Graham seized the opportunity to circulate Wyse's Letter to Morpeth.[14] In July, Wyse again argued the case for higher education, and Peel duly

---

[10] Peel's memorandum, 17 Feb. 1844, Add. MSS 40540, ff. 230-7.

[11] Stanley to Peel, 18 Feb. 1844, Copy, Derby Papers, Box 174/2.

[12] Peel's memorandum, [28 Feb.] 1844, Add. MSS 40540, ff. 40-55.

[13] Gladstone's memoranda, 2 Mar. 1844, Add. MSS 44777, ff. 131-6, Gladstone, *Prime Ministers' Papers*, ii. 238-42.

[14] Ibid: Graham to cabinet, 12 Apr. 1844, Add. MSS 40470, ff. 197-8; Parker, *Peel*, iii. 110.

promised to propose 'means for increasing academical education' early in the next session.[15] The cabinet meetings of November at which the whole question was discussed are worthy of note as the first serious attempt to provide higher education for Catholics and to solve the complex problem of Irish university education. The important documentation which Graham had carefully selected and circulated to the cabinet has not been sufficiently studied.[16] Besides Wyse's letter to Morpeth, it included two well thought-out memoranda on the subject from Dr Henry Maunsell and Dr Cooke Taylor.[17] Blake also submitted a memorandum (which arrived too late for the meeting). These projects foreshadow the many schemes put forward during the next sixty years as statesmen and churchmen struggled with the baffling problem of providing a system of university education that would be acceptable both to Irish Catholics and the British government.

Wyse's letter suggested the establishment of a college in each of the provinces to prepare for entering university or to fit the pupil for his career in life. On the question of degrees Wyse's views were flexible and somewhat unclear. The colleges, he thought, might be empowered to grant degrees under the authority of a central board of examiners. They could be affiliated to a central university. What this central university should be Wyse did not make clear, although in other public statements he favoured the opening-up of Dublin University by the establishment of a sister college to Trinity College. In his letter to Morpeth, he suggested a University of Ireland, along the lines of the University of London. All classes and all religious denominations should be admitted. The colleges should give not merely literary and scientific instruction but religious instruction which should, however, be given separately 'for the several communions under the guidance of their respective pastors'.[18] Later, Wyse told Smith O'Brien that he

[15] *Hansard,* lxxvi. 1121-43, 19 July 1844.

[16] Gladstone was studying these papers on 20 Nov. 1844, see *Diaries,* iii. 413. The editors were unable to trace them. There is a printed copy of them in the Derby Papers, 37/1.

[17] Henry Maunsell (1806-79), Irish physician and journalist; William Cooke Taylor (1800-49), author of several books on history and biography; translated Beaumont's *L'Irlande*; wrote pamphlet on education (1847).

[18] Letter to Morpeth, 8 May 1841; Graham to cabinet, 15 Nov. 1844, Derby Papers, 37/1.

favoured a united or joint university only if it proved impractical to open Dublin University or to found Catholic and Presbyterian universities.[19] Wyse's views on the religious basis of the colleges are important for it was the failure to deal satisfactorily with this issue that was to prove the major stumbling block. Maunsell, on the other hand, opposed the idea of provincial universities on the grounds that they would be merely large schools, centres respectively of Catholic and Presbyterian bigotry and exclusiveness, 'angry and spiteful rivals of their Dublin sister'. He saw the government's task as a threefold one: to let the country as a whole share in the advantage of a national university; to remove Catholic grievances with regard to the exclusively Protestant character of Dublin University; and, finally, to preserve 'a Protestant character to a portion of the university, without sanctioning a monopoly that could be truly designed as unfair.' The best way to achieve these aims would be to set up a new, or 'Queen's College' which, with Trinity College, would form the University of Dublin. This would be acceptable to Catholics, he believed, who 'would have their pride gratified by being admitted into the old, time-honoured, National University, instead of being banished ... into a new, untried and therefore uninfluential and unrespected institution ...' Moreover he claimed that this plan would provide 'an approach to a united education for Protestants and Roman Catholics'.[20] Cooke Taylor's plan also was based on the idea of separating the University of Dublin from Trinity College and affiliating to it other colleges. Unlike Maunsell, however, the colleges which he hoped to affiliate were Maynooth College and the Belfast Academical Institute, together with a new college to be founded in Cork. This new national university would be empowered to grant degrees in arts and law, while divinity degrees would be left to the theological faculties of Trinity, Maynooth, and Belfast.[21] As for religious instruction, apart from suggesting the use of Whately's *Evidences of Christianity* for general students,

[19] Wyse to O'Brien, 14 Feb. 1845, Smith O'Brien Papers, NLI, MS 1317.

[20] H. Maunsell, Memorandum on the Extension of Collegiate Education ... 10 Oct. 1844, Derby Papers, 37/1.

[21] Memorandum of Dr Cooke Taylor on separating Trinity University from Trinity College, and affiliating to it other colleges, n.d. (probably Spring 1844), Derby Papers, 37/1.

Cooke Taylor wanted the two bishops of Cork (where the only really new institution was envisaged) to nominate Protestant and Catholic catechists (who would be paid £50 a year) to give religious instruction to those students whose parents should desire it, on one day a week at their respective churches and chapels.

All three plans had distinct advantages; all would go some way towards bringing Catholics and Protestants into one education system. Cooke Taylor's had the added advantage of leaving the sensitive area of divinity, so closely connected with the training of ordinands, in the hands of the three denominations. In their suggestions of opening up Dublin University without radically changing Trinity College, they were attempting to provide the youth of the country with the best available university tradition and education. It was questionable, however, if such a scheme was feasible in view of the political climate of the country and of the long and close connection between Dublin University and Trinity College. This question was on Graham's mind when he broached the matter to Heytesbury in August 1844 and when, shortly before the cabinet meetings, he told Peel that 'to affiliate [the new colleges] to Dublin Univesity would be the most perfect answer'; but he feared that such a course would be violently opposed 'and not less violently because unreasonably'.[22] Peel viewed the idea favourably, referring Heytesbury to the Irish statutes that left open the possibility of adding new colleges to Dublin University.[23] Such a solution appeared legally possible, for Trinity College was originally intended as the nucleus of a university comprising several colleges, and in 1662 the Act of Settlement had envisaged a second college, to be called King's College. Nevertheless, even if such a solution were legally possible there were many practical difficulties in the way. Already in April Graham had told his cabinet colleagues that it might not be possible to interfere with Dublin University.[24] Although he now felt that a new university would be divisive and would not

[22] Graham to Heytesbury, 13 Aug. 1844, Graham Papers; Graham to Peel, 20 Oct. 1844, Add. MSS 40450, ff. 279-82.
[23] Heytesbury to Graham, 15 Oct. Graham to Heytesbury, 17 Oct. 1844, Graham papers.
[24] Graham to cabinet, 12 Apr. 1844, Add. MSS 40470, ff. 197-8.

confer equal privileges, he reluctantly realized that such a plan
would encounter less opposition than 'adding new cloth to the
old garment'.[25] Before the cabinet met, opposition was already
being voiced. The *Dublin Evening Mail* hinted at 'correspondence
between the Home Office and Dublin Castle' concerning
Trinity, and the primate wrote to find out if any interference
was contemplated.[26] James Henthorn Todd, lecturer in Divinity
in Trinity College, protested privately to Gladstone and publicly
in the *Irish Ecclesiastical Journal* against opening Trinity to
Catholics, although he appeared to have had no great objection
to the affiliation of a new college with Dublin University.[27]
The controversy that seemed likely to erupt in Ireland if an
attempt were made to interfere with Trinity College had already
alarmed Heytesbury, who depicted well the dilemma of the
government: 'we are ... walking upon hot cinders and we must
take great heed lest in conciliating the Catholics we do not stir
up a Protestant fire that will set Ireland in a blaze ...' Furthermore 'by throwing open the university, we shall lose the two
seats in Parliament. They will inevitably fall to the democratic
party.'[28]

Graham carefully abstained, in his memorandum to the
cabinet, from coming down on one side or the other and put the
possibilities before the cabinet in the following order:

Is it expedient to touch Trinity College?

If Trinity College be left untouched, is it expedient to open and remodel
Dublin University?

If Dublin University be left untouched, will you found in Ireland a new
University with Provincial Colleges affiliated to it? If you suspend the establishment of a new University, will you found only Provincial Colleges in

[25] Graham to Heytesbury, 17 Oct. 1844, Graham Papers.

[26] *Dublin Evening Mail,* 1, 18, 27 Nov. 1844; Beresford to Heytesbury, 7 Nov. 1844,
Graham Papers.

[27] Graham to Peel, 4 Nov. 1844, Add. MSS 40450, ff. 309-10; Peel to Graham,
4 Nov. 1844; ibid., ff. 313-14; J. H. Todd, *University of Dublin: remarks on some statements attributed to T. Wyse in his speech in Parliament on academical education in Ireland*
(1844), James Henthorn Todd (1805-69), professor of Hebrew TCD, 1849; librarian
1852; a founder of the Irish Archaeological and Celtic Society 1853; associated with the
Irish scholars John O'Donovan and Eugene O'Curry in classifying many important
Irish manuscripts, some of which he edited.

[28] Heytesbury to Graham, 10 Oct. 1844, Graham Papers.

the first instance, but reserve to the Crown the power of here after converting these colleges into a University ...[29]

Graham also laid before the cabinet a memorial from the General Assembly of the Presbyterian church in Ireland.[30] Although the educational reforms were intended in the first instance for the benefit of Catholics, the claims of the Presbyterians would also have to be taken into account. The dissensions between the orthodox and unitarian wings of Presbyterianism played a part in shaping the final solution to the colleges question.[31] Dissatisfied with unitarian control of the Belfast Academical Institution, the General Asembly of orthodox Presbyterians had met in Cookestown in September 1844 and decided to set up its own college, where students for the ministry could obtain both literary and theological education. The memorial Graham now submitted to the cabinet sought state endowment for this college.

'Without a dissentient voice', the cabinet, on 22 November, decided the main principles of its measure. Trinity College and Dublin University were not to be touched; new colleges were to be established in Cork and in Belfast which would be either separate universities or affiliated to a central university. The reasons why the cabinet decided against opening up Dublin University were the fear of an 'angry controversy', since Trinity was the training-place for ministers of the Established church, and the political consideration of Trinity's parliamentary representation.[32] The decision was almost inevitable when so many cabinet members were staunch supporters of the church. The memory of the appropriation issue was still vivid, and although willing to subsidize the Catholics as regards education of their clergy and laity, they were not prepared to do it by 'stripping the Established Church', as Graham expressed it. Political expediency made it difficult for Peel to take any different line. The first attempt to solve the Irish University

---

[29] Graham's memorandum, 15 Nov. 1844, Derby Papers, Box 37/1.

[30] Memorial of the General Assembly of the Presbyterian Church in Ireland, Nov. 1844, Derby Papers, 37/1.

[31] Moody and Beckett, *Queen's, Belfast*, i. 3-5.

[32] Stanley to Buccleuch, 23 Nov. 1844, Derby Papers, 174/2; Graham to Heytesbury, 26 Nov. 1844, H.O. 45/1656/1, PRO; Peel to Prince Albert, 22 Nov. 1844, Add. MSS 40439, ff. 157-8.

question lost the opportunity for an approach to combined education which would have brought Catholics and Presbyterians into an enlarged Dublin University. The Catholics, moreover, although forming approximately 73 per cent of the population of Dublin, were relegated to the provinces.

The most important remaining problem was the position of religion in the colleges. Education without religion was an idea that found little favour with Peel, Graham, or the Tory party in general as their hostility to the 'Gower Street' college in 1836 and their attitude to other education issues showed.[33] Nevertheless, state support for religious education was becoming increasingly difficult. Already, in 1842, Peel felt obliged to maintain the undenominational national education system in Ireland, and in 1843 his government was forced to drop the educational clauses of the Factory Bill rather than be seen as favouring Anglican education.[34] Peel was also influenced by current glorification of education. When opening the Tamworth Reading Room in 1843, he declared that man 'in becoming wiser will become better'—remarks that called forth a strong reaction from Newman—and during the debate on the academic colleges he appeared to see values even in religionless education.[35] His government, too, was anxious to steer clear of Irish religious dissensions which it feared that the endowment of a denominational university would arouse. It is not surprising, then, that the cabinet decided to follow the lines of the national education system and make the new colleges undenominational. On Peel's suggestion, however, it was agreed that facilities be provided for the private endowment of divinity professorships and for lectures on divinity to be given within the walls of the colleges.[36] By 1 January, Heytesbury had sent Graham the draft of the Colleges Bill. Its approach to the question of religious teaching was somewhat negative and the cabinet meeting of 11 January substituted two new sections, 'for

---

[33] Ward, *Graham*, pp. 175-7, 194; S. Walpole, *History of England* ... iv. 18-19.

[34] See p. 74.; Gash, *Peel*, pp. 376-8.

[35] *The Times*, 26 Jan. 1841; J. H. Newman, 'The Tamworth Reading Room', *Discussions and Arguments* (1918), pp. 254-305; cf. *Hansard*, lxxx. 390-1, 9 May 1845.

[36] Gladstone's memorandum, 25 Nov. 1844; Add. MSS 44777, ff. 206-9, Gladstone, *Prime Ministers' Papers*, ii. 269-70; Graham to Heytesbury, 26 Nov. 1844, HO 45/ 1656/1, PRO.

the better enabling every student ... to receive religious instruction', which assigned the use of lecture rooms for religious classes and positively encouraged private endowment of theological lectures.[37] Peel's influence can be detected here but despite improvement in the wording of the clauses, the colleges were to be, as Gladstone noted, 'neutral colleges' in which all the usual branches of knowledge were provided for except theology. In this important aspect, the scheme had fallen short of what Wyse, Cooke Taylor, or Maunsell had proposed.

Graham instructed Heytesbury to discuss the arrangements with Cooke on the part of the Presbyterians, and with Crolly, Murray, and Blake as representing the Catholics. The negotiations with the Presbyterians proved difficult, since their wish, as the September memorial showed, was state endowment for a Presbyterian college of both theology and general studies. The government rejected their claims, Heytesbury complaining that they wanted 'a Presbyterian Maynooth'.[38] Further negotiations and two deputations to Westminster brought the Presbyterians no nearer their original aim, and in May they decided to reach a compromise with the government by which a satisfactory connection could be effected between the intended Presbyterian faculty and the new college to be established at Belfast.[39] The difficult negotiations with the Presbyterians shed interesting light both on the government's attempt to maintain a balance between the different religious groupings and on the unsatisfactory nature of the negotiations with the Catholics. Despite Graham's instructions, Heytesbury did not approach Crolly, and he consulted Murray only at second hand through Blake.[40] Undoubtedly, the Bequests Act controversy had made it difficult for Heytesbury to contact them, but his failure to do so was to prove of considerable consequence. Blake remained the intermediary, although he had become a highly controversial figure in the eyes of many Catholics. He assured Heytesbury that the Catholics would accept that divinity lectures be left to

[37] Drafts of Colleges Bill, Jan. 1845, Derby Papers 37/1.
[38] Heytesbury to Graham, 28 Jan. 1845, Graham Papers.
[39] Graham to Heytesbury, 25 Mar.; 26 Apr.; Heytesbury to Graham, 29-31 Mar. 1844, Graham Papers; Moody and Beckett, *Queen's, Belfast,* i. 7.
[40] Graham to Heytesbury, 30 Nov. 17 Dec. 1844, Graham Papers.

private endowment, provided that facilities within the walls of the colleges were made available for giving them. It is not possible to ascertain if, in fact, he consulted any other Catholics and certainly the hierarchy as a whole did not delegate him to speak for them. When Sheil renewed his attacks on the exclusiveness of Trinity College, Graham appealed to Blake to dissuade Catholics from such attacks. The situation, he alleged, was not unlike that on the appropriation issue a decade earlier which broke up Lord Grey's government, depriving the Whigs of all power of conferring benefits on the Irish Catholics and of thereby incorporating them with the state. In powerful language, he warned Blake that

this plan of stripping the Protestants, as a condition precedent to clothing the Catholics, had been tried and had signally failed; that if the experiment were now repeated, it would fail again; but that Sir Robert Peel, if he were allowed, without inflicting injury or injustice on the Protestants ... possessed the power ... of conferring on them [the Catholics] lasting advantages quite consistent with the welfare of the entire community; that those who, for factious purposes, defeated such a national settlement incurred a fearful responsibility in the eyes of the Nation and of Posterity ...

Graham further alleged that if the Whig Opposition appealed to religious hatred, they 'would defeat the first opportunity which, since the death of Mr Pitt, had presented itself for laying the foundation of future concord and social improvement in Ireland.'[41] This over-reaction to opposition is characteristic of Graham. He had not been so opposed to interfering with Dublin Univesity a few months earlier, when he had indeed seen it as the best solution. The tone of his letter, and particularly his reference to Pitt, is an indication that he saw Peel and himself as achieving what so many others had failed to achieve—a solution of the Irish problem.

With the Maynooth measure safely out of the way, Graham, on 9 May, moved the first reading of the Academic Colleges bill. Three colleges were to be set up with Cork, Galway, or Limerick, and Belfast or Derry as the probable sites. A capital grant of £100,000 was to be made for the buildings, and each college was to receive an annual grant of £6,000 (later increased

---

[41] Graham to Heytesbury, 9 Feb. 1845, ibid.

to £7,000). Graham, asserting that 'religious differences constitute the great difficulty in the way of a satisfactory adjustment of a general system of education', maintained the necessity to build on the mixed system which had proved so successful for the national schools. The colleges, then, would have no religious lectures or tests but, he added:

It must not ... be supposed that religion will be altogether disregarded ... we propose that ... every facility shall be given for the endowment of professorships in Theology ... and ... that instruction in Theology may be given in the lecture room within the walls of the College.[42]

His speech was well received, although some of the Irish members, notably Wyse, Sheil, and Morgan O'Connell, demanded that Catholics should receive a greater share in the emoluments of the existing university.[43] The main opposition came from the high churchman, Sir Robert Inglis, who denounced the measure as 'a gigantic scheme of Godless education'.[44] His words were to reverberate throughout Ireland.

The evidence does not support the conclusion that the colleges plan was the result of Wyse's long campaign for academical colleges, as Auchmuty implies.[45] It was due, like Peel's other Irish reforms, to the government's desire to break up the solidarity of the Repeal movement and was to be the lay counterpart to the Maynooth Bill. The initiative was Peel's, and to some extent Stanley's, while the detailed preparation of the scheme devolved on Graham. Nevertheless, Wyse's campaign had kept the issue of academic education in the foreground and his Letter to Morpeth provided a working plan. The government accepted Wyse's idea of a college in each of three provinces but its new colleges were to be more akin to university colleges. It would have been wiser as Dr Turton, bishop of Ely, Whately and Wyse had all suggested at different times, to provide more secondary education because all the new university colleges were to suffer from the lack of feeder schools.

The decision to separate the scheme from the Maynooth question was politically wise. The opposition of the hierarchy to a combined lay and clerical college would have been such

[42] *Hansard,* lxxx. 345-66, 9 May 1845.
[43] Ibid., 372-4; 383-6; 396-7, 9 May 1845.
[44] Ibid., 377-80, 9 May 1845.
[45] Auchmuty, *Wyse,* pp. 166-74.

that the government would have forfeited the support of the Irish members and, no doubt, that of Russell and many of the Whigs and Liberals. Both schemes might then well have foundered. For parallel reasons, the decision not to touch Dublin University was also politically wise, at least in the short run, as the 'Hands off Trinity' campaign at the beginning of the twentieth century made clear.[46] Nevertheless, it was regrettable that some formula such as Maunsell's or Cooke Taylor's could not have been adopted which would have preserved unity in the university education of the country. As it turned out, this vital branch of Irish education was to remain both divided and divisive. The exclusion of theology and religion, which in Cooke Taylor's plan were to be an integral part of the colleges system, was unfortunate. Although the utilitarian spirit of the age may have exercised a certain influence on the cabinet's decision, Peel and Graham would certainly have preferred a system based on religion. The combined difficulty, however, of pleasing the different parties in Ireland where religious divisions ran deep, and of extracting more money from the English treasury to subsidize purely Irish and Catholic education appeared to them to constitute unsurmountable obstacles. The decision was to have grave and lasting consequences. Already Inglis's attack was an indication of the type of opposition it would arouse although it is difficult to understand why the official leadership of the Established church did not press its point of view more energetically. Perhaps they were content with keeping a watching brief for their own establishments, perhaps the Factory Bill of 1843 had shown how difficult it was for the church to claim control of education.[47] Whatever the reason, the main controversy concerning the new bill was to come not from the Established church but from within the Repeal Association and the Irish Catholic community both of which were to be sharply divided over the issue.

No sooner was the bill introduced into Parliament than a lively public dispute broke out in Ireland. In the pages of the *Freeman's Journal* and the *Pilot*, the O'Connellites denounced it out of hand: in the *Nation*, the increasingly influential weekly

[46] F. S. L. Lyons, *Ireland since the Famine* (1973), p. 97.
[47] E. R. Norman, *Church and Society in England, 1770-1970* (1976), pp. 114-15.

organ of the Young Irelanders, Davis, while expressing some reservations on the details, gave the principle of the bill an enthusiastic welcome. Lucas, in the *Tablet*, raised his own powerful and intransigent voice against it. Crolly, too, moved quickly. Unwilling to allow the initiative to be snatched from him, as on the bequests issue, and in an endeavour to reunite his splintered hierarchy by 'softening asperities and reconciling, if possible conflicting opinions',[48] he called a special meeting of the bishops to discuss the bill which, he wrote, appeared to be 'pregnant with danger to the faith and morals of the youth of this country'.[49] Despite the short notice, twenty-one bishops attended the meeting in Dublin on 21 May. The absentees were Higgins, McNicholas, Egan, Coen, Keating, and McLaughlin (who was now mentally disturbed). Few details of the meeting are available. On the first day the bishops, declaring that they entertained 'strong objections to certain passages' in the bill, decided to appoint a committee to prepare a memorial pointing out these objections. On 23 May two resolutions were unanimously adopted. Having first placed on record their appreciation of the ministers' 'kind and generous intentions manifested in the endowment of the College of Maynooth', the bishops felt compelled to declare that 'anxious as we are to extend the advantages of education, we cannot give our approbation to the proposed system, as we deem it dangerous to the faith and morals of the Catholic pupils.'[50] The second resolution was that a memorial should be drawn up suggesting such amendments 'as may be calculated to secure the faith and morals of the students', and this memorial was duly presented to the lord lieutenant by Crolly, Murray, MacHale, and French. In it the bishops promised that they were willing to co-operate on the basis of 'such fair and reasonable terms' as they now put forward: a fair proportion of the professors and other office-bearers should be Catholic; they should be appointed by a board of trustees who would include bishops; Catholic chaplains should be appointed, paid by the state but

---

[48] The words are contained in Murray's account of the reasons why the meeting was called: Heytesbury to Graham, 5 June 1845, Graham Papers.

[49] Heytesbury to Graham, 17 May 1845, Graham Papers: Heytesbury was quoting Murray; Crolly to bishops, 14 May 1845, *Catholic Directory*, 1846, p. 239.

[50] *Tablet*, 21 May 1845.

dismissible by their bishops. On the central issue of lectures, the bishops declared that 'the Roman Catholic pupils could not attend the lectures on history, logic, metaphysics, moral philosophy, geology or anatomy, without exposing their faith and morals to imminent danger, unless a Roman Catholic professor will be appointed for each of those chairs.'[51]

These demands were quite extensive and would have gone far to nullify the policy of mixed education. For some of the bishops, the demands were no more than initial bargaining points in what they hoped would be fruitful negotiations with the government. For others, however, these far-reaching demands sprang from a defensive mentality that had characterized the church since the Reformation and from that well-founded fear of proselytism through education that haunted these shepherds of the long-suffering Irish church. When he received the four-man delegation, Heytesbury, while demurring on the questions of a board of trustees and the lectures, told them that the government would do all it could to satisfy them short of abandoning the principle of the measure, pointing out that the bill was only an outline and that many other points might be included in the charter of incorporation and the bye-laws. Heytesbury thought that Crolly, Murray, and French seemed perfectly satisfied, but

Dr MacHale, on rising to leave the room, observed that the Memorial ... had not been drawn up but after earnest and grave deliberation, and that it contained the *Minimum* of the Prelates. Without such concessions, their cooperation could not be relied upon. A smile exchanged between the other members of the Deputation, showed me that in this observation Dr MacHale had probably a little exceeded the limits of his commission.[52]

MacHale's opposition was not to be smiled out of existence. To Murray's horror, the MacHaleites leaked the text of the memorial to the press, where it was trumpeted forth as an ultimatum.[53] An angry Graham complained that its publication 'seriously increased the difficulty of our position' and warned Heytesbury that the government could not yield to the bishops'

---

[51] Memorial of the bishops to the lord lieutenant, 23 May 1845, *Catholic Directory*, 1847, pp. 373-5; Heytesbury to Graham, 17 May 1845, Graham Papers.

[52] Heytesbury to Graham, 25 May 1845, Graham Papers.

[53] *Freeman's Journal*, 26 May 1845; Heytesbury to Graham, 26 May 1845, Graham Papers.

pretensions. He could not bring himself to believe that the memorial was the bishops' ultimatum and told Heytesbury to maintain contact with Murray to see what was 'the real minimun which would satisfy the better portion of his brethren'.[54]

His opportunity to reply to the bishops came a few days later during the second reading of the bill. Lord John Manners had objected to the measure on the grounds that 'without a basis of religion, such learning is worse than useless', a statement that was later to be used by Cullen in his denunciation of the project to Rome.[55] Graham promised that a fair share of the professors would probably be Catholic and that proselytism would be guarded against. He completely rejected, however, the three other points in the bishops' memorial: episcopal involvement in appointments, Catholic chaplains paid by the state, and Catholic lecturers in certain subjects.[56] This was certainly, as the *Tablet* maintained, a flat rejection of the bishops' memorial, and left little middle ground for negotiation.[57] Oddly enough, Gladstone showed more understanding of the bishops' objections, remarking in his abstruse way that: 'it would be monstrous for a majority of that House ... to render, under the name of a boon, that which under other circumstances, would be no boon, but a mockery and an injustice.'[58] In stronger terms, Russell complained that:

I see no reason why the Government should not ... consult those distinguished Roman Catholics who ... must have great influence with their countrymen on a question of this nature. I speak more especially of such men as Archbishop Murray—a man no less distinguished for his moderation of opinion, ... than he is by an unswerving fidelity to his own Church.[59]

Russell demanded that the bishops should be recognized 'as a part of your [the government's] plan'.[60] Despite these criticisms there was little real opposition to the bill which passed its second reading by the overwhelming majority of 311 to 46.

---

[54] Graham to Heytesbury, 28 May 1845, Graham Papers.

[55] *Hansard,* lxxx. 1139, 30 May 1845; Cullen to Propaganda, 31 Jan. 1846, Acta vol. 209, ff. 258-99, Propaganda Fide Archives.

[56] *Hansard,* lxxx. 1144-53, 30 May 1845.

[57] *Tablet,* 7 June 1845.

[58] *Hansard,* lxxx. 1261, 2 June 1845.

[59] Ibid., 1247-8, 2 June 1845.

[60] Ibid., 1247, 2 June; cf. lxxxi. 1359, 30 June 1845.

With the publication of the bishops' memorial and Graham's rejection of its stipulations during the course of the second reading, therefore, the euphoria generated by the Maynooth Grant began to dissipate. The extensive nature of the memorial's demands, especially as regards the subjects for which it required Catholic teachers, and the deliberate leaking to the press, made the government's position difficult. As over the Bequests Act, the main charge that could be levelled against the government was that of legislating *in vacuo* without sufficiently widely-based prior consultations, as indeed Russell implied. Baron Stockmar, confidant of Prince Albert, disclosed to the prince consort about this time his own reflections and considered views on Peel's Irish policies:

That in the Irish question,—the vital one of all,—my good Sir Robert has had, relatively speaking, but a moderate success, troubles me. Again and again I ask myself to what this short-coming is mainly due. I may be wrong, and my opinion I fear, may moreover appear to Sir Robert like presumption, still I cannot refrain from avowing, that to me the main reason of the in-adequate result seems to be this, that a political question which is intimately mixed up with the essence of Christianity is handled by a Protestant Minister and a Protestant majority. By the nature of things Sir Robert cannot get out of his Protestant skin, and just as little can the Protestant majority of the House of Commons do so... Were I an English Minister, before I decided on adopting any...measure, I would cause inquiry to be made by a Catholic... whether the measure were really in substance and form calculated to meet Catholic wants and feelings...'[61]

Stockmar was a well-placed, detached and intelligent observer, anxious to afford Prince Albert his considered advice on all matters of English politics and his shrewd comments on the 'Irish question—the vital one of all' throw light on an important aspect of the difficulties that Peel's policies were encountering. The neglect to consult adequately the leaders of Catholic opinion was evident not merely in the bequest issue but again in the colleges bill. Heytesbury, despite Graham's anxious request, showed remarkable reluctance to consult the bishops who, nevertheless, held the key to the success of the scheme as a measure of reconciliation. When the bill was dividing Irish

---

[61] Stockmar to Prince Albert, 16 June 1845, cited in T. Martin, *The Life of His Royal Highness, the Prince Consort* (1880), i. 264. Baron Christian Friedrich von Stockmar (1787-1863), family adviser of the Coburgs, Prince Albert's former tutor.

public opinion, he was unwilling to see Murray 'because we must not lead the Catholics to imagine that they have a right to be consulted in all such matters.'[62] Graham reminded him, however, that: 'these measures are intended for the special benefit of the Roman Catholic portion of the community and it is important to make them as acceptable as we can and in matters affecting religious instruction of Roman Catholics, prelates of that Church are the guardians of the Faith, and objections are to be heard and considered.'[63] There had been incompetence in the handling of such consultations. Graham was under the impression that Heytesbury had communicated the substance of the colleges plan to Murray 'with the knowledge and by the wish of the Cabinet'.[64] Heytesbury hastened to deny this, referring him to their correspondence of the previous December. No communication was made to the bishops, but 'the heads' of the plan were communicated to Blake, and Heytesbury reminded Graham that 'I gave you no reason to hope that we should be able to draw any opinion from them upon the subject', since neither Crolly nor Murray could speak for the hierarchy.[65] Whether this fact justified the risk involved in not consulting them is debatable. After the publication of the memorial, Heytesbury was still reluctant to show 'any *great anxiety*' to contact Murray, but, pushed by a somewhat worried Graham, he ordered A'Court, his secretary, to call on Murray in order to ask him to come to see him. Reassuringly, Murray told A'Court: 'you must not pay attention to all that Dr MacHale chose to say about the Minimum!'[66] When he called to see Heytesbury a few days later, Murray explained that the memorial was a compromise document drawn up to avoid a split among the bishops. It was never intended as an ultimatum, but as the basis for negotiation with the government. The parts to which the government objected— the appointment of a board of trustees with the power of nominating and removing professors, and the claim for so

[62] Heytesbury to Graham, 13 May 1845, Graham Papers.
[63] Graham to Heytesbury, 15 May 1845, ibid.
[64] Graham to Heytesbury, 14 May 1845, ibid.
[65] Heytesbury to Graham, 16 May 1845, ibid.
[66] Heytesbury to Graham, 30 May, 1 June 1845, ibid.; Graham to Heytesbury, 28, 31 May 1845, ibid.

many chairs for Catholic professors—had originated, Murray explained, with the MacHaleites, who were also responsible for the leak to the press. With the bequests experience fresh in his mind, Murray was reluctant to commit anyone but himself, but, pressed by Heytesbury, he mentioned those improvements which would probably satisfy the moderates: supervision of the halls of residence and religious instruction for the students. Further, the chairs of history and moral philosophy should be entrusted to Catholics. The appointment and dismissal of professors should be confided to a visitatorial body nominated by the government but consisting of a majority of Catholics in any college in which the Catholic students were in the majority. With these changes and with the power to endow theological lectures within the college, Murray thought that the bill would be acceptable both to him and to the majority of his colleagues.[67] It is possible that Heytesbury reported his successful talk with Murray in too optimistic a fashion, but it does appear that the archbishop was guilty of a grave error of judgement in his assessment of the views of his colleagues. Probably, as he claimed, the memorial was a compromise and not an ultimatum, but what scanty information we have of the bishops' meeting where 'grave objections' were raised and where the two resolutions concerning the memorial were passed unanimously, indicate that many of his colleagues considered it as more than a mere basis for negotiation.

Graham, although disappointed that the measure on which he had spent so much care had not received the welcome he expected, determined to press on, feeling, as he told Peel seriously, that 'if we fail to carry this measure, the duty of governing Ireland must be entrusted to other hands.'[68] Although confiding to Heytesbury that 'our object is to keep up the division which we established in the heart of the Episcopacy' and rejoicing to see the discord over the bill in Conciliation Hall, he wanted these reforms for their own sake, regarding each one of them as an integral part of a necessary conciliatory policy for Ireland. He was committed to his programme in a way that contrasts sharply with Stanley's management of the

[67] Heytesbury to Graham, 5 June 1845, ibid.
[68] Graham to Peel, 8 June 1845, Add. MSS 40451, ff. 130-1.

Landlord and Tenant Bill, which was coming to grief at this time; and despite his categorical rebuff to the bishops' memorial, he intended 'to prepare such additions to the College Bill as will remove many of the objections and go far to satisfy Dr Murray and that portion of the Roman Catholic Prelates, who are reasonable enough to be satisfied with any thing.' To this end he consulted Blake, whom he knew to be critical of the draft, and won his approval. He now prepared to propose these 'additions' at the committee stage of the bill.[69]

One consolation which Graham drew from the situation was the open dissension among the Repealers, as evidenced by the sharp reaction of the Young Irelanders to John O'Connell's denunciation of the bill on 12 May in Conciliation Hall.[70] The attitude of Daniel O'Connell himself—which, because of his stature in Irish affairs, was of vital importance—has been the subject of much subsequent discussion. Gavan Duffy and Doheny follow Davis in alleging a sudden change on O'Connell's part.[71] It has been asserted that John O'Connell's speech caught nationalist Ireland by surprise, and that O'Connell, who had originally favoured mixed education, now endorsed his son's attack and so precipitated a quarrel with the Young Irelanders.[72] McGrath rightly throws doubt on the theory of a sudden change in O'Connell's attitude on education but finds difficulty in establishing O'Connell's position between 1825 and 1845.[73] In 1825, O'Connell appeared to favour mixed education; he told the Lords' Committee on the State of Ireland that: 'it would be very much the wish of the Catholic laity to see the clergy of the three principal persuasions educated in the same university as it is very desirable that the laity of all persuasions should be educated together.' When he went on to explain his position, however, his expressions were somewhat ambiguous.[74] There exist other statements by O'Connell before the May meeting of the Repeal Association that merit

---

[69] Graham to Heytesbury, 11 June 1845, Graham Papers.

[70] Graham to Heytesbury, 11 June 1845, Graham Papers; *Tablet*, 17 May 1845.

[71] Duffy, *Young Ireland*, pp. 720-3; M. Doheny, *The Felon's Track* ... (reprint 1920 of orig. ed., 1849), pp. 54-61.

[72] McCaffrey, *O'Connell*, p. 233.

[73] McGrath, *Newman's University*, pp. 48-53.

[74] *State of Ireland; Minutes of Evidence, PP 1825*, ix. 157-8.

being brought to light. In 1839, in the course of the debate on the vote for national education, O'Connell remarked that: 'there was no country in Europe where the children of different persuasions were not educated together ... That was the spirit which ought to exist between Christians.'[75] The statement certainly implied support for mixed education, but it must also be remembered that O'Connell was defending a system that was denominational in all but name. In 1842, however, in his important letter to Cullen, O'Connell listed Catholic education both in schools and at the university level as one of the advantages that Repeal would bring:

... Repeal ... would enable the Irish Catholics either to participate on strictly Catholic principles and subject to the regulation of the Irish Episcopal Synod in the present University ... or to endow under similar regulations another university ... [and] ... would enable the Irish Catholics to endow in every parish, schools for the education, subject to ecclesiastical control and revision, of the Catholic children.[76]

This letter, however, was, as we have seen, a piece of special pleading, part of his move to form a Repeal lobby in Rome to counteract anti-Repeal influences there.[77] The controversy over the Bequests Act undoubtedly played a part in influencing O'Connell against the national system. At the final mass meeting in Dublin on 19 December 1844, when he knew he had been defeated by the government, he declared:

Indeed I am not altogether satisfied with my own conduct with reference to the Education Board. I think that to some extent there was a compromise made for the National Board that had better been avoided. The Presbyterians held out and by holding out firmly carried their point. I am sure that the Catholics by a little more perseverance would have ... secured perfect Catholic education ... That was but a little step towards the state; but what was the second? The present bill.[78]

O'Connell's change of attitude as manifested in this speech was so marked as to merit a comment by Heytesbury in letters to Graham and Peel.[79] O'Connell's reasons were twofold:

[75] *Hansard,* xlvii. 1389, 4 June 1839.

[76] O'Connell to Cullen, 9 May 1842, Cullen Papers.

[77] See pp. 78-9.

[78] *Pilot,* 20 Dec. 1844.

[79] Heytesbury to Graham, 20 Dec. 1844, Graham Papers; Heytesbury to Peel, 20 Dec. 1844, Add. MSS 40479, ff. 216-17.

desire to obtain 'perfect Catholic education' and distrust of any association of the bishops with the state through mixed boards. As the two catholic commissioners for national education, Murray and Blake, had joined the new Board of Bequests despite his pleas, O'Connell's irritation is understandable. When a few weeks earlier at the Repeal Association O'Connell proposed the setting-up of a committee to watch over the progress of any new university, he added that 'the education in literature and religion should not be separated', but that each persuasion should have the means of partaking of both.[80] In February when Dillon Browne denounced the mixed system and Smith O'Brien supported it, O'Connell reserved his own opinion until he could see the government plan, although he also added that he would accept the bishops' decision on it.[81] The bishop he was most anxious to consult was evidently MacHale, somewhat to the annoyance of the Young Irelanders.[82] Even if his own views were fundamentally moderate, O'Connell may have felt obliged to support MacHale; but when MacHale came out violently against the proposed new scheme, O'Connell, while promising his own support for 'truly Catholic education', warned him against a premature condemnation of the project.[83] He also consulted other bishops.[84] O'Connell, then, had gradually moved away from his position favouring mixed education some time before the meeting in May 1845, and the change was neither as sudden nor as unpredictable as has been thought. The other assertion that he was swayed by his son John remains unproven. At the first meeting in Conciliation Hall after the introduction of the bill and later in the decisive meeting on the eve of the bishops' meeting in November 1845, it was O'Connell and not John who launched the attack, just as it was he who fixed on the colleges, Inglis's stigma of 'a gigantic scheme of Godless education'.[85] O'Connell was still too alert to allow John to decide

[80] *Nation*, 7 Dec. 1844.

[81] Ibid., 15 Feb. 1845.

[82] Doheny, *Felon's Track*, p. 51.

[83] O'Connell to MacHale, 19 Feb. 1845, Cusack, *The Liberator*, p. 741.

[84] McGettigan to O'Connell, 29 Jan.; Kennedy to O'Connell, 30 Jan.; Cantwell to O'Connell, 2 Feb. 1845, O'Connell Papers, NLI MS 13649.

[85] *Nation*, 17 May, 22 Nov. 1845.

for him and John too respectful of his father to move without his consent. It is possible that the Young Irelanders attacked John because they shrank at this stage from attacking the undisputed leader of the national movement. O'Connell disliked 'mixed boards', seeing in them as did MacHale and Cooper, a corrupting influence since they would bring the bishops into close collaboration with the government. He also feared state control of education, which for him meant it would be anti-national and anti-Catholic. The struggle in France between the university and the church was in his mind; when Jules Michelet and Edgar Quinet attacked the Jesuits, O'Connell took pains to refute them. He protested that no man can get office in France 'unless he has taken out a degree in an avowedly infidel university'.[86] These reasons rather than any slavish following of his son's views or a desire to discredit the Young Irelanders appear to have been O'Connell's main motives in opposing the new colleges. What he now demanded for Catholics was equal rights:

> While I ask for education for the Catholics, I freely and gladly concede it to the Protestants and Dissenters ... Let the Protestants of the Establishment have the free use of Trinity College ... Let the Presbyterians have the completest control over the education of their children in the Belfast institution, but for the purposes of Catholic instruction, let two more colleges be instituted ... and let the Deans of those establishments be Catholic clergymen, whose appointment shall be vested in the Catholic bishop of the Diocese.[87]

The Young Irelanders, on the other hand, and particularly Davis, saw in mixed education a means of bringing the youth of the country together and alleged that the reasons for separate education were the reasons 'for mutual animosity, for penal laws, for religious wars'.[88] Dissensions came to a head at the Repeal meeting of 26 May. Davis skilfully argued that the bishops supported mixed education in their memorial which was signed, he pointed out, by Dr Murray 'who carries into the academical colleges the same principles that regulate the National Board ...' O'Connell retorted that the proposed system met with the bishops' 'unequivocal and unanimous

[86] Ibid., 22 Nov. 1845.
[87] *Freeman's Journal*, 13 May, 1845; cf. McGrath, *Newman's University*, p. 44.
[88] *Nation*, 17 May 1845.

condemnation'. Then, turning fiercely on his young critics, he declared that 'the section of politicians styling themselves the Young Ireland Party ... support this measure ... Young Ireland may play what pranks they please ... I shall stand by Old Ireland and I have some slight notion that Old Ireland will stand by me.'[89] Although the dispute was quickly patched up both sides clung to their views. The changes which the bishops requested in the bill were so extensive that it is difficult to see how they could be represented as favouring a mixed system—despite Davis's plea that they had accepted the principle. The Young Irelanders organized a petition in favour of their view which they claimed was signed by 'the wealth and intelligence of Dublin'.[90] This claim is hardly borne out by the facts. Only 170 persons signed the petition, 94 of whom were barristers. A mere 7 of the 45 Catholic repealers who were members of Dublin Corporation signed. The signatories included, however, the Lord Mayor, John Arabin, Sir Colman O'Loghlen, and Professor Robert Kane.[91] At much the same time, John O'Connell organized a petition against the colleges and claimed 22,500 signatures from four Dublin parishes. Even allowing for some exaggeration in these figures, the total is impressive. Thus, although some of the professional class supported the petition, the great majority of the middle class followed O'Connell's lead.

In Parliament, O'Connell, ably seconded by Smith O'Brien, made a determined effort to throw out the Colleges Bill not from absolute hostility to the idea but believing that if he succeeded in having it rejected, 'we should get a better, nay a decidedly good one next year'.[92] This was scarcely realistic in view of the overwhelming support for the bill. O'Connell's speech to the House, however, was conciliatory and he assured

[89] Duffy, *Young Ireland*, pp. 702-5; *Nation*, 31 May 1845.

[90] Ibid., 14 June 1845.

[91] J. R. Hill, 'Nationalism and the Catholic Church in the 1840s; views of Dublin Repealers', *IHS*, xix (1975), 385-8; Duffy, *Young Ireland*, pp. 771-2; Sir Colman O'Loghlen (1819-77), educated at Dublin University, called to the Irish Bar 1840; later Judge-Advocate-General in Gladstone's ministry 1868; Robert Kane (1809-90), Dublin-born chemist; nephew of Archbishop Troy; wrote *Elements of Chemistry* (1841-3), and *Industrial Resources of Ireland* (1844); formed the Museum of Industry in Ireland 1846; knighted; president of the Academical (Queen's) College, Cork, 1845.

[92] O'Connell to Smith O'Brien, 9 June 1845, Smith O'Brien Papers, NLI MSS 434.

the members that 'great anxiety exists in Ireland to have such a measure'. Without the bishops' co-operation, it would not succeed, and he implored the government to 'take one step more and consider whether this Bill may not be made to accord with the feelings of the Catholic ecclesiastics of Ireland.'[93] He was strongly supported by Russell and Sheil, both of whom wanted more attention to be given to the requests of the bishops.[94] Graham refused to depart from the principle of a joint scheme. He did, however, bring in amendments which went some of the way towards providing for the moral supervision of the students. The Board of Works was authorized to lend money for the construction of hostels or halls. The other amendment proposed to give the crown the power of appointing visitors to inquire into abuses in the colleges. Russell was not satisfied with these amendments, wanting to make the halls integral parts of the colleges and thus endow the religious instruction given in them.[95] O'Connell did not even regard Graham's new proposals as improvements, since they gave more power to the government; and as for the erection of halls by private endowment, he remarked: 'see what an advantage this gives to the Protestants who are rich, over the Catholics who are poor.'[96]

Privately, O'Connell expressed the view that he detected a great change in the minds of the ministry and was convinced that if the bishops held firm, they would win: 'As to the Bishops, they have the ball at their foot, literally at their foot. If they hold out firmly on the truest Catholic principles, believe me, everything will be conceded ... How I wish I could venture to write to Dr Murray! I wish he knew of what pliable materials the present Government are made.'[97] With this conviction, O'Connell wrote a letter to MacHale which played a part in hardening attitudes. In it he criticized Graham's amendments as making the bill worse and assured the archbishop that 'if the Prelates take and continue in a high, firm and unanimous tone,

[93] *Hansard*, lxxxi. 1096, 23 June 1845.

[94] Ibid., 1358-9; 1366-8, 30 June 1845.

[95] Ibid., 1355, 1375-8, 30 June 1845.

[96] O'Connell to Fitzpatrick, 27 June 1845, O'Connell, *O'Connell Correspondence*, ii. 358-9.

[97] O'Connell to Fitzpatrick, 21 June 1845, ibid., ii. 354.

the *Ministry will yield.* Believe me, that they are ready to yield.'
Warning him of the danger of being outwitted by the government, he repeated in the strongest terms that: 'My object is
that your Grace should know to a certainty that the game is in
our hands if the Prelates stand firm, as I most respectfully
believe they will, to all the Church sanctions relative to Catholic
education.'[98]

This uncompromising advice to one of his closest political
allies, whether or not it was based on a political miscalculation,
came at a critical juncture. The bishops were meeting in
Maynooth to appoint a new president and other members to
the staff and to allot the new bourses made available by the increased grant as well as conduct routine college business. Em-
boldened by O'Connell's exhortation, MacHale, who was in
the chair on 26 June, proposed that advantage should be taken
of the meeting to draw up an Address to Parliament, on the
lines of the May memorial, which should be forwarded as the
final decision of the Catholic bishops. What happened next is
difficult to establish. Cullen's account—and he had spoken to
many of the bishops—was that:

Dr Crolly immediately protested against such a step as they were not assembled to discuss politics. The meeting adjourned in great confusion and Dr
MacHale said he would publish the Primate's letter convoking the other
bishops to consider the education bill, a matter which he now stated to be
purely political. After the meeting was thus separated, Dr Murray interfered
with both sides and brought them together again, when it was agreed to open
the business a second time but after all nothing was done.[99]

Murray's own account is different. He told Heytesbury that
when MacHale made his suggestion, he (Murray) moved
successfully that the discussion upon the affairs of Maynooth
should continue. An annoyed MacHale left the chair and had
to be persuaded to return to it. Next day, Cantwell proposed
that an early date be fixed for a meeting of the bishops to draw
up an address to Parliament, but Murray moved that 'there
appeared to be no sort of occasion for any meeting of the Prelates
before the usual time in November, and that, that time should
be appointed accordingly.' Murray's motion was carried by a

[98] O'Connell to MacHale, 21 June 1845, Cusack, *The Liberator*, p. 743.
[99] Cullen to Kirby, 6 July 1845, Kirby Papers.

'considerable majority'.[100] Whatever the actual details of the confused scene that took place, it appears that Crolly and Murray prevented MacHale from having the discussion he wanted. Although Murray was highly pleased with his success, his manœuvre was scarcely a wise one, for the meeting at Maynooth came at a crucial juncture when the bishops could still have made their common opinion felt. As it was, Heytesbury's own reaction, when Murray told him all, was to breathe a sigh of relief that 'we have now got rid of all interference of the Prelates as a body' until November, when the bill would have become law and hence more difficult to modify. This meeting, too, saw the beginning of a new split within the hierarchy. O'Connell's letter to MacHale was partly to blame, though it must be said that he intended that advice for all the hierarchy.[101] Murray and Crolly bear responsibility for not being prepared to discuss the matter with the MacHaleites and for imagining that mere procedural victory would be of any real use in the long run. MacHale's difficult temperament, and his leaking of the May memorial to the press, hastened the split, but even without him it appears certain that the majority of bishops was not prepared to accept Graham's amendments as sufficient.

The bill passed the Commons by a large majority on 10 July, and the government turned its attention to the difficult problems of staffing the new colleges and of selecting the sites.[102] Two Catholics, Professor Kane and the Revd Joseph Kirwan, were appointed as presidents of the Cork and Galway colleges respectively, and Dr Pooley Shuldham Henry as president of the northern college.[103] The choice had been made after considerable deliberation, and possible candidates—such as O'Malley, Henry Cooke and Dr. Nicholas Wiseman, Roman Catholic

[100] Heytesbury to Graham, 27 June, 1845, Graham Papers.

[101] Duffy, *Young Ireland*, i. 186-7.

[102] *Hansard*, lxxxii. 379, 10 July 1845. The voting on this third reading was 177 to 26.

[103] Heytesbury to Graham, 19, 20 Nov. 1845; Graham to Fremantle 26 Nov. 1845, Graham Papers. Joseph William Kirwan (d. 1849), a distinguished Galway ecclesiastic and preacher; parish priest of Oughterard. In 1844 MacHale had blocked Kirwan's candidature for the see of Galway; O'Reilly, *MacHale*, i. 561, 575; Dr Pooley Shuldham Henry (1801-81), Presbyterian commissioner on the Board of National Education,, 1838-81; Commissioner for Charitable Bequests 1844-67.

coadjutor for the Central District and president of Oscott College—who might not be acceptable to Catholics in Ireland —were set aside. As regards the siting of the colleges, Cork was a clear choice for the south; and despite claims by Limerick and Tuam, Galway was chosen for the west. The selection of a site for the northern college was to prove more difficult.

While the government was thus working out the administrative details of the colleges scheme, new dissensions broke out among the Catholics and nationalists. The first concerned the Bequests Act. Since February Blake and Murray had been in contact with Heytesbury regarding certain amendments that they wanted. Graham was favourably inclined but in view of the furore against the Maynooth Bill, he persuaded Blake and Murray to defer for a time the proposed alterations.[104] In July, however, he mentioned in a reply in the House of Commons that Heytesbury had received representations from the Catholic commissioners stating that the duty had devolved on them of determining which ecclesiastics were entitled to the benefit of bequests and that this duty was at variance with the canons of their church.[105] O'Connell seized delightedly on this admission which seemed to verify his own criticisms of the act, announcing triumphantly at the Repeal meeting that: 'I was ... abused, for offering my humble opinion, that that Bill was uncanonical ... but humble as my opinion is, here it is confirmed by those venerable characters themselves, the Most Reverend and always-esteemed Doctor Murray, the Most Reverend Doctor Crolly and the Right Reverend Doctor Denvir.'[106] O'Connell added the hope that the three bishops would not permit themselves to be committed any longer to the exercise of an uncanonical power. Astutely, he had vindicated himself and embarrassed the bishops. Murray was annoyed with Graham who, he told Hamilton, 'has completely bungled the Bequests affair'.[107] He then wrote a public letter to O'Connell explaining

[104] Graham to Heytesbury, 20, 22 Feb; 13, 22 Mar; 23, 25, 28 Apr. 1845; Graham to Peel, 16 July 1845; Graham's memorandum 23 Mar.; Wellington to Graham, 29 July 1845; Heytesbury to Graham, 9 Mar.; 25 Apr. 1845; Blake to Heytesbury, 23 Feb. 1845 Graham Papers; Graham to Peel 16 July 1845, Add. MSS 40451, ff. 140-2; Blake to Murray, 6, 12, 19, 22 Mar. 1845, Murray Papers.
[105] *Hansard,* lxxxii. 673, 18 July 1845.
[106] *Pilot,* 23 July 1845.
[107] Murray to Hamilton, 24 July 1845, Hamilton Papers, DDA.

to him that: 'the Minister [Graham] must have alluded to objections which had been urged by the opponents of the Act, —objections which, in the opinion of the Commissioner prelates had no solid foundation to rest upon, but which they thought right to bring under the notice of the Government, in the hope that every pretext, ... would be ... taken away.' Murray assured O'Connell, in a gentle remonstrance, of his fixed determination to persevere as a member of the board with the sole view of serving the poor and of protecting the interests of the church.[108] Murray's courage in remonstrating with O'Connell drew the delighted congratulations from some of the minority bishops still smarting at the rough treatment O'Connell and MacHale had meted out to them. Crolly hoped that O'Connell would now realize 'that we are not disposed to submit to his insolent dictation.'[109] Kennedy expressed his satisfaction that O'Connell's arrogance had been checked. 'Will the Archbishop of Tuam now come to the rescue?' he asked tartly.[110] Both bishops were content, however, to let Murray make the running. On the other side, Cooper took the unusual step of appealing to O'Connell to attack his archbishop who, he claimed, 'has laid himself open to a raking fire' and he urged O'Connell not to allow himself 'to be checked in the vigour of your reply by any chilling sense of respect towards the person [Murray] who has thus challenged you...'.[111] The episode is an indication of the bitterness that still existed between the two sides and, although O'Connell did not follow the matter up, it augured ill for the unity of Irish Catholic opinion.

Among the Young Irelanders, too, differences of opinion as to their attitude to the Colleges Bill had arisen. Smith O'Brien, for many years a leading advocate of academic colleges, had become decidely hostile to the bill since his failure to obtain any significant concessions from the government during the parliamentary debate. He warned Davis that the opponents of Repeal 'speculate on being able to overthrow the influence of the Catholic Bishops and of the Repealers by means of these Colleges'. Sensing that Davis still supported the measure, he

[108] Murray to O'Connell, 1 Aug. 1845, *Pilot,* 4 Aug. 1845.
[109] Crolly to Murray, 3 Aug. 1845, Murray Papers.
[110] Kennedy to Murray, 4 Aug. 1845, ibid.
[111] Cooper to O'Connell, 3 Aug. 1845, O'Connell Papers, NLI, 13649.

reminded him that the Young Irelanders were in honour bound to oppose the act because: 'We have declared that we would repudiate the colleges scheme unless it gave security to religious men of all parties that religion should be be excluded wholly from these institutions—and unless public liberty should be protected from the corrupt influences of extensive Government patronage.'[112] Davis, however, was not prepared to regard either of the grounds advanced by O'Brien as sufficient reason for rejecting the act. In a revealing letter he made it clear that he was not committed to the idea that religious teaching was necessary in the new colleges. He told O'Brien that: 'You are mistaken, if you suppose I declared that the Colleges should be stopped by public agitation for the want of religious teaching. I asked and petitioned for such teaching chiefly to conciliate, for I was only in part of the opinion.'[113] Davis's statement accords ill with the wholehearted approval he gave all four points of the bishops' memorial in his great speech at the Repeal meeting of 26 May. It took O'Brien by surprise for he had been under the impression that all the members of the Repeal Association's committee wanted the measure postponed. While lamenting this disunity which he felt would only play into the hands of the enemies of Repeal, O'Brien firmly told Davis that he remained determined to withold his support for the act.[114] Murray's public remonstrance of O'Connell and O'Brien's private disagreement with Davis were overshadowed by another incident in the same month of August which, like the protest the previous year, helped to polarize opinion within the Catholic community. On 14 August, Dr Crolly attended a meeting of Anglicans, Catholics, and Dissenters in Armagh on the new act, and asserted that the government had made 'such arrangements as were calculated to afford general satisfaction'.[115] He then proceeded to argue the case for Armagh as the site of the new Ulster college. He hoped that in Armagh, there would

---

[112] O'Brien to Davis, 3 Aug. 1845, Davis Papers, NLI, MSS 2644, pp. 346-51.
[113] Davis to O'Brien, n.d. Smith O'Brien Papers, NLI, MSS 880. This letter appears to be a reply to O'Brien's letter of 3 Aug. and should be dated Tuesday, 5 Aug. Gwynn, who cites O'Brien's letter in part, places Davis's letter earlier; Gwynn, *O'Connell*, pp. 80-1, 86-7.
[114] O'Brien to Davis, 6 Aug. 1845, Davis Papers, NLI MSS 2644, pp. 359-64.
[115] *Pilot*, 20 Aug. 1845.

be a better balance of the three denominations. To the Anglican primate he held out the enticement of having a university college in the primatial city of Saint Patrick. To the Catholics, he made the point they they would not be submerged in Armagh as they would be in Belfast. His main difficulty lay in convincing the Presbyterians, but he won over some of them. A major argument in his case was that if the new college were in Belfast it would become a purely sectarian establishment rather than one run on the intended lines of mixed education. He achieved some success, for the Anglican primate came out on his side, while Heytesbury, Fremantle, and Graham were attracted by the scheme. Peel remained unconvinced, however, so it was decided to set up a committee of investigation and await its recommendations.[116]

Although Wyse expressed his pleasure at Crolly's move, surprise and, in general, hostility marked the reaction among Catholics.[117] The *Pilot* went so far as to allege that the primate's appearance at a meeting to campaign for an 'infidel college' gave rise to strange surmises as regards his state of mind and that his suggestions at the meeting were so outrageously foolish that they confirmed those surmises, and concluded that 'His Grace's faculties must have undergone some disastrous change since May last'.[118] This offensive comment by the leading O'Connellite paper was too much even for such a bitter critic of the primate's policies as Lucas, and both he and the Young Irelanders joined forces in denouncing the editor of the *Pilot*.[119] Nevertheless, reaction to Crolly's statement was sharp. Cantwell wrote a public letter to John O'Connell, in order 'not to lose a moment in removing your doubts as to the sentiments of the Roman Catholic Prelates, Clergy, and Laity, respecting the Godless Academical Bill'.[120] MacHale in a public letter to Peel, alleged that 'a silence of a sudden surprise has come upon the nation, at the strange rumours ... that the Godless scheme

---

[116] Heytesbury to Graham, 16 Aug. 4, 21 Sept.; 16 Nov. 1845; Fremantle to Graham, 16, 20 Aug. 1845; Graham to Heytesbury, 16, 18, 20 Aug.; 6 Sept.; 18 Nov. 1845; Graham to Fremantle, 18 Aug. 1845, Graham Papers.

[117] Wyse to the Provincial College Committee of Munster, Aug. 1845, cited in Wyse, *Notes,* pp. 80-1.

[118] *Pilot,* 29 Sept. 1845.

[119] *Tablet,* 18 Oct. 1845; Duffy, *Young Ireland,* pp. 772-4.

[120] *Dublin Weekly Register,* 23 Aug. 1845.

of education is to find favour even from those, by whom it was condemned as dangerous to faith and morals'—explicit reference to Crolly's May circular to the bishops.[121] It was not merely MacHale and Cantwell who protested. Kennedy expressed his regret that 'the Primate was so unguarded as to state that the changes in the "Colleges Bill" gave general consent'.[122] Browne of Kilmore expressed the wish that Crolly would recognise 'the necessity of yielding to the general view of the bishops and the people'.[123] Since these bishops had opposed MacHale's views in the past, it was becoming evident, as a friend (Denvir?) warned Crolly, that many of the moderate bishops were displeased by his Armagh statement and were hardening in their opposition to the new colleges. Murray, too, refused to accompany him in his visit to Heytesbury to put the case for Armagh as the site for the northern College.[124] Crolly defended his conduct claiming freedom of action on pastoral and practical grounds:

> I cannot ... concur in the opinion that, because I called the prelates together, on account of the dangers to faith and morals which I apprehended from the new scheme of education ... or because I moved a resolution demanding certain improvements that I therefore, deprived myself of the liberty of taking any other step in the matter until after their next meeting ... If I had this college in Armagh, I would have the Catholic youth lodged in a house selected by myself, in which I could impart religious instruction to them ... I could not defer this application until the meeting of the prelates for in the meantime, Belfast would have been fixed on as the site, and it would then be too late.[125]

Crolly claimed that he understood Ulster better than his critics and denounced as infamous 'the scheme of giving up the Ulster college exclusively to the Protestants, in order to get the southern and western colleges for the Catholics.'[126] Reasonable though his case appeared, he had ignored the solidarity of the bishops. The criticism that followed was not confined to his fellow-bishops.

[121] MacHale, *Letters,* pp. 599-602, see p. 303.

[122] Kennedy to Slattery, 23 Aug. 1845, Slattery Papers.

[123] Browne to Slattery, 2 Oct. 1845, ibid.

[124] —— to George Crolly, 29 Nov. 1850; Archbishop Crolly to —— , 5 Sept. 1845, cited in Crolly, *Life of Crolly,* pp. xcv-xcviii.

[125] Ibid.

[126] Crolly to ——, 16 Sept. 1845, Crolly, *Crolly,* p. xcviii.

Despite their defeat on the charitable bequests issue, Cullen and Kirby regarded the colleges question as too vital to ignore. Cullen (now in Ireland) kept Kirby informed of the state of events, complaining that the bishops 'condemn the college bill ... and then are in a hurry to recommend their friends for situations in those colleges'—a reference to Kirwan's nomination for Galway and Murray's recommendation of O'Malley.[127] On receiving the news from Ireland, Kirby took his own decisive measures, as he related to Cullen: 'I had a long conversation with Mr Rosso Suchetto on the matter, who told me he would talk of the matter with his other friends on Tuesday. Forse si farà qualche cosa.' In Kirby's cipher '*Rosso Suchetto*' was the 'Red Hat' of the Piazza di Spagna, Cardinal Fransoni, prefect of Propaganda and thus the man in charge of the affairs of the Irish Church. Kirby was a devout cleric who had ready entrée into the highest ecclesiastical circles in Rome, and whose views on the complex issues of church and state were uncomplicated. He expounded his simple faith to Cullen at the end of his letter when he contrasted the present deviousness of, presumably, Crolly and Murray with the 'good old saints that planted the faith in the Emerald Isle, and never took any Sasanach gold or Sasanach instruction.'[128] At his urgent request Cullen wrote to Fransoni from Ireland, complaining of Crolly's change of mind and of Murray's collusion:

egli e quattro Protestanti si sono portati la settimana passata dal viceré d'Irlanda per supplicarlo di fare mettere una di dette università nella città di Armagh. Si crede che l'arcivescovo di Dublino seguirà fra pochi giorni l'esempio dell'arcivescovo di Armagh al qual già aderisse in privato.[129]

Kirby, even before the letter had arrived, maintained pressure by sending 'una notizia al sucho [suchetto] rosso in Piazza di Spagna intorno all'educazione.'[130] Kirby, anxious to clinch matters in Rome against 'the minions of government' dramatically appealed to Cullen 'to come home immediately. It is here we must fight.' He warned him, however, not to leave Ireland until he had persuaded the bishops to appeal to the pope.[131]

[127] Cullen to Kirby, 3 Aug. 1845, Kirby Papers.
[128] Kirby to Cullen, 18 Aug. 1845, Cullen Papers.
[129] Cullen to Fransoni, 27 Aug. 1845, SOCG, 968, ff. 76-8, Propaganda Fide Archives.
[130] Kirby to Cullen, 28 Aug. 1845, Cullen Papers.
[131] Kirby to Cullen, 8 Sept. 1845, ibid.

This Cullen was already doing. He visited Mullingar and
Longford, the diocesan seats of those two staunch MacHaleites
—Cantwell and Higgins. He then spent a week in Maynooth, and pleaded with various bishops to denounce the new
scheme to Rome.[132] This done, he returned to Rome where
Kirby, convinced that there was no use looking for peace in
this world, was taking his example from the Lord who came, as
he said, "mittere gladium", which, 'if not to be used in circumstances like the present, I do not know when it is to be used.'[133]

Kirby's gospel metaphor proved apt enough as developments
in Ireland and in Rome soon showed. When Cullen spent the
week in Maynooth the trustees were meeting there for a con-
cursus. The colleges question was not on the agenda although
it was very much in people's minds. Crolly suggested to Slattery
that he ask the government to make his diocesan college at
Thurles the academic college for Munster but Slattery sharply
rejected the idea saying he would rather see his college 'tenanted
by the jackdaws than delivered to such a purpose'.[134] Crolly
left the meeting early to go to Armagh to discuss the location of
the Ulster college. It was a mistake. MacHale, according to
Crolly, waited until he and his friends were gone and then
'drew from the timidity of some and the ill-will of others' their
signatures to a short but significant public document which ran
as follows:[135]

Lest our faithful flocks should be apprehensive of any change being wrought
in our minds relative to the recent legislative measures of academic education, we, the undersigned Archbishops and Bishops, feel it a duty we owe
to them and to ourselves, to reiterate our solemn conviction of its being
dangerous to faith and morals, as declared in the resolutions unanimously
adopted in May last by the assembled bishops of Ireland.[136]

Signed by the seventeen bishops who had opposed the Bequests
Act, this document was also subscribed to by Kinsella—a
notable accession to the majority side. Another moderate, Haly,
added his name a few days later and the number of signatories

[132] Cullen to Kirby, 29 Sept. 1845, Kirby Papers.
[133] Kirby to Cullen, 8 Sept. 1845, Cullen Papers.
[134] Cullen to Kirby, 29 Sept. 1845, Kirby Papers.
[135] Heytesbury to Graham, 21 Sept. 1845, Graham Papers.
[136] *Freeman's Journal,* 20 Sept. 1845.

rose to twenty when the newly consecrated Bishop Maginn also hastened to sign.[137] The primate's stand had been publicly refuted by three-quarters of his colleagues. It is difficult to gauge how much Cullen influenced the bishops' action, for although his presence and encouragement was a source of strength to the majority bishops, it appears that many had already determined to resist Crolly's move. Cullen's influence and that of Kirby proved more direct in an incident that followed soon after. On 20 September, Fransoni, spurred on by Kirby's and Cullen's representations, wrote to Crolly in terms that can only be interpreted as a sharp rebuke:

relatum est mihi A.T. quae antea, bonis omnibus in Hibernia laetantibus, declarandum curaverat nuper inductum adolescentium instituendorum systema a Gubernio propositum, fidei, et moribus Catholicorum periculosum esse, nunc systema ipsum fovere, ac minime perniciosum existimare. Additum est etiam te dare operam ut lyceum, seu Universitas ei systemati accomodata in Diocesi tua statuatur.[138]

Although Fransoni said '*te secreto rogandum censui*', Kirby knew of the letter as soon as it was written, and before long Crolly's adversaries in Ireland were exulting in the rebuke.[139] That the cardinal should thus demand an explanation from the primate on the complaints of two minor dignitaries who did not even live in Ireland is remarkable. It can perhaps be attributed to the importance in Roman circles of personal contact, which the zealous persistence of Kirby exploited, although it is only fair to add that Cullen and Kirby had acquired reputations as excellent priests, devoted to the church. Fransoni was annoyed, moreover, at not being consulted on the colleges scheme and complained to Kirby that none of the bishops had written to him on the question.[140]

Distasteful though such a rebuke was to Crolly, he was at a safe distance from Rome and was not easily shaken from his path. In a vigorous reply to Fransoni, he recalled MacHale's factious opposition to the successful national system of edu-

[137] *Pilot*, 29 Sept. 1845; *Catholic Directory*, 1847, pp. 476-7.
[138] Fransoni to Crolly, 20 Sept. 1845, Acta 1846, vol. 209, f. 288, Propaganda Fide Archives.
[139] Kirby to Cullen, 8 Sept. 1845, Cullen Papers; Cantwell to MacHale, 1 Oct. 1845, O'Reilly, *MacHale*, i. 577-9.
[140] Kirby to Cullen, probably Aug./Sept. 1845, Cullen Papers.

cation, and suggested that the government's intention to exclude from college posts 'viros ecclesiasticos secularibus negotiis implicatos' was the cause of the protests as well as of the false rumours of infidelity in the proposed colleges, and about his own mental health. The May meeting of the bishops never intended to condemn the colleges out of hand, he claimed, but to seek improvements. Then, 'votis nostris annuens Gubernium ... maximi momenti emendationes systematis sancivit.'[141] This assertion that Graham's amendments were of great importance was the crux of Crolly's case, for many of his fellow-bishops did not accept that the government had agreed to their wishes, or that the amendments were 'maximi momenti'. Fransoni, unconvinced by Crolly's case, took the further unusual step of writing to Murray, enclosing his letter to Crolly and asking him whether he considered the amendments 'tales esse, ut sine fidei morumque discrimine adolescentes Catholici ejusdem systematis participes esse possint.'[142] This appeal to Murray was sent at precisely the time when the bishops, meeting in Dublin, were preparing to contact the Holy See officially on the whole matter.

As this annual meeting approached, there was speculation as to what the bishops would decide. 'There is great hope and fear—more of fear' wrote Yore to Slattery, congratulating him on his firm stand. Yore complained that 'the honoured Mitre is much sullied of late in the public eye', and that things would not be better 'while a certain unsteady Pilot is at the head'—an obvious reference to Crolly.[143] Slattery needed no encouragement. He had been in contact with most of the bishops and some leading clergy. He made arrangements to consult Haly and Kinsella on his way to Dublin, and tried to persuade even the ailing Dr Crotty to attend the meeting. Crotty could not travel: 'I might as well undertake a voyage to Australia as a journey to Dublin', but he authorized Slattery to affix his name

---

[141] Crolly to Fransoni, 10 Oct. 1845, Acta 1846, vol. 209. ff. 288-9, Propaganda Fide Archives.
[142] Fransoni to Murray, 25 Nov. 1845, ibid., 288.
[143] Yore to Slattery, 13 Nov. 1845, Slattery Papers.

either to the document which Slattery was circulating or to a memorial to Her Majesty. Crotty had his own solution:

Let the Primate and Archbishop, Dr Murray, in their own names and in those of all the other Bishops send in a Memorial to Government or to Her Majesty explaining fully our objections to the Bill and detailing such changes or amendments in it as they would consider necessary for securing the Catholic people of Ireland, against the introduction into their body of heretical or infidel principles, which they know are every day spreading widely amongst the Protestants of Europe.[144]

Crotty's suggestions show the genuine concern bishops felt lest the colleges propagate infidelity in the continental mode yet it was impractical to imagine that the government would change the act to satisfy these views. Blake fell ill on the point of departing for the meeting, but he promised Slattery his support. He did not believe that Peel wanted to corrupt the Catholics' faith, but 'to so bind our clergy, our educated laity and our people generally to the Government that they shall have no alternative but either to go always with the Government ... or to be deprived of all decent means of subsistence.'[145] Although he was less than generous in his assessment of the government's intentions, he was nearer the mark than those who saw in the colleges scheme a 'gigantic scheme of infidelity'.

The Repeal Association was alive to the importance of the decisions the bishops might take at their meeting. Thomas Davis, the leading advocate of mixed education, had died suddenly on 15 September, weakening the position of the Young Ireland wing of the movement. Now on the eve of the meeting of the bishops when most of them were already in Dublin, O'Connell raised the issue at Concilation Hall, a few hundred yards from the bishops' meeting-place. After referring to the stand taken by the French bishops on 'Godless education' he pointed out that all the Irish bishops had condemned the new scheme, and if one had now changed his mind it was on the inaccurate grounds that Graham's amendments had improved the act. Then, in an appeal reminiscent of his speeches against the veto, he proclaimed: 'I trust the people of Ireland will rally round the second order of the clergy (hear). I trust the people of

---

[144] Crotty to Slattery, 17 Nov. 1845, ibid.
[145] Blake to Slattery, 16 Nov. 1845, ibid.

Ireland will rally round the majority of their prelates, from the Giant's Causeway to Cape Clear.'[146] This was pressure indeed from the most powerful man in Ireland, whose word was law for millions of his countrymen. From the complaint of unfair pressure which the minority bishops made to Rome, one can surmise the anger of Crolly at being singled out in this manner: 'Dum haec in conventu Episcoporum agebantur D. Daniel O'Connell populum convocavit sperans se ejus auxilio et voce publice expressa ad condemnationem legis unanimem nos coerciturum esse, adeo ut vix libera dici posset consultatio nostra ...'[147] This somewhat exaggerated description of O'Connell's pressure was an eloquent tribute to his influence.

When the meeting opened on 18 November, eighteen of the twenty-seven bishops were present.[148] What took place was kept secret. A resolution was passed deploring the refusal of the government to give the securities for faith and morals which the bishops wanted, and laying before the pope 'our former resolutions, and their application to the act in its present form' in order to receive his decision. This resolution had the support of the majority, but no names were given. The minority drew up their own resolution:

Dissentient, because we consider that the following resolution, proposed and supported by us, is a more accurate statement of the case, and more respectful to the Holy See. Resolved—That the bill for Academical Education in Ireland, proposed by the British government, together with the memorial of the assembled prelates in May last, and the bill in its amended form, be submitted to the Holy See for its consideration and decision.[149]

This minority resolution was signed by Crolly, Murray, Denvir, Ryan, McGettigan, and Browne of Kilmore. The voting at the meeting on the colleges question appears to have been twelve to six. When both sides drew up appeals to Rome, however, the majority's document was in the name of eighteen

---

[146] *Nation,* 22 Nov. 1845.

[147] Lettera degli Arcivescovi di Armagh e di Dublino e di altri cinque Vescovi d'Irlanda ... 24 Nov. 1845, Acta, vol. 209, ff. 293-5, Propaganda Fide Archives.

[148] *Nation,* 22 Nov. 1845 gives a figure of sixteen but Murray told Fremantle that there were 18; Fremantle to Graham, 21 Nov. 1845, Graham Papers. Kennedy was in Rome. Blake, Crotty, and McLaughlin were ill.

[149] Meetings of the Irish Bishops, 1826-49, 10 Nov. 1845, DDA; *Catholic Directory,* 1847, pp. 377-8; *Nation,* 22 Nov. 1845.

bishops to the minority's six. Two of the three remaining bishops, Kennedy and Murphy, could be counted on to support the Colleges Act. The third, McLaughlin, was mentally disturbed and Dr Maginn, a determined opponent of the scheme, was administering the diocese. Thus, nineteen prelates opposed the scheme and eight were prepared to accept it, with reservations.[150]

The table on pages 330-1 indicates the attitudes of the bishops to the national education system, the Charitable Bequests Act, the Maynooth Act, and the Colleges Act. It is remarkable that all Murray's suffragans voted against him on the colleges issue, although generally up to then he could count on Haly and Kinsella. Although their decision was reached on lines of principle and policy, one suspects that there was annoyance on their part at Crolly's actions rather than any opposition to Murray. It is remarkable, too, that half Slattery's suffragans refused to follow his lead on the colleges question. The Ulster province was evenly divided—Denvir and Browne remaining loyal to Crolly. McGettigan's case is interesting. He had given some kind of assent to the September document, and although he partly withdrew it, his name was affixed to the statement when it was published. He now sided with Crolly and Murray.[151] The consistency of the Connaught bishops in opposing all government schemes (except the Maynooth Bill) is striking; they were the only bishops who gave undivided loyalty to their metropolitan.

The majority resolved on this occasion to avoid the mistake of the previous annual meeting, when victory had been snatched from their hands, and decided on a joint submission to Rome. The minority thought it prudent to concur in the appeal to Rome for as Murray slyly told Fremantle, 'His Holiness would not be in a hurry to come to a decision upon it'.[152] Heytesbury, nevertheless, was displeased with the 'friendly bishops', for they yielded 'much more than they ought to have done', but

[150] The copies of these documents printed for the use of the Congregation of Propaganda mention eighteen and seven bishops respectively but give only seventeen and six signatures. The final totals remain the same. Acta vol. 209, ff. 289-95, Propaganda Fide Archives.

[151] Slattery to McGettigan, 22, 25, 28, 30 Nov. 1845; McGettigan to Slattery, 25 Nov. 1845, Slattery Papers.

[152] Fremantle to Graham, 21 Nov. 1845, Graham Papers.

Graham eagerly took up the challenge of the majority.[153] 'I do not regret the appeal', he told Heytesbury. Pleased with his victory on the Bequests Act, he sanguinely believed that 'the Holy Father regards the British Government with more favour than he is disposed to show to John of Tuam.'[154] Whether, in the final analysis, it was politic for the government to appeal to the Holy See on what could be regarded as an issue internal to the United Kingdom is doubtful. 'The French Minister at Rome', Graham assured Heytesbury, 'will be instructed to support our Chargé d'Affaires on this occasion.'[155]

It is significant that it was the French government's support and not that of Austria that Graham sought. France, in the 1840s, had become the scene of a violent controversy concerning the rights of the church in education.[156] The French bishops attacked the université's monopoly alleging that infidel teachers were dechristianizing the youth. They fought their case openly in the press and sought to involve Rome with the government, much to the embarrassment of Pope Gregory and Lambruschini, who feared that this strident campaign would endanger their own policy of restoring the alliance between church and state.[157] Thus Lambruschini, while praising the bishops' zeal 'contro il pericolo che minaccia di corrompere tutta la gioventù Francese', told Fornari, the nuncio in Paris, that the public press was not the best place for the bishops to argue their case.[158] Fornari, however, defended the bishops' course of action as being the only one left open to them and, while promising to ask them to temper their attacks, explained that he would have to do so with caution, 'guardandomi sempre di farlo scuoprire al governo acciò non faccia dire ai suoi giornali che la condotta dei vescovi è disapprovata dalla S. Sede.'[159] While the

[153] Heytesbury to Graham, 20 Nov. 1845, PRO, FO 43/38, enclosure with Graham's letter to Aberdeen, 24 Nov. 1845.

[154] Graham to Heytesbury, 25 Nov. 1845, Graham Papers.

[155] Graham to Heytesbury, 25 Nov. 1845, second letter, ibid.

[156] A Prost, *Histoire de l'Enseignement en France 1800-1967* (1968), pp. 166-8; A. Latreille, and R. Rémond, *Histoire du Catholicisme en France*, (1962), iii. 325-47; L. Grimaud, *Histoire de la liberté d'enseignement en France; vol. vi La monarchie de juillet* (1954), pp. 329-708.

[157] R. Aubert, *Le pontificat de Pie IX ...* (1952), p. 19.

[158] Lambruschini to Fornari, 15 Dec. 1843, Archivio Segreto Vaticano, 248, cited in Manzini, *Lambruschini,* pp. 366, 634-5.

[159] Fornari to Lambruschini, 23 Dec. 1843, ibid. pp. 365-6.

Table 5

Irish bishops: place of training and political attitudes

Province		Place of training[a]	National Education Question 1839	Bequests Act 1844	Maynooth Act 1845	Colleges Act 1845	Repeal[b]
Armagh	Crolly	Maynooth	+	+	+	+	+
	Higgins	Paris, Rome	−[c]	−	+	−	+
	McNally	Maynooth	+	−	+	−	+
	Denvir	Maynooth	+	+	+	+	+
	Blake	Rome	+	−	+	−	+
	Browne, J	Maynooth	+	+	+	+	+
	Cantwell	Maynooth	−	−	+	−	+
	McGettigan	Maynooth	+	−	+	−[d]	+
	McLaughlin	Maynooth		+	+		
Dublin	Murray	Salamanca	+	+	+	+	+
	Keating	Maynooth	−	−	+	−	
	Haly	Maynooth	+		+	−	+[e]
	Kinsella	Carlow	+	+	+	−	+
Cashel	Slattery	Carlow	+	−	+	−	
	Egan	Maynooth	+	−	+	−	
	Murphy	Lisbon, Paris	+	+[g]	+	−[f]	
	Crotty	Lisbon			+		+
	Kennedy	Maynooth	+	+	+	+[h]	+

	Bishop	College					
	Ryan	Maynooth	+	+	+	+	+
	Foran	Maynooth	+	−	+	−	+
Tuam	MacHale	Maynooth	−	−	+	−	+
	McNicholas	Maynooth	−	−	+	−	+
	Browne, G	Maynooth	−	−	+	−	+
	O'Donnell[i]	Maynooth	−	−	+	−	+
	Feeny	Maynooth	−	−	+	−	+
	French	Portugal	−	−	+	−	+
	Coen	Maynooth	−	−	+	−	+

+ = those in favour   − = those opposed

[a] Some bishops studied at more than one centre.

[b] No bishop openly opposed Repeal.

[c] McNally was not appointed bishop until 1844.

[d] McLoughlin was not appointed bishop until 1840; in 1845 he was mentally disturbed.

[e] Kinsella said he believed in repeal but did not want to mix in politics.

[f] Murphy was in Rome in 1845. He was a moderate supporter of the Colleges Act.

[g] Crotty was too ill to inform to either the Nov. 1844 or Nov. 1845 meetings.

[h] Kennedy was in Rome in 1845. Although he was critical of Crolly's Armagh speech, he supported the Colleges Act.

[i] O'Donnell was not appointed bishop until 1844.

correspondence between Fornari and Lambruschini shows the delicate nature of the task facing the Roman diplomats, confronted with the conflicting aims of church and state in the matter of education, the persons involved indicate a link with the situation in Ireland. Latreille, writing of the conflict in France, makes the following observation: 'Un homme politique d'une exceptionnelle autorité, Montalembert, a réussi a lui donner pour les catholiques le sens d'une croisade pour la liberté d'enseignement.'[160] Montalembert, who had a long-standing interest in Ireland, had involved himself in Irish Catholic affairs, siding with MacHale in opposing any connection with the government.[161] MacHale, for his part, was a subscriber to the *Univers* then under the direction of a brilliant ultramontane journalist, Louis Veuillot, who was foremost in the attacks on the université. When Michelet defended the université and launched bitter attacks on the religious orders, O'Connell took up their defence.[162] It is not surprising, then, to find O'Connell, MacHale, Cullen, and their supporters citing the evil results of state education in France in justification of their own opposition to the Colleges Act. 'Referimus itidem' wrote the majority bishops in their submission to the Holy See 'ad statum educationis Academicae in Gallia ab omnibus catholicis lugendam.'[163]

When Petre sought the assistance of Acton, the cardinal pointed out that the delicate position in which the Holy See was placed with respect to a similar situation in France added embarrassment in coming to a decision on that of the Irish colleges. Yet Petre found him not unsympathetic: 'agreeing with me that in Ireland political activity was the main source of the opposition and expressing deep sorrow at the language of and conduct of many of the clergy and more especially of Archbishop MacHale.'[164] Petre put the case, not to Lambruschini as the government thought he would, but to Fransoni, a factor which may have influenced the outcome of the case. On his

---

[160] Latreille and Rémond, *Histoire du Catholicisme*, iii. 325.
[161] *The Times*, 12 Mar. 1845.
[162] See p. 312.
[163] Lettera degli Arcivescovi di Tuam e Cashel e di altri sedici Vescovi d'Irlanda ... 25 Nov. 1845, Acta, vol. 209, ff. 289-93, Propaganda Fide Archives. See pp. 328-9.
[164] Petre to Aberdeen, 10 Dec. 1845, PRO FO 43/38.

second meeting with Petre, on 19 December, Fransoni complained that the security against the appointment of undesirable
persons was insufficient. When Petre, alleging that all the
opposing bishops were repealers, suggested that their opposition
proceeded from party spirit rather than from religious zeal,
Fransoni replied that he did not think this was so 'with the
exception of Archbishop MacHale and Bishop Higgins'. Petre
came to the conclusion that Fransoni was 'biased somewhat
towards the prelates of the majority and evidently had not looked
much into the real merits of the question.'[165] As in the bequests
matter, Petre underestimated the curia's awareness of the situation. Disappointed with Fransoni, he determined to see the
influential secretary of Propaganda, Brunelli, who agreed with
him that many of the clergy were asking more 'under fear of
Mr O'Connell' and promised that the question of the colleges
would be put to a general congregation.[166] These were fair
words, but Brunelli, in response to two appeals from the Irish
bishops, had already taken a step of grave significance.[167]

Immediately after the November meeting both parties had
put their case to Rome. The majority's document, drafted
apparently by Slattery with the aid of Fr Patrick Leahy, listed
fifteen objections to the act.[168] A basic complaint was that
although the measure was explicitly intended for the benefit of
the Catholics, the government had neither consulted the bishops
beforehand nor listened to their reasoned pleas after the bill
was introduced into Parliament:

hoc etiam atque etiam rogamus, quare non placuerit catholicos Episcopos
consulere quoad systema educationis in gratiam praecipue catholicorum
proponendum? quare si bona esset ejus fides, suggestiones Episcoporum
aliqua saltem ex parte benigne non exceperit? quare potius eas indigne
rejecerit?

Furthermore, the Catholics were not being accorded equal
treatment although they constituted the vast bulk of the population.

[165] Petre to Aberdeen, 19 Dec. 1845, ibid.

[166] Petre to Aberdeen, 29 Dec. 1845, ibid.; Giacomo Brunelli; secretary for the
Congregation for Extraordinary Ecclesiastical Affairs 1837; secretary for the Congregation of Propaganda 1843-7; titular archbishop of Thessalonika.

[167] See p. 337.

[168] The Slattery Papers contain a draft of the document drawn up by Leahy. Patrick
Leahy (1807-75), archbishop of Cashel, 1857-75.

Objicimus ... quia, cum hoc systema propositum sit a Gubernio pro tota natione Hibernica, cujus ad minus septem partes ex octo Catholicae, oporteret vel catholicam educationem pro catholicis instituere, vel saltem huic systemati tales adnectere conditiones quales ad Religionis catholicae tutamen sufficerent. Hoc justum esset, et eo magis quod, dum catholici ne unam quidem institutionem habent a Gubernio sustentatam pro educatione Academica seculari impertienda, protestantes tamen multas ... habent, nimirum Universitatem Dubliniensem ...

This argument for equal treatment was to remain basic to Catholic demands for a Catholic university. The exclusive power of the crown to nominate officials and lecturers also came in for criticism. Even clause 14 which made provision for religious teachers was open to objection for those teachers had to be recognized by the governing body. There was nothing to prevent the governing body appointing a suspended, excommunicated or laicized (*degradus*) priest. To give substance to their point the bishops instanced cases where the Protestant authorities had nominated to the post of prison chaplain a priest suspended from his sacred functions 'ut alia omittamus, haud ita pridem hoc fecerunt Protestantes in comitatu Corcagiensi qui ad hoc officium, renitente Episcopo, nominarunt Sacerdotem quemdam suspensum, nomine Sullivan.' The bishops feared, too, that their own diocesan colleges, erected at so much expense would be ruined if the new colleges were approved.[169] Turning to the motives behind this plan for academical colleges and the other government measures, the document depicted them as part of the effort to destroy the Catholic faith in Ireland, and as an encroachment of the state on the rights of the church. Open persecution had failed, but the attack was now more insidious; 'Potestas secularis gladium suum in vagina reposuit ... nunc animos hominum delinire orditur per concessiones partim veras, partim fucatas ...' What heightened the bishops' alarm was the government's success in forming a pro-government party to forward its aims: 'etiam nunc in sinu Ecclesiae Catholicae in Hibernia, Gubernium Britannicum quosdam habet suis partibus deditos, quorum adminiculo in Religionis negotio dividere et imperare sperat.'

---

[169] There were at least seven diocesan colleges in existence—Carlow, Kilkenny, Thurles, Tuam, Belfast, Navan, and Armagh. Most of them provided education for both clerical and lay students.

The document finally impressed on the pope the danger of delay in resolving the crisis.[170]

The fear which they expressed for the diocesan colleges may indicate that not all the bishops had grasped the full scope of the new colleges, which were intended in time to constitute a university and as such provide the universal type of education which a university alone affords. More well founded was their complaint of lack of consultation, since it was certainly true, as they claimed, that the scheme was primarily intended for Catholics. Graham failed to grasp the seriousness of the bishops' reaction and by not making more adequate concessions, forfeited the chance of a compromise. His intention was to 'divide and rule', but the bishops' distrust was excessive, for, even if unsympathetic to their Church, he had no anti-Catholic motives. The divisions which he sought were more political in orientation and directed against repealers, lay and clerical. The bishops, given their position as guardians of the Catholic faith, were justified, however, in seeking more precise guarantees for the spiritual welfare of the students. They did not ask for the inclusion of Catholic theology as part of the curriculum for, no doubt, they thought such a demand would be impracticable and they envisaged theology more as part of the training of ordinands than as part of the programme of a national university for the laity. Nor had they as yet worked out a well-formulated argument against 'godless' education on the lines developed by Newman—at Cullen's suggesion—in his lectures when launching the Catholic University in 1852: 'Religious Truth is not only a portion, but a condition of general knowledge. To blot it out is nothing short ... of unravelling the web of University Education.'[171]

The minority bishops' statement, signed by Crolly, Murray, Denvir, McGettigan, Ryan, and Browne (Kilmore), was sent to Rome at the same time and reveals a markedly different approach. O'Connell and MacHale were singled out for attack, the former for bringing popular pressure to bear on the meeting from without, the latter for raising dissension from within. The

[170] Lettera degli Arcivescovi di Tuam e Cashel e di altri sedici Vescovi ... 25 Nov. 1845, Acta, vol. 209, ff. 289-93, Propaganda Fide Archives.
[171] J. H. Newman, *On the scope and nature of university education* (1939 ed.), p. 61.

bishops further accused the popular leaders, who now condemned the colleges as godless, of not hesitating to send their
sons to Trinity College, 'curae ministrorum protestantium qui
pro posse laborabant catholicos alumnos a fide catholica ab-
strahere'. Whoever they had in mind here it was certainly not
O'Connell. The bishops asked how their adversaries' conduct
could be reconciled with Propaganda's rescript enjoining
obedience to the civil power, adding that the outcry against
the colleges was simply due to the fact that the government was
determined to exclude repealers, lay or clerical, from any
position in the colleges. The most positive argument advanced
by the minority in favour of the colleges, and one that was to
remain fundamental to their case throughout, was the parallel
with the national system of education. That had also been an
experiment in mixed education and, although denounced by
MacHale, it had proved its worth. The new colleges 'eodem
principio fundantur quo institutum nationale in beneficium
pauperum jam in omnibus Hiberniae Diocesibus (Tuamensi
excepta) usitatum.' The minority argued that the students'
welfare would not be in danger because their lodgings would be
supervised, and Catholic professors would be appointed. As
regards chaplains, they believed that the power of nominating
them would lie with the bishops. They came then to a more
general and fundamental question. The increased grant to
Maynooth, the state's *innumera beneficia* to the church, not
only in Ireland but in the colonies, along with the appointment
of Catholics as presidents of two of the colleges, were proofs of
the good faith of a government which 'solicitum est ... nostrum
dubia omnia de fidei et morum periculis mota e medio penitus
tollere.'[172] Here they touched on the nub of the question—trust.
The essential differences between the majority and the minority
bishops did not lie so much in the differing arguments they put
forward as in their trust, or lack of it, in Peel's government. To
attribute their opponents' opposition to the exclusion of repealers from college posts showed some bitterness on the
minority's part, and in no way accounted for the position of
moderates like Crotty, Kinsella, Haly, and Slattery. It was

---

[172] Lettera degli Arcivescovi di Armagh e di Dublino e di altri cinque Vescovi
d'Irlanda... 24 Nov. 1845, Acta vol. 209, ff. 298-9, Propaganda Fide Archives.

probably the work of Crolly, for it repeats an accusation he had made a month earlier in his reply to Fransoni.[173] The appeal to the precedent of the national system was a stronger argument and likely to carry weight with Propaganda.

With these documents already in his hands when Petre came to see him, Fransoni now decided that a general congregation was necessary to resolve the issue, and he gave instructions to the secretary to prepare for one. For such important sessions, it was customary to appoint one or two consultors to report on the issue and to make recommendations. On 18 December, Brunelli appointed Paul Cullen one of two consultors. The appointment of one of the principal antagonists of the colleges appears, at first sight, surprising, for Brunelli and Fransoni were probably aware of Cullen's views. Yet no cleric in Rome was as well informed on Irish Catholic affairs as Cullen, who was also regarded as the agent of the Irish bishops. His appointment was a tribute to the prestige he enjoyed in curial circles. To Cullen, it was a heaven-sent opportunity and he set to work energetically to prepare as comprehensive a case as possible which would sink Graham's academical colleges for ever. From the late summer of 1845, Slattery had been emerging, along with Cullen, as the foremost antagonist of the colleges, and as MacHale's leader rather than his lieutenant in this matter.[174] Not that MacHale was inactive, for he sent letter after letter to Rome, but he was prepared to let Slattery do much of the running. In any case, Cullen, who directed the Roman end of the campaign, was more anxious to have Slattery's testimony, for the Munster metropolitan did not have MacHale's controversial record to live down. He welcomed, too, the active support of the many bishops who wrote to him for their letters would prove of considerable use in influencing the congregation. Some of those bishops denounced the proposed colleges with surprising vehemence. Maginn of Derry described them as:

a governmental snare to entrap the young mind of Ireland and make it indifferent to religion ... What they could not do by open violence they intend to do by a masked battery ... Formerly it was the rattlesnake, carrying dismay and death in its noisy track, now it was the not less deadly and venomous aspick, wreathed in flowers.[175]

[173] See p. 325.
[174] Slattery to Cullen, 22 Jan. 1846, Cullen Papers.
[175] Maginn to Cullen, 28 Jan. 1846, ibid.

Browne of Elphin wrote feelingly of the need to protect the youth from the 'perfidious wolves who under the mask of sheep of pretended liberality are with more than Talleyrand craft deceiving ... cajolling some of our venerated prelates'.[176] Blake denounced the *so-called* conciliatory measures and claimed that almost everyone believed 'that they have been dictated by an anti-Irish and anti-Catholic spirit whose tendency was to enslave Ireland's religion and country to the British government.'[177] Cantwell saw the act as having a double object: 'its first is to denationalise; its second as an effectual means to break up the confederacy between clergy and people which must end in de-catholicising Ireland.'[178] McNally saw the colleges scheme as an attempt to subvert totally the Catholic religion. If the government had not the precedent of a Catholic bishop, sitting with all descriptions of sectarians and infidels '*in cathedra pestilentiae*' on the national board, it would never have dared go ahead with the bequests board or the colleges measure.[179] Coen spoke of the necessity of preserving 'the integrity of our Holy Religion against all the machinations of our enemies at home and abroad.'[180] McNicholas urged Slattery to go to Rome with MacHale to press their case against the colleges.[181] Among the priests Yore, Cooper, Cooke, and Leahy all spoke against the colleges scheme with varying degrees of intensity.

Such fierce and general hostility raises the question of its root cause. It could be alleged of MacHale, Cantwell, Higgins, and some others that, as repealers and followers of O'Connell, their opposition was politically inspired, but even for those bishops, the facts were more complicated. Such a theory certainly does not explain the opposition of those bishops who had not joined the repeal movement and who had consistently supported Murray's moderate policies. Haly was never a repealer, nor could Kinsella, Slattery, Crotty, or Egan be termed ardent politicians. Another possible explanation is the bishops' lack of enthusiasm for the provision of education for

---

[176] Browne to Cullen, 4 Feb. 1846, ibid.
[177] Blake to Cullen, 12 Dec. 1845, ibid.
[178] Cantwell to Cullen, 19 Dec. 1845, ibid.
[179] McNally to Cullen, 26 Feb. 1846, ibid.
[180] Coen to Slattery, 15 Dec. 1845, Slattery Papers.
[181] McNicholas to Slattery, 16 Dec. 1845, ibid.

the Catholic middle class. Did they distrust a bourgeoisie which might prove less malleable to their influence than the peasants? Some of the bishops thought along these lines. Writing to O'Connell of the proposed new colleges system, Cantwell deplored that: 'Our middle and high Catholics are not always the most amenable to the salutary influence of the clergy. They are more selfish and less religious than the poor ... Hence I fear that the harvest of immorality, irreligion, and infidelity among the youth of Catholic Ireland would be quick and abundant...'[182] Slattery thought the new colleges unnecessary for 'our middling class, ... in as much as they are ... provided with very excellent institutions for the education of their children.'[183] On the other hand, some bishops such as Ryan, Crotty, Egan, and Murphy had supported the campaign to obtain colleges for the south and west of Ireland in 1838. Egan told Smith O'Brien that 'nothing can contribute more to the prosperity of society and happiness of individuals than the extension of a superior and well regulated system of education.'[184] Crotty declared himself in favour of some such system of higher education, remarking that 'it would be strange if I who had spent more than half a century of my life in College, were an enemy to education.'[185] Cullen was to become one of the greatest providers of education in the United Kingdom in the nineteenth century. The extraordinarily vigorous and sustained effort to establish a Catholic university is proof of the bishops' later commitment to university education, though this could be seen, to some extent, as a reaction to the state's scheme. It is most unlikely, however, that the Irish bishops in 1845 were deeply concerned with the provision of university education. Their flocks were embarrassingly poor and embarrassingly numerous; they themselves were primarily pastors for whom religion, not education, was the first concern. In keeping with the universal attitude of their church, with its belief in a divine commission to watch over the education of its faithful, the bishops wanted to ensure that

---

[182] Cantwell to O'Connell, 2 Feb. 1845, O'Connell Papers, NLI MS 13649.
[183] Slattery to Cullen, 6 Feb. 1846, Slattery Papers.
[184] Egan to Smith O'Brien, 19 Dec. 1838, O'Brien Papers, cited in Gwynn, *O'Connell*, p. 31; see, too, the evidence of Denis Bullen: *Report of ... Commission to Inquire into...the Queen's Colleges... PP, 1857-8*, xxi. 221-3.
[185] Crotty to Slattery, 15 Sept. 1845, Slattery Papers.

whatever higher education was provided would be Catholic or, at least, not anti-Catholic. This more negative, defensive, and yet pastoral attitude emerges clearly from their correspondence with one another and with Rome during this period. Crolly and Murray shared fully in this outlook. The difference between them and the majority was that they would have been content with an active Catholic presence in the educational system whereas MacHale's supporters believed that control was necessary for the protection of their flock.

Such a conclusion fits in with the dominant theme manifested in their opposition to the new colleges—lack of trust in the government. The state and the Established church had made the calamitous mistake of using education for proselytizing purposes from the penal era until Emancipation, and the 'New Reformation' with the zealous and fully publicized work of bible and missionary societies, had sharpened Catholic suspicions considerably.[186] The mark left on the Catholic clergy was indelible. They remained deeply suspicious of the Established church and of the state itself, particularly when the government was in the hands of the Tory party which had such close bonds of unity with that establishment. When Cullen, at the request of the Congregation of Propaganda, drew up a memorandum on the colleges question, the long history of educational proselytism constituted his main argument against the government's scheme.[187] Slattery, a key figure in the opposition to the colleges, denounced them in 1845

as dangerous in the highest degree to the morality and to the religious principles of the Catholic youth ... and on this point my individual testimony must be admitted as unexceptional evidence in as much as from the fact of my having graduated when young in the University of Dublin I am enabled to speak on the subject from my own personal experience.[188]

Similar statements by other bishops abound. A new dimension was added when the danger was seen as coming not merely from aggressive Protestantism but from infidelity in its continental mode. The critical attitude of the Roman curia and the French hierarchy towards state-controlled secular education

---

[186] See pp. 56-7.   [187] See pp. 346-7.
[188] Slattery to Cullen, 6 Feb. 1845, Cullen Papers.

rendered the Irish bishops more wary still of the new colleges which appeared to introduce a new type of education divorced from religion. Wyse, particularly, but also O'Malley and the Young Irelanders were accused of trying to 'prussianize' Irish education.[189] Their distrust of the government's intentions was not justified; Peel and Graham, both religious men, were sincere in claiming that they did not want to exclude religion from the colleges. Nevertheless, the bishops felt that such exclusion would be the practical result, either from the time the colleges were opened or at some later date, and that they— the appointed guardians of the faith of their flock—would be powerless to interfere. One detects, too, in the attitudes of MacHale, Maginn, Cooper, and Cullen a new assertiveness in the Irish Catholic church.

For some of the bishops, and not merely for MacHale, there was a further element in their distrust of the government. Slattery made the point well to Cullen:

But important as this question of Academical Education is, believe me ... that in the present controversy another question of transcendant importance is also indirectly involved viz. whether the Catholic Church in Ireland is to be governed in future by the British Ministry ... through the agency of a few members of the Hierarchy as their Commissioners or by the great body of the Bishops whom the Holy Ghost and the Common Father of the faithful have pleased to rule this portion of the flock of Christ.[190]

As Cooper had remarked a year previously, the majority of the bishops resented the close collaboration of Murray and Crolly with the government.[191] A year later Clarendon, who made every effort to win over the support of the bishops for Russell's government, complained to Blake that the bishops 'always keep aloof and seem to think they must lose caste or be looked upon as traitors to their religion and their flocks if they are suspected even of communication with that natural enemy of both—the government.'[192] Indeed, a detailed report on the situation in Ireland, which Slattery made to Rome, about the

---

[189] *The Voice of Prussia to the People of Ireland, or the Fruits of Government Influence over Education*, translated from the German by William ——, Bishop of —— ... (1845). The translator was probably Bishop William Higgins.

[190] Ibid.

[191] See p. 171.

[192] Clarendon to Blake, 26 July 1847, Clarendon Papers.

same time, bears out what Clarendon suspected and sheds interesting light on the outlook of the majority of clergy and faithful. 'qui sunt ii', Slattery asked with bitter rhetoric, ' ... qui nunc per totam Hiberniam apud Populum et in omnibus Ephemeridibus vulgo cognominantur *Episcopi Gubernii*? Iidem Episcopi Minoritatis.'[193] The terms 'Castle bishop' and 'Castle Catholic' came into wide use at this period and remained marks of opprobium as long as Dublin Castle was the seat of British government in Ireland. Irish Catholics were still deeply suspicious of the government and this deep-seated distrust was at the root of the bishops' opposition. Again and again in condemning the colleges act, the metaphor they employ is that of the Trojan horse, even repeating the identical words: 'Time, Beatissime Pater, time Anglos et dona ferentes.'[194] Despite Peel's olive-branch in the shape of a Bequests Act and an increased grant to Maynooth, he had not yet succeeded in allaying the fears and suspicions of those pastors of the Irish church. On the tactical level, Crolly mishandled the situation. In summoning the May meeting, he had written of the colleges as dangerous to faith and morals and he had concurred in the bishops' joint resolutions. Then, in August, apparently without a word of warning to his fellow-bishops, he had declared that the act as amended was entirely satisfactory and had vigorously canvassed for a college for his cathedral city. Not merely did he expose himself to charges of inconsistency from the MacHaleites but he received a rebuke from Rome and left moderates like Haly and Kennedy aghast at his action.

By the time that the bishops' representations were being seriously considered in Rome, Peel's government was more concerned with its own survival than with Irish concessions. In the autumn of 1845 came the first disquieting news of a potato blight. By October, Peel was considering the repeal of the corn laws. Weeks of cabinet deliberation and public speculation followed, culminating in Peel's resignation on 5 December. Back in office by the end of the month, Peel was in difficulty

[193] Slattery to Pius IX, [n.d. probably early in 1848], Slattery Papers.

[194] Seventeen bishops to Pius IX, 27 Mar. 1848, Acta, 1848, vol. 211, ff. 362-6, Propaganda Fide Archives; Maginn and Derry clergy to Fransoni, 21 Apr. 1846, SOCG, 1846, vol. 968, ff. 655-6, Propaganda Fide Archives; Renehan to Cullen, 6 Mar. 1845, Cullen Papers.

with his Irish government. Lincoln, who had replacd Fremantle as chief secretary, was defeated in the subsequent by-
election, and until May 1846 the chief secretary was without a
seat in Parliament. When Parliament met in January, Peel
proposed an Irish coercion bill and the repeal of the corn laws
both of which encountered strong opposition. Preoccupied
with these matters and conscious from adverse election results
of its tenuous grip on its own supporters, the government had
little time to devote to the Colleges Act. The bill had been
passed, the locations decided on, and the presidents and vice-
presidents chosen. As for the opposition of the bishops, the
government was content with the approval of Crolly and
Murray in Ireland, and confidently left it to them and to Petre
to neutralize MacHale's influence in Rome.

Murray certainly did his best to defend the government's
actions. He told Fransoni that Graham's amendments were of
great importance and reassured him of the government's
intentions: 'Pro certo habeo Gubernium nostrum nihil per
systema illud contra religionem nostram moliri velle, nec alius
quidquam sibi proponere nisi portas scientiarum humanarum
omnibus intrare cupientibus aequa manu aperire.'[195] Murray
was over-trustful in his belief in the single-mindedness of the
government, but when he pronounced the proposed new system
an advance on what was then available, he showed himself
more practical in his approach than the majority of his colleagues. The most telling argument, however, that the minority
advanced in favour of the government's scheme was to represent
it as the natural complement of the successful national education scheme, and MacHale now sought to weaken its force.
Too involved himself, he wisely encouraged Slattery, who had
supported the national scheme, to draw up a letter for joint
signature which would show how different the new colleges
were from the national schools.[196] When Slattery did so, Mac-
Hale signed, acknowledging that 'I should be unreasonable in
declining to sign so well reasoned a document which demon-
strates the utter bad faith of those who would compare the
manifest and necessary evils of the Colleges with the comparatively harmless National System.'[197] This partial acceptance of

[195] Murray to Fransoni, 11 Dec. 1845, Murray Papers.
[196] MacHale to Slattery, 10 Dec. 1845, Slattery Papers.
[197] MacHale to Slattery, 2 Jan. 1846, ibid.

the national system contrasts with a whole series of earlier denunciations by MacHale and says little for his consistency. The document, with the signatures of the two archbishops, was forwarded to Rome in early January 1846. Of the national system, the document argued that the pastors had direct or indirect control of religious matters: there were Catholic commissioners on the board; books injurious to the faith could be excluded and pastors could give religious instruction. Thus the schools in the Catholic parts of Ireland, though nominally undenominational, were in fact Catholic. The same conditions would not at all apply in the new colleges, for there the clergy would have no say whatever as regards supervision, teaching staff, or textbooks. The students would reside unsupervised away from home in close contact with those who might be the occasion of their losing their faith. There was less likelihood of the colleges becoming denominational in practice. In the primary schools, the vast majority of the pupils were Catholic. In the colleges, it was unlikely that the Catholics would number more than a few hundred, and they could well be in a minority to the Protestants. More O'Ferrall, a supporter of Murray's moderate line, voiced the same distinctions made by the majority of the bishops.[198] In view of the fact that Graham based his own case for the new colleges on the success of the national system, it is interesting to note the majority bishops' use of the same argument. Certainly the theory behind both national schools and academical colleges was the same, but the distinction made by the bishops was valid, for the schools, as the government well knew, had rapidly become, and remained, denominational.

All through the early months of 1846, Slattery and MacHale bombarded Rome with letters denouncing the new scheme and imploring an early condemnation.[199] *Periculum est in more* was their constant slogan, since they believed that delay would be the equivalent to indirect approval.[200] The appointments, too, came under their criticism. They denounced Kane for rejecting the selection of a Catholic priest as his vice-president, Fr Kirwan and Fr O'Toole for canvassing for their appointments

[198] More O'Ferrall to Murray, 17 May 1845, Murray Papers. Richard More O'Ferrall (1792-1880) M. P. for Kildare.

[199] 13 Dec. 1845; 2 Jan.; 15 Feb.; 26 Feb.; 13 Mar.; 14 Mar.; 2 June 1846.

[200] Slattery to Fransoni, 2 June 1846, SC Irlanda, vol. 28, ff. 719-20, Propaganda Fide Archives.

against the wish of their bishop, and Henry as belonging to a fiercely anti-Catholic Calvinist sect.[201] They complained moreover of the bad faith of the government with regard to the national system; in 1845 the national board had decreed that all schools receiving building grants should be vested in the board itself, which all the bishops saw as an increase in government control.[202] Other bishops and priests either wrote directly to Propaganda, as did Maginn, or to Cullen who passed on their protests to the curia and used the information thus received in drawing up his case against the scheme.[203] On 12 February, the *Freeman's Journal* published a petition against the colleges signed by the lower clergy. Authenticated by Slattery and MacHale, this formidable list of 1,626 signatures from nineteen dioceses was despatched to Fransoni and was supplemented by signatures from almost all the Derry clergy.[204] Somewhat over 71 per cent of the total number of diocesan priests in the country signed the protest against the colleges.[205] It appears certain that if signatures had been collected in the other seven dioceses, the percentage would have risen to well over 80 per cent, since in the 20 dioceses canvassed the percentage was between 90 per cent and 100 per cent.

A disquieting rumour, however, reached the majority bishops that Pope Gregory intended to come to a decision unfavourable to their point of view. Certainly, Gregory was displeased at the public protests of the French bishops on educational issues, a factor that may have influenced him on Irish matters.[206] But his unexpected death on 1 June 1846 put an end to speculation on this score. His death did not prevent the Congregation from going ahead with its consideration of the matter, and by now a complete dossier had been printed and distributed to its members. This dossier contained a translation of the relevant

---

[201] Slattery and MacHale to Fransoni, 2 Jan. 1846, Acta vol. 209, ff. 294-8, ibid.

[202] MacHale to Fransoni, 14 Mar. 1846, SOCG 968, ff. 681-4, ibid.

[203] Blake to Cullen, 12 Dec. 1845. Cantwell to Cullen, 19 Dec. 1845; 24 Feb.; 18 Mar. 1846; Cooper to Cullen, 12, 16 Jan. 1846; Maginn to Cullen, 28 Jan., 28 Apr. 1846. Browne to Cullen, 4 Feb. 1846; E. Norris to Cullen, 5 Feb. 1846; McNally to Cullen, 26 Feb. 1846, Cullen Papers.

[204] *Freeman's Journal,* 12 Feb. 1846; Slattery and MacHale to Fransoni, 15 Feb. 1846, SOCG, 968, ff. 679-80, Propaganda Fide Archives.

[205] *Freeman's Journal,* 12 Feb. 1846 contained 1,626 names. The Derry priests later signed a similar document bringing the total to some 1710.

[206] Latreille and Rémond, *Histoire du Catholicisme,* iii. 303-4.

passages from the act, the submissions from both the majority
and minority bishops, the decision of Propaganda on the national
education scheme in 1841, and the recommendation of the two
consultors—Monsignor Corboli-Bussi and Cullen.[207] Corboli-
Bussi, who was impressed by the success of the national schools
system, was in favour of continuing the experiment and of
giving the new colleges a chance to prove themselves. Cullen,
on the other hand, put forward the most comprehensive case
yet made against lending any countenance to them.

A fear that students of mixed colleges would be the object of
proselytism or would lapse into indifferentism was uppermost
in his mind. The history of lapsed Catholics in Trinity College
was his prime example. He listed O'Beirne and De Lacy, who
had become dignitaries in the Established church, Mortimer
O'Sullivan, the anti-Catholic preacher, Moriarty, the missioner
to Catholics, and William Carleton, the novelist. There were
others, too, who had lost all religion, such as Nolan who, dying
in Rome, kept a loaded pistol at his side to shoot the first priest
who would dare visit him.[208] Cullen, pointing to the infidelity
that resulted from similar systems of education in Germany,
France, and America, asserted that many Protestants were as
alarmed as the Catholics at the evil effects of such a Godless
system. On a more positive level, he opposed the separation
of the sciences from religion and quoted with approval De
Maistre's words: 'Tout système qui ne repose pas sur la religion
... ne versera que des poisons sur l'état.' He summed up his
detailed reply to all the arguments of the minority bishops,
basing his argument on eternal values: 'i vantaggi che ne
risulteranno saranno sempre di cose temporali, i danni ris-
guarderanno i nostri interessi eterni.' Advising that the bishops
should be told to improve their own existing educational establishments and, if necessary, to found new ones, he made a

[207] Acta vol. 209, ff. 258-99, Propaganda Fide Archives; Giovanni Corboli-Bussi.
(1813-50); secretary for the Congregation of the Consistory 1845; concluded Concordat
with Russia 1847. Corboli-Bussi represented the liberal wing as opposed to the
conservative Lambruschini and became the confidant of Pius IX. He attempted to
form a customs union in Italy, worked with Rosmini for an Italian confederation and
conducted a famous mission to King Charles-Albert in 1848.

[208] Cullen had given details of this case in a letter to his sister twelve years earlier,
Cullen to Margaret Cullen, 28 Apr. 1834, Mac Suibhne, *Cullen*, i. 213.

suggestion that was to influence the thinking of many Catholics on the university question:

Si potrebbe ... scrivere a' medesimi vescovi ... colla raccomandazione, che ...s'impegnino ad ammigliorare ... i collegj cattolici già esistenti, o dove ciò sia necessario di fondarne degli altri ad imitazione de' vescovi del Belgio, che per impedire i danni prodotti dalle università liberali, ne istituirono una cattolica ...[209]

This advice contains the first mention of a Catholic university for Ireland, a project that was later to involve Cullen, John Henry Newman, the bishops, and successive governments.[210] Cullen's views, like those of the bishops, were over-protective, understandable in members of a church fearful of proselytism and overawed by the greater wealth, accomplishments, and educational tradition of the Anglican church. It would take a further generation before Catholics could feel that they could compete in education on equal terms with their Protestant rivals. Cullen, too, aware of the dispute between church and university in France, raised the fundamental question of the validity of any education not based on religion.

In Rome Pius IX and the cardinals were preoccupied with drafting the great amnesty of 16 July 1846 which the pope hoped would herald a new era in the papal states. It was in a city agog with expectation of that political initiative that eleven of the cardinals met again on 13 July to discuss the more arcane question of the Irish academic colleges. Fransoni and Altieri were present but neither Acton nor Lambruschini. Cardinal Ostini made a brief presentation of the documents, carefully balancing both opinions and mentioning the arrival of the petition of the 1,626 priests against the scheme. The conclusion the cardinals arrived at was decisive: the new colleges would be harmful to religion and therefore the Congregation 'si crede in dovere d'avvertire i rispettati prelati d'Irlanda à non prendere parte all' adempimento di tale istruzione.' In a veiled rebuke to the minority, the cardinals expressed regret that some bishops had entered into negotiations with the government without first

---

[209] Voto di Monsig. Paolo Cullen, 31 Jan. 1846, Acta, vol. 209, ff. 272-84, Propaganda Fide Archives.

[210] It is not generally realized that the idea of a Catholic University came from Cullen. Cooper recommended the same project a few months later; Cooper to Slattery, 22 Apr. 1846, Slattery Papers.

consulting the Congregation. Finally, they urged the bishops to set up their own colleges, and taking up Cullen's suggestion pointed to the example of the Belgian bishops in founding the university of Louvain.[211] Despite this decision, all was not yet lost for Murray and Crolly. Pius IX refused to publish the rescript. Nicholson claimed that he had won over Lambruschini to support this action and urged Murray to fight back.[212] Of more weight with the pope in this early liberal period of his pontificate, was the moderating influence of his personal friend, Corboli-Bussi, who was now acting as secretary for state for Lambruschini's appointment had lapsed with the death of Gregory and the new pope had not yet appointed a successor. On his advice, Pius postponed publication of the decision on the plea that he wanted to consult Acton.[213] For a full year he resisted pressure from MacHale, Slattery, and Cullen and finally when he felt that he could no longer refuse their repeated appeals, he first referred the matter back to Propaganda for re-examination to see if any change should be made in the decision.[214] When the Congregation decided that no change was called for, the adverse decision was sent to the bishops, but even then the door was left open for further representations.[215] Although such representations were made during the Whig administration, effectively the decision of 13 July 1846 was to remain the final one and the synod of Thurles in 1850 formally accepted it and made it publicly known. This decision was of no small importance. It could be interpreted as undue inter-ference by the Roman church in the internal and secular affairs of the United Kingdom. Clarendon complained that the pope had 'publicly denounced and directed the Roman Catholic hierarchy to oppose a measure which had received the sanction

---

[211] Acta, vol. 209, ff. 260-2, Propaganda Fide Archives.

[212] Nicholson to Hamilton, 5 Aug. 1846, Hamilton Papers, DDA. Nicholson to Murray, 14 Aug. 1846, Murray Papers.

[213] Corboli-Bussi to Pius IX, July 1846, SOCG, vol. 968, f. 550, Propaganda Fide Archives; G. Martina, *Pio IX, 1846-1850* (1974), pp. 460-2.

[214] The secretary to the cardinals of Propaganda, 13 Sept. 1847, Lettere e decreti della S.C. e biglietti di Monsignore Segretario, 1847, vol. 336, ff. 1192-3, Propaganda Fide Archives.

[215] Fransoni to Slattery, 9 Oct. 1847, reprinted in full in *Decreta Synodi Plenariae Episcoporum Hiberniae apud Thurles habitae, anno mdcccl* (1851), pp. 73-5.

of the Sovereign and Parliament of England.'[216] Palmerston called it 'a mischievous measure' and it contributed to Lord John Russell's intemperate response to the 'papal aggression' of Cardinal Wiseman and Pius IX.[217] Rome, however, had been made a court of appeal by both parties among the bishops, and Graham, too, over-anxious to defeat the MacHaleites and to obtain papal sanction for the government's Irish policies, had contributed to creating a situation where the decision of eleven Italian cardinals nullified, in great measure, the operation of an act of Parliament. The decision of 13 July 1846 effectively crippled Peel's plan to provide academic colleges for the Irish Catholics. The party opposed to Peel's government which had lost on both the bequests and the national education issues had won on this occasion. They certainly fought their case harder. The minority depended on a few letters from the active but now ageing Murray, whereas Slattery, MacHale, Higgins, Maginn, Cantwell, Foran, Cooper, and many others threw their full weight into the struggle against the colleges. Cullen's and Kirby's zealous lobbying and the former's thorough indictment of the colleges in his report played no small part, and Wiseman rightly complained to Greville in 1847 that 'it was all owing to there being no English ambassador at Rome, and no representative of the moderate Irish Clergy.'[218] Whatever the pressures brought to bear on it, however, the fundamental reason why the Congregation took such a decision was the fear that this neutral system of education would harm religion. Later, the Catholic church based one of the canons of its code of canon law on the decision taken against the Irish academic colleges.[219]

By the time the cardinals had come to a decision, Peel and Graham were no longer in a position to carry further their Irish policies. On the day the corn laws were repealed, the 'blackguard combination', as Wellington termed it, used the Irish coercion bill to defeat Peel in Parliament and he resigned

---

[216] Clarendon's memorandum, 20 Nov. 1847, cited in E. Ashley, *The Life and Correspondence of H. J. Temple, Viscount Palmerston* (1877), i. 41.

[217] Palmerston to Minto, 29 Oct. 1847, ibid. i. 40; *Hansard,* cxiv. 183-90, 7 Feb. 1851, Russell.

[218] Greville, *Journal,* 7 Dec. 1847, v. 470.

[219] *Codex Juris Canonici* ... (1917), canon 1379.

on 29 June. His remarkable farewell speech dwelt in part on his Irish reform programme. He avowed that he entirely subscribed and adhered to his earlier sentiments in favour of Irish reforms 'which had practical effect given to them by the Charitable Bequests Bill and by the additional vote for the endowment of the College of Maynooth'. He then outlined the policy that his successors should follow in Ireland:

> ... there ought to be established a complete equality of municipal, civil and political rights ... the favour of the Crown ought to be bestowed, and the confidence of the Crown reposed, without reference to religious distinctions ... the present social condition of the people in respect to the tenure of land, and to the relation between landlord and tenant,... deserves our immediate though most cautious, consideration.[220]

Peel was outlining here the policies he would have hoped to pursue had he remained in power. An astonished O'Connell exclaimed to Smith O'Brien that Peel's was 'a true Precursor discourse', adding that there was a report that 'Peel is inclined to take one turn more and bring in the Repeal.' O'Connell himself discounted this, but remarked that it might come true sooner than people imagined.[221] O'Connell could claim publicly that Peel's speech, in its references to Ireland, 'is only an abstract of half a dozen speeches of mine'.[222] The Young Irelanders declared ecstatically that 'Peel, the future premier, bids for Ireland', adding that 'this declaration of Peel's reminds men that what was a miracle twelve months ago is now come to pass'.[223] It was somewhat late, however, to support Peel when he had left office. Of his policy Peel had this to add: 'I cannot say that justice has been done to our motives, nor has the position of the individual accepting a mark of favour from us been such as to encourage other Roman Catholics to receive similar proofs of confidence.'[224]

This assertion remained true. Justice was not done then (nor has it been since) to Peel's Irish reforms which, considered in the context of the time and of the prejudices of his own party, were remarkable. By putting Catholic charities on an equal

---

[220] *Hansard,* lxxxvii. 1044-5, 29 June 1846.
[221] O'Connell to O'Brien, 30 June 1846, Smith O'Brien Papers, NLI, MSS 437.
[222] *Nation,* 11 July 1846.
[223] Ibid., 4 July 1846.
[224] *Hansard,* lxxxvii. 1045, 29 June 1846.

footing with other charities, he had greatly strengthed the
financial position of the church. His grant to Maynooth had
been generous and his courage in carrying it through parliament
remarkable. By May 1845 the distinct possibility emerged that
his government might succeed in their policy of reconciliation.
He was not to know that the plan for academical colleges would
prove a failure and already by autumn of 1845 the Famine had
struck Ireland bringing with it different priorities for his government's Irish policies.

As Peel also implied in his final speech as prime minister,
justice was not done to Murray, Crolly, and their supporters
who strove to pursue a middle course in Irish politics. Murray,
a few years later, claimed—with justification—that 'as for
Whigs and Tories, I belong to neither Party ... But whichever
Party rules the State, the duty, which Religion imposes on me,
is to render my humble [service?] without respect to Party
towards the preservation of public Order.'[225] To Peel belongs
the credit of being the first Tory premier to make a serious
effort to solve the Irish problem by conciliation; to Murray is
due the credit of responding positively to that initiative in the
face of continual intimidation. Apart from the calamitous
effects of the Famine in deepening mutual suspicions, the
success of the premier and of the archbishop was limited by
their failure to take sufficient account of the views and feelings
of the majority of Irish Catholics—including the clergy. The
loyalty of most Irishmen to O'Connell was too strong and their
political and religious distrust of the Tory party too deep, to be
overcome by the measure of reform which Peel could offer and
Murray agree to recommend. The difference, in Greville's
words, between 'what the people of England could be brought
to consent [to] and what the people of Ireland would be content
to receive'[226] proved too wide to be bridged by a prime minister
whose concessions were met with distrust and an archbishop
whose co-operation was construed as pliant timidity.

[225] Murray to Miley, 10 May 1849, Murray Papers, DDA.
[226] See p. 116.

8

EPILOGUE

Of Peel's three reforms the first two were the most successful. The later history of the Charitable Bequests Board bore out none of the dire forebodings of MacHale, Cooper, and O'Connell. Although the religious orders lost many bequests made in their favour, this was the result of the penal clauses in the 1829 Relief Act; the 1844 act did not worsen their position. The fear that the act would give the Protestant commissioners a right to decide on the legitimacy of the appointment of a parish priest or bishop was never realized; in this sphere, the board functioned most harmoniously and ecumenically from its earliest years. A limited form of *cy-près* was restored to the board by the amending acts of 1867 and 1871. Clause 16 proved, as Cooper predicted, the main weakness in the 1844 act, and the manner of evading it envisaged by O'Connell and Blake and accepted by the law officers was not completely successful. This vexatious clause was finally dropped in 1961 in the Republic of Ireland and in 1964 in Northern Ireland. All in all, however, the act was beneficial, for it did permit the endowment of the church. Fifty years after the controversy, Archbishop Walsh, Murray's successor in the see of Dublin who himself was a commissioner, judged that the act 'with all its drawbacks, was undoubtedly a step in the direction of justice to the Catholics in Ireland'.[1] By then the amount of property held by the Commission had more than quadrupled.

Maynooth College greatly benefited from the trebling of its grant and the generous sum allocated for buildings. Fifty years later, Dr John Healy, a successor to MacHale as archbishop of Tuam, eulogized Peel as a statesman whose memory would be cherished by Maynooth men and of whose patronage they were proud.[2] Peel chose Augustus Welby Pugin, the leading Catholic

---

[1] Walsh, 'Board of Bequests' pp. 893-4.
[2] Healy, *Maynooth*, p. 414.

architect of the day, to design the new buildings at Maynooth, and to this master of the neo-Gothic is due the impressive central section of the present-day College. The salaries of the staff were increased by over 100 per cent and some extra staff provided. Better living facilities and living quarters were provided for them and for an increased number of students (515 in 1853). Paradoxically, as Maynooth began to supply more priests, thus meeting a need which was at the origin of the bishops' plea for an increased grant, the population commenced its steep decline. The number of faithful to each priest which was 2,985 in 1834 dropped to 1,783 in 1861, 1,445 in 1881, and 1,126 in 1901. By 1980 it was 953 to one, a ratio more than three times as favourable as in the decade before the Famine. These figures do not take into account the truly remarkable increase in the number of regular (and missionary) clergy from 200 (approximately) in 1834 to 2,208 in 1980.

Despite the increased grant in 1845 the type of priest Maynooth produced differed little from that which caused complaint in the 1830s. Nor did the political involvement of the clergy

Table 6

Ratio of clergy to Catholic population from 1834 to 1980

	Total diocesan clergy	Catholic population	Ratio of diocesan clergy to Catholic population	Regular clergy [a]
1834	2,156	6,436,060	1 : 2,985	200
1861	2,527	4,505,265	1 : 1,783	528
1881	2,741	3,960,891	1 : 1,445	439
1901	2,938	3,308,661	1 : 1,126	586
1911	3,022	3,242,670	1 : 1,073	715
1976	3,845	3,490,064	1 : 908	2,017
1980	3,816	3,635,693	1 : 953	2,208

[a] The returns for the regular clergy are incomplete in 1834 and 1861. The 1861 figures include chaplains and priests working in schools. The 1976 and 1980 figures include the missionary priests.

Sources: The figures for 1834 are taken from the *First Report of the Commissioners of Public Instruction, Ireland, PP 1835,* xxxiii. The figures from 1861 on are taken from Battersby, *Catholic Directory,* and the *Irish Catholic Directories.*

diminish; if anything it tended to increase.[3] The clergy no longer had O'Connell's guidance, yet in general they followed his constitutional brand of nationalism in condemning Young Irelanders and Fenians alike. In the wake of the 'Papal Aggression', suspicions of the loyalty of the college were again voiced in Parliament, and in 1853 royal commissioners conducted a thorough investigation. They received a favourable impression and affirmed that they saw 'no reason to believe that there has been any disloyalty in the teaching of the College'.[4] Ironically, it remained to Gladstone—with the consent of Cullen—to abolish the grant in 1871 as part of the settlement for disestablishing the Church of Ireland. Although its close links with the state thus came to an end, Maynooth flourished, becoming one of the most important Catholic seminaries and exercising a unique influence throughout the English-speaking Catholic world in the century after the Maynooth Grant. In 1903 King Edward VII thanked the college 'for the training of devoted men to the sacred office of the ministry throughout my dominions and in every English-speaking country in the world', and that praise was repeated in 1979 by Pope John Paul II, the first pope to visit Maynooth, when he commented that 'from here have gone out priests to every Irish diocese and to the dioceses of the far-flung Irish diaspora.'[5] These compliments were merited. Practical in outlook, and less venturous in its approach to philosophy and theology than some of its continental sister-institutes, Maynooth College moulded the profile of the newly-invigorated and mission-minded Irish Catholic church. The question of the Academic Colleges was of more immediate consequence during Russell's administration than either the Charitable Bequests Act or the Maynooth Grant. Both Murray and the government sent agents to Rome to plead for the acceptance of the colleges. They were defeated by a combination of MacHale and Higgins (who travelled to Rome for that purpose) and Cullen, whose influence there was in the ascendant. Crolly, whether through regard for the opinion of

---

[3] Whyte, 'Influence of clergy on politics', pp. 243-55; MacDonagh 'Politicization of Bishops', pp. 51-3.

[4] *Maynooth Commission Report, PP 1854-5*, xxii. 64.

[5] *Kalendarium Collegii Sti Patricii apud Maynooth ...* (1903), p. 182; *The Pope in Ireland: addresses and homilies* (1979), p. 69.

his fellow-bishops or respect for the decision of the Holy See, appeared to abandon his support for the colleges.[6] Nevertheless, by 1849, Murray had won half the bishops to his point of view; thirteen were now prepared to accept the scheme, while thirteen still opposed it. Unfortunately for him, Crolly died suddenly in April 1849 to be succeeded as archbishop of Armagh by Cullen. Cullen's position was further enhanced by his appointment as apostolic delegate to the first national synod held by the church since the seventeenth century. The synod, in itself a sign of the growing strength and confidence of the church, took place at Thurles during August and September 1850. Murray was narrowly defeated by 14 votes to 13 on two counts and by 15 to 12 on another—all concerning aspects of co-operation with the colleges scheme.[7]

Murray held out even after the synod, but the Durham Letter (4 November 1850), in which the prime minister referred to Catholic practices as 'superstitious mummeries', and the Ecclesiastical Titles Bill were blows to his party which had all along protested to the Holy See the goodwill of the government towards the church. The Catholic University, with Newman as Rector, was launched as a counter-blast to the colleges, and Newman, at Cullen's suggestion, delivered his famous *Discourses on University Education* as an attack on 'mixed and religionless education'.[8] The Catholic University failed as did the colleges (with the notable exception of the Belfast college), the former because the government refused a charter, the latter because the Catholic church boycotted them. The lack of an adequate secondary system to provide feeder schools was a further major obstacle to their success. It was not O'Connell who defeated the colleges; indeed it is possible that if Graham had heeded Russell, Smith O'Brien, and O'Connell and taken 'one step more' to conciliate the bishops, the moderates, such as Kinsella, Haly, and Egan would have tilted the balance at the November meeting of 1846 in Murray's favour and Corboli-Bussi's rising

[6] Maginn to Cantwell, 27 Nov.; Cantwell to Slattery, 30 Nov. 1848, Slattery Papers.
[7] Whyte, 'Political Problems', p. 8; Moody and Beckett, *Queen's, Belfast*, i. 78 give slightly different totals. The most recent and most complete account of the synod is given in E. Larkin, *The Making of the Catholic Church in Ireland, 1850-1860* (1980), pp. 3-57.
[8] Cullen to Newman, 20 Sept. 1851; Newman to Ambrose St John, 11 May 1852, Newman, *Letters and Diaries,* xiv. 364-5; xv. 83-4.

influence might have succeeded in counteracting that of Cullen. The bishops, for their part, were unduly suspicious of the government's intentions which were not aimed, as many of them feared, at destroying the faith of Catholics. A compromise might. have been worked out which would have accorded to religious teaching, Anglican, Catholic, and Presbyterian, its due place within the university system. Whatever the reasons for the failure, this unique opportunity to provide university education for all Irishmen was botched; instead of a united national university, there arose rival institutions jealously competing for students and resources. The university problem remained a bone of contention for the rest of the century. An arrangement was finally arrived at in 1908 when an un-denominational National University, comprising three con-stituent colleges in Dublin, Cork, and Galway, was established. Maynooth was joined to the National University as a 'recognised college' for the faculties of Arts, Philosophy, Celtic Studies and Science. A further major revision is now under way.

Thus, of Peel's three reforms, two had proved successful and one a failure. His ulterior hope of breaking up the combination of Irish Catholics had limited success, for within a few years the bishops were able to close their ranks again and exert united and successful pressure on the government. Even the collapse of the Repeal movement is not directly attributable to Peel's policies of concessions. Dissensions, such as the education issue and differing views towards co-operation with the Whigs, had weakened the movement. A month after Peel's resignation, the O'Connells, powerfully supported by the clergy, defeated the Young Irelanders on the key issue of the legitimacy of the use of physical force to achieve freedom. The secession of the Young Irelanders, the Famine and O'Connell's death, completed the dissolution of the movement. Peel's concessions did win over some Catholics, but Peel's own party never fully recovered from the shock administered to it by the Maynooth Grant of 1845. His views on the Irish Catholic question progressed further and in 1848 he told Sheil that he favoured direct endowment of the Catholic clergy.[9] In 1849 he suggested an ambitious programme of social and economic reform which the En-

[9] W. T. McCullagh, *Memoirs of Richard Lalor Sheil* (1855), ii. 387-9.

cumbered Estates Act of that year only partly fulfilled.[10] He died before the 'Papal Aggression', but it is noteworthy that the leading Peelites voted against the Ecclesiastical Titles Bill. Ironically, this act of a Liberal government did much to undo the good impression produced on Catholics by Peel's reforms and evoked protests from the aged Dr Murray who had for so long and at great personal cost, co-operated with successive governments in their policies of moderate reform.[11]

Murray's fate in his declining years was hard. Disappointed by the Liberals, he fell into disfavour with Pius IX for his continuous support for the colleges plan.[12] In view of his attachment to the Holy See and his long years of service to the church, this circumstance greatly upset the ageing archbishop.[13] Before he died in February 1852, matters had been smoothed over.[14] By that time, too, O'Connell, Peel, Crolly, and Anthony Blake were all dead. MacHale maintained his inflexible opposition to the national schools—an attitude that was criticized on the grounds that he thus facilitated the proselytism in Connaught during the Famine. In politics he pursued his own brand of nationalism and remained a thorn in the side of Cullen and successive governments alike until, in the era of Parnell, the Land League proved too much for him.

The future of the Irish church in the nineteenth century lay neither with Murray nor MacHale but with Cullen. Cullen, after following Crolly in 1849 as archbishop of Armagh, succeeded Murray in 1852 as archbishop of Dublin. A devout and vigilant pastor and a skilled organizer, he continued many of Murray's policies, and the improved financial position of the church—due in part to Peel's reforms—made it possible to pursue them more vigorously. Like Murray, education was central to Cullen's policy, although he would accept nothing less than a completely Catholic system for his flock. If he was successful in the sphere of primary and secondary education, a

---

[10] Gash, *Peel*, pp. 641-3.

[11] Meagher, *Murray*, pp. 73-80; Whyte, 'Political Problems', pp. 10-11.

[12] Father Ignatius to Murray, 28 Sept. 1851, Murray Papers, DDA. Father Ignatius (1799-1864), a Passionist priest, was the Hon. George Spencer, brother of Lord Althorp.

[13] Murray to Father Ignatius, 13 Oct. 1851, Murray Papers, DDA.

[14] Pius IX to Murray, 17 Nov. 1851, ibid; cf. Meagher, *Murray*, pp. 197-200.

solution to the university problem eluded him. Cullen completed Murray's reorganization of his diocese and threw himself energetically into the task of reshaping the entire Irish church, in discipline and in devotion, along Roman lines. Maynooth College did not remain immune from his reforming zeal. He strengthened the control of the bishops over the college, introduced Roman devotions among the students, and resolutely rooted out any traces of Gallicanism which he believed still persisted in the teaching of the seminary.[15] In politics, he rejected his predecessor's policy of close co-operation with the government but remained as pragmatic as Murray in his approach to the relationship between church and state. Ironically enough, Cullen, too, curtailed clerical involvement in politics, opposed the policies of MacHale and Lucas and took measures against more advanced nationalists. Under his skilful leadership the hierarchy was able to present a united front on most important issues. At his death in 1878, he left the Irish Catholic church stronger and better organized, if more Roman, than at any previous point in its history. For the success of this programme Murray's diocesan re-organization and pastoral care had paved the way. Peel's enlightened policies too, coming at the critical moment of the Famine, had helped to assure the necessary finances and the trained personnel. Such, however, was the lustre of Cullen's episcopate and its moulding influence on later generations of Irish Catholics that they have obscured Murray's achievement—due in part to Peel's generous and statesmanlike actions—in laying those essential and firm foundations.

---

[15] P. Corish, 'Gallicanism at Maynooth: Archbishop Cullen and the Royal Visitation of 1853', *Studies in Irish History, presented to R. Dudley Edwards*, eds. A. Cosgrove and D. McCartney (1979), pp. 176-89.

APPENDIX

TRANSLATIONS OF THE MORE IMPORTANT LATIN AND ITALIAN DOCUMENTS

p. 25   Murray to Pedicini, 16 August 1834   (cum)

When he writes about these political matters I think his style is too trenchant. It must be borne in mind, however, that he is surrounded by poor people languishing in want and misery; if his comments on the causes of their misery are sharper than I would wish, this should be attributed to his devotion to the poor and his burning zeal for religion, although, according to some, he may have gone beyond the bounds of prudence. It is absolutely certain, however, that he is completely opposed to civil disturbance.

p. 29   Sugrue's comments on his clergy   (De)

I can speak favourably of the qualities of the ecclesiastics; some are very pious, very hard-working and full of zeal; very many give satisfaction by their diligence and preaching.

p. 29   Murray's comments on his clergy   (id)

It is my supreme consolation that the clergy subject to me, unworthy and almost useless as I am, are deeply imbued with zeal for religion, of good morals, and so diligently engaged in preaching the word of God and the other duties of their office that many non-Catholics, through God's grace, are being restored daily to the bosom of holy mother church.

p. 29   Slattery's comments on his clergy   (tam)

both in the administration of the sacraments and in preaching the word of the Lord, each works with commendable diligence, to the best of his ability. They are pastors fervent in zeal and they diligently cultivate the vineyard of the Lord. No scandal requiring serious remedy exists among them.

p. 30   Armagh Synod 1834/5   (qui)

who advise or help lay people to bar the church doors against the parish priest or his lawfully appointed vicar, or who instigate them to withhold the customary fees from them

p. 35   Connaught bishops on priests' fees   (Pro)

For marriages, a sovereign, in addition to the voluntary offerings customary in some places. Where such offerings are not made, the priest may demand, in their place, five English shillings.

p. 36   Leinster bishops on priests' fees   (Post)

Five shillings to be paid after the celebration of baptism, forty shillings after the celebration of marriage; ten shillings for letters of freedom to marry, two shillings for private masses.

p. 93   Fransoni to MacHale, 26 Feb. 1839   (Optarem)
I would indeed strongly desire not only that you avoid taking part in political
controversies, but also that at any meeting or assembly whatever, you refrain
from speaking openly in a way that would signify that you are involved in
political controversies.

p. 101   Altieri to Lambruschini, 5 Nov. 1843   (Il bello)
And the best of it was that the same fierce Tory claimed that such a measure
would have to be counter-balanced by the severe public reprimand that,
according to him, it was the Holy Father's duty to issue to the Catholic clergy
of Ireland forbidding them to support the agitation for the Repeal of the
Union.

p. 101   Altieri to Lambruschini, 5 Nov. 1843   (Nel)
In the heat of his exposition he forgot himself to the point of saying that "the
pope does not think himself obliged to check the Irish *rebellion*, the British
government will not consider itself bound either to refuse assistance to the
Bolognese should they ask for it in support of their claims."

p. 102   Altieri to Lambruschini, 5 Nov. 1843   (Simili)
Such blunders can give some idea of the passions that sway the English
cabinet and its agents.

p. 102   Altieri to Lambruschini, 15 Nov. 1843   (non)
not all the wrong is on the side of the oppressed but that the government has
a large part in it since it does not spontaneously grant them what is theirs in
justice and equity.

p. 102   Altieri to Lambruschini, 15 Nov. 1843   (mentre)
while the Prince assures the British government of the commitment with
which the Holy Father reproves the revolutionary tendencies of the Irish
Catholics, he perhaps takes more liberty than he should in giving them to
understand that the conduct of Mr. O'Connell and his supporters is in all
its aspects judged blameworthy in the eyes of the head of the church and has
therefore met with his severest censure.

p. 104   Promemoria from Lambruschini to Metternich,   (quantunque)
                            Feb. 1844
to what extent it may be hoped that the reports of speeches that were not
written but improvised with passion and heard with corresponding passion
may not always prove to be exact.

p. 105   Promemoria from Lambruschini to Metternich, Feb. 1844   (Ora)
Now on the basis of this consideration which the Holy Father cannot but
regard as an irrefragable canon for the prudent orientation of his pastoral
ministry, it will easily be allowed that a public condemnation of the conduct
of the Irish clergy would be a misguided measure on the part of the Holy See
in the present circumstances.

p. 105   Altieri to Lambruschini, 8 March 1844   (le vie)
the direct and indirect ways that the British government uses to bring the

Holy See to add to the government's material force the highly authoritative efficacy of its voice to suffocate the complaints of the oppressed and unhappy Irish.

p. 109   Altieri reporting Gordon to Lambruschini,   (discorrendomi)
8 March 1844
In his discussion with me regarding O'Connell's condemnation he gave me to understand that if O'Connell together with the Irish Catholic clergy ... instead of fomenting an illegal and unreasonable rising would give up the idea of the Repeal of the Union ... and content themselves with setting out the grievances of which the Irish people complain, it would be easy to accord them the justice that is due to them, especially as he did not deny that they are right to demand it on several points, above all in regard to the burdens they bear to the advantage of the Anglican church.

p. 109   Altieri reporting Gordon to Lambruschini,   (nella)
8 March 1844
in the mouth of one who was forever repeating that his government was not bound to do anything for the Irish, nor inclined to do so.

p. 155   Fransoni to Cullen, 11 Oct. 1844   (cui)
who is very anxious that ecclesiastics should abstain from taking part in political affairs.

p. 159   Acton to Lambruschini, 8 Nov. 1844   (È)
It is uncertain whether a proposal of this kind would have been able, in the present times, to command a majority of the votes. What is certain, however, is that the hopes of the clergy and Catholics of Ireland would have increased at the prospect of seeing the interests of the church defended in Parliament by an orator in whom they had confidence.

p. 159   Acton to Lambruschini, 8 Nov. 1844   (Il)
The ministry chose, and, it must be confessed, most inopportunely, the very time when O'Connell was detained in Dublin Castle to introduce its bill.

p. 160   Acton to Lambruschini, 8 Nov. 1844   (L'effetto)
The outcome, however, has shown that the part taken by some of the Irish Catholic bishops in the running of the said schools kept them from falling exclusively into Protestant hands and served to offset the dangers and disadvantages of the said system.

p. 160   Acton to Lambruschini, 8 Nov. 1844   (non)
there can be no doubt about the expediency of their acceptance, which would be the only means of making up for the disadvantages that have existed for a long time and which the present law has not removed, though it has considerably lessened them. Moreover, the acceptance of the position of commissioner on the part of the bishops does not mean that the law could not, with time, be improved and made more favourable to the church.

p. 161   Vizzardelli's dubium   (se)
whether and in what manner it would be advisable for action to be taken on

the part of the Holy See in regard to the new law. What and in what manner it would be advisable to reply to the English government or to Mr. Petre.

p. 162   Account of meeting of Congregation, 24 Nov. 1844   (prevalse)
on the contrary there prevailed a reflection based on the main thrust and purpose of the law under discussion which, in the final analysis, tends to give the British government control of the future temporalities of the Irish church and thereby begin to strip the church of that independence which, amid the persecutions of the past, she had always preserved.

p. 162   Account of meeting of Congregation, 24 Nov. 1844   (quando)
since none of the Irish bishops had appealed to the Holy See about it, it was up to then not known what they themselves would have decided in their above mentioned meeting in Dublin.

p. 162   Account of meeting of Congregation, 24 Nov. 1844   (Dilatta)
postponed, that is, that for now any instruction to the bishops of Ireland in the matter should be deferred.

p. 162   Account of meeting of Congregation,   (Respondendum)
                              24 Nov. 1844
The reply is that it is not advisable for the Holy See to intervene since up to now the bishops have not consulted it: however, if the bishops should write later, the Holy See will advise them to take a conciliatory approach - on the understanding that this reply be couched in the most informal terms; and it should then be given in writing (without signature) so as not to expose it to the risk of being all too easily altered in the course of verbal communication.

p. 163   Lambruschini to Petre, 29 Nov. 1844   (Il)
The outcome of their meeting will therefore bring out whether they have other reasons for cooperating or not cooperating in the application of the law.

p. 205   Pope Gregory to Count Struwe, 1 Feb. 1845   (Gli fu)
He was also made to reflect on the bad impression occasioned among Catholics scattered around the whole world by the fear of not being protected by the Holy See and by the mere suspicion of secret negotiations and agreements between the Holy See and the respective governments; and in this regard reference was made to the fact of the great alarm of the Irish and English Catholics caused by the mere rumour of a concordat said to have been concluded between the Holy See and the British cabinet.

p. 206   Pope Gregory to Metternich, March 1845   (Conviene)
It is therefore advisable to keep in mind the sinister impression that would be made on Catholics scattered throughout the whole world by the secret negotiation of a concordat in which they would perhaps fear their cause abandoned for partisan political considerations. Most recent is the fact of the great alarm of English and Irish Catholics at the mere rumour of a concordat that had been, or was about to be, concluded between the Holy See and the British cabinet.

p. 206   MacHale to Pope Gregory, 25 Nov. 1844   (ex quo)
from the time that our people was first brought to the faith of the holy, Catholic

and Roman church by your holy predecessor, Celestine, never was that faith in greater peril.

p. 207   Fransoni to MacHale, 30 Dec. 1844   (nonnisi)
only by the mutual cooperation of the venerable prelates, and by their prudent unanimous and calm plan of action, can it be hoped that whatever in the aforesaid law of Her Majesty's government is contrary to the canons of the church or inconsistent with the principles of the Catholic religion, will be eventually emended by the government itself, through the petitions of the bishops presented at the right time and in due form.

p. 227   Bishops to Propaganda, 5 Dec. 1793   (ab)
all voted unanimously that in the training of our clergy or in the erection or administration of our seminaries, we should have no dealing nor anything in common with this Dublin university of the Protestants even though a recent law or act of Parliament enacted the contrary. All the bishops thought that it would be better to die in our own pure simplicity.

p. 322   Cullen to Fransoni, 27 Aug. 1845   (egli)
He and four Protestants last week called on the viceroy of Ireland to entreat him to have one of the said universities put in the city of Armagh. It is believed that the archbishop of Dublin will in a few days follow the example of the archbishop of Armagh with whom he already privately agrees.

p. 324   Fransoni to Crolly, 20 Sept. 1845   (relatum)
I have been informed that your Grace who previously, to the delight of all good people in Ireland, had taken care to declare that the system which the government recently introduced for the education of the youth was dangerous to the faith and morals of Catholics, now encourages the system and deems it in no way dangerous. It was further stated that you are striving to have a college or university conformable to that system established in your own diocese.

p. 325   Crolly to Fransoni, 10 Oct. 1845   (votis)
consenting to our wishes, the government … approved very important amendments to the system.

p. 325   Fransoni to Murray, 25 Nov. 1845   (tales)
were of such a nature that young Catholics could take part in the system without risk to faith and morals.

p. 327   Letter of the Archbishops of Armagh and Dublin,   (Dum)
                    24 Nov. 1845
While this was taking place in the bishops' meeting, Mr. Daniel O'Connell called a meeting of the populace hoping by its aid and its voice publicly expressed to force us to condemn the law unanimously. The result was that our consultation could scarcely be called free.

p. 329   Fornari to Lambruschini, 23 Dec. 1843   (contro)
against the danger that threatened to corrupt all the youth of France.

p. 329   Fornari to Lambruschini, 23 Dec. 1843   (guardandomi)
taking care always that the government not find out about it lest it have its
press say that the bishops' conduct is disapproved of by the Holy See.

p. 333   Letter of archbishops of Tuam and Cashel,   (hoc etiam)
25 Nov. 1845
Again and again we ask, why it was not seen fit to consult the Catholic bishops
with regard to a system of education introduced chiefly in the interests of
Catholics? why, if the government was in good faith did it not courteously
accept, even in some respect, the suggestions of the bishops? why rather did it
scornfully reject them?

p. 334   Letter of archbishops of Tuam and Cashel,   (Objicimus)
25 Nov. 1845
Since the government intended this system for all the Irish nation, seven
eighths of which are Catholic, we object that it did not establish a Catholic
system of education for Catholics or at least attach to this system such conditions as would protect the Catholic religion. This would have been only
what is just all the more since the Catholics do not have a single institution
for secular academic education subventioned by the government, whereas the
Protestants have many ... to wit Dublin University.

p. 334   Letter of archbishops of Tuam and Cashel,   (Ut alia)
25 Nov. 1845
To give one example; lately Protestants in Co. Cork did just that and, in spite
of the bishop, nominated a suspended priest named Sullivan.

p. 334   Letter of the archbishops of Tuam and Cashel,   (Potestas)
25 Nov. 1845
The secular power replaced its sword in its sheath ... now it sets out to woo
men's minds by concessions, partly genuine, partly spurious.

p. 334   Letter of the archbishops of Tuam and Cashel,   (etiam)
25 Nov. 1845
even now in the bosom of the Catholic church in Ireland, the British government has a few committed to its side, by whose support it hopes in religious
matters to divide and rule.

p. 336   Letter of the archbishops of Armagh and Dublin,   (curae)
24 Nov. 1845
to the care of Protestant ministers who strove to the utmost to draw the
Catholic students away from the Catholic faith.

p. 336   Letter of the archbishops of Armagh and Dublin,   (eodem)
24 Nov. 1845
are based on the same principle as the national system for the benefit of the
poor already in use in every Irish diocese except Tuam.

p. 336   Letter of the archbishops of Armagh and Dublin,   (solicitum)
24 Nov. 1845
was anxious ... to remove completely all our doubts concerning dangers to
faith and morals.

p. 342   Slattery to Pius IX, 27 March 1848   (Qui sunt)
who are those who by the people and in all the papers throughout Ireland are
now commonly called government bishops? Those very minority bishops.

p. 343   Murray to Fransoni, 11 Dec. 1845   (Pro certo)
I am convinced that our government had no intention of harming our religion
through this system, and had no object in mind other than to open impartially
the portals of knowledge to all who wish to enter.

p. 346   Cullen's voto (Opinion) 31 Jan. 1846   (i vantaggi)
the advantages arising from it will always affect temporal things, the losses
will affect our eternal interests.

p. 347   Cullen's voto (Opinion) 31 Jan. 1846   (Si potrebbe)
One could write to the same bishops with the advice that they should commit
themselves to the improvement of the Catholic colleges already existing or,
where necessary, found new ones in imitation of the bishops of Belgium who
to counter the damage caused by the liberal universities founded a Catholic
one.

p. 347   Congregation's decision 13 July 1846   (si crede)
believed that it was its duty to warn the venerable Irish prelates not to take
any part in implementing such a scheme of education.

BIBLIOGRAPHY

A   Manuscript Collections
B   Parliamentary Debates and Papers
C   Contemporary Newspapers and Journals
D   Contemporary Works
E   Collections of Printed Correspondence,
    Memoirs, Diaries and Biographies
F   Secondary Sources: (1) Unpublished Theses
                        (2) Published Works
G   Works of Reference

A.   MANUSCRIPT COLLECTIONS

I. IRELAND

DUBLIN

Commission of Charitable Donations and Bequests for Ireland,
128 Lower Baggott Street

These archives contain the annual reports of the Commission from 1846 onwards. The first report (1846) gives information on the operation of the old board and on the new methods adopted by the board established in 1844.

Dublin Diocesan Archives, Archbishop's House, Drumcondra

Charitable Bequests Act:
One bound volume containing news cuttings for 1845 and Murray's pastoral of December 1844.

Cullen Papers:
Papers of Cardinal Paul Cullen (1803-78), archbishop of Dublin. These papers deal almost exclusively with the period after 1852 and were less useful than his earlier papers. *See below under* Archives of the Irish College.

Hamilton Papers:
Correspondence of John Hamilton (*c*.1800-62), archdeacon of Dublin, 29 files. This correspondence covers the period 1820-60.

Maynooth College File:
A single file containing miscellaneous documents for the years 1796-1849.

Meetings of the Irish Bishops 1826-49:
A single handwritten volume containing a record of the meetings and resolutions of the bishops. Occasionally, the minutes of the meetings are given.

Murray Papers:
Correspondence etc. of Daniel Murray (1768-1852), archbishop of Dublin, 43 files: a source of prime importance. The correspondence covers the period 1809-52.

Nicholson Papers:
Correspondence of Francis Nicholson (1803-55), coadjutor archbishop of Corfu, 2 files. The correspondence covers the period 1829-54.

National Library of Ireland

Davis Papers:
Correspondence of Thomas Davis (1814-45).

Duffy Papers:
Correspondence of Sir Charles Gavan Duffy (1816-1903).

O'Connell Papers:
Correspondence of Daniel O'Connell (1775-1847). Through the kindness of Professor Maurice R. O'Connell, I was able to consult the transcripts of his complete edition of the *O'Connell Correspondence.*

Trinity College

Pelham Papers:
Secret ministerial letters from his excellency, Earl Camden, lord lieutenant of Ireland to his grace, the duke of Portland, with some to the right hon. William Pitt, and the right hon. Thomas Pelham, and to Earl Spencer, 1795-7. These letters are a transcription of the originals in the Pelham MSS in the British Library.

HOLLY PARK, CO. GALWAY

Blake Papers:
Correspondence of Anthony Richard Blake (1786-1849).

MAYNOOTH, CO. KILDARE

Archives of St. Patrick's College, Maynooth

Only the more important sources are listed below.

Accounts of Expenditure and of Pensions and Fees of Admission from 1800 to 1845:
These are uncatalogued MSS in the office of the president of the college.

Accounts of the Trustees of the Roman Catholic College 1795-1845, 2 vols.:
These two important volumes contain the balance sheets of the college with
details of expenditure. They are uncatalogued mss in the Bursar's office.

Journal of the Board of Trustees:
This single handwritten volume contains the minutes of the meetings of the
trustees from 24 June 1795 to 29 June 1881.

*Lee, W. M., Index to the Journal of Trustees of Maynooth College,
Vol. 1 from 1795 to [1942]:*
Two handwritten volumes. The original volume was drawn up in 1856,
revised in 1884 and continued in later years.

Ordinations and Prize Lists 1795-1845:
This handwritten volume contains the names of students promoted to
orders and of prize-winners. It also contains information on appointments
and on official visits.

MONAGHAN, CO. MONAGHAN

Clogher Diocesan Archives

Kernan Papers:
Correspondence etc. of Dr Edward Kernan (1771-1844), bishop of Clogher.

McNally Papers:
Correspondence etc. of Dr Charles McNally (1787-1864), bishop of
Clogher.

Donnelly Papers:
Correspondence etc. of Dr James Donnelly (1823-93), bishop of Clogher.

NEWRY, CO. DOWN

Dromore Diocesan Archives, Violet Hill, Newry

This archive contains a few letters of Dr Michael Blake (1775-1860) bishop
of Dromore, of Archbishop Murray, and Archbishop MacHale.

THURLES, CO. TIPPERARY

Cashel Diocesan Archives

Slattery Papers:
Correspondence etc. of Dr Michael Slattery (1783-1857), archbishop of
Cashel. This collection contains valuable papers on the Academic Colleges
question.

Leahy Papers:
Correspondence etc. of Dr Patrick Leahy (1807-75), archbishop of Cashel.

Both collections were consulted on microfilm.

Stencilled calendars, drawn up by Dr M. Tierney, provide a comprehensive guide to both the Slattery and Leahy papers.

II. ENGLAND

LONDON

British Library: Additional Manuscripts

Aberdeen Papers:
Correspondence of George Hamilton-Gordon, 4th earl of Aberdeen (1784-1860); Add. MSS 43151-67.

Gladstone Papers:
Correspondence and papers of William Ewart Gladstone (1809-98):
Add. MSS 44735 Memoranda 1844.
            44735 Memoranda 1845-July 1846.
            44777 Memoranda 1837-51; many deal with the
                         question of Maynooth College.

Peel Papers:
Correspondence and papers of Sir Robert Peel, 2nd Bt. (1788-1850); Add. MSS 40185; 40205; 40281; 40318-40; 40446; 40449-51; 40478-81; 40540; 40551: correspondence with Sir James Graham, Lord De Grey, Lord Eliot, Lord Heytesbury, Sir Thomas Fremantle, and with Queen Victoria and Prince Albert.

Wellesley Papers:
Official and general Correspondence of Richard Colley Wellesley, 1st Marquis Wellesley (1760-1842):
Add. MSS 37306-7   Correspondence, 1832-5.
            37311-13   Correspondence, 1831-42.

Public Record Office

Foreign Office Papers:
FO 7/310 Correspondence from Sir Robert Gordon (1791-1847),
                 ambassador at Vienna; January-June 1843.
FO 7/311 Idem, July-December 1843.
FO 7/316 Idem, January-June 1844.
FO 7/317 Idem, July-December 1844.
FO 43/38 Correspondence from Mr William Petre (1796-1858),
                 government agent in Rome.
FO 43/55 Letters from Petre, July 1844-December 1848.

Home Office Papers:
HO 45/1261   Translation of an article from the *Piedmontese Gazette*
                    on the Charitable Bequests Bill, 1845.

HO 45/1656/1 Cabinet decision on Academic Colleges, November 1844.
HO 45/1656/2 Academic Colleges: sites, courses, staff, August 1845.
HO 45/1656/3 Academic Colleges: charter etc. Secondary schools,
December 1845.
HO 45/1656/5 Schools for middle classes.
HO 45/1702 Report of Visitation of Maynooth College 1846.

Russell Papers:
Correspondence, private and official Papers of Lord John Russell, 1st Earl
Russell (1792-1878):
PRO 30/22/4 A-E Correspondence 1839-45.
PRO 30/22/5 A-C Correspondence 1846.

NETHERBY, CUMBERLAND

Graham Papers:
Papers of Sir James Graham (1792-1861). Consulted on microfilm in the
Bodleian and the National Library of Ireland. A collection of great impor-
tance for this work.

NOTTINGHAM

Nottingham University Library

Newcastle Papers:
Papers of Henry Pelham Pelham Clinton, earl of Lincoln, 5th duke of
Newcastle-under-Lyme (1811-64). Lincoln was chief secretary in Ireland
from February to July 1846. Consulted on microfilm in the National
Library of Ireland.

OXFORD

Bodleian Library

Clarendon Papers:
Papers of George William Frederick Villiers, 4th Earl of Clarendon (1800-
1870). The letterbooks for the period during which he was lord lieutenant
of Ireland (1847-52) are of interest for their lively and often shrewd
comment on many of the church leaders of the day.

Derby Papers:
Papers of Edward George Geoffrey Smith Stanley, 14th Earl of Derby
(1799-1869). Through the kindness of Lord Blake, provost of the Queen's
College, Oxford, I was able to inspect this valuable collection.

PORT ELIOT, CORNWALL

St. Germans Archives:
Correspondence of Edward Granville, 3rd Earl of Saint Germans (1798-
1877).

WINDSOR CASTLE

Royal Archives:
Prime Ministers' Correspondence: Sir Robert Peel 1841-6: Vols. A.C.D. Consulted on microfilm.

III ROME

Archives of the Irish College: Pontificio Collegio Irlandese, via Santi Quattro
Cullen Papers:
Correspondence etc of Cardinal Paul Cullen (1803-78). This collection, which contains the correspondence received by Cullen in the period before 1850, proved particularly valuable. It is cited as 'Cullen Papers'; the Cullen correspondence in the Dublin Diocesan Archives is cited as 'Cullen Papers, DDA'.

Kirby Papers:
Correspondence etc. of Tobias Kirby (1804-95), titular archbishop of Ephesus. Contains important correspondence from Cullen and other Irish ecclesiastics from 1836 to 1895.

Archives of the Congregation of Propaganda Fide
Acta congregationum generalium anni 1846-9, vols. 209-12:
These *acta* constitute a series of registers containing the minutes and decisions of the general meeting of the Sacred Congregation and, as such, are of fundamental importance.

Scritture originali riferite nelle congregazioni generali dell Anno 1846
da Gennaio a tutte Dicembre, vol. 968:
This important volume contains the documents to which reference was made at the general meetings and on which the decisions taken were based.

Scritture riferite nei congressi, Irlanda, dal 1843 al 1846, vol. 28:
The 'congressi' were sub-committees set up by the Sacred Congregation. This volume contains all the papers submitted to the congressi on Ireland during these years.

Lettere e decreti della Sacra Congregazione e Biglietti di Monsignore Segretario -
1845, vol. 332:
This set of registers contain the replies sent out by the Congregation. A few letters are relevant to the present work.

Archivio Segreto Vaticano
Archivio della Nunziatura di Vienna:
Vols 280, 280A, 280B, 280C, 280D, 280E, 280F, 280G. Correspondence of Ludovico Altieri (1805-67), nuncio to Austria, with the secretary for state from 1836-44.
Vols 281Q, 281R, 281S. Correspondence of Luigi Lambruschini (1776-1854), cardinal secretary for state, with Altieri, 1843-5.

Archivio Storico: Congregatio pro negotiis Ecclesiasticis Extraordinariis, Inghilterra. Anno 1844. Pos. 46. Fasc, 18, 19, 20, 21:
This dossier contains the material at the disposal of the Congregation when it took its decision on the Charitable Bequests Act in 1844. It sheds light on the decision-making process of the Congregation and on the views of the cardinals concerning the church in Ireland and the English government. The documentation is extensive, ranging from newspaper reports to submissions from the interested parties and translations of the 1829 Relief Act and the Bequests Act of 1844. The dossier also contains the minutes of the Congregation's meetings of 24 November 1844 and the draft replies to Petre, Murray, and MacHale.

This Congregation, originally established to deal with church affairs in revolutionary France, was placed on a permanent basis by Pius VII in 1814. It was better known under its Italian name: Congregazione degli Affari Ecclesiastici Straordinari (AA.EE.SS.).

B. PARLIAMENTARY DEBATES AND PAPERS

Hansard's Parliamentary Debates. Except when otherwise indicated citations are from the Third Series i-xcvi (1830-48).

Papers presented to the House of Commons relating to the Royal College of Saint Patrick, Maynooth, PP 1808, ix. 371.

Minutes of Evidence taken before the Select Committee appointed to inquire into the Disturbances in Ireland ... PP 1825, vii.

Reports from the Select Committee appointed to inquire into the State of Ireland ... PP 1825, viii.

Minutes of Evidence taken before the Select Committee of the House of Lords, appointed to inquire into the State of Ireland ... PP 1825, ix.

Eighth Report of the Commissioners of Irish Education: Roman Catholic College of Maynooth, PP 1826-7, xiii. 537-998.

Report from the Select Committee on the Irish Miscellaneous Estimates with Minutes of Evidence and Appendix, PP 1829, iv. 127-442.

First and Second Reports from the Select Committee, Commons, on Tithes in Ireland, PP 1831-2, xxi.

First and Second Reports from the Select Committee, Lords, appointed to inquire into the collection and payment of Tithes in Ireland ... PP 1831-2, xxii.

First Report of the Commissioners of Public Instruction, Ireland, PP 1835, xxxiii.

Return of the number of students in the Roman Catholic College at Maynooth, during the years 1840, 1841 and 1842; also the number of professors employed therein, and their respective salaries and emoluments, PP 1843, li. 55-6.

Report from the Select Committee on Mortmain together with minutes of evidence, PP 1844, x. 507-754.

Returns relating to the College of Maynooth, PP 1845, xxviii. 334.

Report of a Visitation held at the College of Maynooth, on 20th day of April, 1846, PP 1846, xlii, 209-13.

Report of Her Majesty's Commissioners appointed to inquire into the management and government of the College of Maynooth..., PP 1854-5, xxii.

Report of Her Majesty's Commissioners appointed to inquire into the Progress and Condition of the Queen's Colleges ... *1857-8*, xxi.

List of the Trustees of Maynooth College from the 5th June 1795 to 13th April 1869, PP 1868-9, xxxiv. 329-31.

C. CONTEMPORARY NEWSPAPERS AND JOURNALS

L'Ami de la Religion
Annual Register
Dublin Evening Mail
Dublin Evening Post
Dublin Monitor
Dublin Review
Dublin Weekly Register
Edinburgh Review
Freeman's Journal
Morning Chronicle
Nation
Pilot
Punch
Record
Tablet
The Times

D. CONTEMPORARY PAMPHLETS, WORKS ETC.

Alvanley, Lord [William Arden], *The State of Ireland considered* (London, 1841).

Authentic report of great Protestant meeting at Liverpool (Liverpoool, n.d.).

Battersby, W. J., *The Catholic priesthood of Ireland vindicated* (Dublin, n.d.).

Beaumont, G. de, *L'Irlande Sociale Politique et Religeuse*, 2 vols. (Paris, 1863).

Bickersteth, E., *Remarks on the progress of Popery* ... (London, 1836).

Blackburn, J., *The Maynooth Grant* ... (London, 1845).

Calumny refuted, or remarks on a pamphlet of the Rev. William Phelan, F.T.C.D., entitled 'The Bible, not the Bible Society'; by a Student of the R.C. College of Maynooth (Dublin, 1817).

Carleton, W., *Traits and stories of the Irish peasantry*, 2 vols. (Dublin, 1843-4).

The Case of Maynooth College considered ... (Dublin, 1836).

Cavour, C. de, *Considerations on the present and future prospects of Ireland* (London, 1845).

Clifford, H. C., *Letters addressed to the Right Hon. Lord Alvanley on his pamphlet entitled The State of Ireland considered* ... (London, 1841).

Colquhoun, J. C., *Ireland: Popery and priestcraft the cause of her misery and crime* (Glasgow, 1836).

—— *Speech at Exeter Hall on the Maynooth College Grant* (London, 1836).

Common sense v. Bigotry: or reasons for supporting the parliamentary grant to Maynooth ... (London, 1845).

Conybeare, W. J., 'The Church in the Mountains', *Essays Ecclesiastical and Social* (London, 1855), pp. 1-56.

Coppinger, W., *Monita pastoralia et statute ecclesiastica, pro unitis diocesibus Cloynensi et Rossensi ... promulgata AD 1775...quae nunc etiam vigent AD 1821, sub ... Gulielmo Coppinger, Episcopo Cloynensi et Rossensi ...* (Cork, 1821).

Crolly, G., *The life of Most Rev. Dr Crolly* (Dublin, 1851).

Croly, D. O., *An essay religious and political on ecclesiastical finance as regards the Roman Catholic Church in Ireland ...* (Cork, 1834).

D'Alton, J., *Letter on the Irish Colleges Bill and on Academic Education generally* (Dublin, 1845).

Dechy, E., *Voyage: Irlande en 1846 et 1847* (Paris, 1847).

Decreta Synodi Plenariae Episcoporum Hiberniae apud Thurles habitae anno 1850 (Dublin, 1851).

Dens, P., *Theologia moralis et dogmatica*, 8 vols. (Dublin, 1832).

Doyle, J., *A letter...in consequence of unjust animadversions against the Roman Catholic Religion* (Dublin, 1822).

Fagan, W., *The Life and Times of Daniel O'Connell*, 2 vols. (Cork, 1848).

Fitzpatrick, W. J., *The Life, Times and Contemporaries of Lord Cloncurry* (Dublin, 1855).

Froude, R. H., *Remains*, 4 vols. (Derby, 1839).

Full report of the great Protestant meeting at the Town Hall, Birmingham, 18 Nov. 1835 containing the speeches ... of Rev Robert M'Ghee and Rev. Mortimer O'Sullivan (Birmingham, 1835).

Grant, J., *Impressions of Ireland and the Irish*, 2 vols. (London, 1844).

Greville, C., *Past and Present Policy of England towards Ireland* (London, 1845).

Hall, Mr and Mrs S. C., *Ireland, Its Scenery and Character, etc.* 3 vols. (London, 1841-3).

Hear both sides: and read the letters which have lately passed between the Protestants and the Roman Catholics in Worcester, on the formation of a Protestant Association there (Worcester, 1835).

Historical statements as to Maynooth College (London, n.d.).

Hope, A. J. B., *The new government's scheme of academical education for Ireland* (London, 1845).

Inglis, H. D., *Ireland in 1834: Journey throughout Ireland during the Spring, Summer and Autumn of 1834*, 2 vols. (3rd ed., London, 1835).

Johnson, J., *A Tour in Ireland*, 2 vols. (London, 1844).

Kelly, O., *Acta, decreta et ordinata sub III^mo. D. Oliverio Kelly, Archiepiscopo Tuamensi ... ejusque Suffragensis, diebus 6ta, 7ma et 8va Mensis Maii, Anno Domini 1817* (Tuam, 1817).

Kelly, T., *Statuta dioecesana in archidioecesi Ardmachensi observanda et a RRmo Thoma Kelly...in sua synodo diocesani edita et promulgata, hebdomeda 3a mensis Aug. AD 1834* (Dublin, 1834).

Lay Protestant, *Strictures on the letter of...Dr Murray ... relative to Dens' Theology* (Dublin, 1836).

Lay Roman Catholic, *The Charitable Bequests Act; a letter to the Most Reverend Doctor Murray* (Dublin, 1844).

Leahy, P., *Thoughts on Academical Education* (Dublin, 1845).

Lever, C., *The Confessions of Harry Lorrequer* (Dublin, 1839).

—— *Charles O'Malley, the Irish Dragoon*, 2 vols. (Dublin, 1841).

—— *St. Patricks Eve* (London, 1845).

Lewis, G. C., *On local disturbances in Ireland and on the Irish Church question* (London, 1836).

Lord, J., *Maynooth College or the law affecting the grant to Maynooth* ... (London, 1841).

Mac Bionaid, A., *Dánta*, ed. T. Ó Fiaich and L. Ó Caithnia (Naas, 1979).

MacDonnell, E., *An appeal to the opponents of the Maynooth Grant* ... (London, 1845).

—— *Letter to the Rt. Hon. William Ewart Gladstone, M.P. respecting the Maynooth Grant* (London, n.d.).

M'Ghee, R. J., *The doctrines promulgated by the Romish bishops in Ireland AD 1832* (London, 1836).

M'Ghee, R. J., & O'Sullivan, M., *Popery in Maynooth as supported by the British government* ... (London, 1839).

Madden, D. O., *Ireland and its rulers since 1829*, 2 vols. (London, 1844).

Martineau, H., *History of England during the Thirty Years Peace*, 2 vols. (London, 1849).

Maynooth College, No. I. Its teaching, collected from its own class-books (London, n.d.).

Maynooth College, No. II. Its teaching, collected from its own class-books (London, n.d.).

Maynooth, The Crown, and the Country (London, 1845).

Meagher, W., *Notice on the life and character of His Grace Most Rev. Daniel Murray late Archbishop of Dublin* ... *with historical and biographical notes* (Dublin, 1853).

Murray, D., *Pastoral address on his return from Rome* (Dublin, 1836).

—— *Pastoral address to the Roman Catholic clergy and laity of the diocese of Dublin* (Dublin, 1844).

—— *Statuta diocesana, per provinciam Dublinensem observanda et a RR.DD. Daniele Murray* ... *Jacobo Keating* ... *Guilielmo Kinsella* ... *edita et promulgata* ... *Mensis Julii, AD 1831* (Dublin, 1831).

Nemo, *A few words on the new Irish Colleges* (London, 1845).

Newman, J. H., *Lectures on the present position of Catholics in England addressed to the brothers of the Oratory in the summer of 1851* (London, 1899).

Noel, B. W., *Notes on a short tour through the Midland counties of Ireland in the summer of 1836* ... (London, 1837).

O'Beirne, E. F., *A succinct and accurate account of the system of discipline, education and theology, adopted and pursued in the Popish College of Maynooth* (Hereford, 1840).

O'Higgins, W., *A warning voice from Prussia: Government influence on education* (Dublin, 1845).

O'Sullivan, M. *The case of the Protestants of Ireland stated, with notes* (London, 1836).

O'Sullivan, M., and M'Ghee, R. J., *Romanism as it rules in Ireland*, 2 vols. (London, 1840).

Parnell, W., *Maurice and Berghetta, or the priest of Rahery* (London, 1819).

Perceval, D. N., *Maynooth and the Jew Bill* (London, 1845).

Perceval, S., *Speech ... on the first Roman Catholic petition ... (13 May 1805)*, ed. D. Perceval (London, 1844).

The popish college of Maynooth ... (London, 1839).

Publications of the Protestant Association, Vol. I. (London, 1839).

The real tenets of the Church of Rome (London, 1835).

Report of the meeting held at Worcester on 13 Jan. 1837 for the purpose of receiving a deputation from the British Society for promoting the religious principles of the Reformation (Worcester, n.d.).

Reports of the Parliamentary Committee of the National Repeal Association of Ireland, 2 vols. (Dublin 1844-5).

A review of the Maynooth Endowment Bill (London, 1845).

Senior, W. N., 'Ireland', *Edinburgh Rev.*, lxxix (1844), 189-226.

—— *Journals, conversations and essays relating to Ireland*, Vol. I. (London, 1868).

Seymour, M. H. and Stoney, W. B., *Letters for conclusive evidence that the doctrines of the Church of Rome as laid down by Peter Dens, so far from being "obsolete" or "exploded" are fearfully in force at this day in the Kingdom of Ireland* (London, n.d.).

Shee, W., *The Act for the more effectual application of Charitable Donations and Bequests in Ireland* (Dublin, 1845).

Sheil, R. L. *Sketches Legal and Political*, 2 vols., ed. M. W. Savage (London, 1855).

Smith, S., *A fragment on the Irish Roman Catholic Church* (London, 1845).

'State Provision for the Irish clergy', *Dublin Rev.*, xvi. (1844), 186-220.

Statement of the views and objects of the Protestant Association (London, n.d.).

Tocqueville, A. de, *Journeys to England and Ireland*, ed. J. P. Mayer (London, 1958).

Todd, J. H. *University of Dublin: Remarks on some statements attributed to Thomas Wyse in his speech in Parliament on academical education in Ireland* (Dublin, 1844).

Trollope, A., *MacDermots of Ballycloran*, 3 vols. (London, 1847).

Wyse, T., *Historical sketch of the late Catholic Association of Ireland*, 2 vols. (London, 1829).

E. COLLECTIONS OF PRINTED CORRESPONDENCE, MEMOIRS, DIARIES AND BIOGRAPHIES

Burke, E., *Correspondence of Edmund Burke*, vol. viii, ed. R. B. McDowell (Cambridge, 1969).

—— *The works of the Right Honourable Edmund Burke*, ed. F. W. Raferty, Vol. v. (Oxford, n.d.).

Cloncurry, *Personal Recollections of the Life and Times with Extracts from the Correspondence of Valentine, Lord Cloncurry* (Dublin, 1849).

Creevey, T., *The Creevey Papers: A Selection from the Correspondence and Diaries of the late Thomas Creevey, M.P.*, ed. H. Maxwell, 2 vols. (London, 1903).

Croker, J. W., *Correspondence and diaries*, ed. L. J. Jennings, 3 vols. (London, 1885).

Curato, F., *Gran Bretagna e Italia nei documenti della missione Minto*, 2 vols. (Roma, 1970).

Doheny, M., *The Felon's Track or history of the attempted outbreak in Ireland ... 1843 to 1848* (Dublin, 1920; reprint of original ed. of 1849).

Fitzpatrick, W. J., *The life, times and correspondence of the Right Rev. Dr Doyle...* 2 vols. (new ed., 1890).

Gladstone, W. E., *Diaries:* Vols. I-IV, 1825-47, ed. M. R. D. Foot and H. C. G. Matthew (Oxford, 1968-74).

—— *The Prime Ministers' Papers*, ed. J. Brooke and M. Sorensen, 2 vols. (London, 1971-2).

Graham, *Life and letters of Sir James Graham, second Baronet of Netherby, 1792-1861*, ed. C. S. Parker, 2 vols. (London, 1907).

Greville, *The Greville Memoirs 1814-1860*, ed. L. Strachey and R. Fulford, 8 vols. (London, 1938).

McCullagh, W. T., *Memoirs of the Right Honourable Richard Lalor Sheil*, 2 vols. (London, 1855).

MacHale, J., *Letters* (Dublin, 1847).

Newman, J. H., *The letters and diaries of John Henry Newman*, ed. C. S. Dessain and V. F. Blehl, xiv-xvi (London, 1964).

O'Connell, D., *Correspondence of Daniel O'Connell, The Liberator*, ed. W. J. Fitzpatrick, 2 vols. (London, 1885).

—— *The Correspondence of Daniel O'Connell*, ed. M. R. O'Connell, 8 vols. (Shannon; Dublin 1972-81).

Ó Laoghaire, P., *Mo Sgéal Féin* (Dublin, 1915).

—— *My own story*, translated by Sheila O Sullivan (Dublin and London, 1973).

Ó Súilleabháin, A., *Cín Lae Amhlaoibh*, ed. T de Bhaldraithe (Dublin, 1970).

Peel, *Sir Robert Peel from his private papers*, ed. C. S. Parker, 3 vols. (London, 1891-4).

Raikes, *A portion of the journal kept by Thomas Raikes from 1831 to 1847*, 4 vols. (London, 1857).

Russell, J., 1st earl, *Recollections and suggestions, 1813-1873* (London, 1875).

—— *The later correspondence of Lord John Russell, 1840-1878*, ed. G. P. Gooch, 2 vols. (London, 1925).

Stewart, R., *Memoirs and Correspondence of Viscount Castlereagh, second Marquess of Londonderry*, ed. C. W. Vane, Marquess of Londonderry, 12 vols. (London, 1848-53).

Torrens, W. McCullagh, *Memoirs of the Right Honourable Richard Lalor Sheil*, 2 vols. (London, 1855).

Trevelyan, G. O., *The life and letters of Lord Macaulay* (London, 1893).

Victoria, Queen, *The letters of Queen Victoria: a selection from Her Majesty's correspondence between the years 1837 and 1861*, ed. A. C. Benson, Vols. 1 and 2 (London, 1908).

Wellesley, *The Wellesley Papers*, by the editor of 'The Windham Papers', 2 vols. (London, 1914).

F. SECONDARY SOURCES

(1) UNPUBLISHED THESES

Acheson, A. R., 'The evangelicals in the Church of Ireland, 1784-1859' (Queen's Univ. Belfast, Ph.D. thesis, 1968).

Bradley, I. C., 'The politics of Godliness: Evangelicals in Parliament 1784-1832' (Oxford Univ., D.Phil. thesis, 1974).

Cahill, G., 'Irish Catholicism and English Toryism, 1832-1848: A study in Ideology' (State University of Iowa, Ph.D. thesis, 1954).

Connolly, S. J., 'Catholicism and Social Discipline in Pre-Famine Ireland' (New University of Ulster, D.Phil. thesis, 1977).

Donajgrodzki, A. P., 'The Home Office, 1822-48' (Oxford Univ., D.Phil thesis, 1973).

O'Donoghue, P., 'The Catholic Church and Ireland in an age of Revolution and Rebellion, 1782-1803' (National Univ. of Ireland, Ph.D. thesis, 1975).

Rennie, I. S., 'Evangelicalism and English Public Life 1832-1850' (Univ. of Toronto, Ph.D. thesis, 1962).

Wallace, P., 'Irish Catechesis - the heritage from James Butler II, Archbishop of Cashel 1774-1791' (Catholic University of America, Ph.D. thesis, 1975).

Wöste, K., 'Englands Staats - und Kirchenpolitik in Irland 1795-1869, dargestellt an der Entwicklung des irischen Nationalseminars Maynooth College'. (Inaugural-Dissertation zur Erlangung der Doktorwürde der Katholisch-Theologischen Fakultät der Rheinischen Friedrich-Wilhelms-Universität zu Bonn, 1976).

(2) PUBLISHED WORKS

Anglesey, *One-Leg: the life and letters of Henry William Paget, first Marquess of Anglesey, K.G. 1768-1854* (London, 1961).

Ashwell, A. R. and Wilberforce, R. G., *Life of the Right Reverend Samuel Wilberforce*, 3 vols. (London, 1880-2).

Akenson, D. H., *The Irish Education Experiment: the National System of Education in the Nineteenth Century* (London, 1970).

—— *The Church of Ireland: ecclesiastical reform and revolution, 1800-1885* (London, 1971).

Auchmuty, J. J., *Sir Thomas Wyse, 1791-1862: the life and career of an educator and diplomat* (London, 1939).

Aydelotte, W. O., 'The disintegration of the Conservative Party in the 1840s: a study of political attitudes', *The Dimensions of Quantitative Research in History*, eds. W. O. Aydelotte, A. G. Bogue, R. W. Fogel (London, 1972).

Barry, P. C., 'The Holy See and the Irish National Schools' *IER*, series 5, xcii (1959), 90-105.

Bell, H. C. F., *Lord Palmerston*, 2 vols. (London, 1936).

Best, G. F. A., 'Popular Protestantism in Victorian Britain', *Ideas and Institutions of Victorian Britain*, ed. R. Robson (London, 1967).

Blake, M. J., *Blake Family Records* (London, 1905).

Bossy, J., *The English Catholic Community, 1570-1850* (London, 1975).

Bourke, U. J., *The life and times of the Most Rev. John MacHale, Archbishop of Tuam* (Dublin, 1882).

Bowen, D., *Souperism: Myth or reality? a study of Catholics and Protestants during the Great Famine* (Cork, 1970).

—— *The Protestant Crusade in Ireland, 1800-70* (Dublin, 1978).

Brady, J. C., *Religion and the Law of Charities in Ireland* (Belfast, n.d.).

Broderick, J. F., *The Holy See and the Irish Movement for the Repeal of the Union with England 1829-1847* (Rome, 1951).

Brynn, E., 'Robert Peel and the Church of Ireland', *Journal of Religious History*, vii (1972-3), 191-207.

Buckley, M., 'Attitudes to nationality in four nineteenth century novelists', *Cork Hist. Soc. Jn.*, lxxviii (1974), 129-36.

Bulwer, H. L. and Ashley, E., *The life of Henry John Temple, Viscount Palmerston: with selections from his correspondence*, 5 vols. (London, 1870-6).

Burke, O. J., *The History of the Catholic Archbishops of Tuam* (Dublin, 1882).

Burke Savage, R., *Catherine McAuley: the first sister of Mercy* (Dublin, 1955).

Cahill, G. A., 'Irish Catholicism and English Toryism', *Review of politics*, xix (1957), 62-76.

—— 'The Protestant Association and the Anti-Maynooth Agitation of 1845', *Cath. Hist. Rev.*, xliii (1957), 273-308.

—— 'Some Nineteenth-century roots of the Ulster problem, 1829-1848', *Irish University Review*, 1 (1971), 215-37.

Chadwick, O., *The Victorian Church*, 2 vols. (London 1966-70).

Coleridge, H. J., *The life of Mother Frances Mary Teresa Ball* ... (Dublin, 1881).

Condon, M., 'The Irish Church and the Reform Ministeries', *Journal of British Studies*, iii (1964), 121-62.

Connell, K. H., *Irish Peasant Society* (Oxford, 1968).

Corish, P. J. ed. *A history of Irish Catholicism*, Vol. v. parts vi-x (Dublin, 1970-71).

—— 'Irish College, Rome: Kirby papers', *Archiv Hib.*, xxx (1972), 29-115; xxxi (1973), 1-94.

—— 'Gallicanism at Maynooth: Archbishop Cullen and the Royal Visitation of 1853', *Studies in Irish History, presented to R. Dudley Edwards*, eds. A. Cosgrove and D. McCartney (Dublin, 1979).

Cowherd, R. G., *The politics of English Dissent* (New York, 1956).

Crosby, T. L., *Sir Robert Peel's administration 1841-1846* (London, 1976).

Crowther, M. A., *Church embattled: religious controversy in mid-Victorian England* (London, 1970).

D'Alton, E. A., *History of the Archdiocese of Tuam*, 2 vols. (Dublin, 1928).

De Brún, P., *Filíocht Sheáin Uí Bhraonáin* (Dublin, 1972).

De hÍde, D., *Abhráin agus Dánta an Reachtabhraigh* ... (Dublin, 1969).

Delany, V. T. H., *The law relating to charities in Ireland* (Dublin, n.d.).

Donajgrodzki, A. P., 'Sir James Graham at the Home Office', *Hist. Jn.*, xx (1977), 97-120.

Drescher, S., *Tocqueville and England* (Cambridge, Mass., 1964).

Duffy, C. G., *Young Ireland: a Fragment of Irish History, 1840-1845* (2nd ed. Dublin, 1880).

—— *Four years of Irish history 1845-1849: a sequel to 'Young Ireland'* (London, 1883).

—— *Thomas Davis, the Memoirs of an Irish Patriot 1840-1846* (London, 1890).

Eversley, G. J. Shaw-Lefevre, first baron, *Peel and O'Connell: A review of the Irish policy of parliament from the act of Union to the death of Sir R. Peel* (London, 1887).

Fitzpatrick, J. D., *Edmund Rice founder ... of the Brothers of the Christian Schools ...* (Dublin, 1945).

Freeman, T. W., *Pre-Famine Ireland, a study in historical geography* (Manchester, 1957).

Gash, N., *Politics in the age of Peel* (London, 1953).

—— *Mr Secretary Peel: the life of Sir Robert Peel to 1830* (London, 1961).

—— *Reaction and Reconstruction in English politics 1832-1852* (Oxford, 1965).

—— *Sir Robert Peel: the life of Sir Robert Peel after 1830* (London, 1972).

Grimaud, L., *Histoire de la liberté d'enseignement en France: La Restauration* (Paris, n.d.).

Gwynn, D., *Daniel O'Connell, the Irish Liberator* (London, 1929).

—— *O'Connell, Davis and the Colleges Bill* (Cork, 1948).

Haller, W., *Foxe's Book of Martyrs and the Elect Nation* (London, 1963).

Halévy, E., *A history of the English people in the nineteenth century, vol. iv: Victorian years, 1841-1895* (London, 1961).

Hamell, P. J., *Maynooth Students and Ordinations 1795-1895; Index: part II* (Maynooth, 1973).

Healy, J., *Maynooth College, its centenary history, 1795-1895* (Dublin, 1895).

Hegarty, W. J., 'The Irish hierarchy and the Queen's Colleges (1845-50)', *Cork University Record*, No. 5 (1945), 35-50.

Hill, J. R., Nationalism and the Catholic Church in the 1840s: views of Dublin Repealers', *IHS*, xix (1975), 371-95.

Hodder, E., *The life and work of the seventh earl of Shaftesbury*, 3 vols. (London, 1880-2).

Hogan, J. F., *Maynooth College and the Laity* (Dublin, 1910).

Hurst, M., *Maria Edgeworth and the public scene: intellect, fine feeling and landlordism in the age of reform* (London, 1969).

Joyful Mother of children: Mother Frances Mary Teresa Ball (Dublin, 1961).

Large, D., 'The House of Lords and Ireland in the age of Peel, 1832-50' *IHS*, ix (1955), 367-99.

Larkin, E., 'Church and state in Ireland in the nineteenth century', *Church History*, xxx (1962), 294-306.

—— 'The quarrel among the Catholic Hierarchy over the National System of Education in Ireland, 1834-41', *Celtic Cross* (1964), pp. 121-46.

—— 'Economic growth, capital investment and the Roman Catholic Church in nineteenth century Ireland', *Amer. Hist. Rev.*, lxxii (1966-7), 852-84.

—— *The making of the Roman Catholic Church in Ireland, 1850-1860* (Chapel Hill, 1980).

Latreille, A., and Rémond, R., *Histoire du Catholicisme en France*, 3 vols. (Paris, 1962).

Lecky, W. E. H., *A history of Ireland in the eighteenth century* (London, 1913).

Lefevre, R., 'S. Sede e Russia e i colloqui dello Czar Nicola I nei documenti vaticani (1843-1846)', *Miscellanea Historiae Pontificiae*, xiv (Rome, 1948), 159-293.

Leetham, C., *Luigi Gentili, a sower of the second spring* (London, 1965).

Lucas, E., *The life of Frederick Lucas, M.P.*, 2 vols. (London, 1886).

Lysaght, M., 'Daniel Murray, archbishop of Dublin, 1822-1852', *Dublin Hist. Rec.*, xxvii (1974), 101-8.

McCaffrey, L. J., *Daniel O'Connell and the Repeal Year* (Kentucky, 1966).

—— *The Irish Question 1800-1922* (Lexington, 1968).

McClelland, V. A., *English Roman Catholics and Higher Education, 1830-1903* (Oxford, 1973).

MacDonagh, O., 'The politicization of the Irish Catholic bishops, 1800-1850', *Hist. Jn.*, xviii (1974), 37-53.

McDowell, R. B.; *Public Opinion and Government Policy in Ireland, 1801-1846* (London, 1952).

—— *The Irish administration, 1801-1914* (London, 1964).

—— 'The Fitzwilliam episode', *IHS*, xv (1966), 115-30.

Mac Eoinín, U. B., 'Coláistí na Bainríona', *Galvia*, vii (1960), 20-39.

—— 'Coláistí na Bainríona: mar glacadh leis an mbille, 1845-49', *Galvia*, viii (1961), 31-41.

—— 'An Dr Mac Éil agus Coláistí na Bainríona', *Galvia*, ix (1962), 20-4.

McGrath, F., *Newman's University: Idea and Reality* (London, 1951).

Machin, G. I. T., 'The Maynooth Grant, the Dissenters and Disestablishment 1845-1847', *EHR*, lxxxii (1967), 61-85.

—— *Politics and the Churches in Great Britain, 1832 to 1868* (Oxford, 1977).

Macintyre, A. D., *The Liberator: Daniel O'Connell and the Irish party, 1830-1847* (London, 1965).

MacNamee, J. J., *History of the diocese of Ardagh* (Dublin, 1954).

Mac Suibhne, P., *Paul Cullen and his contemporaries, with their letters*, 5 vols. (Naas, 1961-77).

Manzini, L. M., *Il Cardinale Luigi Lambruschini* (Vatican, 1960).

Martin, T., *The life of his royal highness, the Prince Consort*, 5 vols. (London, 1880).

Martina, G., *Pio IX, 1846-1850* (Rome, 1974).

Meehan, D., *Window on Maynooth* (Dublin, 1949).

Miller, D. W., 'Irish Catholicism and the Great Famine', *Journal of Social History*, ix (1975-6), 81-98.

Monahan, J., *Records relating to the diocese of Ardagh and Clonmacnoise* (Dublin, 1886).

Moody, T. W., *Thomas Davis, 1814-45* (Dublin, 1945).

—— 'The Irish university question of the nineteenth century', *History*, xlii (1958), 90-109.

Moody, T. W. and Beckett, J. C., *Queen's, Belfast, 1845-1949: the History of a University*, 2 vols. (London, 1959).

Mooney, G., 'British Diplomatic Relations with the Holy See, 1793-1830', *Recusant History*, xiv (1978), pp. 193-210.

Moran, P. F., *The letters of Rev. James Maher, D.D. ... with a memoir* (Dublin, 1877).

—— *Spicilegium Ossoriense: being a collection of original letters and papers illustrative of the History of the Irish Church from the Reformation to the year 1800*, 3rd series (Dublin, 1884).

Morley, J., *The life of William Ewart Gladstone*, 2 vols. (London, 1908).

Murphy, I., 'Catholic education: primary education', *A history of Irish Catholicism*; ed. P. J. Corish, Vol. v, no. 6 (Dublin, 1971), pp. 1-52.

Murphy, J. A., 'The support of the Catholic Clergy in Ireland 1750-1850', *Hist. Studies*, v (1965), 103-21.

—— 'Priests and people in modern Irish history', *Christus Rex*, xxiii (1969), 234-59.

Murphy, M., 'Repeal, popular politics and the catholic clergy of Cork', *Cork. Hist. Soc. Jn.*, lxxxii (1977), 39-48.

Norman, E. R., *Anti-catholicism in Victorian England* (Cambridge, 1968).

—— *Church and Society in England, 1770-1970: a historical study* (Oxford, 1976).

Nowlan, K. B., *The Politics of Repeal: a study in the relations between Great Britain and Ireland, 1841-50* (London, 1965).

—— 'The Political Background', *The Great Famine: Studies in Irish History, 1845-52*, eds. R. D. Edwards and T. D. Williams (Dublin, 1956).

—— 'The relations between Church and State in the age of emancipation', *Proceedings of the Irish Catholic Historical Committee 1960* (Dublin, 1961).

—— 'The Catholic clergy and Irish politics in the eighteen thirties and forties', *Hist. Studies*, ix (1974), 119-35.

Ó Fiannachta, P., ed. *Léachtaí Cholm Cille: ár ndúchas creidimh* (Má Nuad, 1977).

Ó Fiaich, T., *Má Nuad* (Má Nuad, 1972).

O'Hegarty, P. S., *A History of Ireland under the Union, 1801-1922* (London, 1952).

Ó Mainín, M., 'Achran Creidimh in Iarthar Dhuibhneach', *Céad Bliain 1871-1971* ed. M Ó Ciosáin (Ballyferriter, 1973).

O'Neill, T. P., 'The Catholic Church and the relief of the poor, 1815-45', *Archiv. Hib.*, xxxi (1973), 132-45.

O'Reilly, B., *John MacHale, Archbishop of Tuam: his Life, Times and Correspondence*, 2 vols. (New York, 1890).

O'Shea, K., 'Three early nineteenth-century diocesan reports', *Kerry Arch. Soc. Jn.*, x (1977), 55-76.

Ó Súilleabháin, S., *Diarmuid na Bolgaighe agus a chómhursain* (Dublin, 1937).

Prest, J., *Lord John Russell* (London, 1972).

Prost, A., *Histoire de l'Enseignement en France 1800-1967* (Paris, 1968).

Roche, K. F., 'The relations of the Catholic Church and the State in England and Ireland, 1800-52', *Hist. Studies*, iii (1961), 8-24.

Roe, W. J., *Lamennais and England* (London, 1966).

Ronan, M. V., *An Apostle of Catholic Dublin; Father Henry Young* (Dublin, 1944).

—— 'Archbishop Murray', *IER*, lxxvii (1952), 241-9.

Rope, H. E. G., 'Gregory and England', *Miscellanea Historiae Pontificiae*, xiv (Rome, 1948), 373-97.

Seoighe, M., *Cois Maighe na gcaor* (Dublin, 1965).

Silke, J. J., 'The Roman Catholic church in Ireland 1800-1922', *Studia Hib.*, xv (1975), 61-104.

Smith, F. B., 'British Post Office Espionage, 1844', *Historical Studies*, xiv (1969-71), 189-201.

Tierney, M., 'Catalogue of letters relating to the Queens Colleges, 1845-50, in the papers of Archbishop M. Slattery', *Collectanea Hibernica*, no. 9 (1966), pp. 83-120.

Vale, M., 'The origins of the Catholic University of Ireland, 1845-1854', *IER*, lxxxii (1954), 1-16, 152-64, 226-41.

Wall, T., *The sign of Dr. Hay's head; the hazards and fortunes of Catholic printers and publishers in Dublin from the later penal times to the present day* (Dublin, 1958).

—— 'Catholic Periodicals of the Past', *IER*, 5th series ci(1964), 234-44; 289-303; 375-88; cii(1964), 17-27; 86-100; 129-47.

Walpole, S., *The life of Lord John Russell*, 2 vols. (London, 1891).

Walsh, K., *Dom Vincent of Mount Melleray* (Dublin, 1962).

Walsh, W. J., 'The Board of Charitable Donations and Bequests', *IER*, 3rd series, xvi (1895), 875-94; 971-96; 1071-99.

—— *O'Connell, Archbishop Murray and the Board of Charitable Bequests* (Dublin, 1916).

Ward, J. T., *Sir James Graham* (London, 1967).

Ward, W. R., *Religion and Society in England 1790-1850* (London, 1972).

Welch, P. J., 'Blomfield and Peel: a study in cooperation between Church and State, 1841-46', *Journal of Ecclesiastical History*, xii (1961), 71-84.

Whyte, J. H., 'Daniel O'Connell and the repeal party', *IHS*, xi (1959), 297-316.

—— 'The influence of the Catholic Clergy on Elections in Nineteenth Century Ireland', *EHR*, lxxv. (1960), 239-44.

—— 'The appointment of Catholic bishops in nineteenth century Ireland', *Cath. Hist. Rev.*, xlviii (1962), 12-32.

G. WORKS OF REFERENCE

Battersby, W. J., *The complete Catholic Directory, Almanac and Registry ...* (Dublin, 1836-57).

Cleeve, B., *Directory of Irish writers: non fiction* (Cork, 1969).

Crone, J. S., *A Concise Dictionary of Irish Biography* (Dublin, 1937).

Dictonary of National Biography, eds. L. Stephen and S. Lee (London, 1910-).

Dod's parliamentary companion (London, 1833-52).

The Dublin Almanack and General Register of Ireland for the year of Our Lord 1843 (Dublin, 1843).

Gillow, J., *A literary and biographical history or bibliographical dictionary of the English Catholics*, 5 vols. (London, 1885).

Kalendarium Collegii Sti Patricii apud Maynooth ... 1863-1980 (Dublin and Naas, 1864-1980).

Lewis, S. A., *A topographical dictionary of Ireland ...*, 2 vols. (London, 1839).

The Parliamentary Gazetteer of Ireland ... 1844-45..., 3 vols. (Dublin, 1846).

Thom's Irish almanack and official directory (Dublin, 1844-50).

Webb, A., *A Compendium of Irish Biography* (Dublin, 1878).

INDEX